GROUP
DYNAMICS

McGRAW-HILL SERIES IN PSYCHOLOGY

Adams *Human Memory*
Beach, Hebb, Morgan, and Nissen *The Neuropsychology of Lashley*
Von Békésy *Experiments in Hearing*
Berkowitz *Aggression: A Social Psychological Analysis*
Berlyne *Conflict, Arousal, and Curiosity*
Blum *Psychoanalytic Theories of Personality*
Brown *The Motivation of Behavior*
Brown and Ghiselli *Scientific Method in Psychology*
Butcher *MMPI: Research Developments and Clinical Applications*
Campbell, Dunnette, Lawler, and Weick *Managerial Effectiveness*
Cofer *Verbal Learning and Verbal Behavior*
Cofer and Musgrave *Verbal Behavior and Learning: Problems and Processes*
Crafts, Schneirla, Robinson, and Gilbert *Recent Experiments in Psychology*
Crites *Vocational Psychology*
D'Amato *Experimental Psychology: Methodology, psychophysics, and Learning*
Davitz *The Communication of Emotional Meaning*
Deese and Hulse *The Psychology of Learning*
Dollard and Miller *Personality and Psychotherapy*
Edgington *Statistical Inference: The Distribution-free Approach*
Ellis *Handbook of Mental Deficiency*
Epstein *Varieties of Perceptual Learning*
Ferguson *Statistical Analysis in Psychology and Education*
Forgus *Perception: The Basic Process in Cognitive Development*
Franks *Behavior Therapy: Appraisal and Status*
Ghiselli *Theory of Psychological Measurement*
Ghiselli and Brown *Personnel and Industrial Psychology*
Gilmer *Industrial Psychology*
Gray *Psychology Applied to Human Affairs*
Guilford *Fundamental Statistics in Psychology and Education*
Guilford *The Nature of Human Intelligence*
Guilford *Personality*
Guilford *Psychometric Methods*
Guion *Personnel Testing*

Haire   *Psychology in Management*
Hirsch   *Behavior-genetic Analysis*
Hirsh   *The Measurement of Hearing*
Hurlock   *Adolescent Development*
Hurlock   *Child Development*
Hurlock   *Development Psychology*
Jackson and Messick   *Problems in Human Assessment*
Karn and Gilmer   *Readings in Industrial and Business Psychology*
Krech, Crutchfield, and Ballachey   *Individual in Society*
Lazarus, A.   *Behavior Therapy and Beyond*
Lazarus, R.   *Adjustment and Personality*
Lazarus, R.   *Psychological Stress and the Coping Process*
Lewin   *A Dynamic Theory of Personality*
Lewin   *Principles of Topological Psychology*
Maher   *Principles of Psychopathology*
Marx and Hillix   *Systems and Theories in Psychology*
Messick and Brayfield   *Decision and Choice: Contributions of Sidney Siegel*
Miller   *Language and Communication*
Morgan   *Physiological Psychology*
Nunnally   *Psychometric Theory*
Rethlingshafer   *Motivation as Related to Personality*
Robinson and Robinson   *The Mentally Retarded Child*
Rosenthal   *Genetic Theory and Abnormal Behavior*
Scherer and Wertheimer   *A Psycholinguistic Experiment on Foreign Language Teaching*
Shaw   *Group Dynamics: The Psychology of Small Group Behavior*
Shaw and Costanzo   *Theories of Social Psychology*
Shaw and Wright   *Scales for the Measurement of Attitudes*
Sidowski   *Experimental Methods and Instrumentation in Psychology*
Siegel   *Nonparametric Statistics for the Behavioral Sciences*
Spencer and Kass   *Perspectives in Child Psychology*
Stagner   *Psychology of Personality*
Townsend   *Introduction to Experimental Methods for Psychology and the Social Sciences*
Vinacke   *The Psychology of Thinking*
Wallen   *Clinical Psychology: The Study of Persons*
Warren and Akert   *The Frontal Granular Cortex and Behavior*
Waters, Rethlingshafer, and Caldwell   *Principles of Comparative Psychology*
Winer   *Statistical Principles in Experimental Design*
Zubek and Solberg   *Human Development*

John F. Dashiell was Consulting Editor of this series from its inception in 1931 until January 1, 1950. Clifford T. Morgan was Consulting Editor of this series from January 1, 1950 until January 1, 1959. Harry F. Harlow assumed the duties of Consulting Editor from 1959 to 1965. In 1965 a Board of Consulting Editors was established according to areas of interest. The current board members are Richard L. Solomon (physiological, experimental), Norman Garmezy (abnormal, clinical), Harold W. Stevenson (child, adolescent, human development), and Lyle V. Jones (statistical, quantitative).

GROUP DYNAMICS
THE PSYCHOLOGY OF SMALL GROUP BEHAVIOR

MARVIN E. SHAW
PROFESSOR OF PSYCHOLOGY
UNIVERSITY OF FLORIDA

McGRAW-HILL BOOK COMPANY

New York   St. Louis   San Francisco
Düsseldorf   Johannesburg   Kuala Lumpur   London   Mexico
Montreal   New Delhi
Panama   Rio de Janeiro   Singapore   Sydney   Toronto

**GROUP
DYNAMICS**
THE PSYCHOLOGY
OF SMALL GROUP BEHAVIOR

Library of Congress Catalog Card Number   72-125109

ISBN 07-056500-7

8 9 0 K P K P 7 9 8 7 6 5 4 3

TO THE MEMORY OF
JACK C. GILCHRIST AND JACK M. WRIGHT

PREFACE

Group dynamics has become a popular field of study during the past twenty or thirty years, owing largely to the impetus provided by the work of Kurt Lewin and his students. This impetus was amplified by a general interest in group processes. People everywhere are interested in groups, perhaps because we spend so much time in them. The social psychologist is interested in groups because they epitomize social situations and social behavior. Clinical psychologists must know about groups because so many personal problems are rooted in the individual's interactions with others. The businessman wants to know about groups because many of his goals can be achieved only through group action; he needs to know the most effective procedures to help his group or groups achieve these goals. It seems that almost everyone has some reason to want to know about the dynamics of groups.

This book does not purport to meet the needs of everyone who may have some interest in groups. It was written for the student who has been introduced to social psychology, but who has not delved deeply into the study of small groups. In academic terms, it was written for seniors and first-year graduate students. It assumes that the reader is familiar with elementary psychological concepts and has some knowledge of social processes. But even if the reader does not have this background, he should have little difficulty mastering the major ideas presented in this book.

It has been my purpose to examine many aspects of small group behavior, not as isolated phenomena, but as interrelated processes of social interaction. Consequently, the reader will not find the traditional chapter headings, such as Leadership, Group Goals, Social Power, and the like. Instead, the group is viewed as functioning in a number of environments, each of which is related to other environments and each of which influences various aspects of group process. Thus, leadership, conformity behavior, and similar processes are discussed at several points throughout the book. It is hoped that this approach to the analysis of small group behavior reveals something of the complexity and interrelatedness of the variables influencing group process.

Emphasis has been placed upon data obtained from empirical studies rather than upon the theoretical or logical analysis of groups. All kinds of empirical approaches were deemed relevant, providing only that the observations were made under controlled conditions. (This does not mean that the investigator must have *all* relevant variables under control, but only that he knows enough about the situation to make valid inferences about causal relationships.) However, in the review of relevant research, the intent was to be representative rather than exhaustive. Several representative studies are cited to support each of the conclusions drawn about a given process whenever such studies are available, but many relevant studies are not mentioned if essentially the same conclusions can be drawn from those cited.

Finally, each substantive chapter ends with a statement of plausible hypotheses about the phenomena discussed in the chapter. This statement serves as a summary of the data presented in the main part of the chapter and as a guide for future explorations.

I am, of course, indebted to the many persons who contributed to this work. I am especially grateful to Fred E. Fiedler and Guillermo Mascaro, each of whom read the entire manuscript and made many helpful comments and suggestions. Kathy Strobak, Marilyn Sokoloff, Janice Bronowitz, and Maria Llabre each typed significant parts of the manuscript in a professional manner, and I am grateful to them for their assistance. I also wish to express my appreciation to the many authors whose works were cited, directly or indirectly, and to the following publishers who graciously permitted the use of copyrighted materials: Academic Press, Inc.; Acta Psychologica; Addison-Wesley Publishing Company; American Psychological Association; Th Cornell Journal of Social Relations; Duke University Press; Harcourt, Brace & World, Inc.; Harper & Row, Publishers, Inc.; John Wiley & Sons, Inc.; The Journal Press; McGraw-Hill Book Company; Oxford University Press; Plenum Publishing Corporation; Prentice-Hall, Inc.; Psychonomic Journals, Inc.; The Ronald Press Company; and The Society for Research in Child Development, Inc.

MARVIN E. SHAW

CONTENTS

PART III   THE INTERACTION PROCESS

PART I
INTRODUCTION

CHAPTER 1

THE NATURE OF SMALL GROUPS

Man is a social animal. Although this oft-repeated assertion is so obvious that it is almost platitudinous, it nevertheless calls attention to an exceedingly important aspect of human life. The typical human being spends a major portion of his waking life in groups of one sort or another. Life itself may be said to originate in groups; the infant usually is born into a family group and spends his early years as a member of that group. He later enters kindergarten where he becomes a member of other groups. Then come elementary school, high school, college, the work group, and the "golden age" affiliations, along with all the ancillary groupings deriving from those relationships. One can easily call to mind art clubs, swimming teams, bridge clubs, fraternities, sororities, business clubs, professional clubs, community organizations, committees—indeed a plethora of groups which engulf the individual. It has been estimated (Mills, 1967) that the average person belongs to five or six groups at any given time and that the total number of existing small groups may be as high as four or five billion. The social scientist who aspires to understand human behavior cannot avoid the study of groups.

The titles of this book and this chapter indicate that our concern is with *small* groups. It is legitimate, therefore, to ask just how small is a "small group" and how many of the groups in existence fall into this category. Actually, there is no clear-cut dividing line between small and large groups. A group having ten or fewer members is certainly a small group; one with thirty or more members is definitely a large group. But there is a gray area between ten and thirty where the appropriate designation is unclear and often is made on bases other than the number of group members. For example, a group of thirty persons might function as a small group if all its members were closely related to one another and highly motivated to co-operate toward the achievement of a common goal. Fortunately, the maximum size of a small group usually does not become a problem, since the great majority of research studies deal with groups of five or fewer members.

The question concerning the proportion of extant groups that can be considered small is much easier to answer. A survey study of group memberships by James (1951) revealed that 92 percent of all group memberships observed were in groups of two or three persons, and only 2 percent of the remaining groupings included five or more persons. It is important to note that James observed spontaneous groupings in everyday activities. This procedure probably resulted in a bias toward smaller groups. However, his findings strongly suggest that the study of small groups encompasses the majority of group memberships. One cannot infer from these data, however, that small groups are the most important social aggregations, although it seems likely that they are most significant from the standpoint of the individual group member. As shall be seen from studies cited in the following chapters, the small group exerts strong influence on almost every phase of the member's life. The norms (standards of conduct) of the group provide a basis for the determination of "appropriate" behavior in otherwise ambiguous situations; the presence of others often leads to the satisfaction of individual needs for affiliation and may arouse the individual to unusual performance levels; goals can be achieved in groups that cannot be achieved alone; and much more.

Perhaps enough has been said to arouse the curiosity of the reader to the extent that he is willing to examine the data from small group research or at least to ask the question: What is a *group?* This is a fair question. When we presume to discourse upon a significant subject, we should be prepared to define our terms as clearly as possible. It would be easy to state our own definition of group and proceed to more exciting topics. However, there is no single definition that is generally accepted by all (or even most) students of small group behavior. It will be more instructive therefore to consider the diverse meanings of this concept.

DEFINITIONS OF GROUP

It is not our purpose to present a comprehensive listing of definitions of group; rather, we shall sample definitions representing the various approaches to conceptualization. These approaches are not necessarily unique. On the contrary, there is much overlap, and it is evident that different authors are simply looking at different aspects of the same phenomenon. Indeed, some authors are able to discuss group phenomena at great length without presenting a specific definition of the term (for example, Collins & Guetzkow, 1964; McGrath & Altman, 1966; Roby, 1968; Schutz, 1958). These writers have judged that it is more appropriate to specify the characteristics of small groups than to offer a single definition. Others have defined group in terms of one or more of the following characteristics: (1) perceptions and cognitions of group members, (2) motivation and need satisfaction, (3) group goals, (4) group organization, (5) interdependency of group members, and (6) interaction.

IN TERMS OF PERCEPTIONS

Definitions of group in terms of the perceptions of group members are based upon the reasonable assumption that such members should be aware of their relationships to others. The centrality of such perceptions for the identification of the existence of groups is exemplified by the definitions offered by M. Smith and by Bales:

> We may define a social group as a unit consisting of a plural number of separate organisms (agents) who have a collective perception of their unity and who have the ability to act and/or are acting in a unitary manner toward their environment (M. Smith, 1945, p. 227).

A small group is defined as any number of persons engaged in interaction with one another in a single face-to-face meeting or series of such meetings, in which each member receives some impression or perception of each other member distinct enough so that he can, either at the time or in later questioning, give some reaction to each of the others as an individual person, even though it be only to recall that the other was present (Bales, 1950, p. 33).

Each of these definitions requires that group members perceive the group, yet each imposes additional criteria. Smith adds the requirement that unitary action at least be possible, whereas Bales rigorously delimits the situation in which the perceptions occur and specifies precisely the circumstances in which their perceptions may be revealed. Nevertheless, the *sine qua non* in each instance is that group members perceive the existence of the group.

IN TERMS OF MOTIVATION

It is a common observation that individuals join a group because they believe that it will satisfy some need. Thus, the businessman may join civic clubs in order to improve his business opportunities, the college student affiliates with a fraternity to satisfy social needs, and the proponent of civil rights may join action-oriented groups because he believes that such groups can satisfy his motivations to improve society. Groups that fail to satisfy the need or needs of individual group members usually disintegrate. The following definitions are representative of those based upon this aspect of group functioning:

The definition which seems most essential is that a group is a collection of organisms in which the existence of all (in their given relationships) is necessary to the satisfaction of certain individual needs in each (Cattell, 1951b, p. 167).

We define "group" as a collection of individuals whose existence as a collection is rewarding to the individuals (Bass, 1960, p. 39).

Both these definitions specify only need satisfaction as the necessary element for identifying an aggregate as a group. Bass asserted that other characteristics included in other definitions are superfluous. In his view, shared perceptions of unity, commonality of goals, and interaction are irrelevant for purposes of definition unless these ascribed characteristics are related to the potentially rewarding aspects of the collectivity. A practical difficulty in the definition of "group" in terms of need satisfaction is obvious: How does one determine what needs are operating and whether needs are in fact being satisfied by the collection of persons?

IN TERMS OF GOALS

Definitions of group in terms of group goals are closely related to those based on motivation. Presumably, goal achievement is rewarding, and to the extent that this is so, definitions in terms of goals and in terms of motivation are quite similar. Perhaps a single example will suffice:

> Just what *are* these small groups we are referring to? To put it simply, they are units composed of two or more persons who come into contact for a purpose and who consider the contact meaningful (Mills, 1967, p. 2).

It might be noted before we leave this section that the conception of groups in terms of goals is not new. As early as 1936 Freeman pointed out that individuals join groups in order to achieve common goals.

IN TERMS OF ORGANIZATION

The emphasis upon the organizational characteristics of groups occurs most commonly in the sociological literature. This is understandable in view of the greater interest of the sociologist in the group as the unit of analysis in contrast to the psychologist's concern for the individual group member. But this emphasis is not limited to sociologists, as we shall see. Students of group behavior with this orientation are impressed by the structural elements of groups (roles, statuses, norms) and the relationships among them. According to McDavid and Harari, the essential properties of organization which define a group are unitary functioning, interrelated elements, and regulatory mechanisms. They define group as follows:

> A social-psychological group is an organized system of two or more individuals who are interrelated so that the system performs some function, has a standard set of role relationships among its members, and has a set of norms that regulate the function of the group and each of its members (McDavid & Harari, 1968, p. 237).

The definition proposed earlier by Sherif and Sherif is very similar:

> A group is a social unit which consists of a number of individuals who stand in (more or less) definite status and role relationships to one another and which possesses a set of values or norms of its own regulating the behavior of individual members, at least in matters of consequence to the group (Sherif & Sherif, 1956, p. 144).

Definitions in terms of organization seem to limit consideration of structural properties to statuses, roles, and norms, although it is evident that many other structural elements are involved in group structure (for example, power relations, affective relations, etc.). However, the main objection to definitions of this type is that they are merely partial descriptions of one aspect of groups, namely, group structure.

IN TERMS OF INTERDEPENDENCY

Many years ago, Lewin argued cogently that the essential aspect of a collection of individuals which makes it a group is the interdependency of individuals on one another. He was particularly concerned that some writers seemed to view similarity of members as the critical characteristic of groups. In Lewin's view, even definitions of group in terms of group goals are based on similarity. In his words:

> Conceiving of a group as a dynamic whole should include a definition of group which is based on interdependence of the members (or better, of the subparts of the group). It seems to be rather important to stress this point because many definitions of a group use the similarity of group members rather than their dynamic interdependence as the constituent factor.... One should realize that even a definition of group membership by equality of goal or equality of an enemy is still a definition by similarity (Lewin, 1951, pp. 146–147).

A number of current students of group behavior define group in terms of interdependency in the following manner:

> By this term [group] we generally mean a set of individuals who share a common fate, that is, who are *interdependent* in the sense that an event which affects one member is likely to affect all (Fiedler, 1967, p. 6).

> A group is a collection of individuals who have relations to one another that make them interdependent to some significant degree. As so defined, the term group refers to a class of social entities having in common the property of interdependence among their constituent members (Cartwright & Zander, 1968, p. 46).

In the above definitions, the term interdependence can mean a variety of things in the sense that members can be interdependent on one or more dimensions. In many cases, it appears that definitions in terms of interdependency are essentially the same as those based on interaction, which are given in the following section.

IN TERMS OF INTERACTION

Interaction is actually one form of interdependence (Cartwright & Zander, 1968). Many writers believe that this form of interdependence is the essence of "groupness" and hence have based their definitions of group upon this aspect:

We mean by a group a number of persons who communicate with one another often over a span of time, and who are few enough so that each person is able to communicate with all the others, not at secondhand, through other people, but face-to-face (Homans, 1950, p. 1).

A group is a number of people in interaction with one another, and it is this interaction process that distinguishes the group from an aggregate (Bonner, 1959, p. 4).

A group may be regarded as an open interaction system in which actions determine the structure of the system and successive interactions exert coequal effects upon the identity of the system (Stogdill, 1959, p. 18).

Although each of these definitions includes other elements, the central concept in each seems to be interaction among group members. Homans's definition uses the notion of interpersonal communication, but in some sense interpersonal communication can be considered isomorphic with interaction. It is difficult to identify an instance of interpersonal communication that does not imply interaction, and vice versa. Interaction may take many forms: verbal interaction, physical interaction, emotional interaction, etc. Any given group probably involves many types of interaction; hence specification of type of interaction in defining group would be unduly restrictive.

These definitions are all correct in that each points to some important aspect(s) of the concept "group" and/or delimits it in some way. It appears that different theorists look at different facets of the group, and each assumes that his view reveals its essential characteristics. Differences between definitions in some cases appear to be due to variations in levels of analysis, e.g., differences between definitions in terms of perceptions and in terms of organization. In other cases, such differences seem to be due largely to semantic variations, e.g., differences between definitions in terms of interdependency and in terms of interaction. Even when definitions are based upon the same characteristic there often are differences in minor details, such as the requirement that there be face-to-face communication or that some of the consequences of group processes be uniform for all group members. Nevertheless, there is sufficient commonality among definitions to indicate that they are all referring to the same basic concept.

In our view, definitions in terms of interdependency or interaction more directly delineate the basic elements of the concept "group." If a group exists, then it may be assumed that its members (1) are motivated to join the group (and hence expect that it will satisfy some of their needs), and (2) are aware of its existence, i.e., that their perceptions are veridical. Furthermore, it is a common observation that when individuals interact, even for brief periods, differentiations begin to develop. Some persons contribute more to group processes than others, some are valued more than others, and certain approved patterns of behavior appear. In short, group organization begins to take place. Finally, it is not obvious that a common goal is an essential characteristic of a group. It is at least theoretically possible for a group to meet only individual goals. To summarize: Motivations of members may account for the *formation* of a group; the group members may *veridically perceive* that the group exists or that they are members of a group; and organization (the formation and interrelation of roles, statuses, and norms) may be an inevitable *consequence* of group process. But none of these aspects is either necessary or sufficient to define "group." Therefore, for purposes of this book, *a group is defined as two or more persons who are interacting with one another in such a manner that each person influences and is influenced by each other person.* A *small* group is a group having twenty or fewer members, although in most instances we will be concerned with groups having five or fewer members.

Some examples of aggregates that are groups and of some that are not may help to clarify this conception of group. If one person, A, sees another person, B, with whom he wishes to speak and so approaches him, A is influenced by B but not vice versa; hence *interaction* does not occur, and A and B do not constitute a group. However, if B notices that A is attempting to get his attention, B may be influenced to also approach A. In this case, A and B are interacting and so compose a group. Or consider the case of a person, A, who is looking up at the sky and is approached, independently, by two other persons, B and C, who also begin looking in the same direction. Again, no group exists, despite the fact that B and C have been influenced by A, because A has not been influenced by B or C. These three persons become a group if they enter into a discussion (interaction) concerning the object of their attention. It should be clear that interaction requires *mutual* influence, and an aggregate of individuals is a group only if interaction occurs.

Although interaction is the essential feature that distinguishes a group from an aggregate, other aspects of a group are important. In general, the group dynamicist is interested in groups that (1) endure for a reasonable period (longer than a few minutes, at least), (2) have a common goal or goals, and (3) have developed at least a rudimentary group structure.

THE REALITY OF GROUPS

Are groups real? This may appear to be a strange question to raise after devoting several pages to the definition of group. Nevertheless, it is a question that must be considered, since the "realness" of groups has been debated for many years. Some social scientists have maintained that the concept of group is a mere analogy, an abstraction that we use to account for collective individual behavior. F. H. Allport (1924) argued cogently that only individuals are real; groups are no more than sets of values, ideas, thoughts, habits, etc., that exist simultaneously in the minds of the individuals in collectivities. In short, groups exist only in the minds of men. Others (Durkheim, 1898; Warriner, 1956) have argued just as strongly that groups are entities and should be treated like other unitary objects in our environment. Those who take this position assert that group phenomena cannot be explained in psychological terms; hence any valid explanation of group processes must be at the level of the group. Somewhere between these two extreme positions are those theorists who maintain that entities, including groups, vary in the degree to which they are "real" and that the problem is one of determining the degree of being an entity (Campbell, 1958; K. W. Deutsch, 1954; Rice, 1928; Spencer, 1876).

As in many controversies the more moderate position turns out to be the more reasonable one. The most articulate representative of this view is probably Donald T. Campbell (1958). He noted that certain objects in our environment, such as stones and teacups, appear to be more solid and unitary than other objects, such as social groups, and therefore more "real." Somehow, this makes objectionable the use of the same term to refer to both categories of objects. He argued, however, that the differences in objects of this sort are really differences in our perceptions of them. That is, physical objects such as tables and chairs are more solid, have sharper boundaries, and are more multiply confirmed than are social groups. For example, we not only can see a chair, but we can also touch it, feel its temperature, hear the sound that results from tapping it, etc. Information about it can be obtained from multiple sense modalities. Information about a group, however, comes from fewer sources and often seems to be less immediate and compelling than that obtained about physical objects. Therefore, although the process is essentially the same, social groups are seen as less real than physical objects. Campbell suggested that the term "entity" has an all-or-none connotation and hence is inadequate to express the notion of degree of "realness." He therefore coined the term "entitativity" to refer to the degree of having real existence.

Once it is admitted that objects may vary in degree of realness, or at least in the degree to which they are perceived as real, then a question arises concerning the factors determining the perception of entitativity. Campbell has proposed that the gestalt principles of perceptual organization are adequate to account for the perception of entitativity. These well-known principles are proximity, similarity, common fate, and pregnance. Let us examine in greater detail how these principles apply to the perception of the reality of groups.

THE PERCEPTION OF ENTITATIVITY

The identification of an aggregate of several units as an entity is basically a process of establishing boundaries which separate the units belonging to the entity from other units that are not a part of the entity. Thus, through the use of principles of organization Campbell sought to determine the circumstances under which such boundaries are established. He believed that an analysis of this type would be equally applicable to physical objects, e.g., stones and chairs, and to social phenomena, e.g., social groups. According to Campbell, common fate seems to be most important in establishing boundaries, followed by similarity and proximity. Pregnance, which refers to the fact that elements forming a pattern tend to be perceived as the best figure possible, plays a very secondary role in the perception of entitativity. Campbell used this principle only to examine the degree of closure or completeness obtained by application of the other three principles.

In attempting to show how common fate may be used to establish entitativity, Campbell suggested that it might be possible to compute a "coefficient of common fate" which would reflect the degree to which two or more units have been in the same general place at the same time. For example, if a stone is multicolored it may not be immediately obvious that the differently colored parts constitute a single entity. However, if the stone is moved about, it can be seen that the various parts generally move together; that is, the parts maintain their same relative position regardless of the location of the stone in space. The various parts thus experience a common fate, and this is a clue to entitativity. In the same way, we may observe the extent to which a collection of individuals experience a common fate. For example, if we note that a man and a woman are walking down the street side by side, we may be uncertain about their relationship. If they both turn the corner in the same direction, get into the same automobile, etc., then we perceive that they are together, that is, that they constitute a unit or a group. The essence of common fate, then, is that all components of a unit experience similar outcomes. The degree to which the outcomes of several individuals covary serves as an index or cue for the perception of them as a group; the greater the covariation the greater the degree of entitativity attributed to them.

Although similarity does not appear to be as primary as common fate, it does serve an important role in the perception of entitativity. Units that are similar in some noticeable respect tend to be perceived as an entity. Soldiers in military uniform are seen as a group; horses are seen as one group, cats another, etc. Of course, similarity may often lead us to make perceptual errors. Tall persons may be seen as a group (for example, as members of a basketball team) when in fact they just happened to be in the same vicinity at the same time and really do not know each other. Similarity often serves as a preliminary cue for the perception of entitativity, which can later be checked by application of the common fate principle.

The reader may have noted that in the example of tall persons being perceived as a basketball team there was at least the implicit assumption that these similar persons were in close proximity. This is not necessary, however; several tall men might be perceived as belonging to a basketball team even if they were seen in different parts of the city and at different times, assuming that the perceiver had reason to believe a basketball team was in town. But this example does illustrate the role of proximity. The tall men might have been perceived as belonging together even if they were not in proximity to one another, but the probability that they will be so perceived is enhanced by proximity. A collection of individuals occupying a common space is more likely to be perceived as a group than are dispersed individuals, even if there is no other basis for the perception of entitativity. As in the case of similarity, proximity often serves as a basis for preliminary grouping which can be checked by common fate indices.

A collection of individuals who experience a common fate on several different occasions, who are similar in one or more respects, and who are in close proximity will undoubtedly be perceived as an entity. The degree of "realness" attributed to the entity will vary with the strength of these principles of perceptual organization. Since the only basis we have for attributing reality to any object derives from our perception of it, we must conclude (with Campbell) that a group is real to the extent that it is perceived as an entity.

ISSUES IN GROUP DYNAMICS

Although there is disagreement among both psychologists and sociologists concerning the reality of groups, this is not an issue for students of group dynamics. The person who is interested in the scientific study of groups does not doubt that they exist. However, there are a number of issues upon which there is disagreement among group dynamicists. This is not surprising, since group dynamics is a relatively new area of research. It is the nature of the scientific endeavor to continually question and probe for "truth," and the path to truth is never clear. It is inevitable that differences arise regarding the proper questions to be asked and the proper theoretical and empirical procedures to be used in answering them.

If one asked a random sample of group dynamicists to identify the "basic" issues in their field, the number of different lists obtained would probably correspond to the size of the sample. The list provided by Cartwright and Zander (1968) probably is representative. They identified the basic issues in group dynamics as centering around (1) preconceptions about the nature of groups, (2) problems of defining the field of study, (3) the question of an appropriate theoretical orientation, (4) the problem of the proper method or methods of studying groups, and (5) the relation of group dynamics to the larger society. Certainly these are important issues in the study of small groups, although one may question whether they are *the basic* issues. For example, Lana (1969), in writing about the assumptions of social psychology, considered differences in philosophies, theories, and methods. One might also note lesser issues, such as deciding the minimum size of a group. Some writers regard dyads as groups, whereas others maintain that the most significant group phenomena occur only when three or more persons interact and that the minimum size of a true group is three persons.

For our purposes, the major issues in group dynamics today are those associated with the proper approach to the analysis of groups. The disagreements begin with the problem of definition, which was explored in an earlier section. But having accepted a working definition of group, we find that there are still wide differences concerning the most fruitful method of studying groups. At the most general level, there is a division of opinion regarding whether the approach should be theoretical or empirical. Some maintain that the only way we can ever hope to "really" understand group process is by way of theoretical analysis. Others argue that theory is premature at best and, at worst, a waste of time. The extreme empiricist position holds that any phenomenon can be understood only through the careful analysis of empirical observations. (Parenthetically, it might be noted that both the extreme theoretician and the extreme empiricist are wrong; both theory and empirical studies are needed. On the one hand, it is probably impossible to build a theory without some "facts" to use as elements or units of the theoretical structure; and incorrect "facts" lead to incorrect theories. Empirical studies can increase the probability that the elements of the theory are valid. On the other hand, a mass of unorganized and unrelated facts, no matter how correct they may be, is not likely to prove very useful in the understanding of any complex phenomenon. Theory provides the organization of data that is necessary for understanding their implications beyond the specific situations in which the data were obtained.)

In any case, the group dynamicist must decide what theory and/or what empirical methods he will use in his approach to the study of small group behavior. At the level of theory, one may choose among a wide variety of approaches. Cartwright and Zander (1968) listed eight theoretical orientations that have been adopted for the analysis of groups:

1 *Field theory* holds that behavior is the result of a field of interdependent forces. In group dynamics, the major proponent of the field theory orientation was Kurt Lewin, who analyzed both individual and group behavior as parts of a system of interrelated events. The method of analysis is similar to that of physics and assumes that the properties of any given behavioral event are determined by its relations to other events in the same system. Field theory provides an excellent basis for the description of group behavior, but, unfortunately, it has not led to a systematic theoretical formulation of group processes.

2 *Interaction theory* views the group as a system of interacting individuals. In its most common form, three basic elements are identified: activity, interaction, and sentiment. The theory holds that all aspects of group behavior can be understood by spelling out the relations among these three basic elements. This approach has been adopted primarily by socio-

logically oriented social psychologists and has proved to be most useful in the description of natural groups.

3 *Systems theory* adopts a position that is very similar to that proposed by interaction theory, and, indeed, there is some question that these are two different orientations. In both, there is an attempt to understand complicated processes from an analysis of basic elements. The chief difference between interaction theory and systems theory is the kinds of elements that are identified and used for analysis. Whereas interaction theory appeals to activity, interaction, and sentiment, systems theory describes the group as a system of interlocking elements such as positions and roles, with much emphasis upon group inputs and outputs.

4 The *sociometric orientation* emphasizes interpersonal choices among group members. The morale and performance of the group are seen as depending upon the interpersonal relations among group members that are reflected in sociometric choices. This orientation has stimulated much research and, as we shall see later, has contributed to our understanding of certain aspects of group behavior. On the other hand, its effect upon systematic theory has been minimal.

5 The *psychoanalytic orientation,* of course, derives from Freudian psychology. It is concerned with motivational and defensive processes of the individual as related to group life. The psychoanalytic orientation has led to at least one theory of group process and has contributed to many more. It has not, however, stimulated much empirical research; hence, the empirical bases of psychoanalytically oriented theoretical formulations are not as strong as would be desirable.

6 The *general psychology orientation* attempts to extend theoretical analyses of individual behavior to group behavior. Thus, the various theoretical formulations with regard to such individual processes as learning, motivation, and perception are applied directly to group processes. There is some question whether this approach should be called an orientation or merely a denial that there is anything unique about group behavior. We shall see that this denial is incorrect.

7 The *empirical-statistical orientation* holds that the basic concepts of group theory can be discovered through the application of statistical procedures. The work of Cattell (1948) exemplifies this approach. He attempted to

discover the basic aspects of group behavior from a statistical analysis of data about individuals, primarily by means of factor analysis.

8 The *formal models orientation* was most popular during the 1950s. Theorists adopting this approach attempt to construct formal models of group behavior using rigorous mathematical procedures. Model builders are often more concerned with the internal consistency of their models than with the degree of correspondence between model and natural situations. For this reason, perhaps, this orientation has produced only restricted theoretical models which have had limited influence upon group dynamics.

It is clear from this very brief survey that many of the orientations listed by Cartwright and Zander have not contributed greatly to the theoretical analysis of group behavior. In fact, of the eight orientations listed, only three have led to systematic theories of group behavior: systems theory (including interaction theory), the psychoanalytical orientation, and the empirical-statistical orientation. An orientation not mentioned specifically by Cartwright and Zander, *reinforcement theory,* should be added to this list, since it has had important influences upon small group theory. Chapter 2 will present an example of a theory of small group behavior based upon each of these four orientations.

At the empirical level of analysis, the investigator again may select from a large number of possible techniques. The methods available range from loosely controlled descriptive-exploratory studies, on the one hand, to rigorously controlled laboratory or simulation studies, on the other. Proponents of the former approach assert that the more rigorously controlled studies deal with artificial situations and phenomena; hence their findings are irrelevant to "real life." Supporters of the more highly controlled designs take the position that descriptive-exploratory studies can yield only suggestive data; only rigorously controlled studies can provide a degree of certainty that one has established valid principles of group behavior. For them, the question of relevance to "real life"* is an empirical question that

---

* The common expression "real life" is actually inappropriate. Behavior in a laboratory is just as real as behavior in a factory or in the street. The term is usually intended to mean that which occurs in everyday situations, without interference by the investigator. Hence, more acceptable terms would be "natural situations" and "natural groups." In the remainder of this book we will use the more appropriate terms, except when citing the views or statements of others who have used the less accurate phrasing.

can be answered only by testing laboratory-established principles in natural situations.

Methods for studying group behavior may be classified into three major classes or categories, ranging from the most natural and least rigorously controlled to the most "artificial" and most highly controlled: (1) field studies, (2) laboratory experiments, and (3) computer simulation studies.

Field studies, laboratory experiments, and simulation studies are distinguished by the settings in which they occur and by the kinds of subjects typically investigated. Field studies are conducted in naturally occurring situations, i.e., in the field. The units of study are usually experienced groups, i.e., natural groups that have a history, such as family groups or basketball teams. Field studies may vary considerably, however, in purpose and method: They may take the form of descriptive-exploratory studies, natural experiments, or field experiments. The descriptive-exploratory study examines a natural situation for the purpose of describing it and exploring possible relationships among naturally occurring variables. The phenomena under investigation are not interfered with in any way—at least not deliberately. The natural experiment also investigates the phenomena, in this case group behaviors, without interfering with them. It differs from the descriptive-exploratory study in that the investigator tries to take advantage of naturally occurring events in order to study their effects upon group behavior. For example, the researcher might take advantage of forced integration of schools to study racially mixed groups. In the field experiment, the investigator deliberately produces variations in the natural situation in order to study their effects upon the group.

The essential features of a laboratory study are that (1) it is conducted in a laboratory setting and (2) the situation is arranged deliberately for the investigation of specified phenomena. The groups that are brought into the laboratory may be experienced, as in the field study, or they may be naïve in that the members of the group have never interacted with each other before the beginning of the experiment. Such naïve groups may, of course, be formed by random assignment of members or by selecting the members according to specified criteria, such as mental ability, personality characteristics, age, sex, etc.

Computer simulation studies are the most contrived forms of investigation. The variables of interest are programmed, and the group behavior is "enacted" by the computer rather than by groups of actual persons. Computer simulation thus has succeeded in studying the no-person group (E. F.

Borgatta, 1954). The adequacy of this approach clearly depends upon the degree to which the investigator has been able to program the critical variables.

In the following chapter the various approaches to the study of group behavior are examined in greater detail, and some of their strengths and weaknesses are considered. To anticipate, it is evident that the "best" approach depends upon the purposes of the investigator.

PLAN OF THE BOOK

This book will first consider the issues and problems that have arisen in the study of groups and some of the solutions that have been offered. In a sense, this discussion is an introduction to the principles that have been formulated through the scientific study of group dynamics, which is the major concern of this text. It is hoped that the presentation of principles of small group behavior will impose some order on the complex array of interrelationships that have been established by four decades of research. The reader may decide for himself whether and to what extent this goal has been achieved.

The book is divided into four unequal parts. Part I is introductory and deals with the nature of groups (the first sections of this chapter) and approaches to the study of groups (Chapter 2). Part II deals with the origin of groups and coaction (Chapters 3 and 4). It is an attempt to bridge the gap between individual and group behavior. Chapter 3 reviews the early studies on social facilitation, compares individuals and groups on the solution of complex problems, and discusses brainstorming and the risky shift phenomenon as examples of more recent studies of coactive behavior. Chapter 4 is an exploration of the process of group formation and development.

Part III considers the interaction process and constitutes the major portion of the text. Chapter 5 is devoted to the physical setting in which group interaction occurs, and explores the ways in which group behavior is influenced by this environment. Chapter 6 examines the personal characteristics of group members and the relationship of these characteristics to group process. The social environment of the group is considered in the next two chapters. Chapter 7 presents an analysis of group composition effects. The concern here is with particular combinations of persons and personal characteristics as they are related to interaction. Chapter 8 deals with the social structure of the group: the pattern of relationships that emerge during group interaction. The effects of task characteristics and group goals are explored in Chapter 9.

Part IV (Chapter 10) is an attempt to identify some of the major deficiencies of group dynamics and to indicate how some of the principles described in the book can be related to effective group action.

SUGGESTED READINGS

CAMPBELL, D. T. Common fate, similarity, and other indices of the status of aggregates of persons as social entities. *Behavioral Science,* 1958, 3, 14–25.

CARTWRIGHT, D., & ZANDER, A. (Eds.) *Group dynamics: Research and theory.* (3d ed.) New York: Harper & Row, 1968. Pp. 3–20.

CATTELL, R. B. New concepts for measuring leadership, in terms of group syntality. *Human Relations,* 1951, 4, 161–184.

JAMES, J. A preliminary study of the size determinant in small group interaction. *American Sociological Review,* 1951, 16, 474–477.

McDAVID, J. W., & HARARI, H. *Social psychology: Individuals, groups, societies.* New York: Harper & Row, 1968. Pp. 235–241.

MILLS, T. M. *The sociology of small groups.* Englewood Cliffs, N.J.: Prentice-Hall, 1967. Pp. 1–56.

CHAPTER 2

APPROACHES TO THE STUDY OF GROUPS

In Chapter 1 it was noted that group dynamicists sometimes debate whether an empirical or a theoretical approach is likely to be the most productive method for analyzing group process. This controversy often turns out to be no more than a difference in the emphasis placed on theory or research or perhaps only a difference in personal preference for one or the other approach. Probably no one would deny that theorizing and empirical research are interrelated processes and that both are needed for the complete analysis of group behavior. Empiricism provides the evidence necessary for the construction of a meaningful theory. Theory, in turn, organizes and extends known data and thus serves as a framework for further empirical work. Theory often suggests new directions for future research that might otherwise be overlooked. New empirical evidence either strengthens the theory, if consistent with it, or forces rejection or modification if not. Thus, scientific knowledge escalates through successive increments from both theory and research. The important choice, then, is not between theoretical and empirical approaches, but between kinds of theories and between kinds of empirical methods.

THEORETICAL APPROACHES

A theory may be defined as *". . . a set of interrelated hypotheses or propositions concerning a phenomenon or set of phenomena"* (Shaw & Costanzo, 1970, p. 4). Thus, theoretical approaches may vary from very general systems or orientations, such as field theory, psychoanalytic theory, etc., to "small" theories dealing with a specific phenomenon such as leadership or conformity behavior. Shaw and Costanzo (1970) used the term "theoretical orientation" to refer to the more general approach and reserved the term "theory" for the more limited approach. The theoretical approaches examined here deal with "middle range" phenomena, namely, small group behavior.

Many theoretical approaches have been proposed and each has made a contribution to our understanding of group behavior. It is not our purpose here, however, to exhaustively review theories of group process. Instead, selected theories will be described briefly to give the student some familiarity with differing viewpoints and to provide a basis for organizing the empirical data presented in later portions of this text. More detailed accounts of these theories may be found in *Theories of Social Psychology* (Shaw & Costanzo, 1970), but the best source is the original treatise by the author of each theory.

GROUP SYNTALITY THEORY

Group syntality theory was formulated by Cattell (1948). This approach was called "empirical-statistical" by Cartwright and Zander (1968) and "transorientational" by Shaw and Costanzo (1970). Cartwright and Zander were impressed by the method that Cattell used in obtaining the data that went into his theory. Cattell relied heavily on factor analysis as an analytic tool, it is true, but this only provided the raw materials for the theory and probably should not be considered a theoretical approach per se. Shaw and Costanzo, on the other hand, were impressed by the degree to which syntality theory incorporated aspects of different theoretical orientations. For example, Cattell's use of vectors in regard to synergy (group energy) draws upon Lewin's field orientation, whereas his appeal to the law of effect in explaining the acquisition of patterns of group behavior makes use of reinforcement theory. Regardless of its classification, syntality theory represents an interesting approach to the analysis of groups, and one that is strikingly different from the other three summarized in this chapter.

Cattell's theory consists of two interrelated parts, one part dealing with the dimensions of groups and the other with the dynamics of syntality. His dimensions of groups consist of three categories or "panels." These panels were labeled *population traits, syntality traits,* and *characteristics of internal structure.* Thus, each panel is really a set of variables or characteristics which describe some aspect of the group.

Population traits are merely the characteristics of the individual members who compose the group. Such personal characteristics exist independently of the group and are brought to it when the individual becomes a member. In describing the dimensions of the group in terms of population traits, Cattell (1948) used the averages of these characteristics. The population panel of a given group, therefore, consists of average intelligence, attitude, personality, etc., of the members of the group.

Syntality is defined as the personality of the group, or, more precisely, as any effect that the group has as a totality. It is that which makes the group a unique entity. Syntality traits, then, are those effects which the group has, acting as a group. Such effects may be in relation to another group or to the environment in which the group exists. Syntality traits are inferred from the external behavior of the group and may include such behaviors as decision making, aggressive acts, and the like.

Internal structure refers to the relationships among group members, and structural characteristics describe the organizational patterns within the group. Roles, cliques, status positions, communication networks, and the like are examples of characteristics of internal structure.

The three panels are characterized by interdependency. If all the laws of group behavior were known, then it should be possible to predict any one panel from a knowledge of the other two.

Cultural influences are found in all three panels. For example, the characteristics of an individual group member (population traits) are determined in large part by the cultural experiences that the individual has undergone earlier in life. The kinds of interrelationships that develop within a group are also influenced by cultural tradition. Since group syntality is influenced by population traits and structure, it is also indirectly influenced by cultural variables.

Cattell's major concept for analyzing the dynamics of syntality is *synergy*. Each individual joins the group for the purpose of satisfying some psychological need or needs. He thus brings to the group a degree of energy that he has committed to the group's activities. Synergy is the total of this individual energy that is available to the group. Typically, the activities of the group are of two kinds: activities directed toward the maintenance of the group and those directed toward achievement of the group's goal(s). That is, some major portion of the group's synergy must be used to deal with interpersonal relations in the group. In any group there is a certain amount of friction among group members resulting from status striving, power seeking, member incompatibility, etc. The portion of synergy that must be diverted to establishing cohesion and harmony in the group is called *maintenance synergy*. This requirement for synergy is met first, since the group would otherwise disintegrate. After these activities have been supplied with synergy, that which is left over (called *effective synergy*) can be used to achieve the goals of the group.

Seven "theorems" were proposed by Cattell (1948) in his analysis of the dynamics of syntality, which are largely specifications of the characteristics of synergy. Briefly stated, these theorems are:

1   Groups are formed to satisfy individual needs and cease to exist when they no longer serve this purpose.

2   The total synergy of a group is the vectorial resultant of the attitudes of all members toward the group. (Synergy thus depends upon the number of persons in the group, the strength and direction of the satisfactions each person obtains from the group, and the relation of such satisfactions to other groups.)

3   Effective synergy may be directed toward goals outside the group; hence groups may establish patterns of reacting which are subsidiary to some ultimate goal of the group. (For example, a nation may establish an army as a means of attaining its goal of security.)

4   Individual group members may also use groups to achieve personal goals; that is, group activities may be subsidiary to some ultimate personal goal.

(For example, a man may join a trade union (group) in order to join a ship's company (group) in order to travel to see his girl (personal goal).)

5   Patterns of behavior in groups, such as loyalty, subsidiation, and subordination are learned in accordance with the law of effect.

6   Group memberships may overlap, but the total synergy in such overlapping groups remains constant so long as individual energy directed toward nongroup goals remains constant and group activities relative to goal distance do not vary. (Note that this does *not* mean that an individual cannot join a new group without taking energy from groups to which he already belongs. On the contrary, he may do so if the goals of the new group are consistent with his interests. For example, a man who is interested in golf may join a committee to improve the golf course without developing new energy or using energy devoted to other groups. On the other hand, if a person is a member of a group committed to aiding the physically handicapped and joins a group devoted to helping the culturally disadvantaged, some synergy would probably be drained off from the first group, since the source of synergy is the member's concern for hapless persons in both groups.)

7   There exists a close parallelism between the personality traits of the group members and the syntality traits of the group. (For example, individual disposition rigidity parallels syntal conservatism, personal intelligence level parallels syntal integration, etc.)

Many of the terms used by Cattell appear to be unnecessarily recondite. Nevertheless, syntality theory contains some interesting implications for group process. For example, the energies available to groups having common members are interrelated, so that energy which a member commits to one group may detract from that available for use by other groups (theorem 6). This might account for some cases of intergroup conflict. Theorem 7 suggests that the researcher can probably learn as much from the study of the individual group members as he can from studying the group as a whole, and vice versa. This implication is, of course, related to the implications from theorem 5: The law of effect works on individuals, and the patterns of behavior in the group can be established through the reinforcement of selected patterns of individual behavior. For greater detail, the interested reader may wish to refer to Cattell (1951a, 1951b), Cattell and Wispe (1948), and

Cattell, Saunders, and Stice (1953). These reports show how some of the panels of group behavior can be measured and how the ideas discussed above are related to the empirical-statistical orientation discussed in Chapter 1.

A THEORY OF GROUP ACHIEVEMENT

A rather different approach was taken by Stogdill (1959) in the construction of his theory of group achievement. Stogdill was primarily concerned with group productivity and hence did not attempt to account for all aspects of group behavior. Cartwright and Zander (1968) referred to this theory as a systems theory, since Stogdill made use of the concept of "open system" and analyzed group process in terms of inputs and outputs. Shaw and Costanzo (1970) noted that Stogdill's approach included elements of reinforcement theory, field theory, and cognitive theory, and so labeled it a transorientational approach. Again, the label is less important than the structure of the theory.

The structure of the theory consists of three sets or classes of variables: member inputs, mediating variables, and group outputs or group achievement. Each of these classes includes a number of elements. *Member inputs* are identified as *performances, interactions,* and *expectations.* These are the attributes of individuals, alone or in interaction, and they constitute the necessary elements for the description of group behavior. Stogdill defined interaction as an interpersonal situation in which the reaction of any member is a response to the reaction of some other member of the group. Since it is interpersonal, interaction always involves at least two persons, each of whom is reacting to the other. Interaction thus includes actions and reactions, or performances. That is, performance is defined as a response which is a part of an interaction. Performances are, therefore, such things as decision making, planning, communication, and cooperative work. Expectation is defined as a readiness for reinforcement and is introduced to account for such things as group purpose, role differentiation, and group stability.

Performances, interactions, and expectations are seen as interdependent, to varying degrees. Performance and interaction combine to determine structure; performance and continuing interaction produce group identity; performance provides the means by which expectations are confirmed (reinforced); and interaction and expectation combine to produce purpose and the mutual reinforcement of norms. This means that mediating variables are the result of member inputs.

Mediating variables include both *formal structure* and *role structure,* each of which consists of two elements. Formal structure includes functions and status, whereas role structure includes responsibility and authority. Formal structure results from predictable patterns of interactions in the group, which lead to differentiated positions. In the organized group, the structure involves a predictable pattern of action and reaction plus a system of mutually reinforced expectations. Status and functions inhere in these differentiated positions in the group structure. Status is a hierarchical relationship between two or more persons and defines the degrees of freedom that the occupant has in initiating and maintaining goal direction. The function of the positions specifies the nature of the contribution that the occupant is expected to make to the group effort.

Role structure refers to that part of the group structure which is attributable to the particular group members, in contrast to the formal structure, which refers to that part which is largely independent of particular group members. Responsibility is defined as the set of performances that a given occupant of a position is expected to exhibit, whereas authority is defined as the degree of freedom the occupant is expected to exercise. In general, the higher a person's status in the formal structure, the greater his authority, and his responsibility is expected to be related to the functions of the position he occupies.

Group outputs or *group achievement* is the resultant of member inputs and mediating variables. That is, group achievement is the consequence of performances, interactions, and expectations, mediated through group structure and operations. The essential dimensions of group achievement are productivity, morale, and integration. Stogdill defined *productivity* as change in expectancy values as a result of group behavior. Stated differently, member performances and interactions create changes in expectations which are either positively or negatively valued by the group members; the degree of such changes represents group productivity. Group *morale* was defined as the degree of freedom from restraint in working toward the goals of the group. Stogdill believed that morale is lowest in an unstructured group and highest in a structured group in which members know the limits of acceptable behavior. There is, however, an upper limit beyond which increased structure does not increase freedom. Since the degree of freedom may be increased through the reinforcement of goal expectations, such reinforcement also increases group morale. Group *integration,* the third dimension of group achievement, is defined as the degree to which the group can maintain its structure and operations under stress. Group integration is similar to the notion of cohesiveness (Thibaut, 1950) and is reflected by such things as mutual liking among group members, member satisfactions, and other positive reactions to the group. Although productivity, morale, and integration vary together, they are interrelated; hence, when inputs are constant, an increase in one of these dimensions can occur only at the expense of one or both of the others.

In summary, Stogdill proposed that performances, interactions, and expectations (input variables) lead to formal structure and role structure (mediating variables), which in turn lead to productivity, morale, and integration (group achievement). The general trend of events is thus from inputs to mediating variables to outputs, although there are reversals in that each set of variables is influenced by each of the other sets.

EXCHANGE THEORY

Thibaut and Kelley (1959) proposed a much more ambitious theory (or "framework" as they preferred to call it) than that of either Cattell or Stogdill. Their intention was to explain interpersonal behavior and group processes. They viewed their approach as primarily functionalistic, since their focus was upon what is useful or effective from the viewpoint of the group. The theory assumes that the existence of the group is based solely upon the participation and satisfaction of individuals in the group. Therefore, the analysis of group processes must be in terms of the adjustments that *individuals* make in attempting to solve the problems of interdependency. It is not too difficult to see that this viewpoint leads almost inevitably to the adoption of a reinforcement orientation. Although their analysis was limited largely to the dyad, Thibaut and Kelley believe that their theory applies to larger groups as well.

The theory can best be described by examining the authors' analysis of interaction, which involves (1) definitions of the key concepts used in the theory, (2) a consideration of the consequences of interaction, and (3) an analysis of members' evaluations of interpersonal relationships.

The key concepts in the theory are *interpersonal relationship, interaction, behavior sequence,* and *behavior repertoire.* "Interaction" and "interpersonal relationship" are interdependent and hence are defined together. The central feature of interaction is the interpersonal relationship, and two persons are said to have formed a relationship if they interact on several occasions. This statement is meaningful, of course, only when "interaction" has been defined. It is perhaps best to quote Thibaut and Kelley's definition of interaction: "By interaction is meant that they emit behavior in each other's presence, they create products for each other, or they communicate with each other. In every case that we would identify as an instance of interaction there is at least the possibility that the actions of each person affect the other" (Thibaut & Kelley, 1959, p. 10).

For example, if person A meets person B on the street, stops and chats with him about the weather, and listens to his troubles of the day, and then each proceeds on his way, they are said to have interacted; that is, their conversation was an instance of interaction.

The "behavior sequence" was chosen as the unit for the analysis of behavior. Each behavior sequence is said to consist of a number of specific motor and verbal acts that are sequentially organized and directed toward some immediate goal. In the example given above, A's motor and verbal acts during the chat about the weather might be considered a sequence of acts directed toward the goal of being friendly, and hence would be treated as a behavior sequence. Each individual is, of course, capable of enacting a tremendous number and variety of behavior sequences. Thibaut and Kelley used the term "behavior repertoire" to refer to all the possible behavior sequences that a given person might enact during interaction with another person, including combinations of possible behavior sequences. Of course, interaction is selective both with respect to who interacts with whom and with respect to what behavior sequences are enacted. Probably no person interacts with every other person that it would be possible for him to interact with, nor does he enact all possible behavior sequences. For example, it is possible for most persons to enact a behavior sequence leading to murder, but few persons do so.

The consequences of interaction (outcomes) are described in terms of rewards and costs. When two persons interact, each one typically enjoys some part of the interaction, but finds other parts less enjoyable or even unpleasant. The concept of *reward* refers to those aspects which the individual finds pleasurable, enjoyable, gratifying, or otherwise satisfying. "The provision of a means whereby a drive is reduced or a need fulfilled constitutes a reward" (Thibaut & Kelley, 1959, p. 12). *Costs* refer to anything that inhibits the performance of a behavior sequence. That is, the greater the inhibition that the person must overcome in order to perform a given behavior sequence, the more costly the enactment of that behavior.

Rewards and costs may be determined by either exogenous or endogenous factors. Exogenous factors are those things which are external to the interpersonal relationship. For example, rewards and costs that are due to individual characteristics such as values, skills, needs, tools, and the like are regarded as exogenous. If an individual is highly skilled in the performance of a given act, he may find it enjoyable to enact that behavior sequence in the presence of others; if he is unskilled, the enactment of that same behavior sequence may incur a cost. Endogenous factors are those which are inherent in the relationship itself; that is, the reward or cost depends not only upon the actions of the individual but also upon the behaviors of the other person. Two musicians may enjoy a musical interaction only if they harmonize; each one trying to play a different tune would probably be costly to both, owing to response interference. Other kinds of endogenous costs are due to satiation, fatigue, or incompatible responses.

In applying these concepts to the analysis of group behavior, Thibaut and Kelley (1959) made use of a behavior matrix, modeled after game theory formulations. An example of this matrix is shown in Figure 2-1, which represents the possible outcomes of interactions of persons A and B. The

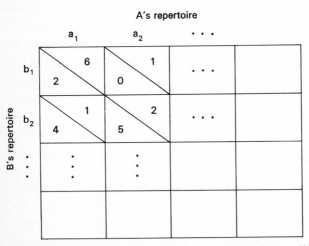

Figure 2-1   Matrix of Possible Outcomes, Scaled according to Overall Goodness of Outcomes. (Reproduced with permission from J. W. Thibaut & H. H. Kelley. *The social psychology of groups.* New York: Wiley, 1959, Table 2-2, p. 15.)

columns of the matrix represent the behavior repertoire of person A and the rows represent that of person B. The numbers in the upper portion of each cell indicate the outcome of the interaction for person A whenever the interaction falls within that cell, and the number in the lower portion indicates B's outcomes for that same interaction. For example, if A enacts behavior sequence a_1 and B enacts behavior sequence b_1, the interaction falls in the upper left-hand corner of the matrix; hence A's outcome is 6 units and B's outcome is 2 units. In this example, these are, of course, arbitrary units which represent the resultant of costs incurred and rewards received during the course of that particular interaction. Parenthetically, it might be noted that the determination of exact values for rewards and costs in a natural situation is one of the unsolved problems for exchange theory and, indeed, for all of psychology.

According to Thibaut and Kelley, interaction outcomes are evaluated by comparison with certain internal standards, which they called the *comparison level* (CL) and the *comparison level for alternatives* (CL_{alt}). The CL is the standard against which an individual evaluates the attractiveness of an interpersonal relationship, or how satisfactory it is. The CL is a subjective standard that is developed as a consequence of the interpersonal relationships the individual has experienced during his lifetime. In general, the CL will be somewhere near the middle of the range of relationships that the person has experienced, ordered according to the goodness of the outcomes. Once the CL has been established, the individual will evaluate positively any relationship that falls above the CL in terms of outcomes, and negatively any relationship that falls below. Presumably, each new experience leads to some modification of the CL, although the increment (or decrement) from any one interaction may be negligible. This conception of the CL is similar to other formulations regarding subjective standards; for example, reference scales (Tresselt, 1947), adaptation level (Helson, 1948), and judgment scales (Sherif & Hovland, 1961).

The CL_{alt} is the standard which an individual uses to decide whether to remain in a relationship or to leave it. The CL_{alt} is the lowest outcome that a person will accept in view of his alternative relationships. Theoretically, an individual might choose to enter into or to maintain a relationship which is unattractive (below his CL) if it is the most attractive one available to him at the time, that is, if it is above his CL_{alt}. For example, if a young man wishes to attend the high school prom, he may elect to escort a young lady who is not particularly attractive to him if she is the best alternative that he has available for that affair. His relationship with her may well fall below his CL but, nevertheless, be above his CL_{alt}. On the other hand, a person may leave an attractive relationship if there are more attractive alternatives. It should be noted that these considerations assume that the relationship is voluntary; the individual may be forced to remain in a relationship that is below both his CL and his CL_{alt}.

This analysis of group interaction can be used to predict the course of interaction if one can identify the rewards and costs in the situation. Thibaut and Kelley proposed that an individual generally repeats a rewarded response but does not repeat a costly response. Consider, for example, the interaction matrix depicted in Figure 2-2. This represents a situation which Thibaut and Kelley called an instance of mutual fate control. In this situation, persons A and B can each determine the other's outcomes regardless of the other's behavior. In this situation, Thibaut and Kelley predict that A will eventually enact a_1 and B will enact b_1 after a series of exchanges. For example, if A enacts a_1 and B enacts b_2, then A is punished (the interaction is costly) and B is rewarded; hence A will tend to change his response and B will tend to repeat the same response. This means that on the next exchange, the interaction will be in the lower right-hand cell, and both persons will be punished. On the next exchange, both should shift responses, putting the interaction into the a_1/b_1 cell. Both are rewarded and the inter-

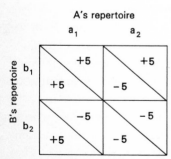

Figure 2-2 An Illustration of Mutual Fate Control. (After J. W. Thibaut & H. H. Kelley. *The social psychology of groups.* New York: Wiley, 1959, Table 7-3, p. 106.)

action should continue in this manner. No matter where the interaction starts, it should always lead to the same final pattern of interaction. Although this example deals with mutual fate control, the same principles should apply to other outcome matrices. Several empirical studies (Bixenstine, Potash, & Wilson, 1963; M. E. Shaw, 1962; Willis & Joseph, 1959) have yielded results opposite to those predicted by the theory; that is, interacting dyads tend to develop an interaction pattern in which the outcomes are *low* for both persons. However, it is unclear whether these findings are due to failure to manipulate rewards and costs or to inaccuracy of the theory.

Exchange theory has many other important implications which cannot be covered here. Its greatest contribution at this stage is probably to the organization of empirical data rather than to the prediction of interpersonal behavior. This is due in part to the difficulty of determining rewards and costs for particular persons and in part to the fact that the theory has not been widely tested as yet.

FIRO

FIRO is a theory of interpersonal behavior that derives from the psychoanalytic orientation. It was formulated by Schutz in 1955 and was later expanded and modified (Schutz, 1958, 1967). FIRO means "Fundamental Interpersonal Relations Orientation." As the name indicates, the theory attempts to explain interpersonal behavior in terms of orientations to others. The theory holds that every person orients himself toward others in certain characteristic patterns, which can be explained in terms of three interpersonal needs: inclusion, control, and affection. These needs are present during childhood, and the characteristic interaction pattern that an individual develops with respect to each need area is a consequence of the way the child was treated by his parents or other adults and of the manner in which he responded to these treatments. The way the individual orients himself to others is a major determinant of interpersonal behavior.

Inclusion refers to the need for togetherness, the need to associate with others. The need manifests itself through behaviors designed to attract the attention and interest of others (Schutz, 1967). The person who has a strong need for inclusion will reveal this through strivings for prominence, recognition, prestige, etc.

Control refers to the decision-making process between people. The need for control varies from the need to dominate others, to have power and authority over them, to the need to be controlled. At one extreme, the person wants to control others completely; at the other extreme, he wants others to control him completely. Again, this need is manifested through the person's behavior vis-à-vis others. The person with a high need to control displays rebellion and refusal to be controlled; the person with a high need to be controlled is compliant and submissive to others.

Affection refers to close personal and emotional feelings between two individuals, and its extremes are represented by love and hate. The person with a strong need for affection will be friendly, make overtures to others, and generally try to establish close emotional ties with others. At the other extreme, the low-need person will avoid close interpersonal relations.

When two or more persons interact, each one typically enacts in each need area the characteristic behavior pattern that he developed in childhood. The interaction patterns of any two given individuals may be either compatible or incompatible. If they are compatible, then the interaction is likely to be easy and productive; if incompatible, difficult and unproductive. Schutz (1958) identified three types of compatibility-incompatibility that could occur in each of the three need areas: interchange compatibility, originator compatibility, and reciprocal compatibility. *Interchange compatibility* is based upon the mutual expression of inclusion, control, or affection. Some persons prefer a great deal of exchange of behavior relevant to the need area under consideration, whereas others prefer neither to receive nor to send inclusion, control, or affection. Interchange compatibility exists when the two persons interacting are similar with respect to the amount of exchange desired; incompatibility results from dissimilarity in this respect.

Originator compatibility derives from the originator-receiver dimension of interaction. In general, two persons are compatible to the degree that the expression of inclusion, control, or affection corresponds to that which the other person wishes to receive in each area. For example, if one person needs to control and tries to dominate another, and that other needs to be submissive, they will be compatible. On the other hand, if one person actively initiates group activities for persons who do not want to be included in such activities, they will be incompatible.

Reciprocal compatibility reflects the degree to which two persons "reciprocally satisfy each other's behavior preferences" (Schutz, 1958, p. 108). If one member of a two-person group is frustrated because the other does not satisfy his needs or if he cannot express his preferred behavior toward the other, the dyad will be incompatible.

The general assumption of Schutz's theory is that compatible groups will be more efficient than incompatible groups. This is reflected in the initial formation of groups, in the degree to which the groups are likely to continue to function, and in the productivity of groups. Research reported by Schutz (1955, 1958, 1967) generally supports the theory.

A BRIEF COMPARISON OF THEORIES

Each of these theories attempts to explain group behavior, although they differ in the range of group processes encompassed. The most comprehensive theory probably is exchange theory, which can be applied to any aspect of group behavior. The most restricted is the theory of group achievement proposed by Stogdill; it does not purport to account for all group behavior, only for the productivity of groups. The other two theories aspire to generality but are not as easily extended to all forms of group behavior as is exchange theory.

The theories also differ in precision, although it is difficult to compare them in terms of overall precision. Syntality theory lacks precision in the definition of some terms and in the measurement of variables. The theory of group achievement lacks precision in that predictions are not unambiguously derivable from its conceptual formulations. Both exchange theory and FIRO permit relatively precise predictions about group behavior, but both suffer from measurement problems. Exchange theory requires the identification and measurement of reinforcers, and this has proved a difficult undertaking. FIRO requires the measurement of needs and the combining of these measures to predict compatibility. Schutz's need scales are moderately satisfactory, but some of the formulas for computing compatibility are of questionable validity.

In spite of these problems, each theory aids in the understanding of group process, and we shall have occasion to refer to each of them again as we explore small group phenomena.

EMPIRICAL APPROACHES

As we noted in Chapter 1, the empirical approaches to the study of small groups fall into three general classes: field studies, laboratory experiments, and computer simulation studies. There are, of course, several variations within each of these categories.

FIELD STUDIES

The basic characteristic of a field study is that the phenomenon under investigation is studied as it exists "naturally." That is, the investigator does not create the situation or situations being studied; instead, he examines the phenomenon as it occurs in natural ongoing social events. The study is conducted "in the field" rather than in a laboratory. The form of field studies may differ, depending upon the purposes and biases of the investigator. If the purpose of the investigator is to explore and describe, the field study is likely to begin with few or no hypotheses, and the researcher will make no attempt to manipulate any aspect of the situation. This is also likely to be the case if the investigator believes strongly that valid data can be obtained only by avoiding any obtrusion into the phenomenon being studied. On the other hand, the investigator may be primarily interested in testing hypotheses and may believe that interference with the phenomenon is the only way one can be certain that the observed relationships among variables are true cause-effect relationships. In this case, the form of the field study will probably be a "field experiment." That is, the investigator manipulates the variable(s) of interest to him, but does so in natural situations rather than in the laboratory. A compromise between these two extreme types of field studies is the "natural experiment." In this approach, the investigator takes advantage of naturally occurring events in order to examine their consequences for group behavior. Let us consider each of these variations.

DESCRIPTIVE-EXPLORATORY STUDIES   The purpose of a descriptive-exploratory field study is to describe the groups under investigation, often with the intention of identifying relationships among variables. The exact purpose served by this approach varies from a mere description of the characteristics of groups to the formulation of precise hypotheses about functional relationships. If the purpose is to formulate hypotheses and/or to establish functional relationships, the researcher may take one of two possible approaches. He may select groups randomly, measure several variables or characteristics of the groups, and look for relationships among them; or he may select groups according to specified criteria, so that they represent different degrees or levels of the variable of interest, and compare sets of groups with respect to other characteristics. An example of the first approach is a study by Polansky, Lippitt, and Redl (1950) of behavioral contagion in groups. These investigators studied eight boys' groups and eight girls' groups in two summer camps. Data consisted of counselor ratings, observations by the experimenters, and questionnaire responses by the boys and girls. The investigators then examined the relationship of the group member's perception of his position in the group and his prestige rating to his influence in the group. High-prestige members attempted influence more often and initiated "contagion" more often than low-prestige members. This observation led to the formulation of hypotheses about the effects of prestige position upon social influence in groups.

The second approach may be illustrated by a study of social welfare agencies conducted by Blau (1959–1960). Among other things, Blau was interested in the effects of the size of the agency upon the behavior of welfare workers. He therefore selected several small agencies and several large ones and examined and compared the role characteristics found in agencies of each size. At the time the study was planned, Blau believed that the differences between large and small agencies could be attributed to the size variable. However, during the study he became aware that the small agencies were located in small towns and the large agencies in large towns. He therefore concluded that differences were due to the environmental setting rather than to the size of the agency.

Exploratory-descriptive studies are attractive to investigators concerned with the relevance of empirical studies to natural situations. Since the situations studied are natural ones, there is no question of relevance to other similar situations. However, since there are many natural settings that might be chosen for investigation and since only a few can be selected, one might still question the generality of the findings. This is a question that can be raised with respect to any empirical study and probably is less serious in this approach than in more restricted approaches. The most serious problem with the exploratory-descriptive approach is the relative uncertainty of the validity of conclusions. The investigator measures only a few of the many uncontrolled variables operating in the field, and he has no good basis for determining cause-effect relations or, indeed, the validity of observed relationships. The study of welfare agencies cited above provides a good example of this problem. Had Blau been less observant, he might very well have concluded that size of welfare agency is a determinant of role characteristics, although it appears more likely that the environmental setting is the major variable.

But even this conclusion may not be valid; some other unnoticed variable may be the real determinant of the role characteristics.

NATURAL EXPERIMENTS   The natural experiment differs from the exploratory-descriptive study in that the investigator takes advantage of naturally occurring changes to study their effects upon group process. This sometimes can be planned in advance if the researcher knows that the change is about to occur or will occur at a definite time. For example, if he knows that certain classrooms will be desegregated on a given date, he can design a before-after study, or he can select other similar classrooms that will not be desegregated and compare those which are with those which are not. In this way the effects of desegregation can be evaluated.

An example of this approach is the study by Cook, Havel, and Christ (1957). They learned that certain foreign students would be selected to attend a summer orientation program in the United States (although they had no voice in the selection) and planned an experiment to study the effects of the orientation on the students. A control group was selected which was roughly matched to the experimental group (those attending the orientation) on such characteristics as nationality, field of study, and age. The two groups could then be compared on the dependent measures of interest to the investigators.

The natural experiment has an added advantage over the exploratory-descriptive study in that cause-effect relationships are somewhat more impelling. However, since the investigator does not have control over the manipulation, uncontrolled and unknown variables may be contaminating the results.

FIELD EXPERIMENTS   The field experiment carries the degree of experimental control one step further: The investigator himself controls the manipulation of variables, but he does so in a field setting. A classic example of this approach is the study of resistance to change conducted by Coch and French (1948). The subjects for this study were four groups of factory workers. Groups contained from seven to fourteen members. At the beginning of the study, the four groups were roughly equivalent on cohesiveness, efficiency, and the amount of change that would be necessary to carry out the study. All groups were subjected to change in work procedure, but preparation for the change was different for different groups. In one group representatives of the workers participated in planning the change, in two groups all workers participated in planning the change, and in the fourth group the members were merely informed of the change. Effects of the various treatments were measured by determining the time required for the groups to attain a set standard of efficiency. Total participation produced the fastest learning of the new procedure, representative participation produced the next best rate, and no participation (the control group) produced the slowest rate of all. This group failed to attain the standard.

A similar kind of field study was conducted by Morse and Reimer (1956). These researchers studied the effect of increasing the decision-making role of the rank-and-file employees in an industrial organization. Four clerical groups were selected to be as similar as possible on a number of characteristics related to group satisfaction and productivity. Two of the groups were randomly assigned to an "autonomy" condition and the other two to a "hierarchically controlled" condition. Members of the autonomy groups were given increased control over their activities, whereas members of the hierarchically controlled groups experienced a decrease in such control. Pre-post measures of satisfaction and productivity indicated that satisfaction increased in the autonomy groups but decreased in the hierarchically controlled groups. All groups increased in productivity, but the increase was greater in the hierarchically controlled groups.*

The advantage of the field experiment over the natural experiment is evident. Since the experimenter controls the introduction of changes in the former, he can be more confident that he has controlled for the effects of unwanted variables. In the latter the change is introduced by natural events or by others. There is still some question about the degree of control over other variables that might influence the phenomena under investigation, but the field approach represents the best compromise between the need to control significant variables and the desire to extend findings to everyday events and situations.

LABORATORY EXPERIMENTS

The major difference between the laboratory experiment and the field study is the locus of the investigation, that is, a self-contained laboratory rather than a natural setting. This difference, however, is highly significant because it carries with it many implications for the control of variables and the

---

* This difference in productivity may have been due to an artifact inherent in the method of measuring productivity. This experiment will be discussed in greater detail in a subsequent chapter.

generality of findings. The greatest advantage of the laboratory experiment is the degree of control that the experimenter can exercise over variables. If the experimenter is ingenuous enough, he can control all or most of the variables that might influence the phenomenon under consideration, except the one(s) that he is interested in studying. Cause and effect can be established with considerably greater confidence than when such controls are lacking. On the other hand, this degree of control makes the laboratory situation unlike any situation that one is likely to encounter in the "real world." Critics of the laboratory approach have used this fact to deny that such studies have any validity for group behavior outside the laboratory. However, Festinger (1953) has argued cogently that the situation in which a group member finds himself is real to him, whether it is in the laboratory or in a natural setting. There are really two issues here: (1) the validity of the behavior, given the conditions under which it occurs, and (2) whether the effects that occur in the laboratory also occur outside the laboratory, i.e., in natural situations. Observations made in either laboratories or natural settings may be valid or invalid, depending upon the conditions under which the observations are made. But the mere fact that data are obtained in the laboratory does not invalidate them. Nevertheless, it is true that the strength of variables operating in the laboratory is usually much less than the strength of similar variables found in natural situations. It is often implicitly assumed that if weak variables produce small effects in the laboratory, strong variables of the same type will produce large effects in natural settings. This is a hazardous assumption which few, if any, investigators would accept when it is stated explicitly, and the careful student of group behavior will be on guard against making such an assumption implicitly.

Whether effects that occur in the laboratory can be generalized to natural situations is a more complex problem. It may be that the variables studied in the laboratory are basically different from those operating in natural settings; if so, laboratory results obviously cannot be generalized to situations outside the laboratory. It is also true that conclusions formulated from laboratory results may not hold in natural settings where many other variables are operating. In natural groups another variable may be so powerful that the effects of the "laboratory variable" are negated.

Like other approaches, laboratory experimentation has many variations. The laboratory experiment most similar to the field experiment is that in which experienced or natural groups are brought into the laboratory and subjected to experimental treatments. The more common method, however, involves the formation of "artificial" or naïve groups for the sole purpose of experimentation. Naïve groups may be formed by random assignment of members or by systematic selection of members to represent specific populations.

EXPERIENCED GROUPS When natural groups are brought into the laboratory, they are already experienced groups; that is, the members of the groups have already established relationships among themselves and many of the processes of group formation have already been completed. This means that the initial phases of group formation cannot be studied with such groups. Often, however, the experimenter is interested in studying processes that are interfered with by group formation processes. Experienced groups are preferable for such studies, as well as for those designed for generalization to natural ongoing groups.

This approach is illustrated by a study conducted by Bowen (1966) in which family groups were brought into the laboratory for the purpose of studying coalition patterns. By bringing three families (father, mother, and teen-age son) into the laboratory at the same time, and systematically rotating group memberships, Bowen was not only able to examine patterns of coalition formation in family groups, but was also able to compare such patterns in family, simulated family (father, mother, and son, each from a different family), and ad hoc groups (three fathers, three mothers, or three sons).

The advantages of using experienced groups are obvious, but it should also be evident that intragroup relationships that are brought with the group into the laboratory may influence the experimental results. That is, there is a greater probability of unknown variables contaminating the results of experiments using experienced groups than of those using naïve groups. Nevertheless, if the intent is to generalize to experienced groups, then the results of studies using such groups are clearly more relevant.

SELECTED NAÏVE GROUPS Often an investigator is interested in studying variables that can be manipulated only through selection. For example, the investigation of group composition effects almost necessarily requires selection of group members. This can be illustrated by an experimental test of FIRO in which Schutz (1955) selected group members according to their scores on need scales. Based on these scores, groups were formed to be either compatible or incompatible, and Schutz was able to show that compatible groups were more effective than incompatible groups when faced with tasks requiring intragroup cooperation. This technique has the advantage of permitting relatively precise specification of group characteristics, but care must be taken to ensure that such selection does not result in the unwitting variation of other significant variables.

RANDOM NAÏVE GROUPS   In laboratory experimentation, the common approach is to use random naïve groups. Subjects are randomly assigned to groups; the groups thus composed are then randomly assigned to sets of groups which are exposed to differential treatments. The purpose of this procedure is to ensure that members of groups exposed to differential experimental treatments are not initially different. Since randomization ensures that each subject has the same chance as any other subject of being assigned to any given group, it is unlikely that any sizable sets of groups assigned to different experimental treatments will be different at the beginning of the experiment. And differences that are observed following experimental manipulations are attributed to the treatment differences. It should be kept in mind, however, that randomization does not guarantee initial comparability of groups. Even strictly random assignment can result in differences in group composition, which in turn can influence experimental results.

Both random and selected naïve groups are subject to the criticism that they are "artificial" and hence have no meaning for the real world. Actually, this is both a strength and a weakness. Just because a group *is* artificial, investigators can contrive situations that do not occur naturally. For example, it is probable that certain combinations of group memberships never occur in a natural group. It would be surprising to find a group composed solely of highly dominant individuals or of submissive individuals. By means of the selected naïve group procedure, however, it is easy to construct such groups in the laboratory. Also, as Cartwright and Zander (1968) pointed out, research on artificial groups in the laboratory can help resolve questions about the direction of causality or about which of several variables may be producing an observed effect found in studies of natural groups. There is, nevertheless, a problem of generalizing to nonlaboratory situations. The best approach is to examine hypotheses in both field and laboratory settings.

COMPUTER SIMULATION STUDIES

The computer simulation approach is a relatively recent development, since its use depends upon the availability of computers. In spite of this, there are several detailed accounts of computer simulation models (Borko, 1962; Gullahorn & Gullahorn, 1964; Roby, 1967; Roby, 1968). Most discussions of computer simulation studies begin with a definition of simulation. Although the need for such a definition is doubtful in this space age with its many TV simulations of space travel, the following definition is offered for those readers who may have successfully avoided the "boob tube." Simulation was originally used to refer to an individual's action and meant the act of pretending to be that which one is not. In research on small groups, it means that the investigator creates a representation or a model of the group process that he wishes to study, without requiring that it be a real group. To some degree, simulation is used in almost all experimental work; simulation is necessarily a part of investigations in which a lone subject is led to believe (through the use of tape recordings, for example) that he is a member of a group. The unique thing in computer simulation is that no subjects at all are required, although subjects may be exposed to computer simulated situations in certain instances. When both human subjects and the computer are used jointly, the method is called "man-machine simulation" (Abelson, 1968).

The use of simulation, of course, brings the research setting one step further from natural situations. Its main strength is that computer simulation permits, at least in principle, the examination of any clearly formulated hypothesis or set of hypotheses, regardless of complexity. This is most advantageous in examining the implications of explanatory systems or theories. Once these implications are clearly spelled out, it is easier to design other types of studies that are more clearly relevant to natural situations. The major weakness, of course, is that relationships established through computer simulation may not have any counterpart in the "real world." The degree to which this is true depends largely on the ingenuity of the researcher.

In applying computer simulation to small group behavior, one encounters a problem that is not usually encountered in simulating individual behavior. Computer programs usually involve sequential organization which is under the control of the main program, called "executive control" (Abelson, 1968). Since the group consists of several people, each of whom represents a center of autonomy, it is difficult to know where to locate the executive control of the group. Abelson identified two techniques that have been used to solve this problem. The approach most frequently used by psychologists is called the *aggregative* approach. The locus of control is considered to reside in each individual group member; hence executive control is distributed among members of the group who take turns generating responses. The second approach is favored by sociologists and organization theorists. It assumes that the group is an entity with its own goals, plans, etc.

As an example of computer simulation applied to social interaction, consider the hypothetical social organism created by Loehlin (1963) and referred to as "Aldous." Loehlin was interested in generating interaction patterns from principles of motivation and learning. He, therefore, endowed Aldous with three emotions (joy, fear, and anger) and three responses (approach, withdrawal, and attack). The response emitted by Aldous in any situation is a function of the relative strengths of the three emotions at that time. The effects of any response vary with the environmental situation in which the response occurs; the consequences, in turn, produce changes in the emotions. Aldous is merely a prototype and can be duplicated as often as necessary. In studying interpersonal behavior, Loehlin (1965) created two Aldouses who interacted with each other. He built in three consequences of responses: injury, satisfaction, and frustration. In this simulation, injury occurred when one Aldous attacked the other without a counterattack, resulting in increased fear or anger, or both. Satisfaction resulted from successful attack, approach, or withdrawal, and could either increase joy or decrease fear and/or anger, depending upon the circumstances in which the response occurred. Frustration was the consequence of withdrawal or attack in response to an approach, or of interference with an attack or withdrawal response. The consequences of frustration with respect to emotions varied widely, depending upon the situation, which Loehlin defined as a sequence of two responses or actions. Using this simulation, Loehlin executed a number of studies relative to two-person interaction.

It should be clear that such investigations demonstrate what outcomes are possible under the specified conditions, but they say nothing about what will happen in similar situations involving actual persons. The relevance of the method would be apparent if outcomes were empirically validated.

The interested reader who may wish to review other attempts to simulate group processes is referred to Coe (1964), Gullahorn and Gullahorn (1963, 1964), McWhinney (1964), Rainio (1966), and Roby (1968).

THEORY AND RESEARCH

Theory and research are complementary processes. A theory organizes information so that its implications can be recognized and subjected to further empirical test. This is really what science is all about. It is an attempt to understand our world through successive approximations to truth. Each theoretical proposition or hypothesis represents one level of understanding, but it must be consistent with known data as well as with data that may accumulate in the future. In one sense, a theory (or better, its propositions) is merely a guess about the nature of the phenomena it purports to explain. To be sure, it is the best guess that the theorist can make at that time with the facts available to him. But the scientist continually questions propositions and attempts to test their validity by comparing them against some external criteria. The empirical methods discussed in the previous section serve this function. Campbell and Stanley (1963) noted that the task of data collection, when its purpose is to test a theory, is primarily one of rejecting inadequate hypotheses. In designing data-collection procedures, one must therefore arrange conditions so that certain results will call for a rejection of the hypothesis being tested. Understanding the nature of this process requires a knowledge of the nature of "proof" as well as an awareness of empirical approaches used in the study of small groups.

THE NATURE OF PROOF

Upon reading a report of an empirical study of small group behavior, the beginning student frequently asks, "What does that prove?" The simple answer to that question is, "Nothing." For no single investigation is sufficient to establish the truth of any but the most limited hypothesis. In order to be absolutely sure that a proposition is true, one must examine every possible instance to which the proposition applies. For example, it cannot be "proved" that the sun always rises in the east, since we obviously have not examined every possible sunrise. It is at least theoretically possible that one fine morning the sun will rise in the west. All would agree that this is an extremely unlikely possibility, but it does illustrate two points about the nature of proof: (1) the impossibility of absolute proof without complete data, and (2) the fact that most of the propositions we accept as "proved" refer to events that have so much supporting evidence that few or no persons reject them.

If we cannot prove a theory or a proposition, then what can we do to establish its validity? Any given phenomenon occurring under a specific set of conditions can be "explained" plausibly by a number of hypotheses. Campbell and Stanley (1963) referred to these several hypotheses as *plausible rival hypotheses,* and they proposed that the purpose of experimentation is to reduce their number. The smaller the number of rival hypotheses, the greater the probability that each of the remaining plausible hypotheses is the correct one. An empirical study designed to test a theory, therefore, should yield evidence that allows the rejection of one or more plausible rival hypotheses.

Reducing the number of plausible rival hypotneses involves a process which Garner, Hake, and Eriksen (1956) called "converging operations." If an investigator observes a specific phenomenon, X, it can usually be explained by a number of hypotheses of the form "X is the result of A," "X is the result of B," . . . "X is the result of E." In attempting to decide which hypothesis is the correct one, he might try to test each hypothesis in turn; if he can show that X occurs in the presence of one factor, say, A, but not in the presence of the others, he would have some basis for concluding that X is due to A. Or perhaps he has reason to believe that A is responsible and can test for X, with A operating and all other factors controlled, or with all others operating except A. In the first instance, such one-by-one testing of hypotheses is likely to be costly in time and energy, or it may not be feasible to separate the variables in this way. The second approach is possible, but the investigator is not apt to be lucky enough to pick the correct hypothesis so easily. In the more typical case, perhaps, he can show that the effect occurs when A, B, and C are operating, with D and E controlled; when A, B, and E are operating, with C and D controlled; and that X does not occur when B, C, and D are operating, with A and E controlled. On the basis of these converging operations he would have some reason for concluding that the correct hypothesis is "X is the result of A." This conclusion, of course, rests upon the assumption that all significant variables have been considered. To the extent that this assumption is not met, gross errors are likely to occur.

Perhaps this process can be explicated more clearly by an example from the research literature. Lewin and his associates (see Lewin, 1953) conducted a series of studies on the effects of group decision* on behavior change.

* "Group decision" was used in these studies to refer to an individual decision made in a group setting.

In the first study (Lewin, 1943) attempted to change the food habits of housewives. Specifically, he was interested in encouraging them to use more undesirable meat products such as kidneys and sweetbreads. The subjects were six groups of Red Cross volunteers; groups ranged from thirteen to seventeen members. Half of the groups were given an interesting lecture arguing for greater use of these meat products, and the other half were led through group discussion to develop the same arguments as those presented in the lecture. At the end of the group discussion, the group leader asked for a show of hands by those willing to try one of the undesirable meat products. A follow-up survey revealed that only 3 percent of those in the lecture groups had served one of these meats, whereas 32 percent of those in the group decision groups had served them. Lewin suggested six factors that might logically account for the observed differences:

1 *The kind of group.* The Red Cross groups had been working together and were well organized. Perhaps organized groups are more responsive to group discussions.

2 *The degree of involvement.* In the lecture situation the audience is essentially passive. Thus the group decision situation might have created greater involvement which could account for the observed difference.

3 *Expectation.* Only the groups in the group decision situation were informed that a follow-up would be made. This expectation of surveillance might have produced the difference.

4 *The act of making a decision.* Presumably, the act of decision is a transition from a state of indecisiveness to one in which the individual is ready to act. This means that one alternative (in this instance, to serve a new meat product) is given greater potency than the other. Since the act of decision occurred only in the group decision situation, this might have accounted for the observed difference.

5 *Leader personality.* The lecturers and the leader of the group discussion were different persons; hence the effect could have been due to differences in leaders' personalities.

6 *Conformity to group standards.* Although the individual is in a group during the lecture situation, he may feel that he is psychologically alone. Thus, the difference might have been due to a greater effect of group standards in the group decision situation.

A second study (Radke & Klisurich, 1947) was conducted with six groups of housewives, with groups ranging from six to nine members. The attempt here was to increase the consumption of milk. The groups were not organized, and the same person served as both lecturer and group decision leader. A follow-up was made after two weeks and again after four weeks. In both instances, the increase was greater in the group decision situation. As in the first experiment, the group decision subjects had been told that a check would be made, but the lecture subjects had not; however, neither group was told that a second check-up would be made. Lewin and his associates concluded from these results that the greater effectiveness of the group decision procedure could not be explained by differences in kind of group, expectation, or leader personality.

A third study was then conducted (Radke & Klisurich, 1947) in which an attempt was made to increase the consumption of orange juice and cod liver oil by babies. The subjects were farm mothers with their first baby. In this study, an individual instruction condition was substituted for the lecture. The investigators reasoned that if the group decision effect was due to greater involvement, then individual instruction should create even greater involvement and thus should be more effective than group decision. Again, the group decision procedure was more effective. It was concluded that the group decision effect was not due to involvement.

Through this series of experiments (converging operations), Lewin et al. were able to reduce the number of plausible rival hypotheses to two: the act of decision and conformity to group standards. The point we wish to make here is not that these two factors are sufficient to account for the group decision effect, but rather to demonstrate the way in which converging operations can reduce the number of plausible rival hypotheses.

SUGGESTED READINGS

CATTELL, R. B. Concepts and methods in the measurement of group syntality. *Psychological Review*, 1948, **55**, 48–63.

COE, R. M. Conflict, interference and aggression: Computer simulation of a social process. *Behavioral Science*, 1964, **9**, 186–197.

FESTINGER, L. Laboratory experiments. In L. Festinger & D. Katz (Eds.), *Research methods in the behavioral sciences*. New York: Dryden Press, Inc., 1953. Pp. 136–172.

HELSON, H. Adaptation-level as a basis for a quantitative theory of frames of reference. *Psychological Review,* 1948, **55,** 297–313.

SCHUTZ, W. C. *FIRO: A three-dimensional theory of interpersonal behavior.* New York: Rinehart, 1958. Pp. 1–80.

SHAW, M. E., & COSTANZO, P. R. *Theories of social psychology.* New York: McGraw-Hill, 1970. Chap. 1.

THIBAUT, J. W., & KELLEY, H. H. *The social psychology of groups.* New York: Wiley, 1959. Pp. 1–99.

WILLIS, R. H., & JOSEPH, M. L. Bargaining behavior. I. "Prominence" as a predictor of the outcome of games of agreement. *Conflict Resolution,* 1959, **3,** 102–113.

PART II

THE ORIGIN OF GROUPS

CHAPTER 3

INDIVIDUALS AND GROUPS

Groups are composed of individuals, and group products are the consequences of individual contributions. But it is not always clear to what extent an individual's contributions are influenced by others. It is at least theoretically possible that each individual group member behaves in the group as he would alone, i.e., that others in the group have no effect upon his contributions to the group product. The evidence indicates, however, that each member's contribution is determined in part by others.

The way in which behavior is influenced by others represents the domain of social psychology. The major question for group dynamics, which is a subdivision of social psychology, is, How is behavior influenced by others *in a group?* The demarcation line between "influence by others in a group" and other aspects of social psychology is indistinct; individual social behavior sometimes merges into group behavior almost imperceptibly. This fact is reflected in the research relative to group processes. The early studies of the influence of others merely required the presence of other persons during the time the actor was performing; only later were interacting groups examined. Initially, these groups were studied only in comparison with individuals, a research area that continues to stimulate interest even today.

Although these types of investigations are not, strictly speaking, studies of group processes, they nevertheless contribute to our understanding of group behavior and provide a transition point between individual social psychology and group dynamics. In this chapter we consider four areas of investigation: social facilitation, individual versus group performance, brainstorming, and the risky shift phenomenon. Social facilitation studies are concerned with the influence of the mere presence of others on individual behavior, whereas the other three deal with comparisons between behavior alone and behavior in psychological groups.

SOCIAL FACILITATION

The study of social facilitation is one of the earliest areas of investigation to be brought into the laboratory. In 1897 Triplett conducted a field study and also a laboratory experiment on social facilitation, although he did not use that term. He was interested primarily in the effects of competition on individual behavior. His studies are most interesting from a historical point of view, but also are enlightening with respect to present-day theory and methodology. Triplett (1897) began by collecting data from the official records of bicycle races as maintained by the Racing Board of the League of American Wheelmen. The League conducted three types of competitions: *unpaced,* in which a single rider attempted to beat an established time on a given course; *paced,* in which a lone rider also attempted to beat an established time, but with a swift multicycle setting the pace; and *competition,* in which several riders competed in an ordinary race. The results of this comparison revealed that the times were fastest for competition, next fastest for paced, and slowest for unpaced events.

Triplett reviewed several theories that had been advanced to account for these differences and proposed one of his own. Consider these interesting proposals:

The Suction Theory held that a vacuum is left by the pacing machine which pulls the rider along without as much effort on his part. In regular races, part of the strategy was to hold back during the early parts of the race and let others set the pace. This conserved energy for the final dash at the end and also allowed the rider to take advantage of the "vacuum" created by the leaders. This is not unlike the strategy employed by present-day automobile race drivers.

The Shelter Theory is similar to the suction theory. It assumed that the front riders provided a shield against wind pressure, and thus less effort was required by those following.

The Encouragement Theory suggested that the presence of a friend keeps up the spirits of the rider and thus encourages a stronger effort on his part.

The Brain Worry Theory explained that it requires greater worry to keep the pace than to follow; the pacer exhausts his energy by worrying about his task.

The Theory of Hypnotic Suggestion proposed that the follower concentrated his attention on the revolving wheel of the pacer, thus becoming hypnotized. The hypnosis created muscular exhaltation, which increased the rider's energy output.

The Automatic Theory held that the leader must use his brain to direct his muscles so that he stays on course, whereas the follower need not attend to such factors. He can ride automatically and thus devote all his energy to pedaling the bicycle.

Triplett admitted that each of these factors might play a part in producing the observed differences between individual performances alone and in the presence of others, but he believed that "dynamogenic factors" probably played a bigger role. He suggested that the presence of others releases latent energy that is not usually available to the individual. In order to test this hypothesis, he constructed a gadget from fishing reels which could be operated by either one or two persons. It consisted of two reels (one for each operator) which were connected to silk bands. By turning a reel, one could move the band around a 4-meter course. After initial practice with the apparatus, forty children were asked to turn the reel at the highest possible rate for four circuits of the 4-meter course. Half of the children worked first alone, then in pairs, then alone, etc., through six efforts. The other half worked in the reverse order. Triplett found that the together (competition) situation produced much faster rates, and thus concluded that this dynamogenic theory was verified.

The Triplett studies contain the prototypes of later investigations of the effects of others on individual performance. These later studies fall into two general classes: those in which the individual performs before a passive audience and those in which the audience is engaged in the same task as the subject.

EFFECTS OF A PASSIVE AUDIENCE

The effects of a passive audience upon eye-hand coordination was studied by Travis (1925). Twenty-two college students were tested on a pursuit-rotor task. Each subject practiced twenty trials per day until Travis judged that the subject had reached maximum efficiency. A passive audience was then admitted, after which the subject was given ten additional trials. The average performance on the ten highest alone trials was compared with the average performance on the ten trials with audience present. Eighteen of the twenty-two subjects had higher average scores with the audience, and sixteen earned their highest single score when the audience was present. The average alone score was 172.76 versus 177.42 for the audience present mean score, although this difference was not statistically significant. The presence of an audience therefore appeared to facilitate the performance of the eye-hand coordination task.

Pessin and Husband (1933) investigated the effects of an audience upon the learning of a finger relief maze. Groups of thirty college subjects were tested either alone with the experimenter or with one or two spectators present. In the spectator situation, subjects were tested either blindfolded or with vision but with the maze shielded from view. No significant differences were found. A study by Begum and Lehr (1963) was somewhat more successful. One group of twenty subjects were tested on a light-monitoring task alone, whereas another group of twenty subjects worked alone but with the knowledge that commissioned or noncommissioned officers would visit them at random. The average detection rate was 45 percent in the alone condition and 79 percent in the observation condition, a highly reliable difference. In this study, however, the subjects were Army National Guard trainees and the audience consisted of their officers. Thus an additional variable was operating in this study.

Evidence that the mere presence of others exerts a consistent influence on individual behavior is not compelling. It appears that the presence of others either has no reliable effect or facilitates performance. From the evidence cited above one might conclude that whether or not a passive audience facilitates performance depends upon the kind of task that the individual must perform. When the primary requirement of the task is motor output, an audience facilitates performance, but when the task involves higher mental processes, an audience has no reliable effect on performance.

EFFECTS OF A COACTING AUDIENCE

By far the greater number of studies of audience effects have employed a coacting audience; that is, several persons work on the same task in a together situation, although each person works as an individual. The early experimental work of Triplett cited above falls into this category. Triplett deliberately introduced the element of competition, however, whereas later investigators usually attempted to eliminate or control the competitive aspect of togetherness. F. H. Allport (1920) appears to have been the first investigator to use the term "social facilitation." He conducted a series of experiments which he believed demonstrated the facilitating effects of the presence of others. In the first experiment, subjects were given a sheet of paper with a single word at the top. Starting with this stimulus word, they wrote as many disconnected words as they could in a given period. Subjects alternated between working alone and working together in the same room. Competition and rivalry were minimized through instructions. Fourteen of the fifteen subjects tested showed a "social increment" (they worked faster) in the together situation, and twelve of the fifteen wrote more personal associations alone.

In the second experiment the procedure was the same except that subjects were required to write only every fourth word that came to mind. Relative to the alone situation, eight subjects gained, four lost, and two were not affected by the together situation. In the third study, subjects wrote every third word; six gained and two lost in the together situation as compared with the alone situation.

In a fourth experiment half of the subjects wrote words about winter and half words about summer. No differences in facilitating effects were found between the situation in which all subjects wrote on the same topic and that in which the two halves wrote on different topics. Subjects in a fifth experiment were asked to write down arguments to disprove certain passages from Marcus Aurelius. Twenty tests were done alone and twenty in a group setting in which subjects were informed that all were working on the same task. Eight of the nine subjects tested wrote more arguments in the group situation, but six of the nine had a higher percentage of ideas rated superior by the experimenter in the alone condition. Two additional experiments involving a cancellation test and a multiplication test gave similar results; subjects produced more in the together situation, but the quality was poorer.

Subsequent studies yielded results that were not altogether consistent with Allport's findings. Weston and English (1926) reported that individuals given intelligence tests consisting of reasoning items generally did much better (eight of ten subjects tested) in the together situation than in the alone condition. This seems to be inconsistent with Allport's results concerning quality of performance; however, Farnsworth (1928) found no consistent differences between the two situations when intelligence testing is the task. He argued that Weston and English had not equated either their groups of subjects or the test forms. When these factors were controlled, no reliable differences were found between alone and together intelligence test scores. Also, Travis (1928) found that stutterers were adversely influenced by the presence of others on a word-association task similar to that used by Allport. His subjects wrote an average of 68.1 words alone versus an average of 65.3 words when they were together.

When one considers all the findings relative to the effects of the presence of others upon individual performance, the results appear quite inconsistent. Whether the presence of others is facilitating, interfering, or irrelevant seems to be unpredictable without knowledge of other factors. Zajonc (1965a) reviewed the findings of social facilitation studies and proposed a possible reconciliation of these seemingly contradictory findings. He suggested that the presence of others has arousal consequences; that is, an audience is drive-producing. This hypothesis is, of course, essentially a revival of Triplett's dynamogenic theory (1897), which held that the presence of others releases latent energy that the individual is unable to release on his own. Zajonc's analysis, however, does have the advantage of being related to a considerable amount of theory and research related to motivation and learning. Zajonc reasoned that if his hypothesis were correct, then the presence of others should have the same effects as those obtained by increasing the generalized drive state. One such effect is the enhancement of dominant responses. A test of this effect was conducted by Zajonc and Sales (1966), with generally positive results. They established different response strengths through training procedures and demonstrated that weaker habits (those less frequently practiced in training) were inhibited and stronger habits (more frequently practiced ones) were facilitated by the presence of others. If this proposal stands the test of further experimentation, it can probably account for discrepant findings. It is known, for example, that stutterers tend to stutter more when they are highly motivated than when they are more relaxed; similar effects might be expected in other kinds of behavior, which could account for the findings of Travis (1928).

Kelley and Thibaut (1969) cited additional evidence to support the notion that motivation level is increased under social conditions. First, subjects report that activity by others produces an urge to greater speed and greater emotional excitement than that experienced when alone. Second, subjects can be aroused to activity even after having been satiated in social isolation, as indicated by studies of children's activities (Burton, 1941). Third, subjects who appear to be least interested in the task itself show the greatest performance gains in the audience situation. And fourth, individual variations from time to time are greater under social conditions. Thus it appears that one strong effect of an audience is to increase motivation for high task performance; the consequences of this high motivation may result either in increased effectiveness or in decreased effectiveness, depending upon the nature of the task, the measure of effectiveness, the initial level of motivation, and other factors. For example, competition seems to arouse higher motivation than either individual or cooperative situations, but this motivation is detrimental to a tracking task, which requires both mental concentration and eye-hand coordination (M. E. Shaw, 1958a). Dashiell (1930) argued that the effects of the audience could be accounted for solely by the fact that the audience instigates competitiveness and rivalry, which, of course, are forms of motivation, although such motivations are not always task-related. These factors must also be considered when we attempt to understand the effects of others upon individual behavior.

INDIVIDUAL VERSUS GROUP PERFORMANCE

The comparison of individual and group performance introduces a new variable into the study of interpersonal effects, namely, interaction. Interacting groups are compared with individuals with respect to their performance on assigned tasks. Studies have centered around three types of tasks: judgment, problem solving, and learning. Brainstorming and the risky shift

phenomenon may also represent types of individual versus group performance, but these have somewhat different implications for group behavior
and are discussed under separate headings.

INDIVIDUAL VERSUS GROUP JUDGMENT

The major question asked by investigations of individual versus group judgment is, To what extent does the quality of group performance exceed that
of individuals? There are two subsidiary questions: (1) Does the quality of
group judgment exceed that of the average individual performance of group
members? (2) Does the quality of group performance exceed that of the most
proficient member of the group? Two general approaches were adopted in
attempting to answer these questions, although methods are not related to
specific questions. The first method has been referred to as the "statisticized"
group technique (Lorge, Fox, Davitz, & Brenner, 1958). The technique compares individual judgments with the result obtained by averaging the products of independent, noninteracting individuals. Actually, this is not a group
at all, but rather an aggregate of individual judgments. This method appears
to have been used for the first time by Knight (1921) in her investigation of
judgments of temperature in a college classroom. She had students estimate
the temperature of the classroom and then computed the average judgment
for the group. The "group" judgment was better than 80 percent of the
individual judgments. A second study was conducted using the same method,
but requiring judgments of intelligence from photographs. The "group"
rank order did not correlate with the true rank order any better than the
individual ranks.

The statisticized group method was employed by Gordon (1923) in a
study of aesthetic judgments and again in a study of the judgment of weights
(Gordon, 1924). Individual judgments of lifted weights correlated .41 with
true weights; "group" judgments yielded much higher correlations, reaching .94 with an aggregate of fifty individual judgments. Gordon concluded
that "group" judgments are distinctly superior to the judgments of the average individual and equal to that of the best individual. An obvious flaw in
this technique is that the number of judgments varies with the size of the
group, and it is well known that the average of several judgments (measurements, estimates, etc.) will approximate the true value more closely than
most single judgments, so long as the error of measurement is random, that
is, so long as any single judgment is just as likely to be too low as it is to

be too high. Thus, Stroop (1932) argued that Gordon's findings could be accounted for by the number of judgments alone, without regard to the source of the judgments. In other words, one would expect the same results from several judgments made by one individual and averaged as one would expect from the same number of judgments made by several individuals, each contributing one judgment, as in the Gordon studies. Stroop confirmed Gordon's results and then conducted a second study in which the same individual made varying numbers of judgments. His findings are compared with those reported by Gordon in Table 3-1. The correspondence between the two sets of results is obvious. Stroop's hypothesis of a statistical artifact therefore seems to be supported.

Investigations using statisticized groups may also be criticized on other grounds. Preston (1938) noted that such studies give no evidence concerning psychological processes in group interaction. Fortunately, the second method of investigation is not so sterile with respect to group behavior. In these studies the judgments of individuals are compared with the judgments of interacting groups or with individual judgments made after group discussion. As early as 1920, Burtt conducted a series of studies of jury decisions in which individual judgments were compared with judgments by the same individuals after group discussion. In the study most relevant to the present issue, confederates "testified" before subjects about an imaginary crime. Some of the confederates lied and others told the truth. Subjects judged the veracity of the "witness" individually. They then discussed the testimony for five minutes, after which they again judged the veracity of the witness. Subjects frequently changed their judgment after group discussion, but they changed in the wrong direction about as often as in the right direction.

TABLE 3-1 A Comparison of Correlations between Actual Weight and Judged Weight as a Function of Size of "Group" and of Number of Judgments

Gordon's findings				
Size of group: 1	5	10	20	50
Correlation: .41	.68	.79	.86	.94

Stroop's findings				
Number of judgments: 1	5	10	20	50
Correlation: .43	.72	.82	.87	.97

A similar study by Marston (1924) produced similar results. Students witnessed a staged classroom incident and were then asked to describe what happened, either individually or in groups acting as a jury. Findings of fact were slightly (but not significantly) less accurate by the jury than by the average individual witness. Marston also found that a trained "judge" was more accurate than a jury. The results of these studies suggest that although group judgments are different from individual judgments, they are not necessarily better, and the judgment of a trained individual may be more accurate than that of untrained groups.

The effect of group discussion on the accuracy of individual judgment was also studied by Jenness (1932). Individuals estimated the number of beans in a bottle, discussed their estimates in groups of three and made a group estimate, and then made a final individual estimate. The discussion groups were selected either to disagree maximally or to agree maximally. Finally, there was a control group in which individuals made two estimates with no intervening group discussion or estimate. With maximum disagreement initially, group estimates were less accurate than individual estimates; however, final individual estimates were better than initial estimates in twenty of twenty-six cases. This represented an average reduction in error of 60 percent as compared with a 4 percent reduction in the control group. When initial agreement was maximum, group estimates were more accurate than initial estimates, but final individual estimates were not significantly different from those of the control group. Again groups are not necessarily better than individuals, and group discussion does not always improve individual judgments. Jenness correctly noted the role of individual differences in knowledge in improving group judgments, a fact that we will have occasion to refer to again in Chapter 6.

A combination of the statisticized group technique and the use of interacting groups was employed by Gurnee (1937). Individuals were required to make their judgments on a written true-false test, after which a vote was taken by a show of hands in groups of 18, 53, 57, and 66. In every group the group judgment was better than the average individual judgment and about equal to the judgment of the best individual. Statisticized group judgments were also computed, but face-to-face groups were generally superior.

In general, it appears that group judgments are seldom less accurate than the average individual judgment and are often superior. This can be accounted for by the number of judgments contributing to the estimate (Stroop, 1932), by the range of knowledge represented by the individual group members (Jenness, 1932), and by the effects of others on the less confident group members (Gurnee, 1937). It is also apparent that the kind of task may determine whether group judgment will be superior to individual judgments. Finally, it is evident that a single capable individual may perform as well as or better than a group (Burtt, 1920; Marston, 1924). The answer to the first question, "Does the quality of group judgment exceed that of the average individual performance of group members?" is therefore a qualified "Yes." The second question, "Does the quality of group performance exceed that of the most proficient member of the group?" must be answered negatively, although under some circumstances the group performance might be better than that of any individual in the group.

INDIVIDUAL VERSUS GROUP PROBLEM SOLVING

Investigators of individual versus group problem solving have used a variety of experimental designs as well as a variety of problems which subjects are asked to solve. The two most common designs are: (1) Individuals are required to solve problems alone and the same individuals attempt to solve similar problems in groups, usually with order and problems counterbalanced, and (2) one sample of individuals attempts a set of problems and another sample of groups attempts to solve the same set of problems. The kinds of problems vary from complex syllogistic reasoning tasks to simple puzzles. There are also variations in the measures of performance, including (1) number of problems solved, (2) time required to solve, either taking into account the number of individuals or not, (3) number of trials, (4) amount of interaction, and (5) quality of solution. Despite all these variations in design and procedure, the results are remarkably consistent when the same measures of performance are compared. A review of several studies may be instructive.

An early study by G. B. Watson (1928) compared individuals and groups on a word-construction task. Beginning with a given word, the subject was to construct as many new words as possible from the letters in the stimulus word. Subjects were 108 graduate students in education. The subjects first worked individually for ten minutes, then in groups (ranging from three to ten persons) for another ten minutes with a secretary recording words for them, followed by a third period in groups, and finally a fourth period as individuals. The best individual in the group averaged 49 words per ten minutes in the individual situation, whereas the groups averaged 75 words per ten-minute period. When the words produced by all individuals in the group working alone were summed to obtain a "group" product, the average was 86.8 words per test period. Note, however, that this procedure did not take into account overlap, that is, the same word produced by several individuals who were grouped together. There was also greater variability among groups than among individuals. Watson concluded that groups are superior to individuals, but that with simple tasks, division of labor, and summation of individual contributions individuals are better. (As noted above, the latter conclusion may be based upon improper procedures.) Watson also concluded that variability among groups depends more upon the ability of the best member than upon others in the group. This was based upon the observation that the performance of the group corresponded more closely to that of the best group member than to the performance of others in the group.

A somewhat more elegant experimental design was employed by Marjorie E. Shaw* (1932) in a now-classic comparison of individual and group problem solving. The subjects were members of a class in social psychology at Columbia University. In the first half of the experiment, half of the students worked in five groups of four persons each and the other half worked as individuals. In the second half, the roles of subjects were reversed, with some substitutions of subjects. The problems in the first part of the study were puzzles, such as the cannibal problem of parlor-game fame. In this particular task, three cannibals and three missionaries must cross a river in a boat that will carry only two persons. One of the cannibals and all of the missionaries know how to row the boat. However, the crossing must be arranged so that the number of cannibals never outnumbers the missionaries —for obvious reasons! The problem is to determine how the crossing can be made in the fewest trips. Another task was similar to this except that the persons involved were husbands and wives. The third task was a disk transfer problem which required that a stack of disks of different sizes be moved from one spot to another, one at a time, using only three positions and never placing a larger disk on a smaller one. The problems in the second half were somewhat more "mentalistic." One required that subjects identify the best location for a school and the best routes for two school buses, given the possible routes, the location and number of children to be picked up, and the capacity of the buses. The second and third problems called for the re-

---

* For those whose curiosity may have been aroused by the similarity of names, there is no relationship between Miss Shaw and the author.

arrangement of letters to form the last sentence of a passage of prose and the last few lines of a sonnet, respectively.

In the first half of the experiment, individuals produced 5 correct solutions of 63 possible (7.9 percent) as compared with 8 of 15 possible (53 percent) for the groups. The time required, however, was greater for groups than for individuals. The average number of minutes for groups was 6.5, 16.9, and 18.3, for problems 1, 2, and 3, respectively, as compared with 4.5, 9.9, and 15.5 for individuals. In the second half, the number of correct solutions was again in favor of groups (27 percent correct as compared with 5.7 percent correct by individuals). The average times, however, were shorter for groups on two of the three problems. Shaw's results indicated, therefore, that groups produced more correct solutions, but often at a cost in time. As we shall see later, this cost is much greater if time per individual is taken into account. In addition, Shaw noted that (1) there was an unequal amount of participation by group members, and (2) in erroneous solutions, groups did not err as early in the process as did the average individual.

The relative superiority of groups with respect to accuracy was interpreted by Shaw as due to the rejection of incorrect suggestions and the checking of errors in the group. She also found that in the group more incorrect suggestions were recognized and rejected by someone other than the one who had made the error. This process is, of course, not available to individuals working alone.

A similar study was undertaken by Husband (1940) in a study contrasting individuals and groups in terms of the man-hours required to arrive at a solution and the quality of the solution. The problems included arithmetic problems, a jigsaw puzzle, and code deciphering. Subjects were 120 college students, 40 of whom worked alone and 80 in pairs. He found that pairs were significantly better on the deciphering task and the jigsaw puzzle, but there was no significant difference between pairs and individuals on the arithmetic problems. On the latter, it appeared that one member of the pair took the lead and did all the work; hence, the comparison was really between two individuals. These findings are consistent with those reported by G. B. Watson (1928) and Marjorie E. Shaw (1932). However, Husband noted that the time saved by pairs was never more than one-third, rather than the one-half needed to equate individuals and groups in terms of man-hours required for solution. He concluded that pairs are relatively less efficient than individuals. This conclusion, of course, fails to take into account the improved quality of the solutions by pairs.

Many other investigators have reported results that are consistent with those cited above. Taylor and Faust (1952) compared individuals with groups of two and four persons on a modified version of "twenty questions," and found that individuals required more time and questions to identify objects than did groups. Again, groups were relatively more costly in terms of man-minutes (an average of 7.40 minutes for two-person groups, 12.60 minutes for four-person groups, and 5.06 for individuals). Marquart (1955) used problems similar to those used by Marjorie E. Shaw (1932) and reported similar results. However, Marquart computed a "concocted" group score by crediting the hypothetical group with a correct solution if any subject solved the problem individually, and found that this score indicated that individuals were superior to groups. Lorge, Aikman, Moss, Spiegel, and Tuckman (1955) tested groups and individuals on four tasks varying in degree of "remoteness from reality," and found that the solutions of groups were superior on all problems. Using a complex intellectual problem, Barnlund (1959) compared the performances of individuals working alone, under majority rule, and as members of discussion groups. Decisions made by discussion groups were better than those made either by individuals or by majority rule. A study by Tuckman and Lorge (1962) also demonstrated that groups of five persons had a greater probability of producing good solutions than did individuals. Finally, Davis and Restle (1963), using three puzzle problems, compared four-person groups with individuals. The proportion of solutions was greater for groups than for individuals on all three problems. There were no differences in overall time, although individuals required fewer man-hours for solution.

The evidence thus strongly supports the conclusion that groups produce more and better solutions to problems than do individuals, although the differences in overall time required for solution are not consistently better for either individuals or groups. When the amount of effort invested, as measured by man-hours required for solution, is considered, individuals are found to be superior. There is at least one investigation, however, that yielded results not in complete accord with the studies cited thus far. Moore and Anderson (1954) compared six individuals with six groups of three persons each on the solution of problems from the calculus of symbolic logic. In general, there were no significant differences between individuals and groups in accuracy or time for solution, although individuals required fewer man-hours. It should be noted that Moore and Anderson's subjects were Navy enlisted men who may not have been experts in the calculus of symbolic logic; if few individuals can solve a problem, it may not help to work together in groups.

A number of hypotheses have been advanced to explain the relative superiority of group problem solving. These include (1) summation of individual contributions (Marquart, 1955; G. B. Watson, 1928); (2) rejection of incorrect suggestions and the checking of errors (Barnlund, 1959; Marjorie E. Shaw, 1932); (3) the greater influence of the ablest group member (G. B. Watson, 1928); (4) the social influence of the most confident member (Thorndike, 1938); (5) the greater interest in the task aroused by group membership (Barnlund, 1959); and (6) the greater amount of information available to the group. All these factors probably contribute to the phenomenon. The degree to which each one operates probably depends upon such additional factors as task characteristics. More will be said about these additional factors later in this chapter.

INDIVIDUAL VERSUS GROUP LEARNING

Implicit in the studies on group judgment and group problem solving is the hypothesis that interaction contributes something to the group product that is more than the mere combination of individual products. This hypothesis suggests that group members somehow exert an influence on their fellow members which leads to behavior that would not occur when members are alone. If this is true, then the effect should not be limited to judgment and problem solving, but should also appear in learning phenomena.

As early as 1926, Barton conducted a study using high school pupils in an algebra class. He selected two sections which were alike in IQ, preliminary training in algebra, and prior test performance. One section worked on assignments on an individual basis and the other section worked on the same assignments in small groups. The groups gained significantly more on subsequent test performance. A decade later, Gurnee (1937, 1939) reported two experiments on maze learning by individuals and by groups. In the first study, groups made fewer errors and achieved a perfect trial sooner than did individuals on the first six trials, but on the seventh trial there were no differences between group and individual performance. The second study was similar in design, but the results were different: On the seventh trial those who had worked in groups did significantly better than those who had worked alone on the first six trials.

Later studies used somewhat more sophisticated experimental designs, with correspondingly more interesting results. Perlmutter and de Montmollin (1952) compared individuals and groups on a nonsense-syllable learning task. The study was conducted at the Sorbonne and the subjects were mostly French students, although some other Europeans were included. Half of the subjects (G-I groups) worked in three-person groups, rested fifteen minutes, and then worked individually but in the presence of others (G-I individuals). For the other half, this order was reversed (I-G individuals and I-G groups, respectively). Order of nonsense lists was also systematically varied. In the group situation, group consensus was required. The results are shown in Figure 3-1. There were no significant differences between the G-I and I-G groups; hence they are combined in Figure 3-1. Note that groups learned more and learned faster than either G-I or I-G individuals. It is also important to note that individuals who had had previous experience in groups (G-I individuals) learned faster than did persons who had not had group

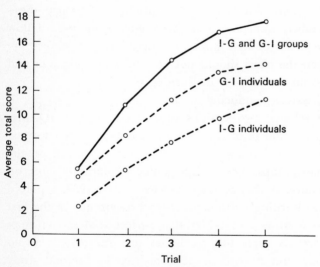

Figure 3-1 Average Curves of Group-learned Products and Individual Learning. (Reprinted with permission from H. V. Perlmutter & G. de Montmollin. Group learning of nonsense syllables. *Journal of Abnormal and Social Psychology*, 1952, **47**, 762–769.)

experience (I-G individuals). These findings demonstrated the superiority of groups over individuals in learning nonsense syllables, as well as the effects of group experience on subsequent learning by individuals.

Similar results were reported by Beaty and Shaw (1965) in a very different kind of learning situation: the probability learning or probability matching situation. In this situation, the subject must choose between two possible outcomes on each trial, such as which of two lights will come on. Individuals learn to "match" their choices to the probabilities associated with each alternative (Gardner, 1957; Gardner, 1958; Goodnow, 1955). Beaty and Shaw reasoned that groups should achieve matching faster than individuals. They compared individual decisions, individual choices made in groups after a two-minute discussion, and group decisions. In the last two conditions, subjects were run in groups of five. The task was to choose which of two lights would come on, where the objective probabilities were 70:30. The results are shown in Figure 3-2. Both groups and individuals in groups learned to match with fewer trials than did individuals alone.

Yuker (1955) demonstrated the same effects in a learning task involving prose materials. He studied 160 subjects divided into forty groups of four persons each. The "War of the Ghosts," a rather bizarre story of ghosts and Indians, was read to individuals in groups, after which they were asked to recall it individually, then as a group, and finally as individuals. Prior to scoring recall data, the investigators segmented story content according to unique ideas. The recall data was scored by assigning a score from 0 (no recall) to 4 (complete recall) to each segment of the story. The recall score was the average for all segments, and could therefore range from 0 to 4. Mean scores were 1.26 for initial individual recall, 1.88 for group recall, and 1.65 for final individual recall. The best initial individual recall in each group averaged 1.64. The group performance was better than the initial individual recall in 38 of the 40 groups and better than the best initial recall in 29 of the 40 groups. Yuker suggested that groups will learn more than individuals on tasks (1) on which several persons can work without getting in one another's way, (2) which can be solved through the addition of individual contributions, and (3) in which the parts of the solution are at least partially independent.

The results of studies of individual versus group learning are remarkably consistent in showing that groups learn faster than individuals, both in natural situations (Barton, 1926) and in contrived laboratory situations (Beaty & Shaw, 1965; Perlmutter & de Montmollin, 1952; Yuker, 1955).

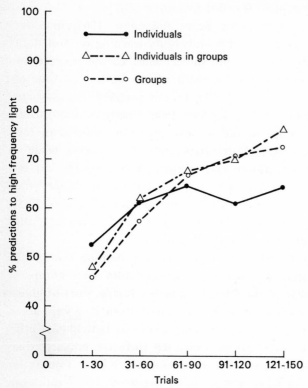

Figure 3-2 Per Cent Frequency of High-probability Responses Plotted against Blocks of 30 Trials. (Reprinted with permission from W. E. Beaty & M. E. Shaw. Some effects of social interaction on probability learning. *Journal of Psychology*, 1965, **59**, 299–306.)

Studies comparing the lecture method with group discussion in the classroom are sometimes cited as evidence that individual learning is sometimes better than group learning (cf. Spence, 1928; Thie, 1925; Zeleny, 1940). However, these studies do not really involve individuals and groups so much as different teaching techniques which seem to depend more on the personality of the teacher than on interpersonal factors.

In summary, whether individuals or groups are more effective depends upon the past experience of the persons involved, the kind of task they are attempting to complete, the process that is being investigated, and the measure of effectiveness. For example, expert and/or experienced individuals may perform better than groups of less expert persons. Groups are more effective than individuals on tasks which require a variety of information, which can be solved by adding individual contributions, and which require a number of steps that must be correctly completed in a definite order; individuals are better on tasks that call for centralized organization of parts. Groups perform better than individuals when the process is learning or problem solving, but not necessarily when the process investigated is judgment. These conclusions are based upon measures of outcome; when the measure of effectiveness is the amount of investment per man, individuals are generally shown to be more efficient.

BRAINSTORMING

The assertion of Osborn (1957) that group participation results in new and radical ideas led to another area of investigation in which individuals and groups are compared. This group participation method of producing new ideas is usually referred to as "brainstorming." The general procedure is to consider a problem, such as new uses for an old product or new products that a company might profitably manufacture, in a group setting in which the procedure is specified by the following rules: (1) Ideas are expressed without regard to quality; (2) no idea may be evaluated until all ideas have been expressed; and (3) the elaboration of one person's ideas by another is not only permitted but actually encouraged.

The reported successes of the brainstorming procedure led inevitably to experimentation. The amount of research, however, is limited and inconsistent. Meadow, Parnes, and Reese (1959) reported results consistent with Osborn's position. Thirty-two college students enrolled in a creative problem-solving course served as subjects. The problems called for the listing of unusual uses of an ordinary clothes hanger and of a broom. All subjects attempted both tasks working alone, one under brainstorming instructions and the other under nonbrainstorming instructions, in counterbalanced order. Each subject was allowed five minutes on each task. Brainstorming instructions produced an average of 7.94 "good solutions" as compared with an average of 3.88 produced by nonbrainstorming instructions. Similarly, Cohen, Whitmyre, and Funk (1960) found that pairs of individuals with prior training in creative thinking and cohesive pairs (two persons who chose to work with each other) were more effective using brainstorming procedures than were nominal pairs (two individuals who worked alone and pooled outputs), pairs who did not have previous experience, or noncohesive pairs.

On the other hand, Taylor, Berry, and Block (1958) compared 12 four-person brainstorming groups with 12 four-person nominal groups composed of individuals who had worked alone under brainstorming instructions. The three problems used required subjects to identify the difficulties we would face if everyone born after 1960 had an extra thumb, to determine how best to attract tourists to the United States, and to formulate methods of dealing with the school enrollment problem. When the products of individuals in nominal groups were combined, their score was higher than the score of real groups on all three problems. Nominal groups produced an average of 37.5 different ideas compared with an average of 19.6 for real groups. This result says nothing about the effectiveness of brainstorming rules, since these rules were followed by both nominal and real group members. However, these findings do cast doubt upon the value of brainstorming in groups.

A study reported by Dunnette, Campbell, and Jaastad (1963) yielded similar results. They used the same nominal group design that was used by Taylor et al., as well as similar problems. Their subjects were forty-eight research scientists and forty-eight administrative personnel in a Minnesota mining company. Subjects were divided into groups of four persons each, selected so that all group members knew each other well. Again, nominal groups produced many more ideas than did real groups.

When experimental procedures are examined, some of the differences in experimental findings become understandable. In the Meadow et al. (1959) and the Cohen et al. (1960) investigations, comparisons were between situations in which brainstorming instructions were followed and situations in which these instructions were not followed, whereas in the other studies all subjects followed brainstorming instructions, either alone or in groups. This difference alone might account for the discrepancies, were it not for the finding by Cohen et al. (1960) that real brainstorming pairs produced more than nominal brainstorming pairs. There is one other procedural factor that might have influenced the results of studies comparing brainstorming individuals with brainstorming groups. In both the Taylor et al. and the Dunnette et al. studies, time for solution was limited. Although the authors of these studies believed that most ideas had been expressed in the allotted time, it is possible that the groups were cut off in the middle of the process. Data suggesting that this may have happened come from a study by Milton Rosenbaum (personal communication) which showed that with longer work periods groups produce more under brainstorming instructions than do individuals. Groups continue to produce ideas indefinitely, whereas individuals "run dry."

Finally, it might be noted that there were differences in the relations among group members: Some subjects knew each other very well whereas others were apparently strangers. That this variable may be an important one is indicated by the findings of Cohen et al. (1960) that cohesive groups and groups composed of individuals with prior training did better than groups without these characteristics. Thibaut and Kelley (1959) noted this variable and suggested that future studies might well be directed toward the study of kinds of groups rather than toward the mere comparison of individuals and groups.

THE RISKY SHIFT PHENOMENON

If the brainstorming process does indeed produce more new and radical ideas, as Osborn claims, the implications for group interaction are exciting—and contradictory to the commonly held belief (e.g., W. H. Whyte, 1957) that group products tend to be conservative and mediocre. An early study by Ziller (1957a) suggested that groups may not be conservative at all and that the common view may be incorrect. He found that decisions made by group-centered decision-making groups were more risky than decisions made by leader-centered groups. He noted that ". . . the group has greater license to make a 'risky' decision since it is their lives they are risking rather than the lives of others" (Ziller, 1957a, p. 388). However, a later study by Stoner (1961) made a more direct comparison of individual and group decision making. He found that decisions made by groups were riskier than prediscussion decisions made by individual members of the group. This research served as the starting point for a series of studies designed to determine the generality of this finding and to explain the process which produces the effect when it does occur.

Wallach, Kogan, and Bem (1962) were taken by surprise by the Stoner findings, and apparently experienced some doubt that the risky shift phenomenon could be reliably demonstrated. They noted that Stoner's subjects were male graduate students in industrial management and that the presence of peers in the group situation might have reminded them of the positively sanctioned role that the business manager is expected to play. That is, business managers are expected to be willing to take risks in their decision making; hence, graduate students in business might simply have been conforming to role expectations in the group decision situation. Wallach et al. also suggested that males, regardless of their professional roles, might make more risky decisions in groups because they perceive risk taking to be an attribute of manliness. They therefore designed a study using as subjects both male and female undergraduates enrolled in a liberal arts college program. They argued that if the risky shift could be demonstrated in both male and female subjects drawn from this population, there would be reason to believe that the phenomenon was not due to the role expectations of the particular subjects used by Stoner. In effect, they were trying not only to test the generality of the phenomenon, but also to reduce the number of plausible hypotheses.

The task used in this study (and in many subsequent investigations) consisted of descriptions of twelve hypothetical situations in which the central person must choose between two courses of action which vary in riskiness and in degree of reward achieved if the chosen course is successful. For each description, the subject must indicate the lowest probability of success that he would demand before recommending the potentially more rewarding alternative. Probabilities were listed as 1, 3, 5, 7, and 9 chances of success in 10, with a refusal category (scored 10) to be used if the subject would never recommend the risky alternative. The following is an example of the kind of description used: "An electrical engineer may stick with his present job at a modest but adequate salary, or may take a new job offering considerably more money but no long-term security" (Wallach et al., 1962, p. 77).

Subjects responded to this questionnaire individually, then as a group (group consensus after discussion), and again individually after the group decision process. Some of the subjects made individual decisions in subsequent sessions held two to six weeks later. The group decision showed a risky shift from the mean initial individual decisions on ten of the twelve items, and an overall shift of −9.4 for both male and female subjects. A similar shift was found between initial and postdiscussion individual decisions. The effect persisted over the two- to six-week period between the postdiscussion individual decision and the final individual test. The shift in a risky direction did not occur in a control group that responded to the questionnaire twice without intervening group discussion. The authors concluded that group interaction and achievement of consensus on matters of risk produce a willingness to make more risky decisions than would be made by individuals working alone. They found a significant relationship between the riskiness of initial individual decisions and the influence the individual had on the group decision; this suggests that the risky shift effect may be due to the influence of risk-taking individuals. Two alternative interpretations of this effect were suggested: (1) Since the individual knows that the responsibility for the decision is spread among several others, he may experience feelings of decreased personal responsibility. This feeling of less personal responsibility might account for the greater willingness to make a risky decision in the group situation and also for the observed relationship between individual risk taking and influence in the group. (2) The influence of the high risk takers could be the cause of the group's shift toward more risky decisions. They favored the first alternative.

The results of these initial studies were generally accepted as demonstrating that the risky shift phenomenon is real, that is, that it can be reliably demonstrated under controlled conditions. Subsequent investigations were directed largely toward either the identification of variables influencing the phenomenon (i.e., its generality) or toward a determination of the process by which the effect is produced. When the Wallach-Kogan-Bem choice-dilemma (CD) questionnaire is the instrument used for investigating the risky shift, it appears to be demonstrable under a variety of circumstances. Wallach, Kogan, and Bem (1964) found that the risky shift occurred when actual risks in the form of monetary payoffs were involved, but only under conditions of group discussion and consensus. An extension of this finding was reported by Bem, Wallach, and Kogan (1965) in a study using aversive stimuli such as olfactory stimulation that might produce unpleasant side effects, chromatic stimulation that might produce severe headache, and the like. Monetary payoffs were varied directly with the probability that the side effects would occur. The risky shift after group discussion was again demonstrated. These experiments seem to demonstrate conclusively that the shift toward risky decisions in group situations is not limited to the particular population, to the particular content of the CD questionnaire items, or to situations in which the risks are hypothetical. The critical element in producing this effect seems to be discussion. Wallach and Kogan (1965) found that discussion, with or without consensus, produced the risky shift; however, consensus without discussion yielded an averaging effect (cf. Teger & Pruitt, 1967).

If the proposition that decisions made after group discussion are more risky than decisions made in the absence of group interaction, a question naturally arises concerning the mechanism that produces this effect. Wallach et al. (1964) argued that it is due primarily to the diffusion of responsibility that occurs in the group discussion situation. However, other investigators have proposed other explanations, suggesting that risk taking is (1) a value attributable to certain roles; (2) a cultural value; or (3) a consequence of the influence of the individual who has the most risky initial opinion. Let us examine the evidence for these various hypotheses.

RISK IS A VALUE FOR CERTAIN ROLES

This hypothesis was proposed as a plausible explanation of Stoner's (1961) findings (Wallach et al., 1962) in view of the fact that Stoner had used only male graduate students enrolled in an industrial management program. It was suggested that both the role of industrial manager and the male role in our society place a high value on the willingness to take risks and to make bold decisions. Several studies yielded results that are inconsistent with this hypothesis. Wallach et al. (1962) found that students in a liberal arts program and females also showed the risky shift in groups, and other studies (Bem et al., 1965; Wallach et al., 1964) also found results that argue against this explanation. The role-value hypothesis appears to be incorrect.

RISK TAKING IS A CULTURAL VALUE

The "risk is a value" theory was proposed by Brown (1965). The general idea is that people in our society value risk, and in the group situation most individuals are willing to take risks in order to enhance their status in the group. Information exchange is therefore essential, since group discussion permits the individual to learn his relative standing as a risk taker. Levinger and Schneider (1969) suggested that most people regard themselves as above average risk takers; if they learn through group discussion that they are only average or below, they shift to be in accord with their self-image, which is determined by the risk-value norm. These investigators attempted to test the value hypothesis by asking 250 subjects to give their own choice on the CD questionnaire, the choice they believed their fellow students would make, and the choice they would most admire. Their results showed that the average student believed his fellow students to be more conservative than himself and that he most admired a choice more risky than his own. The latter finding is especially relevant to the value hypothesis and provides evidence that the underlying assumption of that hypothesis is correct.

Evidence supporting this hypothesis has also been reported by Stoner (1968) and by Wallach and Wing (1968). Stoner reported the risky shift in connection with items on the CD questionnaire for which "widely held values" favored the risky decision, but for items for which widely held values favored a conservative decision there was a conservative shift. Wallach and Wing (1968) found that on a set of six items from the CD questionnaire, male and female undergraduates at Duke University saw themselves as more risky than other students at that university.

Although these findings are consistent with the value hypothesis, the evidence is circumstantial rather than direct. Furthermore, Wallach and Kogan (1965) found that information exchange alone is not enough to produce the risky shift effect. Information about the risk-taking levels favored by peers was not sufficient to produce a shift in the direction of more risky decisions. This suggests that the hypothesis that an individual shifts his decision in order to make it agree with his self-image is probably invalid. This does not rule out the possibility that the individual shifts after group interaction in order to conform to the perceived expectations of other group members. Hence, the cultural value placed upon willingness to take risks probably plays some role in determining the risky shift phenomenon.

THE RISKY INDIVIDUAL IS MOST INFLUENTIAL

Marquis (1962) explained Stoner's findings (1961) in terms of the relatively greater influence on the group of the individual who favored the more risky decision before discussion. If such a person has the greater influence, this could account for the risky shift after discussion. Wallach et al. (1962) examined this hypothesis and found that there was indeed a significant relationship between the initial opinion of the most risky individual and the group decision. Wallach, Kogan, and Burt (1965) reported that even when the risky shift is produced by discussion without consensus, group members judge higher risk takers to be more forceful in group discussions than lower risk takers. Data cited by Rim (1964) are also consistent with this hypothesis.

Unfortunately, evidence of the kind cited above can be interpreted in at least two ways. It may be that the significant relationship between initial high risk by an individual and the group decision is indeed caused by the greater influence of the high risk taker. But it is equally plausible to conclude that the correspondence between the initial individual high risk decision and the group decision is artifactual; if the group's decision is more risky than the average individual decision it must necessarily correspond more closely with the initial opinions of the higher risk takers, regardless of their relative influence. Nor does the demonstration that high risk takers are seen as having greater influence require acceptance of the hypothesis. The fact that the group decision is closer to the high risk taker's opinion may cause the others in the group to perceive him as having greater influence. A recent study by Hoyt and Stoner (1968) was designed to control for the influence of highly risk-prone persons; discussions to consensus still produced the risky shift. It is possible, of course, that Hoyt and Stoner's control of leader influence was inadequate.

There is still another element that may be involved in the question of influence on group decision. Brown (1965) suggested that the high risk taker may have more colorful rhetoric available to him than does the less risky individual. One can advance exciting arguments to support a risky position, whereas the proponent of the conservative position must rely upon relatively drab propositions. If so, this might explain why the high risk taker is more influential (if he is), but it cannot demonstrate that this in fact occurs.

It is probably true that the high risk taker has greater influence and this could account, in part, for the risky shift. But the degree to which this is true is still an open question.

DIFFUSION OF RESPONSIBILITY

As noted earlier in this discussion, Wallach et al. (1962) favored the diffusion of responsibility hypothesis, and they have reported the results of several studies which support their view. Wallach, Kogan, and Bem (1964) examined the risky shift effect under four conditions: personal responsibility-group decision, group responsibility-individual decision, group responsibility-group decision-chance designation of responsible group member, and group responsibility-group decision-group designation of responsible group member. The mean shift indices for the several conditions were 5.6, −1.6, 9.4, and

12.5, respectively, as compared with a mean shift of 2.4 for a control condition. Thus, responsibility for others per se produced a conservative shift, whereas group decision per se produced the usual risky shift. However, when both variables were operating together, a very strong risky shift was found. Wallach et al. (1964) interpreted this as showing that responsibility changes its meaning when linked with group decision. They concluded that group decision brings about a diffusion of responsibility with respect to the decision itself and also reduces the felt responsibility of any group member designated to act as the group's representative. In both instances, the result is to push decisions in a more risky direction.

Most of the evidence reported by Wallach and his associates has been directed toward the systematic rejection of plausible alternative hypotheses. Wallach et al. (1964) and Bem et al. (1965) presented evidence against the role-value hypothesis; Wallach and Kogan (1965) and Kogan and Wallach (1967a) found that exchange of information alone did not produce the risky shift, thus calling into question the cultural value hypothesis; and Wallach et al. (1962) found only low positive correlations between initial risk level and perceived influence ($r = .32$ for males and $r = .22$ for females). Thus, by successively eliminating alternative hypotheses, these investigators have built up a good case for their diffusion of responsibility hypothesis. However, Pruitt and Teger (1969) failed to find a risky shift in groups that were permitted to discuss other issues but not the current issue, a result they interpreted as casting doubt on the diffusion of responsibility theory.

In summary, it seems that three factors contribute to the risky shift phenomenon: the influence of the most risky group member, the cultural value associated with risk taking, and the diffusion of responsibility that occurs in groups. Of these, the diffusion of responsibility hypothesis appears to have the greatest experimental support. It also has somewhat greater plausibility because of the analogous situations observed in more natural situations, e.g., studies of crowd phenomena which show extreme actions by individuals in crowds that do not occur when these same individuals are alone (Turner & Killian, 1957).

PLAUSIBLE HYPOTHESES ABOUT INDIVIDUALS AND GROUPS

The various researches reported in the preceding pages have had the effect of reducing the number of plausible or reasonable hypotheses concerning differences between individual and group processes. The hypotheses that were rejected as a result of research findings are of interest only in a negative way; that is, it is now known that these hypotheses are not valid and need not be considered further. The remaining plausible hypotheses are considerably more significant because they represent the best generalizations that we can make at this time, given the present state of knowledge about individual and group behavior. At this point, it is worthwhile to identify these surviving plausible hypotheses and to state them explicitly so that their implications can be examined and tested more fully. It is well to keep in mind that these hypotheses are generalizations that appear to be valid under most conditions; one should not expect them to hold true under every conceivable set of circumstances. The generality of hypotheses varies greatly, ranging from very general propositions to statements of relationships under very circumscribed conditions. Finally, since they are *hypotheses,* future research may demonstrate that some or all of them are invalid.

Hypothesis 1   The mere presence of others increases the motivation level of a performing individual.

The basis for this hypothesis lies in the studies of social facilitation. The various studies involving motor tasks generally revealed that individuals perform better in the presence of others than they do alone, whether the others represent a passive audience (Travis, 1925) or coacting individuals (Triplett, 1897). Similar findings were reported with verbal tasks, such as word association, that require no complex mental operations (F. H. Allport, 1920). However, on tasks which do require higher mental processes, the presence of others may either have no effect (Farnsworth, 1928; Pessin & Husband, 1933) or have an adverse effect on performance (Travis, 1928). The dynamogenic theory proposed by Triplett (1897) and the arousal hypothesis formulated by Zajonc (1965a) suggest that these findings can be explained on the assumption that the presence of others increases motivation to perform well. An implication of this proposition is that the presence of others should produce effects similar to those produced by increased motivation. Research by Zajonc and Sales (1966) yielded results compatible with this expectation.

Hypothesis 2   Group judgments are superior to individual judgments on tasks that involve random error.

This hypothesis derives from the studies of group judgment that generally show groups more accurate than individuals when the group judgment can be built up from a number of individual judgments (e.g., Gordon, 1923; Jenness, 1932; Knight, 1921). This effect can be accounted for by the increased number of judgments in the group (Stroop, 1932), the wider range of knowledge in the group (Jenness, 1932), and the influence of the more confident (and more accurate) individuals in the group (Gurnee, 1937). The implication of this hypothesis is that several individual judgments are likely to be as accurate as a group judgment when the errors of judgment are expected to be randomly distributed around the true value of the stimulus being judged.

Hypothesis 3 *Groups usually produce more and better solutions to problems than do individuals working alone.*

Data supporting this generalization come from studies by Marjorie E. Shaw (1932), G. B. Watson (1928), Husband (1940), Taylor and Faust (1952), and others. The kinds of problems employed in these investigations varied greatly, but there were sufficient similarities to suggest that the superiority of groups on problem solving is probably limited to tasks having the following characteristics: The contributions of several individuals can be combined; i.e., there can be a division of labor (Marquart, 1955; G. B. Watson, 1928); the creation of ideas or the remembering of information is required (Taylor & Faust, 1952; Yuker, 1955); and it is possible for others to recognize and correct individual errors (Marjorie E. Shaw, 1932). The degree to which the group superiority effect occurs has also been related to the ability of the best group member (G. B. Watson, 1928), to the greater interest in the task aroused by group membership (Barnlund, 1959), and to the influence of the most confident member (Thorndike, 1938). An implication of this hypothesis is that groups should be utilized when the accuracy or quality of the solution is the primary concern.

Hypothesis 4 *Groups usually require more time to complete a task than do individuals working alone.*

An important assumption of the above hypothesis is that the task can be done by a single individual. The general findings indicate that groups often (although not always) require more total time to complete a given task than do individuals, even when the measure is overall time required for completion. The important aspect pointed to by Hypothesis 4 is that the time of several persons is invested in a group action as compared with one person in the individual problem-solving situation. Several persons have noted that individuals are far more efficient than groups in terms of man-minutes invested in the solution (e.g., Davis & Restle, 1963; Husband, 1940; Taylor & Faust, 1952). The implication of this hypothesis is obvious: If one is concerned primarily in cost or efficiency, individuals are better than groups in the solution of problems.

Hypothesis 5   Groups learn faster than individuals.
Data supporting this hypothesis appear to be universally positive (e.g., Beaty & Shaw, 1965; Perlmutter & de Montmollin, 1952; Yuker, 1955). This hypothesis clearly bears important implications for teaching and classroom activities. Greater use of group activities in the classroom should facilitate learning, which, after all, is the primary purpose of teaching. This is already being done in many classrooms (see, e.g., Johnson & Hunt, 1968), although it is not clear to what extent the process is based upon research findings. It should not, however, be confused with the so-called discussion method of teaching.

Hypothesis 6   More new and radical ideas are produced by both individuals and groups when critical evaluation of ideas is suspended during the production period.
The technique labeled "brainstorming" stimulated the several studies supporting the above hypothesis. Although the data fail to tell what effects group participation has in the production of new ideas, they are nevertheless consistent in showing that brainstorming rules produce more ideas (e.g., Cohen, Whitmyre, & Funk, 1960; Meadow, Parnes, & Reese, 1959). From a theoretical point of view, this proposition is important in that it refutes the common opinion that groups produce an averaging effect which leads to mediocrity. Since the research was stimulated by practical application of brainstorming principles, it is scarcely necessary to point to the practical implications of Hypothesis 6.

Hypothesis 7   Decisions made after group discussion are more risky than decisions made by the average individual prior to group discussion.
Although the evidence for this proposition is limited almost entirely to investigations using some form of the choice-dilemma questionnaire, it is nevertheless highly consistent. Hypothesis 7 has been found valid with a variety of situations, subjects, and payoff functions, and hence appears to have some

generality (see, e.g., Bem et al., 1965; Levinger & Schneider, 1969; Wallach et al., 1962; Wallach et al., 1964). This effect appears to be a function of diffusion of responsibility, the influence of the most risky group member, and the cultural value attributed to risk taking. The theoretical and practical implications of Hypothesis 7 are similar to those mentioned in connection with Hypothesis 6. In addition, Wallach and his associates have pointed out that the relative riskiness of group decisions suggests that the common assumption that decisions made in groups are likely to be conservative, and thus to serve as checks and balances, is probably false. A reexamination of several functions of society, such as the jury system, congressional committees, etc., appears to be in order.

Our consideration of individual and group processes has thus suggested a number of interesting plausible hypotheses concerning similarities and differences of individual and group performances. The relationship of these to the internal processes of group interaction should become evident in the following chapters as we examine the various environments in which the group and its members must function.

SUGGESTED READINGS

BARNLUND, D. C.   A comparative study of individual, majority, and group judgment. *Journal of Abnormal and Social Psychology*, 1959, **58**, 55–60.

BEGUM, B. O., & LEHR, D. J.   Effects of authoritarianism on vigilance performance. *Journal of Applied Psychology*, 1963, **47**, 75–77.

KOGAN, N., & WALLACH, M. A.   Risky-shift phenomenon in small decision-making groups: A test of the information-exchange hypothesis. *Journal of Experimental Social Psychology*, 1967, **3**, 75–84.

LORGE, I., FOX, D., DAVITZ, J., & BRENNER, M.   A survey of studies contrasting the quality of group performance and individual performance, 1920–1957. *Psychological Bulletin*, 1958, **55**, 337–372.

PRUITT, D. G., & TEGER, A. I.   The risky shift in group betting. *Journal of Experimental Social Psychology*, 1969, **5**, 115–126.

SHAW, Marjorie E.   A comparison of individuals and small groups in the rational solution of complex problems. *American Journal of Psychology*, 1932, **44**, 491–504.

YUKER, H. E.   Group atmosphere and memory. *Journal of Abnormal and Social Psychology*, 1955, **51**, 17–23.

ZAJONC, R. B.   Social facilitation. *Science*, 1965, **149**, 269–274.

CHAPTER 4

GROUP FORMATION AND DEVELOPMENT

The initial event in group interaction is the establishment of a relationship between two or more persons. This event is often referred to as group formation, although it should be clear that the formation of a group is a continuous process. That is, the formation of the initial relationship is a necessary condition for group existence, but the group during its existence is in a never-ending process of development. The relationships among group members may often appear to be stable, with little change from time to time, and indeed such stability may be possible in certain static groups. In the more general case, however, relationships are modified from day to day. The modifications are relatively large early in the life of the group; after the group has established quasi-stable relationships, the changes may be so slow and of such lesser magnitude as to be almost imperceptible. In this chapter, then, we shall consider not only the initial attraction of group members, but also some of the formative processes that occur in the course of group development.

WHY PEOPLE JOIN GROUPS

If we assume that people join groups voluntarily, the first question that must be asked then is, Why do people join groups? The question can, of course, be answered at many levels. At the most general level, we may say that people join groups because the group meets some individual need. There are some tasks that can be accomplished only by groups, there may exist a personal need for affiliation, etc. In fact, a number of theorists have proposed theories of interpersonal attraction based upon the notion of reinforcement. In Chapter 2, we outlined briefly the exchange theory proposed by Thibaut and Kelley (1959) in which they formulated the concepts of *comparison level* (CL) and *comparison levels for alternatives* (CL_{alt}). According to this theory, the comparison level is the standard which an individual uses to evaluate an interpersonal relationship. If the rewards and costs which accrue from the relationship are above the CL, the relationship is evaluated favorably; if they are below the CL, the relationship is evaluated unfavorably. The CL_{alt} is the standard the individual uses to determine whether to enter into a new relationship or to remain in an already existing one. If the net reward-cost outcome is above that expected from other available relationships, the individual will enter into or continue the relationship; if below available alternatives, he will not enter (or continue) the relationship. Clearly, this theory assumes that the individual establishes and maintains an interpersonal relationship because of the rewards that accrue from it.

A similar theory was proposed by Newcomb (1956), who equated attraction and repulsion to another person with positive or negative attitudes toward that person. These attitudes are established according to reinforcement principles, and hence the individual is attracted or repulsed, depending upon the rewards or punishments that derive from his relationship with another. We will have more to say about these theories after we have discussed some of the relevant research findings.

General explanations have a certain appeal because they seem intuitively correct. But it is not enough to offer general explanations. One may well ask, What are the needs that are satisfied by group membership? What constitute rewards and punishments? The next level of explanation is represented by Cartwright and Zander's (1960) statement that the group itself may be the object of need or the group may simply be the means for satisfying some need that lies outside the group. When these two general classes are examined more closely, it becomes evident that each of them can be analyzed into several smaller classes, which in turn can be subdivided even further. Sources of need satisfaction residing in the group include at least (1) attraction to the members of the group (interpersonal attraction), (2) attraction to the activities of the group, (3) attraction to the goals of the group (i.e., the goals of the group are valued by the individual), and (4) group membership per se. Needs outside the group that may be satisfied through group membership include at least (1) attraction to others outside the group and (2) attraction to goals outside the group. Let us examine these factors in greater detail.

INTERPERSONAL ATTRACTION

The variables influencing the attraction of one person to another have probably been studied more extensively than any other determinant of group formation. The early studies tended to consider secondary determinants, such as propinquity (Festinger, 1953a) and interaction (Bovard, 1956; Palmore, 1955). However, these variables merely provide the opportunity for the operation of primary variables, such as attitude similarity, value congruence, personality characteristics, and the like. Nevertheless, it is instructive to consider some of the environmental factors that make it possible for other variables to exert their effects on interpersonal attraction.

PROXIMITY, CONTACT, AND INTERACTION   Investigations of environmental and group process variables as determinants of group formation and interpersonal attraction are usually discussed under one of three headings: proximity, contact, or interaction. These factors are closely related and represent varying degrees of association rather than unique variables. In general, *proximity* has been used to refer to the physical distance between individuals, *contact* to situations in which individuals are likely to be in each other's presence frequently, and *interaction* to situations in which the behavior of each person influences the other.

In a number of field studies the physical distance between individuals has been found to be related to affiliation. The classical study of the formation of friendships in a student housing complex (Festinger, Schachter, & Back, 1950) clearly revealed the role of proximity in the establishment of interpersonal relationships. Married couples were assigned to housing by the university housing office in order of application, without regard to college major, classification, or other variables that might influence the formation of friendships. Festinger et al. found that such relationships were determined largely by proximity. Persons living next door to each other most frequently became friends. Couples who occupied corner units or end units which faced the street frequently became social isolates. The results of other investigations agree in showing a positive relationship between attraction and proximity; e.g., Maissonneuve, Palmade, and Fourment (1952) observed that propinquity and liking choices were related in boarding school classes; Byrne and Buehler (1955) found that seat neighbors in college classes were more likely to become acquainted; and Sommer (1959) noted that persons who sat near each other in the cafeteria of a large mental hospital interacted more than persons in more distant positions. It is clear, then, that proximity contributes to group formation.

There has been considerable interest in the degree to which contact between minority groups affects the relationships between such groups. Many investigations reveal that contact results in more favorable attitudes toward members of minority groups and an increased willingness to affiliate with them. During World War II, Stouffer, Suchman, DeVinney, Star, and Williams (1949) observed that the degree to which white soldiers thought it was a good idea to have Negroes in the company varied directly with the amount of contact they had had with Negroes. Results consistent with this finding have been obtained in a variety of settings. Deutsch and Collins (1951) compared black-white relations in a housing project in which black and white families were assigned to buildings in segregated areas with those in an integrated apartment house. They found there were more frequent and more intimate interpersonal relations among blacks and whites in the integrated project than in the segregated one. Furthermore, they were able to demonstrate that this difference did not exist prior to residence in the housing projects. Similarly, Jahoda (1961) found a considerable reduction in preferences for residential segregation following black-white contact as neighbors or on the job, and Harding and Hogrefe (1952) found that white persons who had worked with Negroes on an equal basis were more willing to do so again than those who had not.

It has already been suggested that proximity, contact, and interaction probably are not primary determinants of attraction; i.e., proximity makes it possible for individuals to come into contact and interact with each other, and such interaction makes it possible for them to learn about characteristics of others that make them attractive (e.g., their physical attractiveness, their attitudes, etc.). This interpretation is supported by evidence that proximity and interaction do not always lead to increased attraction. Festinger (1953a) described a housing project in which few group memberships existed among residents. In this project, the residents felt they were forced to live in the project because of a housing shortage, and their attitudes toward fellow residents were quite negative. Gundlach (1956) reported similar negative attitudes on the part of white women workers who had been assigned to work with Negroes with similar educations and backgrounds. Experimental studies in which interaction provided no evidence concerning the characteristics of others also yielded generally negative results, i.e., no relationship between amount of interaction and liking (Stotland & Cottrell, 1962; Stotland, Cottrell, & Laing, 1960).

If we are correct in believing that proximity and interaction merely provide the opportunity for individuals to learn about the characteristics of others that make them attractive, it is important to know what these other characteristics are and to explore just how they function to determine attractiveness.

PHYSICAL ATTRACTIVENESS   Probably the most obvious source of attraction between two persons is sheer physical attractiveness. When a person exemplifies the physical characteristics which contribute to the perception of beauty or handsomeness (in a given culture), others are prone to be attracted to him and to want to associate with him. The importance of physical attractiveness in dating behavior, for example, has been demonstrated by Walster, Aronson, Abrahams, and Rottman (1966). They conducted a field study in which subjects were randomly paired at a "computer dance." They found that, regardless of a subject's own attractiveness, how much he liked his partner, how much he wanted to date her again, and how often he actually asked her out again were a function of her physical attractiveness. Scores on the Minnesota Multiphasic Personality Inventory, the Minnesota Counseling Inventory,

Berger's (1952) Scale of Self-acceptance, the Minnesota Scholastic Aptitude test, and high school percentile rank—all were found to be unrelated to how much the partner wanted to continue the interaction. A recent study by Schlosser (1969) also demonstrated that physical attractiveness is a determinant of interpersonal attraction, even when the physically attractive other behaves in a way which interferes with attainment of a common goal.

SIMILARITY   It has been proposed by a number of writers that individuals are attracted to those who are similar to themselves. For example, Newcomb (1956) suggested that it is more likely that an interaction will be rewarding when the two interactors are similar, since one of the rewards deriving from interaction is social support for one's attitudes, beliefs, and opinions. Heider (1958) also theorized that similarity should produce interpersonal attraction. It is important to remember, however, that similarity is not a general quality. It is appropriate to consider similarity only with respect to specified characteristics (see Cronbach & Gleser, 1953). Hence, it is reasonable to expect that interpersonal attraction is related to similarity with respect to those characteristics which are judged important by the persons involved in the interaction. The variable most widely investigated within this general category of significant characteristics is probably *attitude similarity*. For instance, Newcomb (1961) invited students to live in a house rent-free in exchange for serving as research subjects. Seventeen men were selected for each of two years. At the time they moved into the house, no one knew any other member of the group. The men completed a series of attitude and value inventories and also estimated the attitudes of others in the group. Initially, proximity of room assignments was the primary determinant of attraction. Later, attraction was found to be a function of perceived similarity of attitudes.

The effects of attitude similarity on interpersonal attraction have been studied extensively by Byrne and his associates. In an initial study, Byrne (1961) followed Newcomb in assuming that reciprocal rewards and punishments are important determinants of attraction and that perceived similarity-dissimilarity is rewarding-punishing. Byrne devised the following technique for examining the similarity-attraction hypothesis, using twenty-six issues ranging from such relatively important things as integration, God, and premarital sexual relations to such relatively unimportant things as western movies and television programs. Subjects were asked to express their attitudes on these issues on a 7-point rating scale and to indicate how important each item was to them. Two weeks later subjects were falsely informed that the scale had been given as part of a study of interpersonal prediction, that students in another class had taken the same test, and that they were now to be given each other's test with the name removed in the hope that they could learn about one another from this information. Actually, fake scales were made up to represent four conditions: the other's attitudes were (1) the same as those expressed by the subject, (2) exactly opposite to those expressed by the subject, (3) the same on important issues but opposite on unimportant issues, and (4) the same on unimportant but opposite on important issues. The subjects then indicated how well they liked the other person and how much they would enjoy working with him. Attraction was significantly higher when the other person's attitudes were similar than when they were dissimilar according to both measures. Importance of issues had a significant effect only for the liking ratings. Using essentially the same technique, Byrne and Nelson (1964, 1965b) systematically varied both attitude similarity and topic importance, and found only similarity to be related to attraction. However, in a subsequent study, Byrne, London, and Griffitt (1968) demonstrated that importance significantly influenced attraction when topics heterogeneous in importance are associated with one other person.

Several subsequent studies by Byrne and his coworkers have consistently found attitude similarity to be a determinant of attraction (Byrne & Griffitt, 1966; Byrne & Nelson, 1965a; Byrne, Nelson, & Reeves, 1966; Byrne & Rhamey, 1965). The study by Byrne and Rhamey probably illustrates the relationship between attraction and attitude similarity most clearly. They required 180 subjects to read questionnaires purportedly filled out by an anonymous stranger and to evaluate him on a number of variables, including attraction. The stranger's responses agreed with those of the subject on 100 percent, 67 percent, 33 percent, or none of the items. Subjects were also given information about the stranger's evaluation of them, which was positive, neutral, or negative. The attraction scores, which could vary from 2 to 14, are shown graphically in Figure 4-1. It is quite evident that attraction is a positive, increasing function of the proportion of attitudes that are similar to those expressed by the subject. The effects are most strongly operative in the neutral evaluation condition, which suggests that evaluation by the other person also influences one's attraction to him.

That attitude similarity may not always be positively related to attraction has been shown by Novak and Lerner (1968). Forty-eight males and forty-eight females evaluated a "partner" who held either similar or dis-

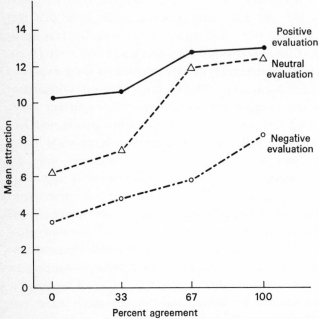

Figure 4-1 Mean Attraction to a Stranger as a Function of Degree of Attitude Similarity and Quality of the Stranger's Evaluation of the Person. (Plotted with permission from data reported by D. Byrne & R. Rhamey. Magnitude of positive and negative reinforcements as a determinant of attraction. *Journal of Personality and Social Psychology,* 1965, **2**, 884–889.

similar attitudes and who was described as either normal or emotionally disturbed. Subjects were less willing to interact with an emotionally disturbed person when he held similar attitudes than when he held dissimilar attitudes.

Similarity with respect to other characteristics has also been shown to be a determinant of attraction. *Similarity of personality* as a determinant of attraction was studied by Griffitt (1966), using the Byrne technique of evaluation of a stranger on the basis of his responses to a self-concept inventory. When the self-descriptions of the subject and those of the stranger agreed on 33 percent of the items, the mean attraction score was 8.76 as compared with a mean score of 11.61 when there was 100 percent agreement. Byrne, Griffitt, and Stefaniak (1967) had 151 subjects examine the responses of strangers to a repression-sensitization scale. The stranger had responded as the subject did on 25 percent, 50 percent, or 80 percent of the items. The subjects then rated the stranger's attractiveness; mean attraction scores were 6.17, 8.29, and 9.70 for the three degrees of response agreement, respectively. The evidence therefore indicates that similarity of personality characteristics is also positively related to interpersonal attraction. This conclusion is supported by Izard (1960a, 1960b), who found that friends were more alike on personality profiles than were random pairs.

There is evidence to suggest, however, that mere similarity may not always be a determinant of attractiveness. Rychlak (1965) examined the effects of similarity and compatibility of needs upon preferences for interpersonal role relationships. Similarity was based upon two persons having the same need (e.g., both have a need for dominance), compatibility upon two persons having complementary needs (e.g., one has a need for nuturance and the other a need for succorance), and incompatibility upon one person's having a need that is inconsistent with that of the other (e.g., one has a need for order and the other a need for change). After participation in two small group problems, subjects selected most and least preferred coworkers for the roles of boss, employee, and neighbor. Rychlak's findings supported the hypothesis that need compatibility is a determinant of attraction, whereas need similarity and need incompatibility are not related to attraction. A study by Jellison and Zeisset (1969) indicated that the degree to which trait similarity is related to attractiveness depends upon the desirability of the trait and also upon the degree to which the trait is common in the general population. When a desirable trait is shared by another, the other is more attractive when the shared trait is uncommon in the general population than when it is common; however, when the shared trait is undesirable, the other person is more attractive when the trait is common than when it is uncommon. A. R. Cohen (1956) found similarity of ego defenses to be related to attraction, whereas similarity based on projection preferences had the opposite effect.

These studies demonstrate that similarity of certain personality characteristics is related to interpersonal attraction, at least under some conditions. However, it should be evident that the similarity of personality traits must be perceived by the individual in order for it to influence his attraction to the other person. The relation between perceived or assumed similarity and interpersonal attraction was investigated many years ago by

Fiedler, Warrington, and Blaisdell (1952). Members and pledges of a college fraternity sorted seventy-six statements descriptive of personality traits four times: (1) describing self, (2) describing how one would ideally like to be, (3) predicting how one's best-liked fellow group member would describe himself, and (4) predicting how one's least-liked fellow group member would describe himself. There was no correlation between real similarity (descriptions of self) and choices of best-liked or least-liked group member. However, subjects perceived persons whom they liked best as more similar to their ideal self and as more similar to themselves than others whom they liked least. A later study by Fiedler, Hutchins, and Dodge (1959) yielded similar findings.

Economic similarity has been shown to be a determinant of attractiveness by Byrne, Clore, and Worchel (1966). High and low economic status subjects evaluated strangers on the basis of responses to economic items dealing with spending money. Ratings of attractiveness were higher when the stranger's responses indicated an economic status similar to that of the subject.

Similarity of race and similarity of sex as determinants of attraction were investigated by Smith, Williams, and Willis (1967). White and black subjects rated a stimulus person on acceptability as a friend. The stimulus person was described as to race, sex, and belief congruence relative to the subject. Race and sex were found to be related to attractiveness, but neither was as strong as belief congruence. Since the investigators' manipulation of belief congruence was essentially the same as the variations used in the studies of attitude similarity-dissimilarity, their findings support earlier studies concerning the importance of attitude similarity as a determinant of attraction.

The *perceived ability* of others also appears to be a determinant of the degree to which an individual desires to affiliate with another. Gilchrist (1952) demonstrated that subjects in a problem-solving situation prefer to work with individuals who have been successful previously in solving problems. This effect was verified in a subsequent study by Shaw and Gilchrist (1955). These studies also showed that although successful persons were initially chosen by both previously successful and previously unsuccessful persons, there was an increasing tendency (over time) for unsuccessful persons to shift to choices of other unsuccessful persons for affiliation. There is some suggestion, then, that similarity of perceived ability may also be a determinant of attraction. Zander and Havelin (1960) reported results consistent with this interpretation; subjects preferred to associate with others having similar ability.

In summary, the degree to which one person is attracted to another has been shown to be due to physical attractiveness of the other person, the degree to which the two persons are similar with respect to a variety of characteristics, and the perceived ability of the other person. Similarity has been studied far more extensively than other determinants of attractiveness and the evidence is highly consistent: Attraction is a function of attitude similarity, belief congruence, personality similarity, race similarity, sex similarity, and economic similarity. It is also evident that under some circumstances similarity of characteristics may lead to reduced attraction, e.g., when the other person is seen as emotionally disturbed or when needs are the characteristics under consideration. In the latter case, need compatibility appears to be the important factor. The implicit assumption in the foregoing discussion is, of course, that attraction between two persons will influence the formation of groups with these persons as members. Undoubtedly, there are many other determinants of interpersonal attraction that we have not considered here.

GROUP ACTIVITIES

An individual may be attracted to a group because he enjoys the things the group members do. A person may join a bridge club, not because he enjoys playing bridge (although he might enjoy it), but because he finds the social activities pleasant. A person may join the Kiwanis Club merely because he enjoys meetings and civic activities, although, of course, he may be in agreement with the goals of the club. One could cite many examples of this kind of attraction to the activities of a group, but data from controlled studies are scarce.

Perhaps the most convincing evidence was provided by Sherif and Sherif (1953), who studied group formation in summer camps for boys. They were able to demonstrate, among other things, that boys who were interested in the same activities tended to form groups. Related evidence has also been provided by Thibaut (1950). He found that the attractiveness of the activities in a group affected the attractiveness of group membership. Thus, although the empirical evidence is not extensive, it generally supports the proposition that group activities constitute one source of attraction to the group.

GROUP GOALS

In many ways it is difficult to separate the activities of a group from its goals, and an individual may be attracted to a group because he both enjoys its activities and values its goals or purposes. For example, a person may join a group formed for the purpose of raising funds to support the local church because he enjoys fund-raising activities and because he believes it is good to support the church. On the other hand, a person who very much disliked soliciting funds might join this group if he valued highly the goal of church support. It is improbable, however, that a person who enjoyed the activities in a particular group would join it if he negatively valued the group's goals and purposes.

The role of group goals in group formation has been demonstrated most clearly in the investigations of group relations by Sherif and Sherif (1953). After initially establishing intergroup hostility and tension through a series of ingenuous manipulations, they attempted to reestablish harmony and integration. In the initial stages of the study, members of a boys' summer camp were formed into two groups on the basis of selected activities. For approximately five days, situations were arranged in which it seemed that one group interfered with or frustrated the other group. For example, following an athletic victory by one group (the Bull Dogs) over the other (the Red Devils), both were invited to attend a party in the mess hall with the stated purpose of reducing intergroup conflict. However, it was arranged so that the Red Devils got to the mess hall first and found ice cream and cake on a table. Half of the refreshments were battered and broken whereas the other half were in good condition. The Red Devils were told to serve themselves and leave the Bull Dogs their share. Without comment, they chose the good half and carried it to their table. The reaction of the Bull Dogs to this treatment was predictable: They called the Red Devils "pigs," "bums," etc., and generally derogated them. When the intergroup conflict created by procedures of this sort had been firmly established, Sherif and Sherif attempted to reduce the conflict and to rearrange group boundaries by introducing common "supraordinate" goals. The most effective of these was a campwide softball game in which a team of best players from both groups were elected by the boys from the entire camp to compete with a team coming from a neighboring camp. Although the supraordinate goal approach did not completely eliminate the hostilities produced by the earlier manipulations, there was a significant reduction in the amount of hostility and tension and some realignment of group boundaries.

The results of this extensive series of studies demonstrate two ways in which attraction to group goals can contribute to group formation. In the early stages of group development, the conflict between groups led to increased group cohesiveness. One element of this cohesiveness was the "common enemy." Or to say it another way, one of the goals of the Bull Dogs was to get even with the Red Devils. More significant, perhaps, is the demonstration that a common group goal can produce new group memberships.

The effects that being in a common predicament has on group attraction are also demonstrated by a study of the consequences of shared stress on interpersonal liking (Latane, Eckman, & Joy, 1966). The investigators proposed that people who are undergoing stress together do something for one another that serves to reduce the stress, thus positively reinforcing each other. Female subjects were assigned to either an experimental condition in which they shared an electric shock or a condition in which each received the same shock but not together. It was found that ratings of liking for the other person were significantly greater in the shared condition, but only when subjects were firstborns. The treatment in such a study is certainly rather weak, and perhaps it is surprising that it had any effect at all. To the extent that it did, however, the results support the hypothesis that attraction to goals constitutes one basis for group attraction.

GROUP MEMBERSHIP

It has also been proposed that membership in a group per se may be rewarding to an individual, quite apart from the particular individuals who are members of the group, the group activities, or the purposes of the group. The results reported by Latane et al. and discussed above might be interpreted as supporting this proposition. It was suggested many years ago that there exists an "affiliation want" (Trotter, 1920), which is one of four instincts that govern man's life. Later theorists have denied the instinctual nature of the need for affiliation, but nevertheless posit such a need as playing an important role in social groupings (McClelland, Atkinson, Clark, & Lowell, 1953; Schachter, 1959). Schachter proposed that one of the functions of affiliation is to reduce anxiety, and his research generally supported this view. Research by others also agrees with this hypothesis. Pepitone and Kleiner (1957) varied the amount of threat experienced by group members and found that high threat yielded greater increases in attraction to the group than low threat. In a second study (Kleiner, 1960) it was found that reduction of threat increased the attractiveness of a confederate who played the role of group member.

Another reason for need affiliation was suggested by Singer and Shockley (1965), namely, that people affiliate in order to compare abilities (cf. Festinger, 1954). Thirty-nine female students were randomly assigned to either a condition in which they had knowledge concerning their performance on an experimental task or one in which they did not have this information. All subjects were then given a choice of waiting for the next part of the study alone or with others. Those who had no knowledge of their performance chose to affiliate significantly more than did those who had such information (6 of 8 versus 2 of 22).

The strongest support for the existence of a need for affiliation is provided by a series of investigations which attempted to show that the need for affiliation can be manipulated through deprivation in the same manner as a physiological need such as hunger.

Gewirtz and Baer (1958b) invited children, aged from three years ten months to five years three months, to play a game using toys. In a deprivation condition, the subject was deprived of social contact for twenty minutes before playing the game. When the child arrived at the laboratory, a familiar adult appeared and announced that the toy was broken but was being repaired. He was given plausible assurance that the toy would be repaired in a few minutes and, since the experimenter did not want the child to miss his turn, he was to wait. The adult then left him alone in a relatively barren room for the twenty-minute period. In the control (nondeprivation) condition, the child began the game immediately upon arrival at the laboratory. Each child played a game which required him to drop marbles into holes in the toy. After a four-minute period to establish a base-line rate, the experimenter dispensed social reinforcements according to a predetermined schedule immediately after the subject had dropped a marble into the least preferred hole (as determined during the base-line period). Reinforcements were verbal expressions of approval such as "good," "fine," "good one," etc. The reinforcements increased the rate of dropping marbles in the nonpreferred hole significantly more in the deprivation condition than in the nondeprivation condition, but only when the experimenter was a member of the opposite sex. In a follow-up study (Gewirtz & Baer, 1958a), a satiation condition was added in which the experimenter maintained a steady stream of conversation with the subject for twenty minutes before the game was started. The effects of reinforcement were significantly greater in the deprivation than in the nondeprivation condition, and greater in the nondeprivation than in the satiation condition. Both boys and girls served as subjects, but only a female experimenter was used. The opposite-sex effect observed in the first study was not found.

Gewirtz and Baer concluded that social deprivation enhances the effectiveness of a social reinforcer, thus supporting the hypothesis that there exists a need for affiliation. However, Walters and Karal (1960) were unable to replicate these findings with college students. Obviously, there is some question whether a twenty-minute period of deprivation is sufficient to arouse the need for affiliation in adults. In a second study (Walters & Ray, 1960), it was found that anxious isolated subjects differed in their response to deprivation whereas nonanxious subjects did not. These investigators concluded that the results reported by Gewirtz and Baer were due to anxiety aroused in the isolated subjects. On the other hand, Stevenson and Cruse (1961) found that social reinforcements were effective in changing behavior, and Stevenson and Odom (1962) demonstrated that the enhanced effects of social reinforcements after social deprivation could not be accounted for in terms of general deprivation. Thus, although there are some conflicting findings, the bulk of the evidence supports the hypothesis that need for affiliation can be manipulated in a manner similar to the manipulation of physiological needs, and that such manipulation has similar effects on responses to reinforcers.

INSTRUMENTAL EFFECTS OF GROUP MEMBERSHIP

It is perhaps unnecessary to note that an individual may join a group in order to achieve some goal outside the group. A young man may join a college fraternity as a means of meeting young ladies who are members of college sororities. In this case, the source of attraction to the group resides in the person(s) of others who are not members of the group; that is, the joiner is attracted to persons outside the group whom he believes he can affiliate with more readily if he becomes a member of the group in question. It is also obvious that a person may join a group because he believes this will be instrumental in the achievement of goals outside the group. For example, a businessman may join a civic club because he believes that such membership will "be good for business." It is not always easy to separate attraction to others outside the group and attraction to goals outside the group. Therefore, we will examine the general proposition that the sources of reinforcement attainable from group membership may reside outside the group itself.

A number of studies have shown that a group may be perceived as a means to an end outside the group. In a study of labor unions Rose (1952) found that members of local unions report that the major benefits from membership are higher wages and greater job security. However, since attainment of such benefits is a major goal of labor unions, this finding could just as easily be interpreted in terms of attraction to group goals. A more direct bit of evidence was provided by Willerman and Swanson (1953) in their study of college sororities. They found that one important reason for joining a sorority was the increased prestige in the college community that can be achieved through sorority membership. A similar study of reasons for belonging to a business organization demonstrated that goals outside the group, such as need for recognition and autonomy, were important factors in the desire to remain in the organization (Ross & Zander, 1957). Although not extensive, the empirical data thus support the hypothesis that individuals sometimes join groups to achieve goals that lie outside the group. Group membership is seen as instrumental in achieving these outside goals.

So, why do people join groups? After reviewing the multitude of factors related to group formation and membership, we find that the answer still seems to be: because the group is perceived as a means of satisfying some individual need or needs. But we have identified and examined some of the things about group membership that are perceived as sources of need satisfaction. For example, Newcomb (1956) has shown how similarity may affect attraction via generalization. It is more likely that an individual will receive reward from another person if that other person is similar to persons who have been rewarding in the past. The effects of need complementarity also may be interpreted in terms of reinforcements. If one person has a need to be dominant and the other a need to be submissive, affiliation will lead to need satisfaction for both. The effects of perceived success of the other person, group activities, group goals, and group instrumentality also may be seen as due to the fact that they satisfy individual needs. Thibaut and Kelley's (1959) analysis of attraction in terms of rewards and costs relative to comparison levels also shows how need satisfaction may be related to such factors as personal success of the other and attitude similarity. For example, the successful person is undoubtedly seen as possessing abilities that will help the group achieve its goals or that may be useful in helping the individual achieve individual goals. In either case, the successful person is seen as contributing to the satisfaction of personal needs, if one affiliates with him. In like manner, the effects of attitude similarity can be shown to be due to the expectation of need satisfaction. One of the rewards or benefits deriving from association with others is the validation of beliefs and attitudes; one may certainly expect validation if the other person holds similar attitudes. Therefore, it appears that interpersonal attraction is a function of the degree to which the person expects affiliation with the other to be rewarding. The difficult task is to identify the many sources of reinforcement in interpersonal relationships.

PHASES IN GROUP DEVELOPMENT

Group formation does not stop with the affiliation of members. The group develops over a moderately long period and probably never reaches a completely stable state. Development proceeds rapidly at first; much structuring and organization may occur in the first few minutes of interaction and certainly within the first several hours. Much early development is oriented toward the establishment of the social structure of the group: the formation of status and role relations, norms, and power relations. We will discuss this aspect of the group in Chapter 8. But there are phases in group development that can be described more or less independently of the particular social structure. It is probable that the kinds, durations, and sequences of phases in group development vary with the kind of group and with the group task. For example, developmental phases have been described in problem-solving groups and in sensitivity-training groups; it is instructive to compare the two.

PHASES IN GROUP PROBLEM SOLVING

The examination of phases in group problem solving conducted by Bales and Strodtbeck (1951) was limited to instances in which the groups worked toward a group decision on a specific problem. They defined phases as ". . . qualitatively different subperiods within a total continuous period of interaction in which a group proceeds from initiation to completion of a problem involving group decision" (Bales & Strodtbeck, 1951, p. 485). Their phase hypothesis was that during the problem-solving period groups move from a relative emphasis upon problems of orientation, to problems of evaluation, and finally to problems of control. *Orientation* refers to the process by which the information possessed by the individual members, and which is relevant to the group decision, is made available to the group and coordinated to the group problem. In a sense, it is an exploratory phase during which the members come to understand the problem and the information relevant to it. *Evaluation* occurs in all instances in which there are differences in values and interests regarding judgment of the facts of the situation and proposed courses of action. It is a subperiod during which group members judge the information relative to the problem and alternative solutions of it. *Control* refers to the regulation of members and their common environment. It involves intermember control as well as control over the group's environment, which, of course, includes the task.

The rationale for the phase hypothesis is that orientation is functionally prerequisite to the solution of problems of evaluation and control. Orientation makes it possible to evaluate and eventually to control the situation. Although Bales and Strodtbeck limited their phase hypothesis to problem-solving groups, they believed that it was compatible with processes of social interaction occurring over longer periods.

In order to test the phase hypothesis, Bales and Strodtbeck examined the interaction pattern of twenty-two problem-solving groups, using Bales's (1950) interaction process analysis. The group interactions were divided into thirds and examined for instances of orientation, evaluation, and control. Of all interactions directed toward orientation, approximately 47 percent occurred in the first period; of those directed toward evaluation, approximately 36 percent occurred in the second period; and approximately 40 percent of interactions relative to control occurred in the third period. Furthermore, the greatest frequency of interactions relative to orientation, evaluation, and control occurred in the order predicted. In the problem-solving situation, therefore, the phase hypothesis is supported by the data.

PHASES IN SENSITIVITY-TRAINING GROUPS

Sensitivity-training groups are markedly different from problem-solving groups. Whereas problem-solving groups have a definite goal, the solution of a specific problem or problems, sensitivity-training groups have only vaguely defined goals, at best. The goals are undoubtedly clear to the trainers who assemble the members, but the participants are typically uncertain about what it is the group is trying to accomplish. Bennis and Shepard (1956), who have been intimately involved with sensitivity training at the National Training Laboratory, have described not only the purposes and goals of such training groups, but also the phases of development of the groups. Their analysis reveals a pattern of group development that seems to contrast sharply with that reported by Bales and Strodtbeck for problem-solving groups. Before considering their analysis, however, we must describe briefly the nature of the training situation and objectives.

According to Bennis and Shepard, sensitivity training has two major objectives: (1) to help people learn how to behave in groups in such a way that they can solve the problems for which they were assembled and (2) to ensure that individuals have a meaningful and rewarding group experience. The goal of the training group is *valid communication*. That is, each member should be able to express freely his own feelings about himself and others and to accept others as individuals who also have the right to express their feelings, beliefs, and values. It is assumed that a group characterized by valid communication will be a "healthy" group that should function with maximum effectiveness.

Sensitivity training groups are typically composed of adults who have responsibility for directing the activities of groups as a part of their regular job. School principals, sociologists, business executives, ministers, etc., are examples of the kinds of persons who may participate in training groups. At the time the groups are assembled by the trainers, the participants are likely to be strangers. The trainer ordinarily does not specify the goals of the group, although he is available for consultation.

Therefore, group members are faced with an ambiguous situation that is undoubtedly unlike any they have experienced before.

According to Bennis and Shepard, two major areas of uncertainty present obstacles for valid communication: dependence (or authority relations) and interdependence (or personal relations). In its development, the group moves from a preoccupation with authority relations to a preoccupation with personal relations. Orientations toward authority are regarded as prior to, and partially determinant of, orientations toward members. The group development thus consists of two phases, the first of which involves problems of authority, and the second problems of personal relations. This pattern appears to be just the reverse of the pattern found in problem-solving groups, but as we shall see, the reversal is more apparent than real.

Within each phase of development there are three subphases. In the authority phase, the members are initially preoccupied with submission (subphase 1). They expect the trainer to establish goals and rules of conduct;

when he does not there is much aimless activity and wonderment about what they are supposed to be doing. After a period of such activity, counter-dependent expressions take over (subphase 2). Typically, two opposed sub-groups develop around the problem of leadership and structure. There is disenthrallment with the trainer, and rebellion is the order of the day. Resolution of the dependence problem (subphase 3) occurs rapidly, or there is a long period of vacillation and indecision during which the group is broken into conflicting subgroups. If and when dependence problems are solved, the group moves into the personal phase, starting with a period of preoccupation with intermember identification (subphase 4). During this subphase the group is happy, relaxed, and highly cohesive. All decisions must be unanimous; all members must be happy with whatever the group does. As time goes on, this harmony becomes more and more illusory and the group progresses to subphase 5, a preoccupation with individual identity. Usually the group will separate into two groups, one favoring and one opposed to close interpersonal relations. Those who oppose close interpersonal relations become anxious that their identities as individuals will be destroyed. Eventually, this conflict should be resolved (subphase 6). The resolution of interpersonal problems involves each group member verbalizing his own private conceptual scheme for understanding human behavior, both his own behavior and that of others. When this is possible, the group has achieved its goal of valid communication.

Bennis and Shepard point out that this is not always accomplished. Some groups become fixated at an earlier phase and hence never attain their goal, i.e., the goal established for the group by the trainer.

At first glance, this pattern of group development seems to be almost the opposite of that found in problem-solving groups. On closer examination, however, it may be seen that the terms used to describe the development are different and the content of the interaction is different (because of task differences), but the functional characteristics of group development are basically the same. In both kinds of groups, the members are attempting to orient themselves to an unfamiliar situation and to organize the information they have so they can deal effectively with the situation as they perceive it. In problem-solving groups, the requirements are much more obvious and the process of orientation is greatly attenuated relative to the highly ambiguous situation faced by training groups. And since the goal of the training group is better understanding of interpersonal relations, the processes of evaluation and control have a content very different from that of problem-solving groups. Again, the two kinds of groups are functionally equivalent; both are directed toward the achievement of the group goal.

These analyses do not necessarily reveal the "true" pattern of group development, but they do reveal clearly that groups follow a reasonably consistent path as they attempt to deal with the problems of group formation.

COALITION FORMATION

The preceding discussions have been concerned primarily with processes leading to uniformity and cohesiveness in groups. But the processes of group development often involve divisive forces as well. This is particularly true when the specific outcome of group process is not agreed upon by the group members. In problem-solving groups the goal is to achieve the "correct" solution or at least the best solution to the problem, and the group is unified with respect to the desired outcome. But in some situations, group members are divided with respect to the desired outcome. For example, at a political convention the members of the party may be divided regarding the person who should be nominated for political office. Each subgroup believes that its own interests (and perhaps the interests of the party) will best be served if its candidate is nominated. If one subgroup is powerful enough to obtain the nomination by its efforts alone, divisiveness is minimized. In most such instances, however, no one subgroup has the necessary votes to win; hence two or more subgroups must join together to produce a result that is more satisfactory to both than an outcome that could be achieved by either alone. Such unions are referred to as coalitions; they occur in such diverse situations as children's groups, university committees, and governmental agencies.

WHAT IS A COALITION?

The term *coalition* has been used in a variety of ways. Sometimes it is applied to mutuality of affective support (Mills, 1953), sometimes to joint activity (M. L. Borgatta, 1961), and sometimes to the joint use of resources to determine the outcome of a decision (Gamson, 1964). The latter usage seems most appropriate for the analysis of formative processes and will be adopted for our discussion. A coalition, defined in this way, is possible only in a certain kind of group situation. We must examine the characteristics of such a situation before we can give a more precise definition of coalition.

In attempting to describe the type of situation in which true coalitions are possible, Gamson (1964) appealed to Schelling's (1958) classification of two-person games. Three kinds of games were identified: pure conflict games, pure coordination games, and mixed-motive games. According to Gamson, we would expect coalitions to occur only in the mixed-motive situation. In such a situation, there is an element of both conflict and coordination. Conflict exists in the sense that there is no outcome that maximizes rewards for every group member; coordination is involved in that there exists for at least two persons the possibility that they can do better by coordinating their efforts than they can by acting alone. For example, consider a small group that is holding an election for the chairmanship. The chairman has control of desirable appointments, such as the treasurer. There are three candidates, each of whom has substantial support but no one of whom has sufficient support to win the election. Thus, there exists the possibility that if one candidate withdraws and throws his support to one of the others, the latter can win the election. Furthermore, the winner can reward the candidate who withdraws by appointing him treasurer. Clearly, there exists the possibility of a coalition which will yield a result for two of the candidates that is better than either could achieve acting alone.

According to Gamson, then, "a coalition is the joint use of resources to determine the outcome of a decision in a mixed-motive situation involving more than two units" (Gamson, 1964, p. 85). Thibaut and Kelley (1959) offered a similar definition: "By coalition we mean two or more persons who act jointly to affect the outcomes of one or more other persons" (Thibaut & Kelley, 1959, p. 205). These definitions make it clear that coalitions occur only when (1) three or more persons are involved, (2) two or more act as a unit against at least one other, and (3) the joint action produces a result superior to any result possible by individual action.

THEORY AND RESEARCH ON COALITIONS

For the most part, research has been directed toward the identification of factors determining coalitions and the prediction of types of coalitions that will be formed under specified conditions. The most common experimental paradigm involves three persons, A, B, and C, each of whom controls resources needed to achieve a desirable outcome. Resources are distributed so that $A > B > C$, $A < (B + C)$. That is, A controls more resources than B, who controls more resources than C, but B and C together control more resources than A alone. The common finding is that, under these conditions, B and C will form a coalition (Caplow, 1959; Kelley & Arrowood, 1960; Vinacke & Arkoff, 1957). However, this outcome does not always obtain, for example, when subjects are female (Uesugi & Vinacke, 1963). Furthermore, the results of the early studies could be accounted for by a variety of theoretical formulations. Gamson (1964) has outlined the various theories and examined how well each is supported by empirical evidence.

THE MINIMUM RESOURCE THEORY   According to the minimum resource theory (Gamson, 1961b), a coalition will form in which the total resources are as small as possible while still being sufficient to determine the outcome of the decision. For example, if person A controls 48 percent of the resources, person B 30 percent, and person C 22 percent, B and C should join together to control the outcome. This prediction is based upon the parity norm, i.e., the expectation that each participant in a coalition is likely to demand a share of the spoils that is proportional to the amount of resources contributed to the coalition. In the above example, if B and C joined together, B could expect approximately 58 percent of the rewards and C 42 percent; if either joined with A, the corresponding proportions would be approximately 38 percent for B and 31 percent for C. According to the parity norm, it is clearly to the advantage of both B and C to form a coalition between themselves instead of either joining A.

Much of the empirical evidence supports the minimum resource theory. The study by Vinacke and Arkoff (1957) tested this theory under three distributions of resources; the predicted coalitions occurred far more frequently than any other coalition. Gamson (1961a) tested the theory in a simulated convention situation. Five-person groups were used (in contrast to the three-person groups in Vinacke and Arkoff's study) with resources (votes) distributed 25-25-17-17-17. Minimum resource theory, of course, predicts a 17-17-17 coalition. Although the probability of this particular coalition occurring by chance is only one in ten, Gamson found that it actually occurred 33 percent of the time. Furthermore, he found that the distribution of rewards corresponded to the parity norm. Players with 17 votes averaged 31 percent of the rewards whereas players with 25 votes averaged 38 percent.

Other investigations have also yielded findings consistent with this theory (Chaney & Vinacke, 1960; Vinacke, 1959).

THE MINIMUM POWER THEORY   The origin of the minimum power theory is not entirely clear, although Gamson (1964) attributes it to game theory. According to the minimum power theory, each person is expected to demand a share of the rewards proportional to his pivotal power; hence, the coalition will form which has the minimum pivotal power that is sufficient to determine the outcome of the decision. The pivotal power of a given person is the proportion of times he can, through his resources, change a losing coalition into a winning one. For example, suppose A controls 10 percent, B controls 50 percent, and C controls 40 percent of the resources relevant to a given decision. There are three possible coalitions: A + B, A + C, and B + C. The A + C coalition cannot win; hence both A and C have pivotal power in only one winning coalition, whereas B has pivotal power in two. In this instance, the two winning coalitions each have a total of three units of pivotal power. The minimum power theory would predict that one of these would form, but it could not predict which. Minimum resource theory, on the other hand, would predict an A + B coalition.

There is little direct support for the minimum power theory, although one study (R. H. Willis, 1962) provided results consistent with it. This study involved four group members, with a 5-3-3-2 distribution of resources. There are four winning coalitions that might be formed: two 5 + 3 coalitions, one 5 + 2 coalition, and one 3 + 3 + 2 coalition. If members of the winning coalition are to share in the rewards in proportion to their pivotal power, the 3 + 3 + 2 coalition would be predicted by the minimum power theory. This occurred about 31 percent of the time, whereas the 5 + 2 coalition (predicted by the minimum resource theory) occurred almost exactly 25 percent of the time. This level of support is not very convincing, despite the argument by Kelley and Arrowood (1960) that the failure to find support for the theory is due to the lack of understanding of power relations by group members.

THE ANTICOMPETITIVE THEORY   This theory holds that coalitions will form along the lines of least resistance. This is based upon the presumed existence of an anticompetitive norm against efforts to make the best deal possible. That is, group members are more concerned about interpersonal relations than about other kinds of rewards. Therefore, coalitions will form in which the distribution of rewards is obvious and relatively equal. Such a coalition, of course, is one in which resources and pivotal power of participants are about equal. For example, if the resources of a group are distributed 4-4-2, the $4 + 4$ coalition is predicted. Evidence for this theory comes primarily from studies using female subjects (Bond & Vinacke, 1961; Uesugi & Vinacke, 1963). It is probable, therefore, that females tend to adopt an anticompetitive norm, whereas males adopt the parity norm.

THE UTTER CONFUSION THEORY   The utter confusion theory is really not a theory at all, but rather an assertion that coalitions are unpredictable. It states that coalitions are determined by chance events, such as a missed telephone call. Since the evidence for this theory consists of failures to understand what determined observed coalitions, it cannot be taken seriously by the student of group processes.

Gamson (1964) suggested that any investigator can find evidence for the theory of his choice simply by arranging conditions appropriately. While there is much to be said for this view, the bulk of the empirical evidence seems to fit the minimum resource theory. In many ways, too, the theory seems to fit our everyday observations about the parity norm. Furthermore, Leventhal and his associates (Leventhal, Allen, & Kemelgor, 1969; Leventhal & Bergman, 1969) reported that subjects who receive a proportion of rewards that deviates from an equitable distribution will usually increase or decrease their share in the direction of parity. On the other hand, Chertkoff (1966) has pointed out that the coalition formation process is probably not as simple as indicated by the minimum resource theory and the experiments designed to test it. He suggested that in natural situations in which rewards are great we must consider other possible factors, such as differing political philosophies and probability of success. In a simulated political convention, he found that when the probabilities of future success favored the strongest person in the group, the weakest members preferred the strongest. An equitable share of the rewards has no meaning if the coalition does not achieve the rewards in the first place.

In summary, coalitions often form during the process of group formation and development. They are influenced by the initial resources held by group members, by the norms of the group, and by the probability that the coalition will be successful in achieving future goals. When it is clear that the coalition will be a winning one, most males seem to adopt the parity norm, and coalitions form according to the minimum resources theory; most females adopt the anticompetitive norm and form coalitions that are least disruptive of social relationships. In either case, coalitions may be expected to shift from time to time with changing circumstances.

PLAUSIBLE HYPOTHESES ABOUT GROUP FORMATION AND DEVELOPMENT

The investigations of group formation and development have not answered all the questions about these processes, but they have reduced the number of plausible hypotheses. Again, the reader should recognize that these propositions are the most reasonable interpretations that can be made at this time, but any or all of them may be rejected as new evidence becomes available.

Hypothesis 1   People join groups in order to satisfy some individual need.
This is the most general proposition that we can derive from the empirical data concerning group formation. To a large extent, Hypotheses 3 through 7 are specifications of the sources of need satisfaction that inhere in groups.

Hypothesis 2   Proximity, contact, and interaction provide an opportunity for individuals to discover the need satisfactions that can be attained through affiliation with others.
Studies by Festinger, Schachter, and Back (1950), Maissonneuve, Palmade, and Fourment (1952), and Byrne and Buehler (1955) show the effects of proximity upon the formation of friendships in a variety of environmental settings. The effects of contact and interaction upon interpersonal attraction have been shown by Stouffer et al. (1949), Deutsch and Collins (1951), Jahoda (1961), and Harding and Hogrefe (1952), among others. The interpretation of these findings as showing that proximity, contact, and interaction merely provide the opportunity to learn about sources of satisfaction is further supported by the finding that attraction is reduced if contact fails to induce the belief that affiliation will be satisfying (e.g., Festinger, 1953a; Gundlach, 1956).

Hypothesis 3   Interpersonal attraction is a positive function of physical attractiveness, attitude similarity, personality similarity, economic similarity, racial similarity, perceived ability of the other person (his success or failure), and need compatibility.

Substantial empirical support has been reported for each of the factors listed in Hypothesis 3, but attitude similarity has been studied most extensively, with the generally consistent finding that interpersonal attraction is a positive function of degree of attitude similarity (Byrne, 1961; Byrne & Nelson, 1964; Byrne & Nelson, 1965a; Byrne & Nelson, 1965b; Newcomb, 1961; and many others). Studies supporting the other factors listed in Hypothesis 3 are as follows: physical attractiveness (Walster et al., 1966); personality similarity (Byrne et al., 1967; Griffitt, 1966; Izard, 1960a; Izard, 1960b); economic similarity (Byrne, Clore, & Worchel, 1966); racial similarity (Smith et al., 1967); success-failure (Gilchrist, 1952; Shaw & Gilchrist, 1955); and need compatibility (Rychlak, 1965).

Hypothesis 4   *An individual will join a group if he finds the activities of the group attractive or rewarding.*
Evidence for this hypothesis is not as strong as the evidence for Hypothesis 3, but it is moderately convincing (Sherif & Sherif, 1953; Thibaut, 1950). Furthermore, it is intuitively plausible.

Hypothesis 5   *An individual will join a group if he values the goals of the group.*
Again, the empirical support for this hypothesis is less than adequate, probably because it does not seem to require empirical demonstration. However, results of the studies of Sherif and Sherif (1953) and Latane et al. (1966) are consistent with the hypothesis.

Hypothesis 6   *There exists a need for affiliation which renders group membership rewarding.*
Empirical evidence consistent with this hypothesis has been reported by a number of investigators (e.g., Gewirtz & Baer, 1958a; Gewirtz & Baer, 1958b; McClelland et al., 1953; Pepitone & Kleiner, 1957; Schachter, 1959; Singer & Shockley, 1965; Stevenson & Odom, 1962).

Hypothesis 7   *An individual will join a group if he perceives it to be instrumental in satisfying needs outside the group.*
The basis for this hypothesis is primarily self-reports by members of existing groups (e.g., Rose, 1952; Ross & Zander, 1957; Willerman & Swanson, 1953). As in the case of Hypotheses 4 and 5, Hypothesis 7 seems so obviously true that few investigations have been made to test its validity.

Hypothesis 8   Group development follows a consistent pattern which may be characterized as orientation-evaluation-control.

There is some reason to believe that the kind of group, the goals of the group, and other factors may influence this pattern of development. However, the evidence to date is consistent with the proposed hypothesis (Bales & Strodtbeck, 1951; Bennis & Shepard, 1956).

Hypothesis 9   Coalitions form in situations in which two or more persons can achieve greater rewards through joint action than can either acting alone.

Hypothesis 10   When it is clear that the coalition can succeed, males adopt the parity norm and form the coalition with minimum but sufficient resources, whereas females adopt the anticompetitive norm and form coalitions that are least disruptive of social relationships.

Hypotheses 9 and 10 are interrelated in that the first states the conditions for coalition formation and the second specifies the type of coalition that is likely to form. Although the evidence is not always consistent, the results of empirical observations make the above hypotheses more plausible than alternative ones (Bond & Vinacke, 1961; Caplow, 1959; Gamson, 1961a; Gamson, 1961b; Gamson, 1964; Uesugi & Vinacke, 1963; Vinacke, 1962; Vinacke & Arkoff, 1957.

SUGGESTED READINGS

BENNIS, W. G., & SHEPARD, H. A. A theory of group development. *Human Relations*, 1956, **9**, 415–437.

BYRNE, D., & RHAMEY, R. Magnitude of positive and negative reinforcements as a determinant of attraction. *Journal of Personality and Social Psychology*, 1965, **2**, 884–889.

DEUTSCH, M., & COLLINS, M. E. *Interracial housing: A psychological evaluation of a social experiment.* Minneapolis: University of Minnesota Press, 1951.

GAMSON, W. A. Experimental studies of coalition formation. In L. Berkowitz (Ed.), *Advances in experimental social psychology.* Vol. 1. New York: Academic, 1964. Pp. 82–110.

GILCHRIST, J. C. The formation of social groups under conditions of success and failure. *Journal of Abnormal and Social Psychology,* 1952, **47,** 174–187.

GUNDLACH, R. H. Effects of on-the-job experiences with Negroes upon racial attitudes of white workers in union shops. *Psychological Reports,* 1956, **2,** 67–77.

NEWCOMB, T. M. The prediction of interpersonal attraction. *American Psychologist,* 1956, **11,** 575–586.

SHERIF, M., & SHERIF, C. W. *Groups in harmony and tension.* New York: Harper & Row, 1953.

STEVENSON, H. W., & ODOM, R. D. The effectiveness of social reinforcement following two conditions of social deprivation. *Journal of Abnormal and Social Psychology,* 1962, **65,** 429–431.

WALSTER, E., ARONSON, V., ABRAHAMS, D., & ROTTMAN, L. Importance of physical attractiveness in dating behavior. *Journal of Personality and Social Psychology,* 1966, **4,** 508–516.

PART III

THE INTERACTION PROCESS

CHAPTER 5

THE PHYSICAL ENVIRONMENT OF GROUPS

Groups do not function in isolation. They are embedded in a complex environmental setting that exerts a strong influence on almost every aspect of the group process. Because of its complexity, this setting should be regarded as several environments rather than a single one. Obviously, the group must exist in a *physical environment*. The buildings, rooms, chair and table arrangements, communication channels, and the like are different for different groups, and such factors affect the functioning of the group in several important ways. There are other environments that are less obvious, perhaps, but nevertheless are significant factors with respect to group process. The personal characteristics that group members individually bring to the group may be considered one aspect of the environmental setting (a *personal environment*), since they may be an important determinant of the group's operational characteristics. Once the members have assembled and begun interaction, a whole set of interpersonal relationships become established; this *social environment* exerts a strong influence upon the group. And finally, the group is usually formed for a purpose. Its task or set of tasks constitute the *task environment,* which is an important factor in shaping group behavior. In this chapter, we are concerned with the physical environment; in the remaining chapters, we will examine the characteristics and effects of the personal, social, and task environments.

Although many aspects of the physical environment are potential determinants of group behavior, relatively few of them have been examined systematically. We will restrict our consideration to those aspects which have been studied extensively enough to permit sound conclusions about their effects on group process. Particular attention will be devoted to territoriality, personal space, spatial arrangements, and patterns of communication channels. Studies of territoriality and personal space reveal the psychological significance of the physical environment for the individual; studies of spatial arrangements and patterns of communication reveal how elements of the physical environment can influence group interaction along a variety of dimensions.

TERRITORIALITY

It is a common observation that individuals tend to appropriate space and assume proprietary rights to it in almost all situations in which several people come together over a period of time. For example, when seats are not assigned in the classroom, each student typically selects a particular chair or desk which he occupies day after day. If another student sits in the chosen chair, the "proprietor" usually does not hesitate to point out that the other student is occupying his seat. Furthermore, the other student ordinarily recognizes the proprietary rights of the first student and moves to another chair without argument. By *territoriality,* therefore, we mean the assumption of a proprietary orientation toward a geographical area by a person or group. This proprietary orientation is distinguished from ownership by the fact that the individual or group has no legal right to the geographical area in question. The territory is simply occupied, either permanently or intermittently, by an individual (or group) who then acts as if the property belongs to him. That is, he uses the "territory" for his own purposes, and he defends it from invasion by others.

The orientations that individuals adopt toward geographical areas and objects in these areas have highly significant implications for small group behavior. When a group member assumes a proprietary right to a particular object, the smooth functioning of the group depends upon the degree to which other group members respect that person's assumed territorial right. For example, if one member adopts a particular chair as his own and another member sits in it and refuses to move, intragroup conflict is inevitable. Even if the offended member yields to the new occupant, ill feelings are likely to develop between the two members to the detriment of good interpersonal relations. Similarly, when one group assumes territorial rights to a given geographical area, good intergroup relations depend upon other groups respecting that assumed right. Evidence concerning these orientations derives primarily from investigations that focus upon individual territoriality. However, in the following discussions, the reader should keep clearly in mind the consequences of these individual orientations for group behavior.

INDIVIDUAL TERRITORIALITY

Individuals typically assume territorial rights over spatial objects, such as tables, chairs, and beds, as well as over larger spatial areas, such as rooms. This has been well documented in a number of carefully controlled observational studies. W. F. Whyte (1949) conducted an extensive study of the social structure of restaurants and found, among other things, that kitchen workers held proprietary attitudes toward the kitchen area. When other workers entered the kitchen, the normal pattern of interaction was disrupted. If the "invader" had lower status, the kitchen workers openly attempted to block his participation in the work they normally carried out. Higher-status persons were not openly resisted, but their presence typically disrupted relations in the kitchen.

Altman and Haythorn (1967a) studied the interactions of isolated dyads. During the period of isolation the members of the dyad gradually withdrew from one another and established strong preferences for a particular chair, table, and/or bed. These preferences were rigidly respected by both members of the dyad. The degree to which this occurred varied with need compatibility; when both members were either very high or very low on need for dominance, the "territorializing" was much more marked than when dominance needs were more compatible (i.e., one member high and the other low on need for dominance).

The tendency to assume a proprietary orientation toward public geographical areas has been explored by Lyman and Scott (1967). They called attention to public areas that are taken over by groups or individuals for their own purposes. Examples included children's clubhouses, tree houses, coffeehouses, and similar territories appropriated for individual or group activities. These territories become the "property" of the occupants, who resent any implication that they have no right to occupy the area and will defend it against intruders. The current fad of establishing "people's parks" is a modern example. Similar proprietary orientations were observed in seventeen British old folks' homes (Lipman, 1968). Most of the inmates had chairs that they regarded as their own property. If a newcomer sat in a chair claimed by an inmate, he was asked in a preemptory manner to move. Furthermore, others respected a particular inmate's right to the chair and often defended it for him. New patients sometimes had difficulty finding a seat that did not "belong" to someone, and various initiation rites were sometimes required to teach the new inmate the norms of the home.

As indicated above, the occupants of a territory will ordinarily defend it against invasion by outsiders. Sommer (1969) described a series of studies designed to examine the ways individuals defend their territory against intruders. In one study, twenty-four students were shown diagrams of a rectangular table with three, four, or five chairs per side. They were asked to show where they would sit if they wanted to be as far as possible from the distraction of other people. By a large majority, they chose end positions. Another twenty-one students were shown the same diagrams and asked where they would sit to discourage anyone else from sitting at the table. These students almost unanimously chose the middle chair. Thus, different types of territories were defended by different techniques. In another study, an attractive young lady attempted to maintain privacy in a room which was a part of a soda fountain. For twenty-minute periods, on various days, she sat facing the door and gave the appearance of studying. On other days, she watched the room from a distance, in both instances keeping records of the number of people entering, where they sat, and how long they stayed in the room. She was able to keep the room completely to herself on only one of ten occasions; however, she was successful in keeping her table private on nine of ten occasions. This one unwanted visitor compared with thirteen who sat at that table during control sessions.

On the basis of these findings, Sommer concluded that territorial defense is not an all-or-none proposition, and further studies supported this conclusion. For example, one young lady attempted to assert her right to a table in a soda fountain even when she was not physically occupying it. After a person had sat at the table for varying lengths of time, she would approach and inform him that he was occupying her table. If the occupant had been there only a short time, he typically moved to another table without question. But if he had been there for a longer time, he suggested she must be mistaken—that he had been there for a long time. Similar studies in a busy library revealed that territory can be "reserved" by tokens (coats, books, etc.) for long periods.

It is clear then that individuals assume territorial rights over physical space and objects in that space and that they will defend this territory against intruders. We will see that groups also establish this orientation.

GROUP TERRITORIALITY

Group territoriality differs from individual territoriality in a number of ways. First, and most importantly, it is the group qua group that establishes territorial rights and defends against invasions. Second, the areas are usually larger and sometimes less clearly delimited than in the case of individual territoriality. Whereas the individual occupies a chair, a room, or perhaps a vacant lot, the group frequently occupies a much larger geographical area, such as a city subdivision or sometimes a whole town. In the well-known studies of street-corner gangs (W. F. Whyte, 1943) it was found that gangs typically establish a territory that they defend to the death against rival gangs. More recently, Mack (1954) and Marine (1966) have reported evidence of group territoriality. Mack described a residential situation in which Swedes and Italians lived in adjacent areas, but in almost complete social segregation. This separation apparently served the function of reducing conflict. Marine described a number of cities in which racial segregation produced similar effects. Although no one required that certain groups reside in certain areas, the separation into territories was nevertheless rigid and precise.

In addition to reducing or preventing conflict, group territoriality, as well as individual territoriality, serves to protect the individual against other people; it provides a bit of privacy that might not otherwise be obtainable. In certain cases, territoriality is a way of asserting the dominance of one group or individual over another group or individual. The close relationship between status and certain ecological factors has been detailed by Sommer (1969) and will be discussed in greater detail later in this chapter.

PERSONAL SPACE

Personal space is distinguished from territoriality in that it is relative to the person's body. Unlike a territory, personal space is carried about with the individual; it is not tied to a geographical area. Also, its boundaries are not fixed, but expand and contract under varying conditions. Little defined personal space ". . . as the area immediately surrounding the individual in which the majority of his interactions with others take place" (Little, 1965, p. 237). But there is more to personal space than this definition implies. Personal space is that space surrounding the individual which he regards as private—the space that others may not enter. Unwanted intrusion evokes negative reactions which vary from subdued expressions of displeasure to strong retaliatory actions, depending upon the characteristics of the intruder and the circumstances in which the invasion occurs.

As was mentioned above, personal space has flexible boundaries which vary with the personal and social relationships between the person and others, as well as with the nature and purpose of the interpersonal contact. The area of personal space, as indicated by comfortable approach distances, is smaller in relation to impersonal than to personal objects, and it is smaller in relation to intimate others than to others with whom the person is less intimate. It also varies with the status of the person and with the kind of interaction.

Like territoriality, personal space has important consequences for group process. When one group member invades the personal space of another member, for example, negative reactions are inevitable. Groups in which members are insensitive to the personal space of other members are likely to experience intragroup conflict and poor interpersonal relations. Again, the studies discussed in the following sections have concentrated upon the individual aspects of personal space, but it should not be too difficult to understand the significance of the findings for group behavior.

SITUATIONAL IMPERSONALITY

When persons are in certain role relationships, personal space may become very small indeed. The dental patient submits to direct personal contact with the dentist with no negative reactions toward him; the physician is permitted unusually intimate contact with the patient; etc. These role relationships define the situation as impersonal, and the dentist and physician may be defined psychologically as nonpersons. The effects of the impersonal-personal dimension on interpersonal distance have been explored in a number of studies. Horowitz, Duff, and Stratton (1964) instructed mental patients to walk over to either a person or a hat rack, and measured the distance between their stopping place and the object. They found that each patient tended to establish a characteristic individual distance and that this distance was relatively stable across situations. They also observed that subjects approached the hat rack more closely than they did another person. In a similar study (Argyle & Dean, 1965), subjects were asked to stand as close as comfortable to see well a variety of objects, including two photographs of a person, one with eyes open and one with eyes closed. They found that subjects stood closer to the photograph with the eyes closed. Presumably this photograph represented a more impersonal object than the one with the eyes open.

The effect of impersonality of setting on the perceived interaction distance on line drawings of same-sex figures was investigated by Little (1965). In one study, the figures were said to have been talking for about two minutes, and subjects were asked to arrange the figures on a background setting and to tell what they had been talking about. The settings varied in degree of impersonality: a living room, an office, or a street corner. Little predicted that the interfigure distance would be least in the living room and greatest on the street corner. This prediction was supported when the subjects were female, but not when the subjects were male. A second study in which the settings were an office, a lobby in a public building, an office waiting room, and a scene called "on the campus" revealed that the maximum distances occurred in the office. Thus, the hypothesis that distance should increase with increasing impersonality of the settings was only partially verified.

A rather different procedure was followed by McBride, King, and James (1965) in a study of emotional reactions to being touched by persons and by impersonal objects. They used the galvanic skin response (GSR) as a measure of emotionality, since it was well known that changes in skin conductivity, which are revealed by the GSR, are related to changes in emotionality. They found that being touched by another person produced a greater GSR than being touched by an inanimate object. This may be related to a finding reported by Rosenfeld (1965). Female subjects who were instructed to play an approval-seeking role sat closer to a confederate than subjects who were instructed to play an approval-avoidance role. The effects of impersonality are further revealed by the fact that subjects sat farther from a person who was described as cold and unfriendly than from one who was described as warm and friendly (Kleck, 1969).

The general trend of these empirical data is clear. Personal space contracts in the presence of impersonal objects and expands in relation to more personal objects (including other persons). The more impersonal the object, the less the social implications of close personal contact with them.

INTERACTION DISTANCE

Just as individuals tend to establish an approach distance which varies as a function of impersonality, there is also a characteristic individual distance that is most comfortable for interaction with others. This interpersonal distance appears not only to be an individual matter, but also to vary systematically with the intimacy of the relationship between the person and others and the circumstances under which the interaction occurs. Although interaction distance is an important aspect of interpersonal behavior, relatively little careful research has been done to establish the limits of comfortable interaction or the variables related to it. Results of the few investigations reported in the literature, however, are enlightening. F. N. Willis (1966) recorded the speaking distance between two persons under a wide range of circumstances. Forty investigators obtained data on 755 persons in such diverse places as homes, places of business, and halls of university buildings. Each investigator obtained measures of initial speaking distances in twenty encounters. When an investigator was approached by another person who began a conversation, the investigator remained at a fixed point. At the start of conversation, he measured (with a cloth tape measure) the nose-to-nose distance between himself and the other person, and categorized his relationship to the other person according to one of the following definitions: *stranger*—the investigator had never met the other person; *acquaintance*—the investigator had met the other person but did not know him well enough to call him by name; *friend*—the investigator knew the other person well enough to greet him by name; *close friend*—the investigator's best same-sexed friend, or person of opposite sex he had dated or was married to. There were not enough subjects in some categories to permit meaningful comparisons. However, it was found that women investigators were approached more closely (mean = 21.58 inches) than men (mean = 24.46 inches). Compared with males, female subjects stood very near to "close friends" when speaking, but stood back from "friends." Persons the same age as the investigator stood closer (mean = 23.87 inches) than persons who were older (mean = 26.67 inches), and acquaintances stood closer (mean = 23.80 inches) than strangers (mean = 27.33 inches). On the other hand, parents stood as distant as strangers (median = 27 inches in both instances).

Interaction distances were measured by Little (1965) in a study designed to determine the relationship between such distances as measured by a projective method and by live-person interactions. In one situation, pairs of plexiglass silhouettes were presented to subjects and described as either strangers, acquaintances, or friends. Subjects were asked to place the figures on a blank background (which they were to imagine represented various settings; see page 123) so that they faced each other and to tell what was going on between the figures. A second situation was essentially the same except that live actresses were used instead of plexiglass silhouettes. Subjects were asked to assume the role of theater director and to place the actresses in situations similar to those used in the first part. Considering all conditions, the mean interaction distance was 14.1 for the silhouettes (measured in eighths of an inch) and 25.6 inches for the actresses. The important finding for the present discussion is that the interaction distance varied with the relationship. The average distance for the actresses was 15.5 inches for friends, 27.2 inches for acquaintances, and 34.3 inches for strangers. The distance scores were similar for the silhouettes: 8.7, 15.0, and 18.5 for friends, acquaintances, and strangers, respectively. There was also some variation as a function of the setting, as already mentioned. Note, however, that this study dealt with perceived interaction distances rather than distances in actual interactions. Little suggested that actual face-to-face interaction distance may be influenced by a variety of factors, such as odor and depth perception, which were not present in his experimental situations. However, it is reasonable to assume that the distances in real interactions would be relatively the same as those reported in this study.

Some evidence concerning interpersonal distance in real interactions has been provided by Justice (1969), who was primarily interested in interperson distance as a function of the person's field dependency and as a function of the intimacy of the topic being discussed. He selected twenty-four field-dependent subjects (i.e., subjects who scored high on a test designed to measure the degree to which they relied upon situational and environmental factors) and twenty-four field-independent subjects (who scored low on the field-dependency test). Subjects were asked to write about either their favorite hobby or their concerns about relationships with members of the opposite sex. Then each subject was asked to present the topic orally to the experimenter. On a bell signal, the subject walked down a hall toward the experimenter, stopped, and made the oral presentation. Each subject was given four trials, and the distance (in inches) between subject and experimenter measured on each trial. Mean distances on the four trials were 25.67, 25.08, 28.63, and 30.38 for the field-dependent subjects, and 33.88, 34.46, 38.79, and 40.21 for the field-independent subjects. The average distance was therefore greater for the field-independent subjects than for the field-dependent subjects on all trials, as expected. Field-dependent subjects need closer relations than field-independent persons. These distances are only slightly greater than those reported by Little (1965). The greater distance for real interactions is probably due to the fact that they are more personal than projected interactions.

In summary, for comfortable interaction, persons establish a characteristic distance which varies with the setting and, especially, with the relationship between the person and the other. This interaction distance is undoubtedly influenced by many variables that have not yet been studied.

INVASION AND DEFENSE OF PERSONAL SPACE

Implicit in the several studies of personal space that have been cited is the assumption that the distance an individual places himself from other persons and impersonal objects defines the limits of his personal space. We have seen how the boundaries of this space vary with the situation and the relationship of the person to others. But we should not assume that personal space has regular boundaries, such as a circle around the person's body, which merely expand or contract with circumstances. Instead, personal space seems to form an irregular pattern about the person. McBride et al. (1965), in the study cited earlier, found that the GSR was greatest when the subject was approached frontally and least when approached from the rear. An approach from the side elicited an intermediate response.

The results reported by McBride et al. suggest that approaches to the person that are closer than the distances typically established by him should elicit defensive reactions by that person. Sommer (1969) described a number of investigations of reactions to invasion. The first study was conducted in a 1,500-bed mental institution, which was located in a parklike area. Since most of the wards were unlocked, it was easy to find patients seated alone on a bench or knoll. When a male patient was observed alone and not engaged in any definite activity, Sommer walked over and sat beside him without saying a word. If the patient selected as the victim moved his chair or slid further down on the bench, so did Sommer. Control patients were selected from similar situations but some distance away from the observer. The typical reaction to invasion was simply to leave the scene. During the first nine minutes, half of the victims had departed as compared with only 8 percent of the control subjects. Although flight was the most noticeable reaction to intrusion, Sommer reported other less obvious responses. A typical immediate reaction included facing away, pulling in the shoulders, and placing elbows at the side. Other evidences of discomfort included rubbing the face, breathing heavily, looking at watch, and flexing fingers.

In another study cited by Sommer, Nancy Russo invaded the privacy of students in a college library. She selected female students who were sitting alone with one or more books before them and empty chairs on either side. In any given instance of invasion, one such person was selected as the victim and another in the same kind of situation as a control. The invasion consisted of sitting alongside the victim, directly across from her, or in some other position contrary to seating norms in the library. Again, departure was the most common reaction to intrusion, although this was often preceded by defensive gestures, shifts in posture, and similar behaviors.

In these situations, it is easy for the person to defend his privacy through flight. But many other kinds of behaviors appear to be designed to protect against invasion beforehand. The person may select a position that is as inaccessible as possible, such as an isolated chair or a fenced-in area. Sommer (1969) reported a number of attempts to explore ways in which offensive display and avoidance protect spatial privacy. In one study, subjects were given charts of tables and chairs with instructions to select the position they would want in order to either retreat from others or defend themselves against others. With retreat instructions, 76 percent of the subjects chose a chair with its back to the wall, whereas only 38 percent chose a wall chair under defensive instructions. In other studies, retreat instructions elicited choices of rear seats in preference to front seats, small tables over large tables, and tables against the wall rather than tables with aisles all around.

When the room was described as crowded, choices were similar to those produced by retreat instructions.

The conclusion to be drawn from these studies is that individuals devise various techniques to guard against invasion. If these techniques fail, the intrusion of another into the personal space evokes discomfort, unease, and other negative feelings which are revealed in various defensive responses, ultimately ending in flight.

INTERPERSON DISTANCE AND STATUS

The personal space of an individual serves both personal and interpersonal functions. We have already seen how personal space can affect the emotional state of an individual and his comfort in the situation. But personal space also has important connotations for interpersonal behavior. One of the important functions of spatial relations among persons is the establishment and communication of status differences. In general, the high-status person occupies the best position, and, conversely, the person who occupies the better position is seen as having higher status. For example, Lott and Sommer (1967) conducted a questionnaire study in which subjects were asked to indicate where they would sit in relation to peers, higher-status, and lower-status persons. When the table had obvious status positions, such as "the head of the table," the high-status person was placed there, but when the table was square (all positions equal) the positions selected placed greater distance between the person and both higher- and lower-status others than between the person and his peers.

The role of interperson distance in the perception and communication of status differences was demonstrated in a study conducted by Hutte and Cohen (cited in Sommer, 1969). They prepared a series of ten one-minute silent films in which two actors portrayed a simple interaction sequence. In each film, one man is seated at a desk sorting through a card index when he is interrupted by the telephone. The next scene shows the second man, who knocks at the office door, enters, approaches the man at the desk, and discusses something with him. Ratings of the relative status of the two men were obtained from audiences that viewed the films. The caller was rated most subordinate when he stopped just inside the door and least subordinate when he walked directly to the desk. When he walked halfway into the room, he was seen as less subordinate than when he stopped at the door but more subordinate than when he walked all the way to the desk.

It seems clear that interperson distance is related to the perception of the relative statuses of individuals. The distance that a person maintains between himself and another person communicates something about his status relative to that other. However, the direction of the difference often depends upon other factors. The study by Lott and Sommer suggests that individuals tend to place distance between themselves and persons having both higher and lower status; hence interperson distance alone does not indicate which person has the higher status. For example, in the Hutte and Cohen films, the situation in which the interaction occurred provided clues to the direction of the status difference. In most instances, the variations in situation and/or behavior of the person involved serve as indicators of differences in status level.

Although these investigations demonstrate a relationship between interperson distance and status, it is not clear whether the relationship is caused by expansion of the personal space of the higher-status person in the presence of the lower-status individual or is merely due to culturally established patterns of interaction. That is, in many situations the higher-status person is physically separated from those of lower status. The leader sits at the head of the table, the professor at the head of his class, the politician before the crowd, and so on. It is possible that long familiarity with such situations has produced a cultural expectation of greater interperson distance between high- and low-status persons than between peers. We will see that the interperson distance-status relationship is found also in studies of the effects of seating arrangements.

SPATIAL ARRANGEMENTS

In the preceding pages we have been concerned with the orientations that individuals adopt with regard to the space about them and to other persons and impersonal objects in that space. It is now time to consider some of the consequences of certain spatial arrangements in group situations. Although relatively little research has been devoted to this important aspect of group interaction, there is good evidence that spatial arrangements in groups exert significant influences upon the perception of status, the patterns of participation, leadership activities, and the affective reactions of group members. It is not surprising, then, that there are consistent position preferences in group situations; that is, the choices that people make with regard to where they position themselves in the group are consistent with what is known about the effects of spatial arrangements on group process.

SEATING PREFERENCES

When persons are free to choose their position in a group, their choices usually reflect the cultural import of various locations. Persons who perceive themselves to have relatively high status in the group select positions that are in accord with this perception. For example, Strodtbeck and Hook (1961) analyzed data obtained from experimental jury deliberations and found that jurors from professional and managerial classes selected the chair at the head of the table significantly more often than did persons from other classes. Similarly, Hare and Bales (1963) found that subjects who scored high on a pencil-and-paper measure of dominance tended to choose the more central seats in the group situation.

Sommer and his associates examined seating preferences in a number of investigations ranging from questionnaire studies to actual participation in group activities (Sommer, 1969). In one study, subjects were asked to choose from a number of alternatives the seating arrangement at a rectangular table (see Figure 5-1) that they most preferred for four different activities: conversing, cooperating, coacting, and competing. A corner-to-corner or a face-to-face arrangement was chosen for casual conversation, whereas cooperating individuals preferred the side-by-side arrangement. Competing pairs tended to choose a face-to-face arrangement, although some chose a more distant setup (e.g., across and at opposite ends of the table). Coacting pairs were consistent in choosing a pattern that minimized intimacy, such as the distant arrangement referred to above. A second questionnaire study using round tables yielded results that were in accord with those found in the first study.

The next step was to try to verify the results of the questionnaire studies by examining seating preferences in real groups. Pairs of children were placed in cooperative, competitive, and coacting activities to see how they would arrange themselves. In general, cooperating pairs sat side by side, competing pairs sat at adjacent corners, and coacting pairs sat at a distance. Very few pairs used the face-to-face arrangement which had been prominent in the questionnaire results. In still another investigation, adult subjects were told that they would be either competing or cooperating with another person who was already seated at a table. In the cooperative situation, thirteen of

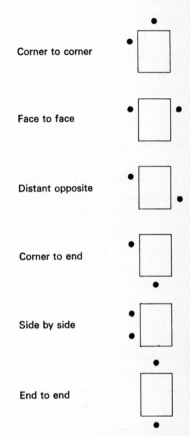

Figure 5-1 Seating Arrangements at Rectangular Tables. (Adapted with permission from R. Sommer. *Personal space: The behavioral basis of design.* Englewood Cliffs, N.J.: Prentice-Hall, 1969.)

twenty-four subjects sat on the same side of the table as the decoy, whereas in the competitive situation nineteen of twenty-three subjects sat opposite the decoy. The experimental findings and the questionnaire results are therefore consistent in showing that individuals prefer the side-by-side arrangement for cooperation and the face-to-face arrangement for competition. These results are also in substantial agreement with findings reported by Myers (1969) in a counseling setting. Counselees overwhelmingly preferred an informal "knee-to-knee" arrangement to a formal face-to-face arrangement.

It is not possible to determine from investigations of this kind whether the preferences for seating arrangements are due to cultural expectations concerning the appropriate spatial relationship in a given setting or to the feelings that various arrangements produce in the individual under certain conditions. Sommer's subjects in the questionnaire studies explained their choices in terms of task efficiency. That is, they suggested that casual conversation is facilitated by both physical proximity and eye contact; hence they chose arrangements that would maximize these factors. It is always possible, however, that explanations of this sort are rationalizations rather than true causes of the observed phenomenon. Evidence reported by Myers (1969) suggests that preferences may be caused by the feelings aroused by the particular seating arrangement. He found that subjects in a formal seating arrangement scored significantly higher on a scale designed to measure situational anxiety than subjects in an informal arrangement. Thus, certain spatial relationships may produce unpleasant affective responses which result in conditioned avoidance reactions. Also, it is not difficult to see that the position-status relationship should make some positions positively rewarding and others negatively rewarding (unpleasant, punishing). Therefore, the most plausible explanation of spatial preferences is in terms of the reinforcement probabilities associated with various spatial positions.

SEATING ARRANGEMENT AND INTERACTION

The rewarding values of spatial positions derive in part from their consequences for group interaction. Obviously, it is difficult to interact with another person at a great distance, and certainly interaction with a person one cannot see is less satisfactory than face-to-face interaction. For example, most people find a telephone conversation less satisfactory than a face-to-face conference, largely because the nonverbal parts of communication are not available during a telephone conversation. But there are consequences of spatial arrangement which are not so obvious. For example, the flow of communication in a group is a function of the spatial relationships among group members. When members of a group are seated at a round table, there is a strong tendency for members to communicate with persons across the table and facing them rather than with persons adjacent to them. Steinzor (1950) tabulated the number of times persons removed 5, 4, 3, 2, and 1 seats from others in the group followed each other in making verbal statements. He found no consistent relationship between interperson distance and following, but members across the table followed each other significantly more often than chance. A similar effect was reported by Strodtbeck and Hook (1961) in their study of twelve-man juries seated at rectangular tables. Persons sitting at end positions participated more and were seen as having more influence on the group decision than persons seated at the sides.

This so-called "Steinzor effect" was verified in a study in which group members were seated at a square table (Hearn, 1957). Hearn found that, with minimum direction from a designated leader, members of a face-to-face discussion group directed more comments to persons sitting opposite them than to those on either side. However, he found that in groups with a strong directive leader, the opposite occurred; that is, more comments were directed to neighbors than to those sitting opposite. This latter finding does not negate the hypothesis that seating arrangement influences the pattern of communication in the group, but it does specify some of the limiting conditions of the Steinzor effect.

Seating arrangement also has an effect on the quality of the interaction. Russo (1967) presented diagrams of five seating arrangements at a rectangular table (see Figure 5-2). In each case, two persons were seated on either side of the table and one person at each end. She was interested in subjects' perceptions of the social relationships existing between two persons occupying different spatial relationships at the table. The spatial relationships of the two designated persons were: side-by-side, near corner-to-end, on opposite sides and facing, distant corner-to-end, and end-to-end. The two designated persons were identified as members of the same sex. Subjects were asked to rate the couple on four dimensions: intimate-unacquainted, hostile-friendly, talkative-untalkative, and equal-unequal. In general, the more distance there was between the two persons, the less friendly, acquainted, and talkative they were perceived to be. This was qualified by the fact that situations permitting easy eye contact showed less of the interperson distance effect.

The same kind of qualitative effect probably accounts for the relationship between attitude and seating preferences cited by Campbell, Kruskal, and Wallace (1966) in their study of integrated classrooms. They reported

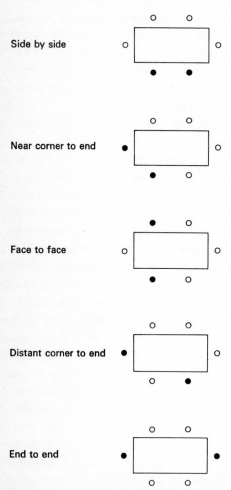

Figure 5-2 Seating Arrangements in Russo's Study of Perceived Social Relationships. Filled-in Circles Represent Critical Positions and Open Circles Represent Empty Chairs. (Adapted with permission from N. F. Russo. Connotations of seating arrangements. *Cornell Journal of Social Relations,* 1967, **2,** 37–44.)

that the number of black-white seating adjacencies departed significantly from randomness. An index of aggregation reflecting this lack of randomness in seating arrangements showed the expected differences between two schools selected to represent differing attitudes toward integration.

In summary, it is clear that spatial arrangement has a profound influence not only on the pattern of communication in the group, but also upon qualitative aspects of group interaction. These effects, in turn, have important consequences for the emergence of leadership and for status in groups.

SEATING ARRANGEMENT AND LEADERSHIP

The relationship between status and interperson distance has already been discussed, and since the leader usually has high status in a group, it is not surprising that there is also a relationship between spatial arrangements and leadership. The leader usually occupies the head of the table, for example, and conversely the person who sits at the head of the table is usually perceived as the leader. These facts mean that the spatial position which a person occupies in the group will have important consequences for his chances of emerging as a leader and the amount of influence that he exerts on group process.

One of the first demonstrations of the effects of spatial arrangements on leadership status was conducted by Bass and Klubeck (1952). They were interested in the effects of seating position on leadership emergence in a leaderless group discussion situation (Bass, 1949). The leaderless group discussion is a procedure designed to evaluate leadership potential. Small groups are formed and assigned a discussion task, during which observers rate group members on leadership potential. This leadership rating has a moderately high correlation with leadership status attained in natural settings, such as industrial organizations. Bass and Klubeck examined data from 467 participants in sixty-eight half-hour leaderless group discussions involving subjects drawn from such diverse populations as college students and ROTC cadets. Two seating arrangements were involved: a rectangular table with four chairs on either side and an "inverted V" arrangement with three chairs on each side plus a seventh chair at the apex of the V. Two samples drawn from college students had sat at rectangular tables, one sample consisting of three groups and another of four groups. In one of the samples, but not in the other, the person sitting at an end position attained a significantly higher leadership score than persons in middle positions. For groups in the V arrangement, there was little evidence that seating position had a significant influence on leadership status, although one sample did yield significant differences in favor of end positions. It must be remembered, however, that all these studies were conducted for another purpose, and a number of variables, such as participants' own choice of seating position, were confounded with seating arrangement. This fact makes the Bass and Klubeck findings difficult to interpret, to say the least.

A study designed specifically to test the hypothesis that seating arrangement influences leadership emergence (Howells & Becker, 1962) provided more reliable evidence that spatial position in the group is an important determinant of leadership status. The rationale for this hypothesis was that spatial position determines the flow of communication, which in turn determines leadership emergence. The experimental situation involved five-person groups seated at a rectangular table, with three on one side of the table and two on the other. Since interaction is more likely to occur across the table than around it, the investigators expected that each of the two persons on one side would influence three persons on the other, whereas the three could influence only two other persons. Therefore, it was predicted that members from the two-person side of the table would emerge as leaders more frequently than members from the three-person side. The data supported the prediction; fourteen persons emerged as leaders from the two-seat side of the table as compared with six from the three-seat side.

When these findings are related to those concerning spatial position and status and to those concerning spatial position and interaction, it becomes evident that seating arrangement has an important influence upon the interaction process. The physical arrangement of group members determines to a significant degree the flow of communication and interaction in the group, the status assigned to group members, and the emergence of leaders. These effects are caused in part by the cultural patterns of interaction which typically place persons in physical positions that correspond to their leadership or other status positions. It also seems clear that spatial arrangement exerts a more direct influence upon the flow of communication, both verbal and nonverbal, which in turn influences a person's chances to attain status in the group. The many studies of communication networks in small groups provide further evidence of these effects of the physical environment on group process.

COMMUNICATION NETWORKS

In the preceding pages, we have been concerned primarily with the physical distance between persons and the ways interperson distance affects individual and group behavior. In the discussion of spatial arrangements, we noted that the particular pattern of physical distance could influence the flow of communication, the perception of status, and the emergence of leadership. In some instances, not only distance but also the particular body orientations among group members determined many facets of group process. In a similar way, the number and arrangement of communication channels among group members exert a powerful influence upon the group. In fact, one may say that communication lies at the heart of group process (M. E. Shaw, 1964). If the group is to function effectively, its members must be able to communicate easily and efficiently. This fact has long been recognized by organizational planners, who try to arrange communication networks in such a manner as to permit the free flow of ideas, knowledge, and other information throughout the organization. Such attempts are exemplified by the military "chain of command," the industrial "table of organization," etc. There can be little doubt that factors affecting communication within the group also influence the efficiency of the group and the satisfaction of its members.

Organizational planners have usually assumed that it is possible to determine logically how the communication channels should be arranged for maximum efficiency, and they have generally concluded that a hierarchical arrangement is most efficient. However, the validity of this assumption is open to question. Years ago Alex Bavelas (1948, 1950) raised several important questions which led to a series of investigations concerning the effect of fixed communication patterns upon group process. For example, what effects do various patterns of communication have upon leadership emergence? Organizational development? Problem-solving efficiency? The ability of the group to adapt to environmental changes?

It is well to note at this point that we are concerned with the physical *arrangement* of communication channels among group members. In a sense, we are dealing with topological space, rather than Euclidean space. It does not matter where the individual group members are located with respect to others. What is important is the distribution of communication channels among them, that is, who can communicate with whom, whether the communication is direct or via another group member, etc.

Following Bavelas's lead, numerous investigators conducted studies of these questions as well as others that arose during the course of research.

The major findings concerned the effects of imposed communication networks upon leadership emergence, organizational development, problem-solving effectiveness, and member reactions. Before exploring the research related to these processes, we will consider the experimental method which was typically used to study communication patterns.

RESEARCH METHODS

The usual method of research is to impose various communication networks upon groups in order to determine their consequences for group process. The communication networks that have been investigated are diagramed in Figure 5-3. The circles represent individual group members (or positions in the group), the lines represent channels of communication between positions, and the arrows indicate one-way channels. All lines that do not have arrows represent two-way communication channels. The most common technique for imposing communication networks was first suggested by Bavelas (1948). Group members are placed in cubicles which are connected by slots in the cubicle walls, through which written messages can be passed. When all channels (slots) are open, every group member can communicate directly with every other member. This is the comcon (completely connected) pattern shown in Figure 5-3. Other patterns may be formed merely by closing the appropriate channels. Alternative techniques use telephone lines or messengers as communication channels.

In most experiments, free (continuous) communication is permitted within the limits imposed by the network; that is, each member is free to use his open channels as much as he wishes during the course of the group interaction. However, some investigators have restricted each group member to single messages transmitted at a designated time. Also, group members usually are assigned a task to perform working together as a group under conditions which require communication for completion. The kind of task assigned the group varies from simple identification problems to complex sentence-construction and discussion problems. This variation in task characteristics is an important consideration in understanding the effects of communication patterns on group process, a fact which will become evident as we discuss empirical findings. Measures of problem-solving efficiency include time to solve, number of errors, number of messages, etc. In addition, the investigator may obtain measures of the group members' reactions to the situation and/or an index of organizational development.

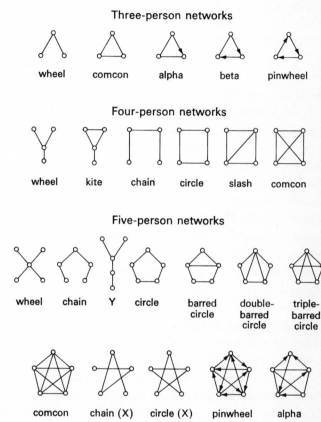

Figure 5-3 Communication Networks Used in Experimental Investigations. Dots Represent Positions, Lines Represent Communication Channels, and Arrows Indicate One-way Channels. (Reprinted with permission from M. E. Shaw. Communication networks. In L. Berkowitz (Ed.), *Advances in experimental social psychology*. Vol. 1. New York: Academic, 1964. Pp. 111–147.)

LEADERSHIP EMERGENCE

One of the first experimental investigations of communication networks (Leavitt, 1951) compared the five-person wheel, chain, Y, and circle patterns (see Figure 5-3). The task was a symbol-identification task which required that the group identify which of several symbols (stars, triangles, circles, etc.)

appeared on each and every card held by group members. This is a relatively simple task involving only the collation of information for solution. Each group was given fifteen trials. When these trials had been completed, each member was asked, "Did your group have a leader? If so, who?" In the wheel pattern the person in the central position was named by twenty-three of twenty-five persons, whereas no one in a peripheral position was named as leader. The persons in the more central positions of the chain and Y patterns were also named considerably more often than peripheral members (seventeen in the Y and twelve in the chain). In the circle, no position was identified as leader significantly more frequently than any other position. Thus it appears that the person who occupies a central position in a communication network has a high probability of emerging as the leader of the group. This finding has been verified in a number of studies. For example, M. E. Shaw (1954b) compared the four-person wheel, slash, and circle patterns shown in Figure 5-3 and found that a leader emerged more frequently in the wheel pattern. Similarly, Shaw and Rothschild (1956) investigated leadership emergence in four-person wheel, slash, and comcon patterns, and found that a leader emerged in only two of eight groups in the comcon and in the slash, whereas a leader emerged in all wheel groups. The criterion of leadership emergence was the naming of an individual as leader by at least three of the four persons in the group, where a group member could vote for himself. The cultural generality of this finding is indicated by the results of a study using Japanese subjects (Hirota, 1953) which replicated Leavitt's findings.

It seems clear, then, that the person who occupies a central position in a communication network has a high probability of emerging as a leader. When the network consists of positions of approximately equal centrality, a leader is less likely to emerge, at least in experimentally assembled groups. The reasons for the centrality–leader-emergence relationship probably are availability of information and the related possibility of coordinating group activities. This interpretation is supported by the fact that this relationship can be modified by giving a member in a peripheral position access to more information initially than a member in the central position (M. E. Shaw, 1954b).

ORGANIZATIONAL DEVELOPMENT

The emergence of leadership is, of course, one aspect of organizational development. Another aspect, emphasized by investigators of communication networks, is the mode of operation of the group. That is, the group may develop any one of several alternative methods of attacking the task assigned to them. In general, a group is said to have developed an organizational pattern when it follows a consistent pattern of information exchange during the course of problem solution. In other words, an organizational pattern is the informal communication pattern that the group establishes within the limits imposed by the communication network. Four organizational patterns may be distinguished: each-to-all, each-to-all plus check, centralized, centralized plus check (Shaw & Rothschild, 1956). Actually, there are two basic patterns, each-to-all and centralized, with the check variation of each. In the each-to-all pattern, all available information is transmitted to all group members, each of whom solves the problem independently. The each-to-all plus check pattern is essentially the same, except that answers are transmitted to other group members for checking before the answer is accepted. In a centralized organizational pattern, all information is funneled to one person who solves the problem and distributes the answer to other group members. The centralized plus check pattern is the same as the centralized except that the central person transmits his solution to at least one other person for checking before it is accepted by the group.

Leavitt (1951) reported that the wheel, Y, and chain networks adopted a centralized organization, whereas the circle showed no consistent operational organization. However, his definition of organization did not include the each-to-all pattern. M. E. Shaw (1954b) found that all his groups used either the centralized or the each-to-all form of organization. Centralized organization was employed by 73 percent of the wheel groups, 7 percent of the slash groups, and 7 percent of the circle groups, whereas each-to-all organization was used by 27 percent of the wheel groups, 93 percent of the slash, and 93 percent of the circle. Another study in which groups met for an hour per day for ten days (Shaw & Rothschild, 1956) found that all groups in the wheel adopted either a centralized or centralized plus check organization; two groups in the slash developed each-to-all, one used a centralized pattern, and five developed no discernible organization; and two groups in the comcon developed each-to-all, three each-to-all plus check, and three developed a centralized form of organization. Similar results have been reported by Schein (1958), Guetzkow and Dill (1957), Cohen (1961, 1962), and others.

These experimental findings clearly indicate that the imposition of a centralized communication network predisposes groups to develop a centralized organization. However, when the communication network is unrestricted, as in the comcon, or does not place any person in a highly centralized position, as in the circle, the tendency is to develop an each-to-all organizational pattern. This latter is not merely lack of organization, as might be supposed; it involves a consistent procedure for ensuring that all members receive all available information. As we shall see later, these differences in organizational development are related to differences in group effectiveness but do not seem to be determinants of group efficiency. That is, both form of organization and group effectiveness are determined by other variables.

GROUP MEMBER REACTIONS

It is inevitable that variations in availability of communication channels will affect the reactions of group members to the group and its activities. In general, a person who occupies a centralized position with its abundance of communication channels is better satisfied with his position than are persons who occupy peripheral positions with limited communication facilities. And since the morale of the group depends upon the satisfaction of its members, group morale (or group satisfaction) is greater in decentralized communication networks (e.g., circle, comcon) than in centralized networks (e.g., wheel, chain). This consequence has been reported by almost all investigators who have examined satisfaction in communication networks. In Leavitt's study, for example, the mean rating of job satisfaction for persons in the most central positions was 7.8 as compared with a mean rating of 4.6 for those occupying peripheral positions. Similarly, the average ratings by networks were 5.4, 5.8, 6.0, and 8.0, for the wheel, chain, Y, and circle networks, respectively. Comparable differences have been reported by M. E. Shaw (1954b), Shaw and Rothschild (1956), Cohen (1961, 1962), Lawson (1965), and others.

PROBLEM-SOLVING EFFICIENCY

Although the student of group process is interested in all aspects of group interaction, the emergence of leadership, organizational development, and member reactions are in some ways secondary to the operational efficiency of groups. Certainly the great bulk of research on communication networks has been directed toward the analysis of problem-solving efficiency. This is probably the result of practical considerations, such as how best to organize office committees, work teams, and similar task-oriented groups in order to achieve the group's goal most efficiently. The emergence of a leader and organizational development are often viewed as intervening variables which account for differences in group effectiveness, although there is reason to believe that there is little or no causal relation between these variables and effectiveness (see pages 145–146).

The initial study by Leavitt (1951) indicated that a centralized network was most efficient for problem solution. The circle network was least efficient in terms of time required for solution, number of errors, and number of messages; the wheel and Y patterns were most efficient by these criteria, although the chain was almost as effective. The generality of these findings is limited by the size of the group, the subject population, and the kind of task. Of these, task seems to be the most critical variable. It will be recalled that Leavitt used a simple symbol-identification task which required only that information be collected by at least one position. Such a task makes no demand upon problem-solving ability of group members; it requires no manipulation of information. When the task is more complex, as in the case of mathematical problems, the decentralized network is usually found to be most efficient. For example, M. E. Shaw (1954b) compared the wheel, circle, and slash networks with respect to solution of arithmetic problems. He found that the circle was most efficient and the wheel least efficient in terms of time required for solution. Mean times were 12.3 minutes for the wheel, 12.0 minutes for the slash, and 11.5 minutes for the circle. On the last of three problems attempted, the differences in time required were greater; mean times were 9.7 minutes for the wheel, 8.6 minutes for the slash, and 8.0 for the circle. The circle groups also corrected more errors than did the more centralized groups. On the other hand, the wheel groups required fewer messages to reach a solution than did the others; however, this difference can be accounted for by the number of communication channels available. There were no differences among networks in number of messages per channel.

The differences among networks reported by Shaw are just opposite to those reported by Leavitt, a difference which has been shown to be a consequence of the kind of task (M. E. Shaw, 1954a). When the task is relatively simple and requires only the collation of information, a centralized network is most efficient, but when the task is more complex and requires that operations be performed upon the information (for example, mathematical manipulations), the decentralized networks are more efficient in terms of time and errors. Research by others generally supports these conclusions.

For example, on simple identification problems, Hirota (1953), Guetzkow and Simon (1955), and Lawson (1964a), among others, found centralized networks faster than decentralized networks; on more complex problems, Mulder (1960) and Lawson (1964b), among others, found the decentralized network faster. M. E. Shaw (1964) examined the findings from eighteen studies in which the assigned task could be classified as either simple or complex. The results of this tabulation are shown in Table 5-1. It is clear that the complexity of the task is a critical factor in determining the relative effectiveness of different communication networks.

The interesting aspect of these findings is that they are contrary to the usual assumptions about the most effective arrangement of communication channels in a group. Since most of the problems that groups are faced with are more complex than the most complex task used in laboratory experiments, it is evident that a decentralized communication network is most likely to be effective in natural group situations. It should be kept in mind, however, that the centralized-decentralized dimension of communication networks does not correspond to centralized-decentralized decision structures

TABLE 5-1 Number of Comparisons Showing Differences between Centralized (Wheel, Chain, Y) and Decentralized (Circle, Comcon) Networks as a Function of Task Complexity

	Simple problems*	Complex problems†	Total
Time			
Centralized faster	14	0	14
Decentralized faster	4	18	22
Messages			
Centralized sent more	0	1	1
Decentralized sent more	18	17	35
Errors			
Centralized made more	0	6	6
Decentralized made more	9	1	10
No difference	1	3	4
Satisfaction			
Centralized higher	1	1	2
Decentralized higher	7	10	17

* Simple problems: symbol-, letter-, number-, and color-identification tasks.

† Complex problems: arithmetic, word arrangement, sentence construction, and discussion problems.

SOURCE: Reprinted with permission from Shaw (1964).

(cf. Mulder, 1960). Therefore one should be cautious about making inferences concerning other kinds of organizational relationships from the data on communication networks.

EXPLANATORY CONCEPTS

If it be granted that communication networks partially determine group effectiveness, we would like to understand the processes by which this influence occurs. As mentioned earlier, some theorists have sought to explain the effects of communication networks by treating organizational development as an intervening variable. For example, Guetzkow and Simon (1955) and Guetzkow and Dill (1957) proposed that networks affect the efficiency of group interaction only indirectly by governing the group members' ability to organize themselves for efficient task performance. In the first test of this hypothesis (Guetzkow & Simon, 1955), five-person groups were tested in the wheel, circle, and comcon networks, using symbol-identification tasks. Groups were given task-free periods between trials for the purpose of organizing themselves for efficient task performance. The results showed that the organizational opportunity did *not* eliminate differences among networks as required by the hypothesis. However, when groups that organized themselves centrally were compared, there was no difference attributable to networks. The investigators believed that this supported their hypothesis. In the second study (Guetzkow & Dill, 1957), groups were allowed time to organize in a comcon network and were then tested in a circle network. The performance of these groups was compared with that of the circle groups in the first experiment. Again, the expected differences did not occur, but when groups were divided into organized and unorganized categories, the organized groups were found to be more effective. Similar findings were reported by Mulder (1959a, 1960), who found that groups with more centralized decision structures performed better than groups with decentralized decision structures.

Unfortunately, the interpretation of these data is not easy. There is a methodological problem that arises whenever comparisons are made between groups that are selected on the basis of some aspect of their behavior during the experimental period. It is always possible that the same, but unnoticed, variable is affecting both the criterion for selection and the criterion for evaluating the differences between the selected groups. This appears to be exactly what happened in the Guetzkow et al. studies and probably in

Mulder's experiments as well. In a series of studies reported by Schein (1958), the development of both organization and efficiency was traced over time. Again, it was found that the groups developing a strong organization were the most effective, but efficiency was achieved *before* the organization had developed. It must be concluded, therefore, that the organization could not have caused the efficiency of the groups, even though organization and efficiency were highly correlated.

Two other explanatory concepts have been suggested that are more useful: independence and saturation. The concept of independence was first suggested by Leavitt (1951) to account for differences among network positions. His view was that differences in answer-getting potential would structure group members' perceptions of their roles in the group. For example, group members of a wheel network can readily perceive the degree of information accessibility and the nature of their own roles; the central person is autonomous and controls the group. In a decentralized network, such as the circle, no group member is entirely dependent upon any other member, and his role is not clearly different from anyone else's role. Morale is higher because of the greater independence in the decentralized network, which permits the gratification of culturally supported needs for autonomy. Thus, Leavitt concluded that communication networks determine behavior via their effects upon independence of action, which in turn produces differences in activity, accuracy, satisfaction, and other behaviors.

Subsequent research made it clear that Leavitt's original formulation was too limited. Consequently, it has been expanded (M. E. Shaw, 1964) to include freedom from all restrictions on action. As expanded, the term *independence* refers to the degree of freedom with which the individual may function in the group. A group member's independence of action may be influenced not only by accessibility of information but also by situational factors, by the actions of other group members, and by the person's own perceptions of the situation. So defined, independence is related to both group efficiency and member satisfaction, although its strongest effect seems to be on satisfaction (M. E. Shaw, 1955).

The concept of *saturation* was first formulated by Gilchrist, Shaw, and Walker (1954) to refer to the communication overload experienced by group members in centralized positions in communication networks. They observed that when the number of messages that must be handled by a position passed a certain optimal level, the communication requirements began to counteract the effects of the more favorable network position. At this point, the position was said to be "saturated." This suggests that saturation is an all-or-none process, but such is not the case. Positions vary in the degree to which they are overloaded by communication, so we may speak of degree of saturation. In general, the greater the saturation the less efficient the group and the less satisfied the group members, although saturation probably influences effectiveness to a greater extent than it does satisfaction.

Gilchrist et al. distinguished two kinds of saturation: channel saturation and message unit saturation. Channel saturation refers to the number of channels with which a position must deal, and message unit saturation refers to the number of messages which a position must handle. These two kinds of saturation are correlated and are usually combined to determine the total saturation of a position. Like the concept of independence, the saturation concept, as originally formulated, was too limited. The requirements imposed upon an occupant of a position in a communication network call for action, regardless of the source of the requirements. Thus, the total saturation of a position derives not only from communication requirements but also from other requirements, such as organizational decisions and data manipulation that may be required for task completion.

The notion of saturation accounts for most of the effects on group performance that have been observed in communication networks. For example, the central position in a wheel network is more vulnerable to saturation than any position in a decentralized network, such as the circle. When the group is faced with a simple task, the communication requirements are not excessive and the central position does not become saturated. The favorable arrangement of communication channels for information collation in a wheel network thus renders it more effective for simple problems, unhampered by saturation effects. However, when the group is faced with a more complex task, such as a human relations problem or an arithmetic problem, the communication demands upon the central position are great and the position quickly becomes saturated, thus reducing the efficiency of the group. Decentralized networks, being less subject to saturation, are more effective in solving complex problems.

The negative consequences of saturation can be seen in a variety of other empirical findings. Macy, Christie, and Luce (1953) found that groups were less effective in identifying a "noisy" marble (a marble having many different colors) in a centralized than in a decentralized network. Centralized networks are less effective in dealing with irrelevant information than are decentralized ones (M. E. Shaw, 1958b). In short, anything that increases the demands upon the group is likely to interfere with centralized networks more than with decentralized networks. These effects are, of course, predicted by the saturation hypothesis.

The effects of saturation are not limited to laboratory groups. In a large state university, for example, classrooms traditionally had been assigned to academic departments, which were then free to schedule classes as they chose (a decentralized system). Although a few complications arose at the beginning of each new term, room assignments were handled efficiently. One year, the administration of the university decided that the system was inefficient and could be improved by centralization. All rooms were withdrawn from departments and assigned by a central office. Anyone who needed a room for a new class or for a larger class could, theoretically, obtain one by calling the central office. On the first day of class after the new centralized procedure had been installed, chaos reigned. Requests for room assignments were met with the statement that there were several hundred requests and that things would be straightened out in a few weeks! Although this is anecdotal evidence, it does illustrate the effects of saturation in a natural situation.

In summary, the arrangement of communication channels in the group has been shown to determine leadership emergence, organizational development, member satisfaction, and group efficiency. In general, centralized networks as compared with decentralized networks enhance leadership emergence and organizational development, but impede the efficient solution of complex problems and reduce member satisfaction. These effects are mediated through independence and saturation processes which appear to be operative in both laboratory and natural situations.

PLAUSIBLE HYPOTHESES ABOUT THE PHYSICAL ENVIRONMENT OF GROUPS

We have seen how individuals and groups are influenced by their physical environment. Personal space and individual territoriality have important consequences for group behavior, and spatial arrangements in groups are important determinants of status, satisfaction, and performance. We are now ready to formulate some more precise plausible hypotheses that have survived the test of empirical data.

Hypothesis 1 *Individuals and groups typically assume a proprietary orientation toward certain geographical areas which they defend against invasion.*

Individual territoriality has been observed in a variety of situations. Altman and Haythorn (1967a) found that isolated dyads developed strong preferences for a particular table, chair, and/or bed. Similar evidences of territoriality were reported by Lipman (1968) in his study of old folks' homes. That individuals defend against invasion has also been demonstrated in a number of empirical studies (Sommer, 1969). Similarly, group territoriality has been shown by studies of street-corner gangs (W. F. Whyte, 1943), residential areas (Mack, 1954; Marine, 1966), etc.

Hypothesis 2 *Individuals typically establish personal space into which others may not enter.*

The notion of personal space has been implicit in the writings of many theorists, although Katz (1937) appears to have been the first to use the term. The existence of personal space is inferred from the results of many studies. For example, Sommer (1969) reported evidence of great discomfort when experimenters approached others more closely than was permitted by cultural norms.

Hypothesis 3 *The boundaries of personal space vary with the personalness of the situation, the intimacy of the person-other relationship, and the status of the person relative to the other.*

Personal space is not fixed, but expands and contracts according to circumstances. For example, McBride et al. (1965) noted that individuals registered a greater GSR when touched by another person than when touched by an inanimate object. The effects of situational impersonality were also observed by Argyle and Dean (1965) in that individuals stood closer to a photograph than to a real person and closer to a photograph of a person with eyes closed than to one with eyes open. The effects on the boundaries of personal space may be inferred from demonstrations that various degrees of acquaintanceship result in varying degrees of comfortable approach (Little, 1965; F. N. Willis, 1966). Finally, it will be recalled that Lott and Sommer (1967) found that status was perceived as closely related to spatial position in the group. The high-status person usually occupies the best position, and, conversely, the person who occupies the favored position is seen as having high status.

Hypothesis 4   *Invasion of personal space evokes discomfort and negative
feelings which are revealed by various defensive reactions on
the part of the victim, the person whose space is invaded.*

This hypothesis has considerable empirical support. Sommer (1969) reported numerous studies of invasion of personal space which revealed the feelings of discomfort produced by such invasion. Typical reactions included change in body orientation, rubbing the face, and similar behaviors. When these defensive responses proved ineffective, the victim usually left the scene.

Hypothesis 5   *There is a positive relationship between status and the favorability of spatial position in the group.*

There is reliable evidence that high-status individuals not only prefer certain positions in the group, but also that occupants of certain positions are accorded higher status than occupants of less favored positions. An analysis of experimental jury deliberations (Strodtbeck & Hook, 1961) revealed that jurists from professional and managerial classes tended to choose the head of the table. Similarly, Hare and Bales (1963) found that persons high on dominance chose central positions in the group. The perception of high status as a function of position was demonstrated clearly by a series of investigations by Lott and Sommer (1967) and Sommer (1969).

Hypothesis 6   *Persons interact more frequently with persons seated facing them than with persons seated adjacent to them.*

Steinzor (1950) analyzed the interaction process of groups seated at round tables and found that group members sitting across the table from each other followed one another in speaking significantly more often than they followed persons in other positions. A similar result was obtained by Strodtbeck and Hook (1961) using rectangular tables. Persons sitting at the ends of the table participated more than others in the group.

Hypothesis 7   *Seating arrangement influences the quality of group interaction.*

This general hypothesis summarizes the finding that the relationships of persons seated at a table are perceived as qualitatively different as a function of their relative positions at the table. These interpersonal relationships are undoubtedly reciprocal, since people who are well acquainted tend to sit near each other, etc. However, the research has considered primarily the effects of seating arrangement upon subsequent interaction. Russo (1967) reported that, in general, the more distance between two persons the less well acquainted, the less friendly, and the less talkative the dyad was seen to be. When the relative position permitted eye contact, however, there was less effect of interperson distance on the quality of perceived interaction. Since the evidence relative to Hypothesis 7 is limited to questionnaire data, further research is needed for validation.

Hypothesis 8 *A leader is more likely to emerge in a centralized communication network than in a decentralized network.*

This finding is well substantiated in a number of investigations. In his initial study, Leavitt (1951) observed that a leader emerged significantly more often in a wheel network than in a chain or Y network, and more frequently in the latter two than in a circle network. In other words, the frequency of leadership emergence varied directly with the degree of network centrality. This finding has been verified in a number of subsequent investigations (for example, Hirota, 1953; M. E. Shaw, 1954b; Shaw & Rothschild, 1956).

Hypothesis 9 *Organizational development occurs more rapidly in a centralized than in a decentralized communication network.*

This hypothesis is supported by Leavitt's research, as well as by that of many others. Leavitt (1951) found that groups in wheel networks organized themselves into centralized patterns whereas circle groups failed to organize at all. When a different definition of organization is applied, however, organization develops in decentralized as well as in centralized networks (Shaw & Rothschild, 1956). But again, development occurs earlier in the more centralized network. The hypothesis is also supported by the work of Schein (1958), Mulder (1959a), and others. However, there is reason to believe that this organizational development is not causally related to group efficiency.

Hypothesis 10 *Group members have higher morale in decentralized than in centralized communication networks.*

This hypothesis has general support from research on communication networks. Leavitt (1951) found that ratings of satisfaction were negatively correlated with network centralization; the highest ratings occurred in the circle and the lowest in the wheel. Other investigations have verified these results (for example, A. M. Cohen, 1961; Lawson, 1965; M. E. Shaw, 1954b). All these studies used tasks that probably had low relevance for group members, at least outside the experimental situation. It is an open question whether the same relationship would be found with more ego-involving tasks.

Hypothesis 11   A decentralized communication network is most efficient when the group must solve complex problems, whereas a centralized network is most efficient when the group must solve simple problems.

In Hypothesis 11, the term "simple problems" refers to tasks that require only the collection of information; when all the information is available in one place, the solution is obvious. Problems of this sort include symbol-, letter-, number-, and color-identification tasks. Many studies have shown that centralized networks are more efficient than decentralized networks with this kind of task (Guetzkow & Simon, 1955; Hirota, 1953; Lawson, 1964a; Leavitt, 1951; and others). The term "complex problems" means that the information must be collected in one place *and* operations must be performed upon it before the solution can be known. Examples of this type of problem are word-arrangement tasks, discussion problems, arithmetic problems, etc. Centralized communication networks are typically more efficient with this type of task (Lawson, 1964b; Mulder, 1960; M. E. Shaw, 1954b; and others). Table 5-1 shows the frequency with which the empirical data support Hypothesis 11.

Hypothesis 12   A centralized communication network is more vulnerable to saturation than a decentralized network.

The term "saturation" refers to the degree to which one or more positions in the group have more requirements placed upon them than can be handled efficiently. It has been demonstrated that a centralized communication network typically places greater demands upon the central position than are placed upon any position in a decentralized network; hence a centralized network becomes saturated more quickly than does the decentralized. For example, groups in centralized networks are impeded more than those in decentralized networks by "noisy" marble-identification tasks (Macy et al., 1953), irrelevant information (M. E. Shaw, 1958a), and similar interferences. These effects are observed in natural situations as well as in the laboratory.

SUGGESTED READINGS

BAVELAS, A. Communication patterns in task-oriented groups. *Journal of the Acoustical Society of America,* 1950, **22**, 725–730.

HEARN, G. Leadership and the spatial factor in small groups. *Journal of Abnormal and Social Psychology,* 1957, **54**, 269–272.

LITTLE, K. B. Personal space. *Journal of Experimental Social Psychology,* 1965, **1**, 237–247.

LYMAN, S. M., & SCOTT, M. B. Territoriality: A neglected sociological dimension. *Social Forces,* 1967, **15**, 236–249.

MARINE, G. I've got nothing against the colored, understand. *Ramparts,* 1966, Vol. 4.

SHAW, M. E. Communication networks. In L. Berkowitz (Ed.), *Advances in experimental social psychology.* Vol. 1. New York: Academic, 1964. Pp. 111–147.

SOMMER, R. *Personal space: The behavioral basis of design.* Englewood Cliffs, N.J.: Prentice-Hall, 1969.

STRODTBECK, F. L., & HOOK, L. H. The social dimensions of a twelve man jury table. *Sociometry,* 1961, **24**, 397–415.

WILLIS, F. N., Jr. Initial speaking distance as a function of the speakers' relationship. *Psychonomic Science,* 1966, **5**, 221–222.

CHAPTER 6

THE PERSONAL ENVIRONMENT OF GROUPS

Individuals bring their personal characteristics with them when they join a group, and these characteristics exert a powerful influence upon group process. A person's manner of behaving, his typical reactions to others, and his skills and abilities determine not only his behavior patterns but also to a major extent the reactions of others to him as a group member. In other words, the personal characteristics of each group member serve as stimuli for all other members, and those of other members serve as stimuli for each individual member. The characteristics of individuals who compose the group thus constitute a personal environment in which the group must operate.

One cannot hope to fully understand group process without knowing the ways in which this personal environment influences group behavior.

Individual characteristics influence group processes in two ways. First, the characteristics of each group member determine to some extent what his own behavior in the group will be and how others will react to him. For example, a person who has a special knowledge of the task may be expected to use this knowledge to help the group achieve its goal, and the dominant individual may be expected to enact behaviors designed to give him control over others. A second way in which individual characteristics influence the group's behavior is a consequence of the particular combination of individual characteristics. In this case, it is not a question of whether the individual has special knowledge of the task, but whether he has more or less knowledge than the others in the group. The relationships among the attributes of group members may be of greater consequence for group action than the attributes as such. For example, the fact that a dyad is composed of one person high on dominance and one low on dominance may be more significant than the absolute degree of dominance exhibited by either member of the dyad. Since this aspect of group composition has to do with relationships among persons, it constitutes a social structure or environment in which the group must function. We will consider the effects of group composition as an aspect of the group's social environment in Chapter 7.

For purposes of the present discussion, we will divide personal attributes into three categories or classes: biographical characteristics, abilities, and personality traits. This division is somewhat arbitrary, since the categories are interrelated in several important ways. Biographical characteristics partially determine the personality traits the person reveals by his behavior. Special abilities that the individual has developed may also be a consequence of certain background characteristics, such as the amount of education that has been available to him. Abilities are sometimes regarded as aspects of the personality, since they reflect unique properties of the individual. Despite these interrelations, it is convenient to discuss these personal factors separately in order to see more clearly their consequences for group behavior.

BIOGRAPHICAL CHARACTERISTICS OF GROUP MEMBERS

This category includes a wide range of background influences, some of which are biological (for example, age and sex) whereas others are more sociological (for example, education and socioeconomic status). Although the effects of such characteristics upon group process are pervasive they are often difficult to identify and document. Consequently, there are many unanswered questions concerning them. The evidence available, however, makes it clear that they are important in the determination of group process.

CHRONOLOGICAL AGE

It is obvious that persons of different ages behave differently; children do not act like adults, although senile adults may behave like children. Nevertheless, it is of interest to see how age differences are reflected in group behavior. Unfortunately, age has been a neglected variable in the study of group behavior, perhaps because its effects are so obvious that controlled studies seem unnecessary. In spite of this neglect, there are some significant studies relative to age effects, and the results of controlled investigations do not always agree with the "obvious."

AGE AND INTERACTION BEHAVIORS   Age is an important determinant of the kinds of behaviors an individual group member will display in the group. The kinds of contacts individuals make, the friendships resulting from such contacts, and the quality of behavior engaged in during contacts have been shown to vary with the age of group members. As early as 1932 it was noted in an observational study that the number and percentage of social contacts mentioned by individuals increased with chronological age (Beaver, 1932). Social participation in school activities was also found to correlate with age (Parten, 1932), and an observational study by Green (1933b) revealed that the amount of group play activity increased with age. A somewhat more sophisticated motion-picture technique was used to study the behavior of preschool children of three age groups (Bernhardt, Millichamp, Charles, & McFarland, 1937). This investigation failed to show the usual correlation between age and frequency of social contacts, perhaps because of the particular age groups studied. However, qualitative differences as a function of age were observed. With increasing age there was a tendency to restrict contacts to certain individuals and to certain types of contact and to increase the complexity of the interaction pattern.

The increasing complexity of interaction patterns with increasing age has been reported by several investigators. For example, Dymond, Hughes, and Raabe (1952) measured empathy in two age groups and found that eleven-year-olds had greater perceptive ability than seven-year-olds. The older children were more sensitive to the feelings of others than the younger children, a difference which appeared to be related to age differences in popularity. Similarly, Leuba (1933) studied the behavior of children aged two to six years. Children worked either alone or together on a pegboard task which required that they place pegs in holes as rapidly as possible. Evidences of rivalry did not appear before the age of five; that is, children did not appear to be sensitive to the behavior of others before that age. Observations of behavior in nursery schools and in kindergarten have revealed that dominating behavior decreases with age, whereas integrative behavior increases with age (Anderson, 1939). This might also be interpreted as showing an increased sensitivity to others and an increased tendency toward more complex behavior patterns with increasing age.

Differences among older age groups have also been reported. Bass, Wurster, Doll, and Clair (1953) studied behavior in seven sororities and found that older women were more active in extracurricular pursuits than younger women (r = .53 to .60) and were esteemed more highly by their sorority sisters (r = .20 to .28). Although these correlations are not great, they do indicate that age is a significant variable not only in children's groups but also in adult groups.

AGE AND LEADERSHIP   Differences in leadership behavior as a function of age have been studied extensively by investigators using the trait approach to the study of leadership. Unfortunately, the investigations have differed in the way leadership was defined, the kinds of groups studied, and the method of study. The definition of leadership commonly varied with the experimental method. For example, the two most common methods of investigation were (1) the selection of leaders and nonleaders, who were then compared with respect to age (or other characteristic of interest to the investigator), and (2) the correlation of ratings of leadership ability with chronological age (or other trait). When the first method was used, there was a marked tendency to define the leader as the person who occupied a position of leadership, such as the foreman of a factory work group, the president of an organization, etc. When the latter method was chosen, there was a strong tendency to define the leader as the person so named by the members of his group or by superiors in his organization. The groups represented by these studies also varied greatly, ranging from social groups, such as fraternities or sororities, to formal organizations, such as industrial work groups. It is well to keep these differences in mind as we consider the data obtained from such studies.

Stogdill (1948) reviewed studies of leadership and found nineteen investigations that had examined the relationship between age and leadership. The findings were quite inconsistent, although more often than not leaders were found to be older than nonleaders. Specifically, ten studies reported that leaders were older than nonleaders, six that leaders were younger than nonleaders, two that there was no age difference between leaders and nonleaders, and one that age differences depended upon the particular situation. Reported correlations between leadership effectiveness and chronological age ranged from −.37 to .71. In view of the large differences in the definition of leader, the kind of group, the measure of leadership effectiveness, etc., it is not surprising that the findings were so inconsistent. Nevertheless, these results fail to support the hypothesis that there is a strong relationship between age and leadership. To the extent that there is such a relationship, it probably means only that an individual must live long enough to achieve his leadership potential. Unless one marries the boss's daughter, time is required to attain a position of leadership in most groups.

AGE AND CONFORMITY   Conformity is one of the most prominent forms of behavior in groups. When individuals interact, pressures toward uniformity are generated and the individual member tends to behave in a manner which conforms to that of the modal group member. Although blind, unreasoning conformity can be debilitating, in most instances conformity serves the useful function of establishing order and stability in our interactions with others. For example, if every automobile driver decided for himself which side of the road to drive on, it would be impossible for anyone to move efficiently from place to place. The fact that most of us conform to normative expectations in our interactions with others means that there is order in a world that otherwise would be chaotic, and this order permits us to respond appropriately to the demands of the social situation on most occasions.

Conformity behavior is usually assumed to be the result of developmental processes (Berg & Bass, 1961). At minimum, the individual must learn the norms of the group or groups of which he is a member, and presumably this learning occurs as a part of the socialization process; that is, as the individual grows older he learns more and more about group norms. Hence, it might be expected that conformity would increase with increasing age, at least up to some minimum age level. However, Piaget's extensive research (1954) with children suggests that although social development progresses through an orderly sequence of stages, the consequences for conformity behavior may not be linear. Piaget's analysis of the way the child learns the "rules of the game" indicates that at an early age the child is not influenced by rules, but gradually begins to follow them more and more until about age eleven or twelve. At about this age, the child internalizes the rules and recognizes that they are not absolutes, that they are made for convenience, and hence can be broken or modified whenever this appears desirable. This kind of evidence led Costanzo and Shaw (1966) to hypothesize a curvilinear relationship between age and conformity, with conformity increasing to a maximum at about age twelve and decreasing thereafter.

The prior experimental evidence for this hypothesis is not altogether consistent. For example, Marple (1933) found that high school students conformed more to majority or expert opinion than either college students or adults, and Patel and Gordon (1960) reported that conformity decreased from the tenth to the twelfth grade. Both studies employed postadolescent age groups. A study by Berenda (1950) conducted in a classroom revealed that subjects in a seven- to ten-year age group conformed more than those in a ten- to thirteen-year group. This finding would be contrary to the Costanzo-Shaw hypothesis except that social pressure was exerted by either the brightest children in the class or by the teacher. Hence there is some question whether the sources of pressure in these studies can be interpreted as normative.

A more extensive range of ages was studied by Iscoe, Williams, and Harvey (1963). They examined four age groups (seven-, nine-, twelve-, and fifteen-year-olds) in a simulated conformity situation. Subjects were asked to count the number of metronome clicks in a series after being confronted by unanimously incorrect judgments by simulated group members. Conformity of females increased up to age twelve followed by a decrease at age fifteen, whereas that of males increased up to age twelve with no significant change from age twelve to fifteen.

Costanzo and Shaw (1966) tested their hypothesis by examining conformity behavior in groups ranging in age from seven to twenty-one years. Since this is a wider age range than has been examined in other investigations, their procedure will be presented in some detail. The experimental design included both male and female subjects who were randomly assigned to one of four age groups. The four age groups were: seven to nine years, eleven to thirteen years, fifteen to seventeen years, and nineteen to twenty-one years. They were tested with the Crutchfield apparatus (described in Chapter 8; see page 249) in which subjects are seated in isolated booths, but receive simulated information about the choices of others. The stimuli used were the Asch lines, which require that the subject choose which one of three lines is the same length as the standard. Subjects were tested in four-person groups, each of which was homogeneous with regard to sex. The results of the study, shown in Figure 6-1, indicate that conformity increased with age to a maximum level at age eleven to thirteen and decreased thereafter, in close agreement with the hypothesis that age and conformity are curvilinearly related. This conclusion is probably valid only when group pressure is exerted by peers. When pressure is exerted by authority figures, for example, the degree of conformity might be negatively related to age, or the age of maximum conformity might be shifted toward lower age levels. More research is needed before this question can be answered definitively.

In summary, there is good evidence that the chronological age of the group member is related to several aspects of group interaction. With in-

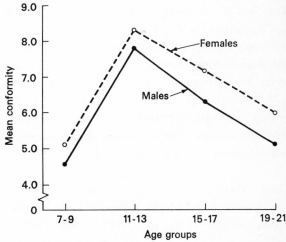

Figure 6-1 Mean Conformity as a Function of Age. (Reprinted with permission from P. R. Costanzo & M. E. Shaw. Conformity as a function of age level. *Child Development,* 1966, **37**, 967–975.)

creasing age, the individual has an increasing number of contacts with others, and there is a change toward greater selectivity of contacts and greater complexity of the interaction pattern. Conformity increases to a maximum at about age twelve and decreases thereafter, at least in peer groups. There is little evidence that age and leadership are related in any simple way. To the extent that age is related to behavior in groups, it provides the time required for the individual to learn appropriate social responses. That is, in most cases it is not the mere fact that the individual has aged that is important, but rather that he has had greater experience in social situations.

SEX OF GROUP MEMBERS

The sex of the individual group member is another fairly obvious determinant of behavior in groups. Women and men behave differently in groups, and this has important implications for group process. Differences in behavior are usually assumed to be due to role differences imposed upon men and women by the culture in which they live. Extensive studies of cultural influences on sex roles (Mead, 1949) strongly indicate that role differences are molded by culture during infancy and childhood. The results of such cultural influences are far-reaching and strongly affect the basic personality characteristics of men and women. For example, a comprehensive study of sex differences in personality (Terman & Miles, 1936) revealed that males are more aggressive, self-assertive, and fearless. They are also likely to display more roughness of manner, language, and sentiments than women. On the other hand, women are likely to express themselves as more compassionate, sympathetic, fastidious, and emotional than men.*

As with age differences, relatively little careful research has been directed toward identification of the consequences of sex differences for group interaction. The following discussion can do no more than indicate the kinds of effects that occur.

SEX AND INTERACTION BEHAVIORS   The sex differences in personality mentioned above suggest some of the differences that might be expected in interaction behaviors. Since males are generally more aggressive and self-assertive than

---

* These findings are limited to the American culture and may not represent sex differences in other cultures. Also, the student should note that this study was conducted in 1936. In view of the changing roles of men and women, the findings may no longer be valid even in American culture; however, it seems probable that sex differences in personality will exist for some years at least.

females, we might expect them to behave more aggressively in groups, and indeed this is the case. Among younger children, boys are more "quarrelsome" than girls, and the amount of quarreling among girls reaches a peak and declines earlier than among boys (Green, 1933a). A comparable difference has been observed among adults. For example, Ort (1950) observed that females report fewer role conflicts in marriage than do men. Partly because of these sex differences in aggressive-assertive behavior, men are often seen as more influential in a group than are women (Stewart, 1947). The research dealing with coalition formation (see Chapter 4) also reveals sex differences that are consistent with greater ascendancy by men. It will be recalled that women more often than men adopt an anticompetitive norm and attempt to operate so that everyone will benefit. For example, Uesugi and Vinacke (1963) found that women subjects adopted rotation systems and alliances which included everybody, in contrast to men subjects who made the best deals they could under the circumstances.

Interaction is frequently mediated through nonverbal communication, such as body orientation, eye contact, etc. Communication through the eyes is especially relevant to interpersonal behavior, as evidenced by the significance placed upon eye contact in different cultures. In the American culture, a man who fails to "look you in the eye" is not to be trusted; what red-blooded American male has not been stirred by the "come-hither look" in the eyes of an attractive female? In other cultures, eye contact may be avoided because of various social taboos. For example, among certain African tribes a man may not look at his mother-in-law, and in some Eastern countries women wear veils which prevent eye contact. Recent experimental investigations have revealed the expected sex differences in the frequency of eye contact in social situations. Exline (1963) observed sixteen groups of three men and sixteen groups of three women as they attempted to decide upon the best name for a new soap product. Some of the groups were composed of persons high on need for affiliation, and some were of persons low on this need. Also, half of the groups were given instructions designed to arouse competitive motivations, and half were given instructions designed to arouse cooperative motivations. Two observers recorded the frequency of mutual eye contact during the discussions. Females engaged in greater visual interaction than did males under all conditions. However, the effects of sex, affiliation, and competitive-cooperative instructions on mutual visual interaction were interrelated. Competition seemed to inhibit mutual glances among high affiliators and to increase visual interaction among low affiliators. This effect was much stronger in female than in male groups. In a follow-up investigation, Exline, Gray, and Schuette (1965) reported that females look at others more than males, regardless of the sex of the other person.

The eye-contact studies to date have been useful in showing a sex difference in the amount of visual interaction, but there is little sound data concerning the meaning of eye contact for men versus women. Undoubtedly the meaning of mutual glances is different for men and women, depending upon the circumstances surrounding the interaction. Studies on these differences are badly needed.

SEX AND CONFORMITY   In the previous section it was stated that men are usually more dominant and self-assertive than women. It has also been noted (Reitan & Shaw, 1964) that in the American society females play a relatively submissive role, whereas men play a relatively dominant role. These considerations suggest that women should conform to the norms of the groups more than men, and experimental evidence supports this expectation (e.g., Beloff, 1958; Costanzo & Shaw, 1966; Reitan & Shaw, 1964; Tuddenham, 1958). The regularity of sex differences in conformity can be seen clearly in Figure 6-1.

Sex differences in conformity behavior may simply reflect cultural differences in sex roles, as suggested above, or they may reflect other cultural influences. For example, it has been suggested that there exists in our society a stereotypical belief that men are superior to women in certain areas of cognitive functioning (Tuddenham, Macbride, & Zahn, 1958). If men are seen as more competent, then it is not surprising that they conform less than women. In line with these expectations, Tuddenham et al. reported that women were more conforming when they were concerned about their answers not appearing peculiar to others, whereas men conformed more when they were concerned about completing the task quickly. This becomes especially significant in explaining sex differences in conformity behavior when the different orientations of men and women are considered. Berg and Bass (1961) cited evidence that college men tend to be task-oriented and concerned with getting the task completed, whereas college women tend to be much more interaction-oriented and concerned with establishing harmonious relations with others.

Clearly, in many situations females are more conforming than males. It is probable that these differences are due to the differential cultural influences exerted upon men and women. Regardless of the causes of this sex difference, however, it is a significant factor in the determination of group process.

PHYSICAL CHARACTERISTICS OF GROUP MEMBERS

Physical characteristics, such as size, weight, height, and general health, influence the behavior of the individual group member and the responses of other group members to him. Relative to other variables, these factors are generally weak and can be overcome by the effects of more powerful variables such as personality and ability. Nevertheless, it is worthwhile to examine briefly the consequences of physical differences among group members.

SIZE OF GROUP MEMBERS   Early studies of leadership indicated quite clearly that physical size is related to the attainment of leadership status. In his review of studies of personal factors in leadership, Stogdill (1948) found a generally positive relationship between leadership and weight, height, and measures of physique. Fourteen studies investigated the relation between height and leadership; nine found leaders taller than nonleaders, two found leaders shorter, two reported no difference, and one reported that differences depended upon the situation. Correlations between leadership status and height ranged from −.13 to .71. Eleven studies examined weight in relation to leadership. Seven reported that leaders were heavier than nonleaders, two that leaders were lighter than nonleaders, and two that there was no difference in weight between leaders and nonleaders. Reported correlations averaged .23. Twenty-five investigations dealt with general physical characteristics, with twenty-one reporting a positive relationship between physique and leadership, and four reporting that physique was not a factor. Reported correlations between leadership and measures of physique ranged from .11 to .62. Obviously, all these factors are intercorrelated; tall men tend to be heavier than short men, for example. Nevertheless, these findings indicate that physically superior men have a slightly better chance of *becoming* leaders than others. Note, however, that there is no evidence that size is related to the *performance* of leaders.

Relatively little attention has been devoted to the investigation of the effects of physical size on other aspects of group behavior, although it is evident that size may be a variable in determining the acceptability of an individual by others. It is a common observation that the tall, handsome man or the beautiful woman elicits a more favorable response from others.

The skinny group member or the overweight individual may be less acceptable in groups, and hence less effective as a group member. Indeed, Burgess and Cottrell (1939) found that the wife being overweight correlated negatively with marital adjustment. However, this is another set of variables that seems to have been neglected by researchers.

ABILITIES OF GROUP MEMBERS

In the preceding discussions, we have been concerned primarily with the characteristics which determine what the individual may *choose* to do in group situations. But equally important is the question of what the individual *can* do. The abilities of the group member determine how effectively he can perform the acts that he wishes to perform in the group, and this in turn influences how others react to him as a group member. Abilities, of course, may be general (intelligence) or they may be specific to the particular situation or task faced by the group.

INTELLIGENCE OF GROUP MEMBERS

When we discuss the effects of intelligence upon group process, we are referring to "test intelligence," or the general ability that is measured by intelligence tests. In a sense, this intelligence is an estimate of the individual's ability to deal with a variety of situations and problems. It is presumed to be determined by both innate ability and the experiences that the individual has had during his lifetime. The data regarding this general ability and behavior in groups are based upon measures of intelligence obtained by means of standard intelligence tests.

As in the case of biographical characteristics, the most extensive studies involving intelligence and group behavior have been in the field of leadership. Stogdill (1948) identified thirty-two studies dealing with the relationship between intelligence and leadership. Of these, twenty-two found that leaders were brighter than nonleaders, five that leaders and nonleaders were not different in intellectual ability, and five that too great a difference between the leader and other group members was undesirable from the standpoint of effectiveness. All reported correlations between intelligence and leadership ability were positive (average r = .28). Similar results have been reported in studies conducted since that review was completed. For example,

Bass and Wurster (1953a, 1953b) examined the correlations between intelligence and LGD (Leaderless Group Discussion) scores of oil refinery supervisors and obtained correlations ranging from .34 to .61. Hollander (1954) found that the ACE (American Council on Education) test scores of 268 naval cadets in preflight school correlated .30 with leader choice scores, i.e., the extent to which the cadet was named as leader by his group. These data make it clear that there is a low positive correlation between tested intelligence and leadership behavior. However, emphasis should be placed upon the word "low" in the above statement. It seems reasonable to conclude that intelligence accounts for approximately 10 percent of the variance among leadership scores.

Intelligence has also been found to be related to general activity, popularity, and conformity of individual group members. Bass et al. (1953) reported low positive correlations between general participation in LGD discussions and ACE scores (r = .21), and Zeleny (1939) reported similar findings. A positive relationship between intelligence and popularity was found by Mill (1953). Mann (1959), in a review of the literature, reported that of thirteen studies reviewed, 81 percent indicated a positive relationship between intelligence and popularity. However, caution must be used in interpreting these results, first, because Mann included studies using a variety of measures of intelligence, such as scholastic grade-point average, and second, because the highest correlation reported was only .37, with the median correlation about .10.

Studies of the effects of intelligence on conformity behavior are somewhat more convincing. Crutchfield (1955) reported a correlation of −.63 between the "assessment staff's rating of intellectual competence" and estimates of conformity, and a correlation of −.51 between the Concept Mastery Test (a measure of superior mental ability) and conformity. Nakamura (1958) obtained similar results using the analogies portion of the Concept Mastery Test as the measure of intelligence. Correlations between intelligence and conformity ranged from −.22 to −.44. Results consistent with the hypothesis that conformity and intelligence are negatively correlated have also been reported by Wyer (1967).

In summary, the evidence indicates that the more intelligent individual tends to be more active and less conforming in groups than the less intelligent person. As a partial consequence, he is more effective as a leader than the less intelligent group member. These effects are generally weak and probably can be outweighed by other factors.

SPECIFIC ABILITIES OF GROUP MEMBERS

Since intelligence as measured by intelligence tests is a composite of specific abilities, it is not surprising that its effects upon group behavior are somewhat variable and less than robust. Specific abilities are more directly related to behaviors in the group and hence exert a more powerful effect upon group process. The specific abilities that are of interest include not only those which may be reflected in general ability, but also special skills and knowledges. As we shall see, some of these special knowledges are essentially unrelated to general ability, although the use that the individual makes of them may be determined in part by intelligence.

Supervisory aptitude as measured by pencil-and-paper tests was examined by Bass and Wurster (1953b) in their study of oil refinery supervisors. They found correlations between supervisory aptitude scores and LGD scores ranging from .07 to .54, with an average r = .30. The higher correlation was between supervisory aptitude and LGD scores derived from a case history discussion task, whereas the lower correlation was between aptitude scores and LGD scores derived from a group discussion of in-plant leader specifications. General education and LGD scores were also found to be positively related (r = .47 to .63).

The relation between task-specific ability and effective leadership was also investigated by Palmer (1962a, 1962b). Ability with respect to the group task was measured by a multiple-choice test, after which subjects worked at the task in four- or five-person groups. Successful leadership was defined as the degree to which the individual influenced the group's decision, and effective leadership was defined as the exchange of accurate information. Task ability correlated .66 with successful leadership and .83 with effective leadership.

These task-related abilities undoubtedly reflect the possession of special knowledges and skills which enable the individual to aid the group in achieving its goal. This has been demonstrated in a number of studies in which the individual group member was provided with task-relevant information by the experimenter. For example, Maier (1950, 1953) has shown that a leader who knows the correct solution to the group problem is more effective in leading a group to the solution than is a leader who does not know the solution. Similarly, Shevitz (1955) has shown that the exclusive possession of expert knowledge results in more attempts to lead and higher status in the group. In a series of investigations, the author has shown that the amount of influence an individual has in the group, his satisfaction with the group, and the amount of effort he expends in helping the group achieve its goal—all are related to the probability that his information will lead the group to a valid conclusion if it is accepted by the group (M. E. Shaw, 1961a; Shaw & Penrod, 1962a; Shaw & Penrod, 1962b). The performance of the group also varies directly with the probability that an informed member's information will lead to the correct solution if accepted by the group. However, if there is reason to believe that the informed group member is not to be trusted or that his information is incorrect, then he will be unable to use his knowledge to aid the group in achieving its goal (Shaw & Penrod, 1962a; Shaw & Penrod, 1962b).

In general, if the individual has specific abilities that are related to the group task, he will be more active in the group, will make more contributions to the group's attempts to complete the task, and will have more influence on the group's decisions. As a consequence of these behavioral effects, the individual is more likely to emerge as a leader and the group's performance is improved. The person himself is better satisfied with the group's cooperation and performance, probably because he is accorded a special place in the group and because the group is more successful as a result of his contributions.

PERSONALITY CHARACTERISTICS OF GROUP MEMBERS

As Haythorn (1968) noted, to say that an individual's personality characteristics are related to his behavior is almost a tautology, because a personality trait is usually defined as a tendency or predisposition to behave in a particular manner in differing situations. Hence, to say that a person possesses a particular personality trait is equivalent to saying that we expect him to behave in a particular way in many different situations. We do not necessarily expect that he will behave this way in *all* situations, nor do we always know precisely how the trait will be expressed. But to the extent that the personality characteristic exists, there should be some degree of behavior consistency.

Researchers have not neglected personality variables in the study of group behavior. In reviewing the literature, Mann (1959) found that researchers had used over five hundred different measures of personality. Unfortunately, fewer than one-quarter of these measures were used in more than one investigation. Mann's findings lead to two possible conclusions:

(1) There is a tremendously large number of different personality attributes, or (2) different investigators often use different names and measures for the same attribute. Although personality is exceedingly complex, it is doubtful that meaningful results or theories can be achieved by subdividing personality into so many parts. Furthermore, it is clear that basically the same characteristic is given many names and many different measures have been devised to measure it. Indeed, Mann concluded that empirical work indicates that the multitude of measured personality attributes can be subsumed under seven dimensions of personality. Although his dimensions may not be entirely accurate, it is evident that personality can be represented by fewer characteristics than have been employed in the past.

In our discussion, we will group the various personality characteristics that have been studied into five broad categories or classes: interpersonal orientation, social sensitivity, ascendant tendencies, dependability, and emotional stability. Excluding intelligence and masculinity-femininity, our five categories correspond reasonably well to those Mann identified. The effects of intelligence have already been discussed; data concerning the effects of masculinity-femininity are sparse and generally contribute very little to our understanding of group process. We are, however, using labels which we believe more nearly reflect the kinds of characteristics included in our categories.

INTERPERSONAL ORIENTATION AND GROUP PROCESSES

An individual typically adopts a particular way or ways of viewing or reacting to other persons. This interpersonal orientation is reflected in the individual's typical behavior toward others in a variety of situations, although, of course, it does not by itself determine his behavior. It is only one of several personality attributes that, along with many nonpersonality factors, influence his behavior. Nevertheless, empirical investigations have revealed consistent effects of the group member's interpersonal orientation on group process and on the individual's behavior in the group.

In Table 6-1 we have listed the personality characteristics that are subsumed under the general orientation category, along with some representative findings concerning the relationships among characteristics and behaviors. Whenever available, the correlations between personality measures and behavioral measures are given; in other cases, only the direction of the relation-

TABLE 6-1 Relationships between Interpersonal Orientation and Group Processes

Personality characteristic	Behavior variable	Relationship	Reference
ASo/LPC of leader	Group effectiveness	—.67 to .69	Fiedler, 1964, 1967
ASo/LPC of leader	Group effectiveness	Positive	Sample & Wilson, 1965
Authoritarianism	Conformity	.39	Crutchfield, 1955
Authoritarianism	Conformity	Positive	Beloff, 1958
Authoritarianism	Conformity	.48	Nader, 1959
Cyclothymia	Cohesiveness	.37	Haythorn, 1953
Cyclothymia	Competitiveness	—.45	Haythorn, 1953
Cyclothymia	Morale	.24	Haythorn, 1953
Adventurous cyclothymia	Cohesiveness	.29	Haythorn, 1953
Adventurous cyclothymia	Social interaction	.62	Haythorn, 1953
Paranoid schizothymia	Cohesiveness	—.69	Haythorn, 1953
Paranoid schizothymia	Friendliness	—.57	Haythorn, 1953
Message/source orientation	Conformity	Message > Source	McDavid, 1959

ship can be indicated. As might be expected, the magnitudes of the correlations are not great, but the pattern of relationships is quite consistent.

ASo/LPC OF LEADER   Years ago, Fiedler (1951) became interested in the perception of similarity or "assumed similarity," which he believed correlated with liking and warmth in interpersonal relations. Later, he became interested in the relationship between assumed similarity of opposites (ASo) as a predictor of leadership behavior (Fiedler, 1954). In measuring ASo, the investigator asks the individual to evaluate his most preferred coworker (the coworker he has liked best in the past) and his least preferred coworker (again as recalled from past experiences) using a common set of questionnaire items. The difference between the two sets of responses reflects the degree to which opposites are seen as similar. Since the score is basically a difference score, the higher the score the more *dissimilar* opposites are seen to be. It was later discovered that the LPC score (the rating of the least preferred coworker) correlated very highly with ASo (.70 to .93), so the two measures are now used interchangeably. Persons with high ASo/LPC scores tend to see others, even a poor coworker, in a relatively favorable manner. As leaders, high LPC persons behave in a relationship-relevant manner in situations which are unfavorable for them; that is, they are concerned more with their relationship to others in the group than with the task. On the other hand, persons with low ASo/LPC scores tend to see others in a relatively unfavorable light. As leaders, they tend to act in a task-relevant manner in situations which are unfavorable to them. The unfavorable situation elicits different behaviors in high and low LPC persons.

It can be seen in Table 6-1 that correlations between ASo/LPC scores of the leader and measures of group effectiveness ranged from moderately high negative to moderately high positive. These correlations were obtained from a variety of groups that were faced with widely different tasks in various settings. Thus, the direction of the relationship between the ASo/LPC scores of group leaders and the effectiveness of the group depends upon the circumstances under which the group activity takes place. The nature of these circumstances and their interaction with the leader characteristics will be discussed in some detail in Chapter 8.

AUTHORITARIANISM   The authoritarian person believes that it is right and proper that there should be status and power differences among persons. It is "in the nature of things" that some persons occupy more powerful positions than others. Therefore, when the authoritarian is in a position of authority and power, he uses his power. He is demanding, directive, and controlling in his relations with those less powerful than himself. When he is in a subordinate position, he is submissive and compliant; he accepts his subordinate role as natural and appropriate. The nonauthoritarian (or equalitarian), on the other hand, believes that there should not be status and power differences among individuals; hence he rejects both the superior and the subordinate roles. There is some doubt concerning the extent to which true authoritarians or true nonauthoritarians actually exist in the general population. It seems likely that the behavior of individuals varies in the extent to which it reflects authoritarian tendencies.

Authoritarianism is usually measured by the California F-scale or some variation of it (Adorno, Frenkel-Brunswik, Levinson, & Sanford, 1950). This scale has been criticized because agreement with statements in it always reflects authoritarianism, and hence the score may be contaminated by acquiescence, and because it correlates negatively with intelligence. Nevertheless, it has been shown that the scores earned by individuals correlate in the expected way with behavior in groups (Haythorn, Couch, Haefner, Langham, & Carter, 1956a). For example, leaders emerging in groups composed of highly authoritarian persons behaved more autocratically than leaders emerging in groups composed of highly nonauthoritarian individuals. More will be said about this research in Chapter 7.

Also implicit in the concept of authoritarianism is the notion of adherence to rules and norms of the group. Therefore, it follows that the authoritarian should show greater conformity behavior when faced with a unanimous majority judgment. The data cited in Table 6-1 show that this expectation has been verified by research. Furthermore, this correlation cannot be completely accounted for by the common correlation of F-scale scores and intelligence scores with conformity.

In general, there is evidence that the authoritarian behaves differently from the nonauthoritarian in group situations. The authoritarian is autocratic and demanding; he tends to conform to the norms of the group more closely than the nonauthoritarian. However, the most significant effects of authoritarianism are consequences of the particular combinations of individuals in the group and the kind of structure the group has established or had imposed upon it. These effects will be discussed in subsequent chapters.

APPROACH-AVOIDANCE TENDENCIES   The characteristics labeled cyclothymia, adventurous cyclothymia, and paranoid schizothymia in Table 6-1 refer to a person's tendency to approach (like, esteem, trust) or to avoid (dislike, distrust) other people. Persons who score high on measures of cyclothymia tend to be cooperative, trustful, and adaptable; they prefer situations involving interaction with others. Low scorers prefer situations involving inanimate objects. Adventurous cyclothymia describes the extent to which individuals like people. Paranoid schizothymia refers to the avoidance aspect of interpersonal tendencies. Persons who score high on this dimension are said to be suspicious and jealous of others. They are dour and rigid, and tend not to accept suggestions from others.

The representative studies cited in Table 6-1 reveal the expected pattern of correlations with respect to behavior in groups. Approach tendencies (cyclothymia, adventurous cyclothymia) enhance social interaction, cohesiveness, and morale in groups, and suppress competitiveness. Avoidance tendencies (paranoid schizothymia) suppress friendliness and cohesiveness in groups.

SOCIAL SENSITIVITY AND GROUP PROCESSES

Social sensitivity refers to the degree to which the individual perceives and responds to the needs, emotions, preferences, etc., of the other person. This sensitivity to others has been labeled empathy, insight, social judgment, and the like. It seems obvious that this personality attribute should lead to positive effects in the group. The representative studies listed in Table 6-2 are entirely consistent with this expectation. Empathy, social insight, social judgment, and similar characteristics are positively correlated with leadership attempts and success, acceptance in the group, amount of participation, and group effectiveness. Independence and resoluteness are essentially opposite to social sensitivity in that the person who possesses these characteristics is unconcerned about others. They correlate negatively with friendliness and social interaction, as expected.

The only trait listed in Table 6-2 that may require further discussion is parmia. This term was used by Cattell and Stice (1960) to label a dimension reflecting outgoing sociability and expressed emotional responsiveness. From their description, it seems evident that this personality characteristic is one aspect of social sensitivity.

TABLE 6-2 Relationships between Social Sensitivity and Group Processes

Personality characteristic	Behavior variable	Relationship	Reference
Empathy	Leadership	.19 to .25	Bell & Hall, 1954
Independence, resoluteness	Friendliness	−.33	Haythorn, 1953
Independence, resoluteness	Social interaction	−.42	Haythorn, 1953
Parmia	Acceptance in group	.27 to .34	Cattell & Stice, 1960
Parmia	Participation	.16 to .28	Cattell & Stice, 1960
Sociability	Attempted leadership	.39	Bass, Wurster, Doll, & Clair, 1953
Sociability	LGD participation	.22	Bass, McGehee, Hawkins, Young, & Gebel, 1953
Sociability	Group performance	Positive	Bouchard, 1969
Social activeness	Group effectiveness	.23	Greer, 1955
Social insight	Leadership	Positive	Stogdill, 1948
Social judgment	Leadership success	.36	Meyer, 1951
Social skills	Leadership	.10 to .98	Stogdill, 1948

ASCENDANT TENDENCIES AND GROUP PROCESSES

Individuals vary markedly in the extent to which they wish to be prominent in group situations, the degree to which they assert themselves as individuals, and the extent to which they wish to dominate others. All these tendencies reflect an individualistic orientation, or at least a tendency to emphasize self in contrast to submission to oblivion in the group. This general ascendant tendency is referred to variously by such terms as ascendancy, assertiveness, dominance, and individual prominence. Although each of these terms refers to a slightly different aspect of the ascendant predisposition, there is enough commonality to consider them as a set.

Table 6-3 lists a number of investigations that have examined the relationships between ascendant tendencies and certain group processes. Persons who possess the personality characteristics associated with ascendancy generally behave as one would expect from the description of the dimension.

TABLE 6-3   Relationships between Ascendant Tendencies and Group Processes

Personality characteristic	Behavior variable	Relationship	Reference
Ascendance	Attempted leadership	.39	Bass, Wurster, Doll, & Clair, 1953
Ascendance	LGD participation	.37	Bass, Wurster, Doll, & Clair, 1953
Assertiveness	Assertive behavior	.42	Borg, 1960
Assertiveness	Popularity	.25	Borg, 1960
Assertiveness	Good follower role	—.22	Borg, 1960
Assertiveness	Rigid behavior	.22	Borg, 1960
Assertiveness	Creativity	.42	Borg, 1960
Assertiveness	Leadership	.39	Borg, 1960
Dominance	Conformity	—.23 to —.50	McDavid & Sistrunk, 1964
Dominance	Cohesiveness	.26	Haythorn, 1953
Dominance	Social interaction	.33	Haythorn, 1953
Dominance	Dissatisfaction with leader	—.19	Cattell & Stice, 1960
Dominance	Leader emergence	.17 to .18	Cattell & Stice, 1960
Dominance	Negative social-emotional remarks	.35	Cattell & Stice, 1960
Dominance	Leadership status	.20 to .29	Stogdill, 1948
Individual prominence	Influence on group decisions	Positive	Shaw, 1959
Individual prominence	Participation	Positive	Shaw, 1959

They attempt leadership, participate in group activities, are assertive, and are creative. They tend to emerge as leaders, promote group cohesiveness, influence group decisions, conform to group norms, and are popular. They also tend to be dissatisfied with the leader—when the leader is someone else!

Two relationships shown in Table 6-3 do not appear to be consistent with the general pattern of relationships: Assertiveness was found to correlate positively with rigid behavior (Borg, 1960), and dominance correlated positively with negative social-emotional remarks (Cattell & Stice, 1960). Although Borg stated that the correlation between rigidity and assertiveness was predicted, it nevertheless does not appear to be consistent with a positive correlation between assertiveness and creativity, since rigidity and creativity are usually presumed to be incompatible. Similarly, the positive correlation between dominance and negative social-emotional remarks does not seem in agreement with the positive correlations between dominance and cohesiveness and between assertiveness and popularity. However, these inconsistencies may be due to the particular measures used or to the particular circumstances under which the data were collected.

DEPENDABILITY AND GROUP PROCESSES

The average group member is probably attracted to others who are dependable both with regard to personal integrity and ability and with regard to behavioral consistency. A person who is self-reliant and responsible for his actions probably will be viewed as a desirable group member and will contribute to the effectiveness of the group. Similarly, an individual who can be expected to behave in conventional ways is unlikely to disrupt the group, whereas an unconventional person is likely to cause disorder and dissatisfaction. These two aspects of personality are placed in a single category, labeled dependability, because both aspects seem to predict responsible, dependable behavior. Table 6-4 lists representative studies of this dimension of personality.

SELF-RELIANCE AND RESPONSIBILITY   The tendency toward dependable, responsible behavior is identified by such traits as integrity, self-esteem, responsibility, self-reliance, and will control. Each of these represents a unique aspect of personality, but there is a common core that reflects dependability in the personal area. Self-esteem fits the category least adequately; it refers to the degree to which the individual respects himself as a person. The

TABLE 6-4   Relationships between Dependability and Group Processes

Personality characteristic	Behavior variable	Relationship	Reference
Integrity	Leadership	.32 to .41	Stogdill, 1948
Responsibility	Leadership	.10 to .87	Stogdill, 1948
Self-esteem	Conformity	Curvilinear	Gergen & Bauer, 1967
Self-reliance	Group effectiveness	.23	Greer, 1955
Unconventionality, undependability	Group productivity*	—.61	Haythorn, 1953
Unconventionality, undependability	Interest in job	—.43	Haythorn, 1953
Will control	Group productivity*	.41	Haythorn, 1953

* Ratings of performance on reasoning, mechanical assembly, and discussion tasks.

person's self-esteem should lead him to behave in a way which would enhance his self-esteem, that is, in a dependable and responsible manner.

The representative findings shown in Table 6-4 suggest that persons who are high with respect to dependability are likely to emerge as leaders and to be successful in helping the group to be effective in accomplishing its task. The finding with respect to self-esteem is unclear, since the curvilinear relationship was observed only when the task was of low or moderate difficulty, and with female subjects. This unusual result may be due to these factors, or it may be that self-esteem is basically different from the other characteristics considered in this category.

It is probable that the dependability of the person has other important effects on his behavior vis-à-vis others. The dependable person will probably be more attractive to others, more popular as a group member, more active in the group, and so on. Such effects would have significant consequences for group process.

UNCONVENTIONALITY   The unconventional person cannot be depended upon to behave in typical or expected ways in his relations with others. Hence, others are always a bit uncertain about his behavior in social interaction. This lack of behavioral stability can be expected to reflect a disinterest in the group's task and consequently to lead to lowered group productivity. The data given in Table 6-4 strongly support these expectations. Unconventionality is negatively correlated with interest in the job and with group productivity.

Again, it is expected that unconventionality is related to other behaviors that are important for group interaction. For example, it is a common observation that the deviant who consistently fails to conform to the
group norms is rejected by the other group members (Schachter, 1951).

EMOTIONAL STABILITY AND GROUP PROCESSES

The emotional stability of the individual in relation to group processes has
been studied more extensively than any of the other categories we have
examined. And it is reflected by more different labels and measures than any
other category. In general, emotional stability refers to a class of personality
characteristics that are related to the emotional or mental well-being of the
individual. It is reflected by such positive characteristics as adjustment, emotional control, and emotional stability, and by such negative characteristics
as defensiveness, depressive tendencies, and neuroticism. Representative
studies relating emotional stability to group processes are listed in Table 6-5.

ANXIETY   Anxiety may be defined as a general worry or concern about some
uncertain or future event. Although it is not necessarily associated with a
definite event, it is often related to a specific kind of situation or event, as
in the case of "free-floating anxiety." In any case, the person who experiences
anxiety feels a vague unease, a nagging worry and concern, which is psychologically unpleasant and which interferes with his responses to the demands of everyday living. Such a state, if chronic, as is suggested by labeling
it a personality characteristic, undoubtedly influences interpersonal behavior.

The kinds of anxiety that have been studied most extensively in relation to groups are *manifest anxiety* (J. A. Taylor, 1953) and *test anxiety*
(Mandler & Sarason, 1952). Manifest anxiety is the level of anxiety that the
individual reveals (manifests) at any particular time, whereas test anxiety is
anxiety that is associated with test taking or with the evaluation process.
Manifest anxiety is measured by the Manifest Anxiety Scale (MAS) developed by Taylor, largely by selecting items from the Minnesota Multiphasic
Personality Inventory (MMPI). Test anxiety is also measured by a pencil-and-
paper test (the Test Anxiety Questionnaire or TAQ) which was developed
by Mandler and Sarason (1952). When reviewing the data shown in Table 6-5,
the reader should keep in mind that such tests or scales may be less than perfectly valid and reliable. Achievement anxiety may be considered one form
of test anxiety, and peripheral nervousness a form of manifest anxiety.

TABLE 6-5 Relationships between Emotional Stability and Group Process

Personality characteristic	Behavior variable	Relationship	Reference
Achievement anxiety	Risky shift	Positive	Kogan & Wallach, 1967a
Manifest anxiety	Response latency	Negative	Cervin, 1956
Manifest anxiety	Performance variability	Negative	Ryan & Lakie, 1965
Test anxiety	Aspiration level	Negative	Beckwith, Iverson, & Render, 1965
Test anxiety	Conformity	Positive	Meunier & Rule, 1967
Test anxiety	Satisfaction with group	Positive	Zander & Wulff, 1966
Adjustment	Group effectiveness	.31	Greer, 1955
Emotional control	Leadership	.18 to .70	Stogdill, 1948
Defensiveness	Risky shift	Negative	Kogan & Wallach, 1967
Depressive tendencies	Cohesiveness	—.33	Haythorn, 1953
Depressive tendencies	Morale	—.49	Haythorn, 1953
Depressive tendencies	Motivation	—.26	Haythorn, 1953
Emotional stability	Job interest	.43	Haythorn, 1953
Emotional stability	Morale	.57	Haythorn, 1953
Emotional stability	Group productivity*	.47	Haythorn, 1953
Emotional stability	Leadership status	.21	Bass, Wurster, Doll, & Clair, 1953
Neuroticism	Opinion change	Negative	Cervin, 1956
Neuroticism	Response latency	Negative	Cervin, 1956
Paranoid tendencies	Group effectiveness	—.32	Greer, 1955
Peripheral nervousness	Group effectiveness	—.25	Greer, 1955
Pathology	Communication efficiency	Negative	Bixenstine & Douglas, 1967

* Ratings of performance on reasoning, mechanical assembly, and discussion tasks.

The pattern of relationships between measures of anxiety and measures of group process variables is generally consistent, in spite of the differences in measures and their potential deficiencies. The anxious individual reveals an overall picture of inadequacy in his relations to others and to the group. He has lower aspirations for the group, his responses are slower and more variable, he conforms to the norms more closely, he alters his judgment in response to the group more readily, and he is better satisfied with the group than the nonanxious individual. His personal concerns apparently cause him to be unusually dependent upon the group and, at the same time, lead him to expect less from the group. Since he expects little from the group, he is better satisfied with whatever outcome is obtained than is the individual who sets higher group goals. Conformity to norms may be one means of reducing anxiety or at least preventing it from increasing. Such behaviors can scarcely contribute to effective group functioning.

ADJUSTMENT   All the characteristics in the second set of general tendencies are more or less related to personal adjustment, that is, the degree to which the individual's personality reflects adequate organization relative to his environment, including other people. These characteristics are often labeled and measured negatively; they include such traits as depressive tendencies, paranoid tendencies, pathology, and the like. Each trait, whether stated positively or negatively, has to do with the degree to which the individual has adjusted to his world and achieved a personality organization that enables him to function effectively in that world.

Again, the pattern of correlations between adjustment measures and measures of group process is quite consistent, although the size of the correlations is not impressive. Group effectiveness, cohesiveness, morale, group motivation, and communication efficiency are positively related to such attributes as adjustment, emotional control, and emotional stability, and negatively related to such attributes as depressive tendencies, neuroticism, paranoid tendencies, and pathology. In short, the well-adjusted person is an asset to the group and the maladjusted person is a liability.

To summarize the findings relative to personality characteristics and group processes, there is good, though limited, evidence that behaviors in groups are caused, in part, by the personality characteristics of the group members. Personality attributes of leaders exert strong influences on group process, and the personality characteristics of individual members have been found to be both facilitative and inhibitive with respect to group process. The magnitude of these effects is not great, however, and relatively little has been done to reduce the number of plausible hypotheses about the effects of personality on behavior in groups.

PLAUSIBLE HYPOTHESES ABOUT THE PERSONAL ENVIRONMENT OF GROUPS

Although the effect of any given personality characteristic on behavior in groups is relatively weak, it is clear that such attributes have profound consequences for group process. Many of the following hypotheses are in agreement with "common sense" expectations, and many must be stated in terms of behavioral tendencies. Nevertheless, it is important to state them explicitly so that the effects of personality characteristics upon group process can be examined more completely.

Hypothesis 1 Social participation increases with increasing chronological age.

Numerous observation studies have shown that the number and percentage of social contacts (Beaver, 1932; Green, 1933b) and the amount of social participation in school activities increase with age. This increase in social participation is presumed to be a consequence of increased opportunity for social contact as well as increased development of cognitive and motor skills.

Hypothesis 2 Social interaction becomes more highly differentiated and complex with increasing chronological age.

As the child grows older, the contacts he makes with others become more complex. As a partial consequence of this increased complexity, the older person often becomes more sensitive to others, more popular, and more highly esteemed by associates than younger persons (Bass et al., 1953; Dymond, Hughes, & Raabe, 1952; Leuba, 1933).

Hypothesis 3 There is a tendency for the group leader to be older than other group members.

Although the older person does not always emerge as the leader, there is a slight trend in this direction (Stogdill, 1948). The low positive correlation between age and leadership status probably means only (or primarily) that a person must live long enough to achieve whatever leadership potential he may have. However, this does *not* imply that all persons who live long enough get to be leaders.

Hypothesis 4 Conformity behavior increases with chronological age to about age twelve, and decreases thereafter.

The empirical evidence for this hypothesis is reasonably good. The clearest support comes from the study by Costanzo and Shaw (1966), which revealed a curvilinear relationship between age and conformity (see Figure 6-1). However, the findings by researchers who observed the influence of nonpeer majorities on conformity at different age levels (Berenda, 1950) suggest that this effect may be limited to pressure from peers.

Hypothesis 5   *Women are less self-assertive and less competitive in groups than are men.*

Sex differences in assertive, competitive behavior were noted by Terman and Miles (1936), and studies of sex differences in group behavior agree with this finding. For example, Ort (1950) found that women reported fewer role conflicts in marriage than men, and the studies of sex differences in coalition formations demonstrate quite clearly that women more frequently than men adopt an anticompetitive attitude toward others (Uesugi & Vinacke, 1963).

Hypothesis 6   *Women use eye contact as a form of communication more frequently than do men.*

Although the evidence is unambiguous in showing that women engage in eye contact to a greater extent than do men (Exline, 1963; Exline et al., 1965), the meaning of this for interpersonal behavior remains an enigma.

Hypothesis 7   *Females conform to majority opinion more than males.*

Again, the evidence is unambiguous with respect to a sex difference in conformity (Costanzo & Shaw, 1966; Reitan & Shaw, 1964; Tuddenham, 1958), but the interpretation of this difference is still controversial. The most probable explanations are: (1) The female role in the American culture requires that the woman be more submissive than the male. (2) Men are usually regarded as superior to women on the kinds of tasks used in most conformity studies; hence the sex difference is the result of differences in perceived competence on the task.

Hypothesis 8   *There is a slight tendency for physically superior individuals to become leaders.*

In his review of the literature, Stogdill (1948) found leadership status to be positively correlated with height, weight, and physique, although a few negative correlations were reported. The correlations were generally low and may only reflect the fact that physically superior persons are usually more energetic and active than physically inferior persons.

Hypothesis 9   *Leaders are usually more intelligent than nonleaders.*

The studies comparing leaders and nonleaders reviewed by Stogdill (1948) overwhelmingly indicated that the leader was, on the average, more intelligent than the average nonleader. However, the correlations between intelligence and leadership status were generally low and averaged only .28. Studies of leadership behavior in leaderless group discussions (Bass & Wurster, 1953a; Bass & Wurster, 1953b) also revealed a positive correlation between intelligence and leadership scores. Thus it is clear that intelligence contributes to leadership potential, but the size of the contribution is small. Also, there is some reason to believe that too great a difference between the intelligence of the leader and that of other group members may be detrimental to group effectiveness.

Hypothesis 10   *The more intelligent group member is usually more active in the group than less intelligent group members.*
A number of investigators (e.g., Bass et al., 1953; Zeleny, 1939) have reported a positive correlation between general activity in the group and intelligence.

Hypothesis 11   *The more intelligent group member is usually more popular than less intelligent group members.*
Mann (1959) reported thirteen studies dealing with the relationship between intelligence and popularity, most of which showed a positive correlation. The correlations were very low, however, and averaged only .10. Therefore, intelligence does not appear to play an important role in determining popularity in groups.

Hypothesis 12   *More intelligent persons are less conforming than less intelligent persons.*
Again, the evidence is consistent and unambiguous in supporting this hypothesis (Crutchfield, 1955; Nakamura, 1958), but the correlations between conformity and intelligence are only moderately high, ranging from $-.22$ to $-.63$. The more intelligent person apparently feels more confident that his judgment is accurate, and perhaps does not feel the need to have the support of others in the group.

Hypothesis 13   *The individual who possesses special skills (abilities, knowledges, information) relative to the group task usually is more active in the group, makes more contributions toward task completion, and has more influence on the group decision.*
Activity in the group, contributions to the task, and influence on group decision have been grouped together in Hypothesis 13 because all these behaviors seem to be related to task-oriented activity in the group. Several studies have contributed to the support of this hypothesis (for example,

Bass & Wurster, 1953b; Palmer, 1962a; Palmer 1962b; Shaw & Penrod, 1962a; Shaw & Penrod, 1962b; Shevitz, 1955); however, it must be limited to the situation in which the other group members have reason to believe that the informed person's knowledge is accurate. He must be accepted and trusted by other group members if he is to use his special skills effectively.

Hypothesis 14   *When the situation is unfavorable to the leader, high ASo/ LPC leaders tend to behave in a relationship-relevant manner whereas low ASo/LPC leaders tend to behave in a task-relevant manner.*

This hypothesis is based upon the results of a long series of investigations of the behavior of persons scoring high or low on Fiedler's assumed similarity questionnaire. Hypothesis 14 is an attempt to summarize one of the more significant conclusions from the results of studies by Fiedler and his associates.

Hypothesis 15   *The authoritarian is autocratic and demanding of others in the group.*

Hypothesis 15 is basically a statement that the concept of the authoritarian personality is validated by the behavior of individuals in groups (Haythorn et al., 1956a).

Hypothesis 16   *The authoritarian conforms to the majority opinion more than does the nonauthoritarian.*

Evidence from experimental investigations reveal low positive correlations between authoritarianism (as measured by the F-scale) and conformity behavior. These correlations are on the order of .40, and hence authoritarianism accounts for only a small percentage of the variance among individual conformity scores.

Hypothesis 17   *Individuals who are positively oriented toward other people enhance social interaction, cohesiveness, and morale in groups, whereas individuals who are positively oriented toward things inhibit social interaction, cohesiveness, and morale.*

A number of personality characteristics reflect general approach-avoidance tendencies with respect to other people. The person who tends to like others, trusts them, wishes to cooperate with them, etc., produces favorable group atmospheres; the one who tends to prefer things to people, who is suspicious and jealous of others, etc., produces undesirable group atmospheres such as low cohesiveness and low morale (Haythorn, 1953).

Hypothesis 18 *Socially sensitive persons behave in ways which enhance their acceptance in the group and group effectiveness.*
This hypothesis is a brief summary of the pattern of relationships revealed in Table 6-2. For example, persons who score high on measures of empathy are more likely to emerge as leaders (Bell & Hall, 1954); sociability and social insight correlate positively with group effectiveness (Bouchard, 1969; Greer, 1955); and parmia (outgoing sociability and emotional responsiveness) correlates positively with acceptance in the group and with participation (Cattell & Stice, 1960).

Hypothesis 19 *Ascendant individuals are dominating and self-assertive in groups and generally facilitate group functioning.*
In general, the empirical evidence cited in Table 6-3 indicates that the ascendant, dominant individual, to a greater extent than others, attempts leadership, participates in group activities, asserts himself in the group, and conforms to group norms. Partly as a consequence of these behaviors, dominant individuals promote group cohesiveness, are popular, and influence group decisions. It seems probable, however, that extremely assertive-dominant persons would have an adverse effect upon group functioning.

Hypothesis 20 *The more dependable the group member, the more probable it is that he will emerge as a leader and that he will be successful in helping the group achieve its goal.*
Dependability is reflected by such personality characteristics as integrity, responsibility, and self-reliance. Table 6-4 shows clearly that attributes of this sort are related to leadership emergence and group effectiveness (Greer, 1955; Haythorn, 1953; Stogdill, 1948). This research merely verifies common sense expectations, and Hypothesis 20 makes explicit the relationships between dependability and group process.

Hypothesis 21 *The unconventional group member inhibits group functioning.*
Unconventional behavior means that the person's actions cannot be predicted with any degree of accuracy, and hence the unconventional person cannot

be relied upon to behave in socially acceptable ways. This behavior disrupts group functioning (Haythorn, 1953).

Hypothesis 22   *The anxious group member inhibits effective group functioning.*

The person who scores high on tests of anxiety tends to set relatively low goals for the group (Beckwith, Iverson, & Render, 1965), responds more slowly and less consistently than low scorers (Cervin, 1956), shifts his opinion more readily than others (Kogan & Wallach, 1967a; Meunier & Rule, 1967), and is better satisfied with the group's performance than nonanxious group members (Zander & Wulff, 1966). All these response patterns may be expected to interfere with group efficiency.

Hypothesis 23   *The well-adjusted group member contributes to effective group functioning.*

Hypothesis 23 appears obvious, and indeed it is almost a tautology. Nevertheless, it is important that personal adjustment be recognized and made explicit in the study of group process. To summarize, adjustment indicators (for example, emotional stability and emotional control) are positively correlated with cohesiveness, morale, and group effectiveness (Greer, 1955; Haythorn, 1953), whereas indicators of maladjustment (for example, depressive tendencies and neuroticism) are negatively correlated with these group processes (Cervin, 1956; Greer, 1955; Haythorn, 1953).

In conclusion, it is clear that the personality characteristics of group members play an important role in determining their behavior in groups. The magnitude of the effect of any given characteristic is small, but taken together the consequences for group process are of major significance.

SUGGESTED READINGS

ASCH, S. E. *Social psychology.* Englewood Cliffs, N.J.: Prentice-Hall, 1952. Chap. 16.

BASS, B. M., McGEHEE, C. R., HAWKINS, W. C., YOUNG, P. C., & GEBEL, A. S. Personality variables related to leaderless group discussion. *Journal of Abnormal and Social Psychology,* 1953, **48**, 120–128.

BORG, W. R. Prediction of small group role behavior from personality variables. *Journal of Abnormal and Social Psychology,* 1960, **60**, 112–116.

COSTANZO, P. R., & SHAW, M. E.   Conformity as a function of age level. *Child Development,* 1966, **37**, 967–975.

EXLINE, R. V., GRAY, D., & SCHUETTE, D.   Visual behavior in a dyad as affected by interview content and sex of respondent. *Journal of Personality and Social Psychology,* 1965, **1**, 201–209.

FIEDLER, F. E.   A contingency model of leadership effectiveness. In L. Berkowitz (Ed.), *Advances in experimental social psychology.* Vol. 1. New York: Academic 1964. Pp. 149–190.

HAYTHORN, W. W.   The composition of groups: A review of the literature. *Acta Psychologica,* 1968, **28**, 97–128.

MANN, R. D.   A review of the relationship between personality and performance in small groups. *Psychological Bulletin,* 1959, **56**, 241–270.

MEUNIER, C., & RULE, B. G.   Anxiety, confidence, and conformity. *Journal of Personality,* 1967, **35**, 498–504.

STEWART, F. A.   A study of influence in Southtown: II. *Sociometry,* 1947, **10**, 273–286.

STOGDILL, R. M.   Personal factors associated with leadership: A survey of the literature. *Journal of Psychology,* 1948, **25**, 35–71.

CHAPTER 7

THE SOCIAL ENVIRONMENT: GROUP COMPOSITION

Ample evidence has already been presented showing that the individuals who compose a group are highly significant determinants of group process. The mere presence of others is sufficient to alter the behavior of individuals (Chapter 3); the formation of groups depends, in part, upon the attractions among individuals and the rewards they provide one another (Chapter 4); the spatial relations among individuals contribute to the interactions among them and the kinds of relationships they establish (Chapter 5); and legions of personal characteristics are correlated with almost all aspects of group functioning, as well as with many individual behaviors in the group (Chapter 6). There can be no doubt that the kinds of individuals who make up a group constitute a set of powerful determinants of group behavior.

In the preceding chapter, attention was given to the consequences of the individual's characteristics upon group process without regard to the characteristics of others in the group. The correlations between personal attributes and behavior in groups were considered under conditions of random or undetermined group composition in an attempt to establish general effects of personal characteristics upon group process. In a sense, these correlations reflect consequences when other members in the group are average or typical with respect to personal attributes, that is, the effects of personal characteristics in the modal group. In this chapter, we are concerned with the *relationships* among the personal characteristics of group members and the consequences of these relationships for group functioning. It is not the particular characteristics of an individual group member that are of interest, but rather the *relative* characteristics of the various persons who compose the group. For example, when we discuss intelligence, it is not the intelligence of individual members that we are concerned with, but the differences in the intelligence of the various individuals in the group.

The first question the investigator should raise in connection with group composition effects is: Does the particular composition make *any* difference, or can differences among groups treated alike be explained on the basis of individual characteristics alone? For example, suppose that fifty persons are available for assignment to ten groups of five persons each. Does it make any difference how these fifty persons are distributed among the groups? Or can they be assigned at random with no gain or loss in group achievement? The answer, as we shall see, is that it does make a difference how the groups are formed.

The next questions concern the particular combinations of individuals and the effects of these combinations on group process. Investigators have employed various approaches in studying these aspects of group composition. Some were concerned with interpersonal attraction (cohesiveness) and similarity versus complementarity of personal characteristics; others were concerned with compatibility of needs; and still others with the heterogeneity-homogeneity dimension of group composition. These approaches have much in common, but the interests and techniques of the investigators vary considerably. For example, Winch (1955) was interested primarily in need complementarity in mate selection, and therefore limited his investigations to dating and married couples. Students of cohesiveness have been interested in group problem solving and small group interaction, and hence have concentrated on the small group. In the following sections, we will first consider the empirical evidence supporting the conclusion that the particular combination of individual characteristics does produce a significant effect upon group process. Subsequent sections consider the effects of cohesiveness, compatibility, and heterogeneity-homogeneity of group membership upon group behavior.

THE ASSEMBLY EFFECT

The term *assembly effect* refers to the variations in group behavior that are a consequence of the particular combination of persons in the group, apart from the effects produced by the specific characteristics of group members. Consider an instance in which four persons, two of whom tend to dominate others and two of whom tend to be submissive toward others, are to be assigned to two dyads. It seems obvious that a better overall result will be obtained by pairing each dominant person with a submissive person than by pairing the two dominant persons and the two submissive persons. This may seem so obvious as not to require verification. Indeed, Haythorn (1953), in the extensive study of the effects of personality characteristics on group process discussed in Chapter 6, assumed that such effects must be eliminated from the data in order to identify personality effects per se. He therefore designed his experiment so that each subject worked in five unique four-person groups, and no other subject was a member of more than one of them.

The serious student of small group behavior, however, is careful not to make many assumptions; he therefore wants verification of all hypotheses, even those which appear obvious. It was probably this concern with verification of the apparently obvious proposition that stimulated a study by Rosenberg, Erlick, and Berkowitz (1955) which contributed the most convincing evidence that assembly is indeed a determinant of group behavior. Two samples of nine persons each were drawn from a large pool of Air Force enlisted men. Each sample of nine was subdivided into three groups of three persons each. The membership of these groups was shifted from trial to trial so that each individual in the sample worked with every other individual in that sample. Hence, every triad differed in composition from every other triad, although any given arrangement included the same individuals as any other arrangement. Therefore, any differences in the functioning of triads could not be accounted for by differences among individual group members. That is, when different arrangements or assemblies of the same individuals are compared, any nonchance differences must be attributed to the effects of group composition.

The task assigned these differently assembled groups required a group version of the ball and spiral apparatus. This apparatus consisted of a hexagonal base from which a track or channel spiraled upward through five levels to a circular receptacle at the top of the channel. Six handles were attached to the base, so that it could be manipulated by the three members of the group. A golf ball was placed at the bottom of the channel, and the group's task on each trial was to manipulate the spiral in such a way as to move the golf ball to the receptacle at the top. An error was recorded for the group each time the ball fell off the track, and a performance score was recorded as the average height attained before the ball fell. The effectiveness of the triads differed on both measures, although the difference in perform-ance scores was minimally reliable. The results of this investigation thus verified the hypothesis that individuals contribute differently to the group product, depending upon the particular other individuals with whom they are grouped.

GROUP COHESIVENESS

Now that it is clearly established that group composition is a significant variable in group process, we must turn to an examination of the specific interpersonal relationships that contribute to this effect. One such inter-personal relationship is the degree to which the members of the group are attracted to each other, or the degree to which the group coheres or "hangs together." This aspect of the group is usually referred to as *group cohesive-ness*. Unfortunately, at least three different meanings have been attached to the term "cohesiveness": (1) attraction to the group, including resistance to leaving it, (2) morale, or the level of motivation evidenced by group members, and (3) coordination of efforts of group members. Most persons who use the term, however, agree that it refers to the degree to which mem-bers are motivated to remain in the group. Members of highly cohesive groups are more energetic in group activities, they are less likely to be absent from group meetings, they are happy when the group succeeds and sad when it fails, etc., whereas members of less cohesive groups are less concerned about the group's activities. In our discussion, we will accept the definition advanced by Festinger: Group cohesiveness is "the resultant of all the forces acting on the members to remain in the group" (Festinger, 1950, p. 274). According to this definition, all those factors contributing to interpersonal attraction which were discussed in Chapter 4 also contribute to group cohesiveness. The chief difference between the study of interpersonal attraction and group cohesiveness is that the former emphasizes individual attractions, whereas the latter emphasizes the number, strength, and pattern of attractions within the group.

Group cohesiveness is reflected by many different behaviors of group members; hence, it is not surprising that the operational measures of cohesiveness vary considerably from investigation to investigation. The most common technique for assessing cohesiveness is sociometric choice. Group members are asked to name the person or persons they would most prefer as associates for various activities, and the number of ingroup choices is presumed to reflect the degree of cohesiveness of that group. This measure is based upon the attraction of group members and disregards other forces that may be acting on a person to remain in or to leave the group. Variations in the application of this technique may also be important in understanding the relationship of cohesiveness to other aspects of group process. For example, some investigators count only positive choices, whereas others may ask individuals to name the least preferred as well as the most preferred, and then subtract the negative choices from the positive to estimate cohesiveness. Still others may take into account mutual choices. In addition, cohesiveness has been estimated by the relative frequency with which group members use "we" and "I" in their discussions, by the regularity of attendance at group meetings, and by direct questions about members' desires to remain in the group. These different measures of cohesiveness reflect different aspects of group cohesiveness, and none takes into account all aspects of group spirit. These variations in measurement techniques should be kept in mind as one attempts to evaluate research findings relative to cohesiveness.

The cohesiveness of the group has been supposed to influence a wide range of group activities, but perhaps its most significant influence is on group maintenance. According to most theories (cf. Cattell's syntality theory [Chapter 2] and Bennis and Shepard's theory of group development [Chapter 4]), the first demand that must be met by a group is the resolution of internal problems. Indeed, unless it solves these problems the group will cease to exist. Therefore, there must be some minimum degree of cohesiveness if the group is to continue to function as a group. To the extent that this minimum requirement is exceeded, it may be expected that the degree of cohesiveness will be related to other aspects of group process.

Although group cohesiveness has been related both theoretically and empirically to numerous process variables, the major ones are interaction, social influence, satisfaction, and group productivity. It will be instructive to consider the relationship of cohesiveness to each of these processes.

COHESIVENESS AND INTERACTION

It is a common observation that we interact, both verbally and nonverbally, with those others who are attractive to us. However, this relationship between interaction and interpersonal attraction is usually associated with opportunity for interaction, since we choose to join groups composed of attractive persons and to live and work in social environments composed of others who are attractive to us. It is theoretically possible that interaction is merely a by-product of affiliation and is only indirectly influenced by attraction or cohesiveness. There is good evidence, however, that both the quantity and quality of interaction are related to the cohesiveness of the group. Lott and Lott (1961) obtained groups of six to ten friends from student organizations at the University of Kentucky and Kentucky State College, representing religious, academic, athletic, and social activities. Groups of strangers were also obtained from introductory psychology courses. At the beginning of each group meeting, each person was asked to indicate, on a 9-point rating scale, how much he liked each other individual present.

Each member was paired with every other member and the difference in each pair's ratings of each other was averaged. A group cohesiveness index was then computed as the average of the scores earned by each pair. Each group then discussed a topic concerning student attitudes while an observer tallied the frequency of member communication. These procedures resulted in an estimate of group cohesiveness and a measure of quantity of communication activity for each of the fifteen groups. A rank difference correlation of .42 was obtained between cohesiveness and communication level. Although not exceedingly high, this correlation is statistically reliable and indicates that cohesiveness and amount of communication are related, even when opportunity for interaction is the same for all groups.

Behavior in accord with the findings reported by Lott and Lott has also been observed in a radically different setting (Moran, 1966). The subjects for Moran's study were 233 dyads obtained from nine Dutch industrial training groups. High- and low-cohesive dyads were identified on the basis of expressed ability to work together. Amount of communication between members of each dyad was obtained by asking each person to mark 70-millimeter rating scales showing how often he communicated with every other member in his training group. The communication level of each dyad was computed as the sum of the two members' perceptions of the amount of communication each had received from the other. The relationship between quantity of communication and cohesiveness was determined by comparing the relative number of high- and low-cohesive dyads that were above and below the median communication level for all dyads. There were 112 high-cohesive dyads above the median as compared with four low-cohesive dyads above the median. Clearly, then, cohesiveness is a factor in amount of verbal interaction.

Perhaps the quality of the interaction is of greater significance for group functioning than mere quantity, and there is good evidence that cohesiveness and quality of interaction are related. An early study by French (1941) showed some of the qualitative differences that may be observed between cohesive and noncohesive groups, although he did not use cohesiveness to label the differences in his groups. He compared eight organized (athletic teams) with eight unorganized groups (Harvard undergraduates who did not know each other). Each six-person group attempted to solve three problems that were said to be insoluble: (1) combining four 4s in such a way as to equal values from 65 to 90, inclusively; (2) moving disks from one position to another, via a third position, one at a time, and never placing a larger disk on a smaller one; and (3) the ball and spiral problem. Observers kept records of behavior categories and verbatim remarks (as well as records of other types that are not relevant here). Analysis of the verbatim remarks revealed greater usage of "we" than "I" in the organized groups, thus supporting the present interpretation that the organized groups were more cohesive than the unorganized. Observers' records of behavior categories revealed that, relative to the unorganized groups, the organized groups engaged in more objective problem-solving behavior (mean = 131.2 versus 121.6), less friendly behavior (mean = 4.7 versus 8.0), more aggression toward others (mean = 45.4 versus 6.0), and more self-aggression (mean = 7.5 versus 3.5). Not all differences were statistically reliable, but it was clear that the behavior pattern was different for the two kinds of groups.

Differences in the pattern of communication within groups as a function of cohesiveness was also noted by Back (1951) in a study designed to measure the effects of cohesiveness on pressures toward uniformity. Each member of each dyad was given a set of three pictures believing the two sets were identical, although in fact there were slight differences. They were asked to discuss the sequences of pictures and to write a story about them. Two observers recorded the discussion using a twenty-category recording system. High- and low-cohesive dyads were created through instructions, based upon either attraction to the partner, attraction to the task, or attraction to the group itself (prestige). A subsequent check revealed that the experimental inductions produced the wanted differences in cohesiveness. In general, members of low-cohesive groups tended to act independently, with little consideration for the other member of the dyad, whereas the cohesive group members were active in seeking facts and in reaching agreement. Also, within the high-cohesive groups the interaction patterns were quite different for different kinds of cohesiveness. When cohesiveness was based upon interpersonal attraction, members of the dyad wanted to prolong the discussion and to engage in pleasant conversation; when cohesiveness was based upon task performance, they wanted to complete the task quickly and efficiently; and when cohesiveness was based upon group prestige, members of the dyad acted cautiously and attempted to avoid any actions that might endanger their status.

Differential patterns of interaction as a function of cohesiveness have also been observed in children's groups (Shaw & Shaw, 1962). Three-person groups varying in degree of cohesiveness were formed on the basis of choice preferences for work partners in a classroom situation. The groups were then assigned the task of learning to spell lists of words, working together in groups. The teacher, who did not know the cohesiveness scores, observed and recorded the behavior of each group. Differences between high- and low-cohesive groups were observed in four categories: group atmosphere, method of study, leadership behavior, and nontask behavior. High-cohesive groups were cooperative and friendly, and the members praised one another for accomplishments; low-cohesive groups were hostile and aggressive, and members were delighted when others made errors. High-cohesive groups initially devoted time to planning their method of study, and all group members followed the agreed-upon plan; low-cohesive groups usually began immediately to test each other, with no preliminary planning. A strong leader emerged in both high- and low-cohesive groups, but in high-cohesive groups the leader behaved in a democratic manner whereas in the low-cohesive groups the leader was "bossy" and autocratic. Initially, both high- and low-cohesive groups devoted most of their time to the assigned task, but by the third task period the high-cohesive groups engaged in much more nontask (social) activity, whereas the low-cohesive groups developed interpersonal conflicts and tended to break up and study as individuals.

In summary, it is clear that cohesiveness is related to both quantity and quality of group interaction. Members of high-cohesive groups communicate with each other to a greater extent, and the content of group interaction is positively oriented. Members of high-cohesive groups are cooperative, friendly, and generally behave in ways designed to promote group integration, whereas low-cohesive group members behave much more independently, with little concern for others in the group.

COHESIVENESS AND SOCIAL INFLUENCE

Groups characterized by friendliness, cooperation, interpersonal attraction, and similar indications of group cohesiveness exert strong influences upon members to behave in accordance with group expectations. Members of cohesive groups are motivated to respond positively to others in the group, and their behavior should reflect this motivation. For example, French (1941) found that organized groups were more highly motivated than unorganized groups, as indicated both by observers' ratings and by group member questionnaire responses. Hence, members of cohesive groups theoretically should conform to group norms and respond positively to attempted influence by others in the group. Empirical observations generally support these theoretical expectations. Festinger, Schachter, and Back (1950) found that members of cohesive groups in university housing units held uniform opinions and usually acted in conformity with group standards. Thus, pressures toward uniformity increased with increasing group cohesiveness. In the laboratory study described in the preceding section, Back (1951) found that members of highly cohesive dyads changed their opinions more toward their partner's position than did members of the less cohesive dyads. Back interpreted this as showing that influence through social communication was greater in cohesive than in noncohesive groups.

The greater effectiveness of attempted influence in cohesive than in noncohesive groups under certain conditions was also demonstrated in an investigation by Schachter, Ellertson, McBride, and Gregory (1951). These investigators examined the effects of positive and negative inductions in high-

and low-cohesive groups. Cohesiveness was manipulated by telling the members of some groups that their responses to questionnaires indicated that they were members of extremely congenial groups (high cohesiveness); members of other groups were told that, owing to scheduling difficulties, it was impossible to assemble congenial groups and hence there was no reason to think that others in the group would like them. Each group member was assigned to a different room and given the task of cutting cardboard parts which ostensibly were to be used by the other group members to make checkerboards. Influence attempts were introduced by written notes which the subject believed came from other group members, although in fact they were prepared by the experimenter. During the first sixteen minutes of the work period each group member received five notes that made no attempt to influence productivity. During the final sixteen minutes, each group member received six notes that attempted to either increase or decrease productivity. Positive influence attempts were equally successful in both high- and low-cohesive groups, but the negative induction was much more effective in the high-cohesive than in the low-cohesive groups. Schachter et al. theorized that two forces were acting upon the subject, a force to please the experimenter and do well on the assigned task and a force to be accepted in the group. In the positive induction condition both forces were acting in the same direction, whereas in the negative induction condition they were operating in opposite directions. This would explain the overall greater effect of the positive induction, but the reason for the failure to find differences between high- and low-cohesive groups in the positive induction condition is not clear.

Somewhat different results were reported by Berkowitz (1954), although the procedure was essentially the same as that followed by Schachter et al. The subjects were male ROTC students and students in economics who were told either that they would be in congenial groups or that they would not find others congenial. The task was to assemble ashtrays, although each member actually cut out disks from desk blotters. In some groups, a high productivity standard was established through experimenter-controlled communications, whereas in others a low standard was established. In this experiment, however, members of high-cohesive groups were influenced more than the low-cohesive groups by both the positive and the negative inductions. The reasons for this difference with respect to positive inductions in high-cohesive groups are not immediately evident, but it may be due to subject differences. The Schachter et al. subjects were female and so might have been more positively oriented toward the task than the male subjects used by Berkowitz. If so, the positive induction in the low-cohesive female groups may have produced maximum productivity, in which case the high-cohesive subjects could do no better even if they were more strongly influenced by the requests from fellow group members.

The differential effects of social influence as a function of cohesiveness are shown most clearly in studies of conformity. An early study by Festinger, Gerard, Hymovitch, Kelley, and Raven (1952) found that groups who were told that they would find each other congenial and interesting exerted greater pressures toward uniformity of opinion than did groups that had been given no such instructions. In the Lott and Lott (1961) study cited earlier, the group cohesiveness index correlated .54 with a measure of conformity to contrived group opinion. Using a more traditional approach to conformity, Wyer (1966) found that group members conformed more to a contrived group majority judgment of the number of dots on a card in high-cohesive than in low-cohesive groups, although the magnitude of the cohesive effect varied with other conditions. A positive relationship between cohesiveness and conformity was also reported by Bovard (1951), but in another study (1953), he found no difference in conformity as a function of cohesiveness. Failure to find positive results was also reported by Downing (1958), using the autokinetic task (judgment of movement of a stationary light in a dark room), and by Seashore (1954), using agreement of members of industrial groups regarding production standards as the measure of conformity. In both of the latter studies, however, other factors were so strong that the effects of cohesiveness were undoubtedly suppressed.

The general conclusion from these studies is that cohesiveness leads to increased social influence, which in most cases produces greater conformity to group standards. However, other variables may be sufficiently strong to negate the effects of cohesiveness. Some of these other variables have been identified by Thibaut and Strickland (1956). Subjects in an experiment involving two levels of cohesiveness (high and low), three levels of confidence (high, medium, and low), and two psychological sets (task set and group set) were 234 male students. High-cohesive groups were made up of freshman pledges from social fraternities on a college campus; low-cohesive groups were composed of strangers. Levels of confidence were created in connection with the group task. Each member was seated in a cubicle facing a square board divided into four quadrants, each of which contained twenty-four thumb-tacks arranged in different ways. The tacks were arranged so that quadrants could be rank-ordered according to any one of four criteria. Subjects were instructed to imagine that the tacks in each quadrant represented four groups of people and were told to rank-order the groups on the basis of friendliness. Ten simulated balloting trials were given, during which each subject circled one of four alternative orders and indicated his degree of confidence in his judgment on each of five cards to be transmitted to other group members. The ballots were intercepted by the experimenter, who replaced them with pre-marked ones which varied the level of confidence and communicated a majority decision different from that of the subject. Psychological set was manipulated through instructions. Task set instructions emphasized the importance of problem solution, whereas group set instructions were designed to make social evaluation within the group as salient as possible.

Across all experimental conditions, the high-cohesive groups conformed approximately 51 percent of the time as compared with 41 percent for the low-cohesive groups. However, the amount of conformity varied systematically with other variables in the situation. Figure 7-1 provides a graphic representation of the amount of conformity under the various conditions. It can be seen that when the majority expresses low confidence in its judgment, there is little difference in conformity as a function of cohesiveness. When the majority's confidence is high, however, the high-cohesive groups conformed more than the low-cohesive groups under both psychological sets. It is also interesting that high-cohesive groups conformed more than low-cohesive groups at all levels of confidence under group set conditions, although the difference in the low majority confidence condition is probably not reliable.

In summary, there is good evidence that group cohesiveness is related to social influence in the group. When group members are attracted to the group, they are motivated to behave in accordance with the wishes of other group members and in ways that facilitate group functioning. These motivations are reflected in greater responsiveness to group inductions and in greater conformity to group norms and standards. It must be recognized, however, that many other variables are related to social influence processes, and under some circumstances these other variables may be strong enough to negate the effects of cohesiveness.

COHESIVENESS AND PRODUCTIVITY

Group members who are attracted to the group work harder to achieve the goals of the group; one consequence of this is higher productivity by more

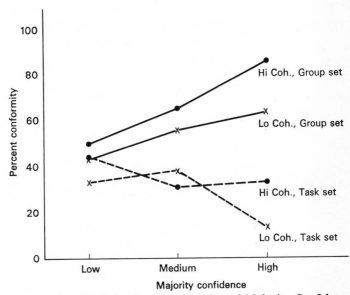

Figure 7-1 Conformity Behavior as a Function of Majority Confidence and Psychological Set. (Plotted with permission from data reported by J. W. Thibaut & L. Strickland. Psychological set and social conformity. *Journal of Personality,* 1956, **25**, 115–129.)

cohesive groups. This assertion states an apparently obvious fact about group process, yet a considerable amount of research has been devoted to determining whether or not it is valid. After we have reviewed some of this research, we can say more about the empirical data on the relationship of cohesiveness to productivity. To anticipate, it appears that the cohesive group can achieve goals that it accepts more efficiently than the noncohesive group. The problem often is that groups do not set the same goals for themselves that outside agencies (experimenters, boards of directors, etc.) set for them. Hence a cohesive group may achieve its own goals, but be relatively unproductive with regard to the goals of the researcher. But let us examine some of these studies.

Relatively few laboratory studies have been designed for the primary purpose of examining the relationship between cohesiveness and productivity, although there is some evidence on this issue from studies designed for other purposes. In the studies concerned with the effects of cohesiveness on social influence, for example, base-line measures of productivity were obtained before the influence attempts were introduced. These data showed no differences between the high- and low-cohesive groups in the Schachter et al. (1951) experiment and only small increments in favor of the high-cohesive groups in the Berkowitz (1954) study. Since the group members were working in separate rooms with no knowledge about the expectations of other group members, it is perhaps not too surprising that the group atmosphere had little effect upon group productivity.

More acceptable evidence derives from field studies and field experiments. A field study of twelve 6-man squads in the United States Army was conducted by Goodacre (1951). Prior to participation in a military problem conducted in the field, squad members were asked to indicate their choices of buddies in various social and tactical situations. These choices were used to compute measures of cohesiveness for each group. The correlation between the measures of group cohesiveness and the scores earned on the military problem ranged from .62 to .78. An overall group cohesion score correlated .77 with the field score. Hemphill and Sechrest (1952) also studied military personnel. They tested ninety-four B-29 bomber crews in combat in the Pacific area. Each person was asked to select an air crew from the squadron by naming one man for each crew position. They then computed an "on-crew" versus "off-crew" index of cohesiveness for each air crew; this index was then correlated with bombing accuracy scores obtained from official records. The correlation was positive but was not as high as that obtained by Goodacre (r = .36). Strupp and Hausman (1953) also reported a positive relationship between cohesiveness and productivity for aircraft maintenance crews, but a study by Roby (1952) yielded equivocal results. Nevertheless, evidence from field studies in military situations generally supports the proposition that cohesiveness and productivity are positively correlated.

Evidence from studies in industrial settings is also generally in accord with the hypothesis. In a series of studies, Van Zelst (1952a; 1952b) reported positive relationships between measures of cohesiveness and productivity indices. In the first study, carpenters and bricklayers were asked to list three choices for teammates. Voluntary regrouping was permitted on the basis of these choices, after which the men worked together for five months on a construction job. Compared with a nine-month period prior to regrouping, the rate of turnover dropped and there was a 5 percent savings in total production costs. In a second study, sociometrically constructed work groups of carpenters and bricklayers were compared with control groups during a three-month work period. Experimental groups were superior to control groups with respect to turnover rate, an index of labor cost, and an index of materials cost. Similar results were reported by Speroff and Kerr (1952) in a study of accident reduction through sociometric grouping. Negro and Spanish-speaking manual workers in a steel mill were asked to name the person they would most like to work with and the person they would least like to work with. An index of desirability was computed by subtracting the square of number of least-like choices from the square of number of most-like choices. This index correlated −.54 with the number of accidents during the three previous years. Thus, cohesiveness is demonstrably related to behavior in the industrial realm.

Finally, there is evidence that cohesiveness is related to group effectiveness in the classroom. In the study by Shaw and Shaw (1962) cited earlier, second graders were grouped according to sociometric choices in such a way as to form groups varying in cohesiveness. Each pupil was asked to name the three persons he would most like to study with and the three he would least like to study with. A cohesiveness index was computed for each three-person group by assigning a weight of 1 for a rejection, a weight of 2 for no choice, and a weight of 3 for a positive choice. For example, consider a group composed of persons A, B, and C, in which A had chosen B as most preferred and B had rejected C. The cohesiveness index would therefore be 12, since there were four possible choices that were not made, plus one rejection and one positive choice. Each group was tested on two word lists, with group effectiveness being measured by the number of words that the group could spell which it could not spell before the study period; that is, the sum of individual gains over pretest scores. Altogether, four sets of groups were tested, resulting in four correlations for each test period. In the initial test period, correlations between cohesiveness and performance were all positive, ranging from .16 to .56 and averaging .47. In the second test period, however, the correlations ranged from −.56 to .47 and averaged only −.01.

This study is presented in some detail because it makes a point about the experimental study of cohesiveness and productivity. It will be recalled that the interaction patterns were different in the high- and low-cohesive groups and that this pattern changed during the course of the study. In the second test period the more highly cohesive groups engaged in much more social activity and devoted less time to the assigned task, whereas the less cohesive groups broke down and studied individually. This differential pattern of interaction during the second test period effectively destroyed any relationship between cohesiveness and performance. In other words, the more cohesive groups set social activity as their goal, and they apparently achieved this goal!

In spite of some equivocal evidence, it seems evident that the empirical data support the hypothesis that high-cohesive groups are more effective than low-cohesive groups in achieving their goals. The cohesive group does whatever it tries to do better than the noncohesive group. Indeed, Seashore (1954) reported that among industrial groups cohesiveness was related to either high or low productivity, depending upon the production standards established by the group.

The effect of cohesiveness upon the performance of the group is undoubtedly mediated by motivational factors. According to Cattell's syntality theory (see Chapter 2), it might be inferred that cohesiveness increases the effective synergy in the group in two ways: It increases the total synergy of the group by producing more favorable attitudes toward the group on the part of its members, and it reduces the amount of synergy that is needed to maintain the group. The resulting increase in effective synergy enables the group to attain its goal or goals more efficiently. Data concerning the relationship between cohesiveness and member satisfaction (reported in the next section) are generally in accord with this interpretation.

COHESIVENESS AND SATISFACTION

Members of cohesive groups are generally better satisfied with the group than are members of noncohesive groups. Indeed, the concept of cohesiveness almost demands that this be the case, for it is highly unlikely that an individual will experience forces to remain in a group that he is dissatisfied with. Of course, it is possible that a person will be attracted to some aspects of a group, such as group goals, without being satisfied with the group as a whole. Nevertheless, the general theoretical expectation is greater satisfaction with increasing cohesiveness.

The empirical data are entirely consistent with this proposition. In the study of carpenters and bricklayers cited earlier, Van Zelst (1952b) found that members of groups formed on the basis of sociometric choice had higher job satisfaction than members of control groups. Similar findings were reported by Marquis, Guetzkow, and Heyns (1951) in a field study of decision-making conferences. The participants in seventy-two conferences in business and government were observed at the University of Michigan, and a cohesiveness index computed for each group determined from observer ratings of liking among group members. Group members rated their satisfaction with several aspects of the conference. The cohesiveness index correlated positively with members' satisfaction with the group process and with the meeting. Gross (1954) reported a positive relationship between cohesiveness of Air Force groups and their satisfaction with the Air Force and its goals.

The findings from field studies have also been supported by data from more traditional laboratory studies. Exline (1957) told some participants that they were in groups that were well matched and congenial, and told others that it was not possible to arrange a congenial group for them. Persons assigned to presumably congenial groups expressed greater satisfaction with their group's progress than did those given the opposite orientation.

The general findings with respect to group cohesiveness and group process are therefore reasonably consistent, despite the many inadequacies in the operationalizing of cohesiveness. Relative to low-cohesive groups, high-cohesive groups engage in more social interaction, engage in more positive interactions (friendly, cooperative, democratic, etc.), exert greater influence over their members, are more effective in achieving goals they set for themselves, and have higher member satisfaction.

GROUP COMPATIBILITY

It should be clear from the preceding discussions that high-cohesive groups are composed of members who are compatible; hence, group cohesiveness is one form of group compatibility. The questions asked about the behavior of cohesive groups, however, are not based upon the proposition that they are either compatible or incompatible, at least not beyond the compatibility implied by interpersonal attraction. But a number of theorists and researchers have been interested in the consequences of compatibility per se. These scholars have generally attempted to formulate theoretical propositions about the characteristics of individuals that make them compatible or incompatible with particular other individuals. Groups varying in degree of compatibility are then formed and studied under controlled conditions. In this way, the theoretical hypotheses can be tested and empirical relationships between compatibility indices and group process variables can be established.

Although approaches to the analysis and study of compatibility are varied, they can be classified into two general categories: need compatibility and response compatibility. These two approaches are basically similar in that both are concerned with personal characteristics of group members which reflect response tendencies that are either compatible or incompatible. They differ in the kinds of characteristics they consider important.

NEED COMPATIBILITY

Individuals have differing needs the satisfaction of which may be either facilitated or interfered with through group interaction. When the needs of two or more persons can be mutually satisfied through interpersonal activities, they are compatible in terms of needs; when their needs cannot be satisfied through interaction or when the satisfaction of their needs is interfered with through the interaction process, they are incompatible. Obviously, groups whose members are incompatible are likely to be unhappy and the effectiveness of group members will be adversely affected; when member needs are met (i.e., when the group is compatible), the opposite effects should occur.

This simple notion of compatibility was applied to mate selection by Winch (1955) in his theory of complementarity of needs. Basically, Winch theorized that individuals choose mates whose personal characteristics complement their own characteristics. For example, assertive persons should marry receptive or submissive persons, since the need to assert oneself can be satisfied through interaction with a person who needs to be submissive. To test this theory, Winch conducted "need interviews" with twenty-five married couples. On the basis of these interviews, he identified the needs of each person and correlated them to determine whether the expected relationships occurred. The correlations were generally in the predicted direction, and thus tended to support Winch's theory. However, data from case history interviews and from the analysis of responses to Thematic Apperception Test cards failed to support the hypothesis. Winch discounted these data because the need scores were unreliable. He therefore concluded that his data supported the hypothesis that marriage partners choose each other to satisfy complementary needs.

Other investigators have not been so successful in obtaining support for the Winch hypothesis. Kelly (1955) studied 300 engaged couples to test the hypothesis that "opposites attract." He administered a battery of tests designed to measure attitude, interest, and social values, and computed correlations between the scores of the engaged couples. Since these correlations ranged from —.02 to .58, he concluded that there is no evidence that opposites attract. However, the characteristics studied did not include the kinds of needs investigated by Winch. Inconclusive evidence was also reported by Gross (1956) from a study of groups at Air Defense Command bases. Groups were analyzed for composition with regard to seventeen variables, such as marital status, religion, education, and source of income. He found that some groups were composed of men having dissimilar or contrasting characteristics, whereas others were composed of men having similar characteristics. Again, it is questionable whether these findings are relevant to the need complementarity hypothesis. The general conclusion that can be drawn is that complementary needs lead to mate selection, but similarity with respect to such characteristics as interests, attitudes, and other social attributes may be more important (see Chapter 4).

The most ambitious attempt to analyze need compatibility in groups is Schutz's three-dimensional theory of interpersonal behavior (also called FIRO), which was outlined briefly in Chapter 2 (Schutz, 1955, 1958). It will be recalled that Schutz proposed three interpersonal needs—inclusion, control, and affection—which he believed were necessary and sufficient to explain interpersonal behavior. Certain combinations of needs were presumed to produce group compatibility and others incompatibility. In general, the more compatible a group the more it would approximate goal achievement.

In the early stages of theory development, Schutz (1955) attempted to construct compatible and incompatible groups on the basis of three individual characteristics of group members: dependence, assertiveness, and personalness. These three attributes were measured by specially constructed scales, and groups were composed according to the pattern shown in Table 7-1. Intelligence was used as a control variable. According to the theory, compatible groups can be constructed by selecting as group members persons who favor the personal orientation and who disfavor the dependent orientation, like those shown in Table 7-1. In addition, Schutz assumed that the group would need a focal person to initiate the appropriate atmosphere. Thus, in Table 7-1, the person identified by the symbol FP_p should play this role, since he is high on assertiveness and all other members are low to medium on assertiveness. An incompatible group can be formed by establishing two opposing subgroups. Thus, the group shown in Table 7-1 includes one compatible subgroup made up of a focal person and a compatible member, and a second subgroup which favors the power orientation over the personal orientation. This subgroup also has a focal person, FP_c, who initiates the power-oriented atmosphere for his subgroup. Therefore, the incompatible

TABLE 7-1 Characteristics of Members Used in Constructing Compatible and Incompatible Groups

Variables	Compatible group members				
	FP$_p$	MS$_p$	M$_p$	M$_p$	M$_p$
Personalness	H*	H	H	H	H
Dependence	L,M	L,M	L,M	L,M	L,M
Assertiveness	H	L,M	L,M	L,M	L,M
Intelligence	H	H	L,M	L,M	L,M
	Incompatible group members				
	FP$_p$	S$_p$	FP$_c$	S$_c$	N
Personalness	H	H	L	L	M
Dependence	L,M	L,M	H	H	M
Assertiveness	H	L,M	H	L,M	L
Intelligence	H	L,M	H	L,M	L,M

Personal subgroup   Counterpersonal dependent subgroup

Antagonistic subgroups

* H—roughly highest quartile; M—roughly second or third quartile; L—roughly lowest quartile.

SOURCE: Reproduced with permission from W. C. Schutz, What makes groups productive? *Human Relations*, 1955, 8, 429–465.

group is composed of a personal subgroup and a counterpersonal subgroup which are antagonistic. The compatible groups were expected to be more productive than the incompatible groups when the group task was a complex one requiring cooperation among group members. Groups were required to solve three problems, varying in complexity. The most complex task was a plotting problem designed to require cooperation through a division of labor. Essentially, the group was required to plot the track of many planes on a large plotting board, with the planes arranged in such a way that different group members had different tasks to complete at the same time. The second most complex problem, the intercept problem, required agreement among group members for each decision made by the group. The final problem, and the least complex, involved two intellectual problems, a decoding exercise and a logical exercise, neither of which required a great deal of group cooperation. The results showed clearly that the compatible groups were more productive than the incompatible ones, and this effect was greater as task complexity increased. Evidence from questionnaire results also indicated that the group members felt more positive toward the compatible groups and that the focal person emerged as a leader more frequently than others. Since the groups were matched with respect to intelligence, these differences in productivity must be attributed to differences in compatibility. The results of this initial study thus generally supported Schutz's hypotheses regarding the differences between compatible and incompatible groups.

As the theory was developed more fully, Schutz (1958) identified three types of compatibility: interchange compatibility, originator compatibility, and reciprocal compatibility. These types of compatibility are described in more detail in Chapter 2. A compatibility index can be computed for each of these types within each of the three need areas; indices for the three types can be computed by summing the appropriate index for the three need areas; inclusion, control, and affection indices can be computed by summing the indices for the three types within the appropriate need area; and an overall compatibility index can be computed by summing the three type indices or the three need indices. Thus, it is possible to compute sixteen different compatibility indices. Schutz cited a number of studies relating the various types of compatibility to group productivity and group cohesiveness. These studies generally supported the view that compatibility is positively related to these group processes, although in some cases the results were equivocal. In a later study, Schutz (1961) found that members of compatible groups are more aware of the interactional characteristics of their group than are members of incompatible groups.

Positive results supporting the hypothesis of a relationship between compatibility and productivity were also reported by Moos and Speisman (1962). On the other hand, Shaw and Nickols (1964) administered the Schutz scales to a large population of subjects, formed groups at random, and observed them in problem-solving situations. All possible compatibility indices and all possible correlations between these indices and measures of group productivity and group satisfaction were computed. Only a few of the correlations were significant, and these could have been due to chance factors. However, it was noted that the range of compatibility scores was not great, which might have accounted for the low correlations. It appears from these results that extremely compatible or extremely incompatible groups probably do not occur naturally.

The predicted effects of need compatibility failed to occur in an extensive study reported by Altman and Haythorn (1967b). They investigated compatibility-incompatibility based upon need achievement, need affiliation, and need dominance, and found the expected compatibility effects only with respect to need affiliation. They predicted that dyads homogeneous with respect to need achievement or need affiliation would be more compatible than dyads heterogeneous with respect to these needs, and therefore that homogeneous groups should perform more effectively than heterogeneous dyads. Homogeneous need-affiliation dyads performed better than heterogeneous need-affiliation dyads, as expected, but heterogeneous need-achievement dyads performed better than homogeneous need-achievement dyads, contrary to expectations. On the other hand, *heterogeneous* need-dominance dyads were expected to be more compatible and hence to perform better than homogeneous need-dominance dyads, but the opposite effect was observed. Altman and Haythorn noted that their Greco-Latin square experimental design does not permit the assessment of interactions among need variables; hence some of the observed effects may be the result of such interactions rather than of compatibility-incompatibility. It is also possible that the particular needs in question, especially need achievement, are related to effective performance quite independently of group composition; hence, compatibility-incompatibility effects are at least partially confounded with such individual effects. It is also possible, of course, that Altman and Haythorn's assumptions regarding need compatibility were incorrect, although this would be difficult to explain with respect to need dominance, particularly. Despite these possible flaws in design and prediction, the results of this study raise questions about the generality of need compatibility-incompatibility effects on group effectiveness.

A somewhat different approach was taken by Sapolsky (1960). He investigated the effects of verbal reinforcement on acquisition and extinction as a function of the compatibility-incompatibility of experimenter and subject. He selected five female experimenters on the basis of their scores on the Schutz scales, such that all were high on need for control but varied with respect to need for inclusion and affection. Subjects were then selected to be either compatible or incompatible with the experimenter with whom they worked. Each subject was asked to make up sentences using words presented on cards. During this procedure, E verbally reinforced the use of first-person pronouns by saying "mmm-hmm" at the end of any sentence that began with either "I" or "We." The acquisition period was followed by an extinction period during which no reinforcement was given. The results are shown in Figure 7-2. It is clear that the subjects in the compatible dyads responded to verbal reinforcement more than subjects in incompatible dyads, and that this effect continued for some time after reinforcement was discontinued. This may be a partial explanation of the greater productivity and satisfaction of

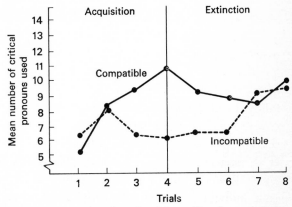

Figure 7-2   Curves Showing the Mean Number of Reinforced Pronouns Used by the Compatible and Incompatible Groups. (Reprinted with permission from A.
Sapolsky. Effect of interpersonal relationships upon verbal
conditioning. *Journal of Abnormal and Social Psychology,*
1960, **60,** 241–246.)

compatible groups; reinforcements provided by compatible others enhance
the motivation and efforts of individual group members.

RESPONSE COMPATIBILITY

Another group of investigators have been interested in patterns of behavior
predicted from personality characteristics. The basic assumption is that certain personality attributes predispose the individual to behave in typical ways,
and that these ways of behaving may produce either group compatibility or
group incompatibility. We noted some of these considerations in Chapter 6
and in the first part of this chapter. It will be recalled, for example, that the
authoritarian person is autocratic and demanding, ascendant individuals are
assertive and dominating, etc. (see Table 6-3). A person who is autocratic
would probably be compatible with a person who is submissive but he would
be incompatible with a person who behaves in a dominating manner himself.
It is therefore important to know how the various combinations of personality
characteristics are related to compatibility-incompatibility and hence how
they influence the performance and satisfaction of groups. Unfortunately,

relatively little work has been done on the effects of response compatibility as determined by personality characteristics. What has been done is limited almost entirely to studies of authoritarianism and dominance.

Perhaps the most extensive examination of response compatibility based upon authoritarianism was made by Haythorn, Couch, Haefner, Langham, and Carter (1956b). The California F-scale was used as the measure of member authoritarianism, and groups were composed of various leader-follower combinations: leader high on authoritarianism, followers high (Ff groups); leader high, followers low (Fd groups); leader low, followers high (Df groups); and leader low, followers low (Dd groups). Although Haythorn et al. discussed their predictions in terms of similarity-dissimilarity of leaders and followers, their hypotheses were based upon the assumption that the same individuals would behave differently depending upon the characteristics of others in the group. For example, they expected that leaders would be less directive and autocratic with democratic followers (low scorers on the authoritarianism scale) than with autocratic followers (high scorers). With authoritarian followers, leaders were predicted to be more decisive and directive because these kinds of followers expected the leader to behave this way. In general, similar group members should be compatible, and dissimilar group members should be incompatible.

The four-person groups formed according to the above design were required to perform a task which called for discussion of a human relations problem presented by film, after which they composed and recorded dialogue for similar problems. Observers recorded the interaction, and postexperimental questionnaires were administered to obtain reactions to the group. The results revealed the usual differences between the behavior of authoritarian and democratic leaders, with the authoritarian leaders less concerned with group approval, less sensitive to others, and more autocratic than the democratic leaders. There were also differences that depended upon the particular combinations of leader-follower personality. Leaders with authoritarian followers were rated by observers as higher on autocratic behavior, and their groups were rated as more dominated by the leader than the groups with democratic followers. Under democratic leadership, followers were rated by observers as having more influence, more effective influence, and equal participation in group activities. Homogeneous groups (presumably the more compatible ones) revealed less personality conflict than the heterogeneous groups (presumably the less compatible ones). Furthermore, followers in the homogeneous groups were rated as more secure and as striving for goal achievement more than those in the heterogeneous groups.

A somewhat similar study was conducted by M. E. Shaw (1959b), although he was concerned primarily with compatibility of group membership with respect to the structure of the group. As in the Haythorn et al. study, groups were composed of varying combinations of leader-follower authoritarianism; however, the measure of authoritarianism was the acceptance of authority scale devised by Bales (1956). Groups of four persons each were assigned to either a centralized communication structure (the wheel network) or a decentralized communication structure (the comcon network). Groups were required to solve a series of three arithmetic problems requiring written communication among group members. It was expected that groups composed of authoritarian members would perform better and be better satisfied in the centralized than in the decentralized structure, whereas groups composed of nonauthoritarian members would be more effective in decentralized networks. Theoretically, then, the most efficient combinations should be authoritarian leaders and followers in a centralized structure and nonauthoritarian leaders and followers in a decentralized structure. Unfortunately, measures of authoritarianism are negatively correlated with intelligence, so that a direct test of these expectations is not valid. Therefore, correlations were computed between the leader's authoritarianism score and the performance of the group, with intelligence partialed out, and between the average authoritarianism score for all group members and the group's performance score, with intelligence partialed out. The partial correlations between group authoritarianism and performance (time to solve) were −.18 in the centralized structure and .22 in the decentralized structure. This difference was in the predicted direction, but was not statistically reliable. The partial correlations between leader authoritarianism score and group performance were −.29 in the centralized and .38 in the decentralized structure, a highly significant difference. This finding is important because it suggests that the effects of group member characteristics may depend upon the roles that group members are expected to play in the group.

In summary, the evidence concerning response compatibility predicted from authoritarianism is disappointing, not so much because it is negative, but because of its paucity. The very limited amount of evidence available indicates that certain combinations should be more effective than others, at least under certain circumstances, but considerably more work is required before definitive statements can be made about the most effective combinations under specified circumstances. This research probably must await the development of more adequate measures of authoritarianism.

Investigators in the area of dominance have had better success in showing that compatible groupings lead to more effective group action. Smelser (1961) theorized that different combinations of dominant-submissive individuals would determine the extent to which such individuals can use salient interpersonal techniques, and that the use of such techniques is related to anxiety reduction. When the situation, including the other person in the group, permits the use of techniques consistent with the person's predispositions, anxiety is reduced and the performance of the group is enhanced. If the individual cannot use habitual modes of response, anxiety is likely to occur and group performance will be inhibited or interfered with. Subjects selected on the basis of the dominance scale of Gough's California Psychological Inventory were paired with others who were either similar or dissimilar to them with respect to dominance-submission. Some of the pairs were assigned roles (one dominant, the other submissive) and some were not; within pairs that were assigned roles, personality and roles were congruent for some subjects and not for others. Subjects were given the task of simultaneously operating two trains on a common set of tracks. Switches controlling trains, crossovers, sidings, etc., were controlled by each person; hence, carelessness of either could interfere with the performance of the other. Group scores were based upon mutual round trips, so achievement scores depended upon cooperation.

Smelser was primarily interested in the congruency of personality and role, but his data also provide evidence concerning the compatibility of group composition. Other things equal, a pair consisting of one dominant and one submissive member should be compatible, whereas pairs composed of either two dominant or two submissive individuals should be incompatible. When dominant-submissive pairs were compared with the other two combinations in the no-role-assignment condition, they were found to be more effective (mean performance score = 141.2) than submissive-submissive pairs (mean = 130.2) but approximately equal to the dominant-dominant pairs (mean = 142.0). Under conditions of role assignment, personality and role could be completely congruent only in dominant-submissive pairs; that is, in both dominant-dominant and submissive-submissive pairs, one of the two members was assigned a congruent role and the other an incongruent role. When the dominant-submissive congruent-role pairs were compared with the other two, the dominant-submissive were clearly more effective (mean $=$ 160.4 versus means of 153.3 and 142.9). The dominant-submissive pairs assigned to incongruent roles were least efficient (mean $=$ 116.4).

Essentially similar results were obtained by Fry (1965) in a study of various combinations of ascendant group members. In the first study reported, subjects were divided into quartiles according to scores on the Allport and Allport (1928) A-S Reaction Study for ascendance, matched for intelligence and authoritarianism. Groups of four persons, one from each level of ascendancy, reported to the laboratory for each experimental session. Each subject played a game requiring coordination with each of the other three subjects on three successive trials. The results showed that subjects with discrepant ascendance scores performed better than did those with similar ascendance scores. In a second experiment, subjects were paired as similar if they came from adjacent quartiles and as dissimilar if they came from more remote quartiles. The differences were the same, although not as great as in the first study, a variation that may have been due to the grouping procedure. Considering the results from the investigations of both Smelser and Fry, it is clear that compatible groups with respect to dominance-ascendance are more effective than groups that are incompatible in this respect.

Compatibility based upon ego-defense preference has also been shown to influence interpersonal relations (A. R. Cohen, 1956). Cohen hypothesized that when two persons have a similar type of psychosexual disturbance and this disturbance is aroused, they react to each other in terms of their defenses against the disturbance. Using the Blacky Pictures Test and its auxiliary Defense Preference Inquiry, he identified the following defenses against psychosexual disturbances: projection, avoidance, regression, reaction formation, and intellectualization. Subjects were paired according to type of disturbance and preferred defense against it so that three kinds of pairs were formed: pairs of projectors, pairs with similar defenses other than projection, and pairs with dissimilar defenses. Each pair then discussed material related to their psychosexual disturbance, after which they rated various aspects of the group process. The results revealed that members of projector pairs experienced their interaction as more negative than other pairs, and the more intense the disturbance the greater was the composition effect. Since this negative reaction occurred only when projectors were paired with each other, it appears that it is due to composition of the group rather than to member projection per se. Cohen interpreted this effect in terms of the anxiety aroused through the projection process.

In summary, when group members have personality attributes that predispose them to behave in compatible ways, the group atmosphere is congenial, the members are relaxed, and group functioning is more effective. On the other hand, when member attributes lead to incompatible behaviors, members are anxious, tense, and/or dissatisfied, and group functioning is less effective.

HOMOGENEITY–HETEROGENEITY OF GROUP MEMBERSHIP

It is evident from the preceding discussions that in many studies the incompatible groups were heterogeneous with respect to needs and personality attributes and the compatible groups were homogeneous with respect to these characteristics. Examination of Table 7-1 reveals that the compatible groups composed by Schutz were much more homogeneous than the incompatible ones. Similarly, the groups formed upon the basis of authoritarianism and of dominance also varied with respect to homogeneity-heterogeneity. These types of composition can be distinguished from those we are about to discuss primarily because compatibility theorists assumed that certain homogeneous groups might be compatible and others incompatible; the emphasis was thus placed upon the relationships among particular characteristics rather than upon the mere fact that group member characteristics were homogeneous or heterogeneous. On the other hand, many theorists believe that the homogeneous-heterogeneous dimension is the most important one and so have concentrated their research upon this aspect of group composition. The general assumption is that most group activities require a variety of skills and knowledges; hence, the more heterogeneous the group, the more likely the necessary abilities and information will be available and the more effective the group is likely to be. Indeed, some investigators (for example, Hoffman, 1959; Hoffman & Maier, 1961) assert that heterogeneous groups are generally more effective than homogeneous groups. However, the reader should keep in mind that the distinction between compatibility and homogeneity-heterogeneity is somewhat arbitrary. It should also be remembered that groups are homogeneous or heterogeneous with respect to specific characteristics, not all of which are relevant to the group's activities.

The most common approach to homogeneity-heterogeneity of group composition is a simple comparison of homogeneous and heterogeneous groups, where homogeneity is defined in terms of a single characteristic. For example, groups composed of persons of the same sex are compared with mixed-sex groups, or groups composed of members having similar abilities are compared with groups composed of members having diverse abilities. This has been referred to elsewhere as *trait homogeneity* (M. E. Shaw, 1966). In contrast, some studies have considered several characteristics of group members in defining homogeneity and heterogeneity. In these studies, personality profiles are usually compared to determine degree of correspondence of member characteristics. *Profile homogeneity* may be considered a more powerful determinant of group process than trait homogeneity because of the greater number of characteristics used in the identification of group differences. It is obvious that the effects of one variable can be obscured by uncontrolled variables. On the other hand, different variables reflected in the personality profiles of group members may have opposite effects, and thus some will cancel out others. That is, homogeneity of some traits may facilitate group functioning whereas heterogeneity of other traits may be desirable. These effects can not be ascertained if the investigator considers only profile homogeneity. The best approach is the simultaneous investigation of both profile and trait homogeneity. Unfortunately, this approach is rarely used, as we shall see in the following discussions.

TRAIT HOMOGENEITY

Trait homogeneity may be measured in several ways, all of which are based upon variability of scores earned by group members on some standard measure. In some cases, such as sex composition, the measure may be only visual inspection and the degrees of homogeneity-heterogeneity limited by the number of persons in the group. That is, a two-person group is either homogeneous or heterogeneous; a four-person group may be homogeneous, or it may vary in degree of heterogeneity since there may be three of one sex and one of the other or two of each sex, etc. In the case of personality characteristics, however, the degree of heterogeneity is limited only by the characteristics of the personality measure and the method of computing variability among members' scores. Any standard measure of variability may be used, such as range, standard deviation, or average deviation, or an average of the discrepancy between the scores of each pair of group members may be used. All measures should yield comparable scores, although they would not be perfectly correlated.

The number of characteristics that have been investigated is not great, despite the obvious significance of this aspect of group composition. A review of the literature reveals studies dealing with ability, sex, conceptual systems, authoritarianism, individual prominence, and "interpersonal comparability." Several of these are represented by only one investigation, and none has been studied extensively.

ABILITY HOMOGENEITY-HETEROGENEITY   One early investigation of ability composition was reported by M. E. Shaw (1960), with largely negative results. In an experiment designed for another purpose, four-person groups solved problems in either a centralized or a decentralized power structure, or in either a centralized or decentralized communication network. Homogeneity-heterogeneity scores were computed for each group as the average deviation among member scores on the Scholastic Aptitude Test. These scores were then correlated with achievement scores and ratings of member satisfaction. Correlations between homogeneity-heterogeneity and performance ranged from —.07 to .38; none was statistically reliable. The correlations of homogeneity scores with ratings of satisfaction ranged from —.49 to .30. The —.49 correlation was statistically reliable and occurred in the centralized power structure. Considering the number of correlations computed, this one reliable correlation could have been due to chance factors.

A different approach was taken by Goldman (1965), who was interested in the relative performance of individuals and two-person groups. Subjects from a college population were given the Wonderlic Intelligence Test and divided into high (H), medium (M), and low (L) intelligence levels on the basis of their test scores. Subjects were paired in the following combinations: HH, MM, LL, HM, HL, and ML. The pairs were given a different form of the same intelligence test and instructed to work together on the test, discuss each item, and reach consensus regarding the correct answer. Although Goldman was interested in differences between the performance of pairs and that of individuals, we are interested here primarily in the differences between the homogeneous and the heterogeneous pairs. An examination of Goldman's data reveals that the heterogeneous pairs did slightly better than the homogeneous pairs; however, the HH, HM, and HL did not differ significantly from one another, and the ML and LL did not differ, although the MM was significantly better than either. The results of this study do not reveal a clear superiority of either homogeneous or heterogeneous groups, but improvement on intelligence tests is a rigorous test of group effectiveness, and homogeneous and heterogeneous groups were not equated on intelligence.

A very similar study was conducted by Laughlin, Branch, and Johnson (1969), again for the primary purpose of comparing individual and group performance. Subjects were administered the first part of the Concept Mastery Test (Terman, 1956) and divided into high (H), medium (M), and low (L) intelligence categories. Triads of the following combinations were formed: HHH, HHM, HHL, HML, HMM, HLL, MMM, MLL, and LLL. Again, performance of triads on a second administration of the test was taken as the measure of group effectiveness. This means that there is a problem in comparing homogeneous and heterogeneous triads, because a part of the differences among triads can obviously be attributed to differences in the abilities of members of triads. However, if one compares the average score of HHH, MMM, and LLL groups with that of HML groups, the over-all level of ability should be the same for homogeneous and heterogeneous groups. Examination of data presented by Laughlin et al. reveals that the heterogeneous groups were clearly superior to the homogeneous groups (means = 63.75 and 49.83, respectively). Of the three types of homogeneous groups, only the HHH group (mean = 79.94) performed better than the HML group.

Empirical evidence regarding ability homogeneity and group effectiveness is not entirely consistent, although many of the comparisons were not as well controlled as would be desirable. The best evidence probably is that provided by Laughlin et al., which shows clearly that, other things equal, groups composed of members having diverse abilities perform more effectively than groups composed of members having similar abilities.

SEX HOMOGENEITY-HETEROGENEITY   It is a common observation that women's groups behave differently from men's. Groups of men are commonly believed to be task-oriented and businesslike, and women's groups social-oriented and interested more in gossip than in getting the job done. Despite these stereo- typed beliefs, there is little factual information about sex composition and group process. As early as 1927, it was observed that a same-sex committee is usually more efficient than a mixed one, since same-sex groups spend less time on social-emotional activity (South, 1927). Nevertheless, the small group researcher has responded to these beliefs about sex composition effects by introducing experimental controls rather than by attempting to identify the nature of such effects. That is, he has studied either all-male or all- female groups so that the effects of the sex of group members are the same for all experimental conditions. However, there is limited evidence concerning sex composition and performance and concerning sex composition and conformity behavior.

When members of a group have differing perspectives, the quality of the group's problem solving is likely to be higher than when group members are homogeneous in this regard. We have already seen that males and females have differing viewpoints and behaviors in social situations; hence, mixed-sex groups should be more effective problem solvers than same-sex groups. Hoffman and Maier (1961) compared same-sex and mixed-sex groups as they interacted in case discussions, problem solving, and role playing. Three problems that the groups attempted could be scored quantitatively for quality of solution: the mined road problem, the student assistance fund problem, and the painter-inspector argument problem. The mined road problem required the group to devise a plan for getting five men across a heavily mined road; the student assistance fund problem was a role-playing task requiring that group members decide how to distribute a $3,000 student assistance fund among five students (the group members), each of whom needed and qualified for $1,500 for the next academic year; and the painter-inspector argument task required the group to settle an argument between a painter and an inspector, both of whom were members of the group. Three sex compositions were studied: all-male groups, groups composed of three males and one female, and groups composed of two or three females and one or two males. Mixed-sex groups generally performed more efficiently on all three problems than did same-sex groups. Unfortunately this study was concerned primarily with homogeneity-heterogeneity of personality, and it was not always clear which effects were due to that variable and which to sex composition. The fact that no all-female groups were included also clouds the interpretation of these findings, since it is unclear to what extent the differences may have been due to sex differences per se.

Conformity behavior as a function of sex composition has been studied somewhat more extensively, and the findings are somewhat more readily interpretable. However, there is a methodological problem which complicates the study of sex homogeneity-heterogeneity as it affects conformity behavior: Females typically conform more than males (see Chapter 6), and a heterogeneous group should therefore conform more than a homogeneous male group but less than a homogeneous female group, assuming that there are no composition effects. Any comparison of homogeneous and heterogeneous groups based on sex must take this factor into account. The most common way of doing this is to compare the amount of conformity of members of a given sex in same-sex and mixed-sex groups. In studies using this approach, the results are somewhat conflicting, although the general conclusion that both males and females conform more in mixed-sex than in same-sex groups seems justified. Luchins and Luchins (1955) found that men conformed more to erroneous judgments of a female partner than to those of a male partner. However, from the data obtained in a more complicated experimental situation, Tuddenham, Macbride, and Zahn (1958) concluded that men conformed more in same-sex groups than in mixed-sex groups. Several sex compositions were examined: five men; three men and two women; two men and three women; and five women. These groups were asked to make judgments of visual stimuli (e.g., which line was the same length as a comparison line), information problems (e.g., percentages of persons in the United States over age sixty-five), and opinions (e.g., that most people would be better off if they had never gone to school), after being exposed to unanimously incorrect judgments (or discrepant opinion judgments) by other group members. Although there were some variations in conformity as a function of kind of judgment, the best evidence is probably the total conformity score for all tasks. These data showed that men conformed less in the two-men–three-women groups (mean = 2.12) than in either the all-male groups (mean = 3.80) or the three-men–two-women groups (mean = 4.00). On the other hand, women conformed more in the three-women–two-men groups (mean = 6.60) or in the all-female groups (mean = 5.81), although none of these differences were statistically reliable.

The relationship between sex composition and conformity behavior was also studied by Reitan and Shaw (1964). Groups composed of four men, four women, or two men and two women were tested in the Crutchfield apparatus, which exposed them to unanimous wrong judgments by other group members. The results of this study clearly revealed that all group members, regardless of sex, conformed more in the mixed-sex groups that in the same-sex groups (medians = 2.5 and 2.1, respectively). The interpretation of these results is bolstered by questionnaire responses by group members which showed that members of mixed-sex groups were more concerned about disagreements and were more doubtful of their accuracy than were members of same-sex groups. Reitan and Shaw interpreted these findings as showing a greater concern for interpersonal relations in the mixed-sex groups; men may not wish to be in a position of disagreeing with a woman, or the distracting influences of members of the other sex may reduce an individual's confidence in his judgments.

Although there are some inconsistent findings, the empirical data generally support the hypothesis that individuals conform more in mixed-sex than in same-sex groups, and this effect applies to both men and women. When the group is homogeneous with respect to the sex of its members, group members are task-oriented and hence are more concerned with effective performance than with social-emotional problems. The judgments of others in the group therefore serve as a source of information to be considered along with other relevant information about the task. When there is a conflict between social information and objective information about the task, objective information is weighted more heavily, and less conformity occurs. On the other hand, members of mixed-sex groups are more concerned with social-emotional activity and with a desire to conform to the expectations of others in the group. The majority opinion thus becomes of greater importance than objective information, and greater conformity occurs.

HOMOGENEITY-HETEROGENEITY OF CONCEPTUAL SYSTEMS   In a careful analysis of personality, Harvey, Hunt, and Schroder (1961) identified four conceptual systems which reflect the individual's level of cognitive functioning. System I individuals are said to function at the lower level of abstractness or integrative complexity, whereas System IV individuals, at the other extreme, function at the highest level of integrative complexity. The System I individual finds ambiguity threatening; hence, he invokes authority and normative standards to avoid ambiguity. He tends to use few dimensions or categories in organizing information about his world. System IV individuals, on the other hand, perceive many dimensions of information and use several ways of organizing their world. Their processing of information is flexible and permits many alternative interpretations.

Groups composed of individuals who function at the same conceptual level (homogeneous groups) may be expected to behave in similar ways and thus to perform more effectively on tasks requiring uniformity and less effectively on tasks requiring diversity of opinion than groups composed of individuals differing in level of conceptual functioning (heterogeneous groups). Unfortunately, few researchers have examined this particular aspect of group composition. Studies regarding conceptual system composition have based their analyses upon the relative effectiveness of individuals, largely irrespective of others in the group. In general, predictions have been based upon the relative number of System I and System IV individuals in the group; the more System IV individuals in the group, the better the performance is expected to be. For example, Tuckman (1967) examined the performance of three-person groups of homogeneous System IV's, homogeneous System I's, heterogeneous System IV's composed of one System I and two System IV individuals, and heterogeneous System I's composed of two I's and one IV. He predicted that the groups having the greatest number of System IV members, the homogeneous IV's and the heterogeneous IV's, would perform more effectively than homogeneous I's and heterogeneous I's on "abstract" tasks, but not on "concrete" tasks. The abstract task required the group to make a number of decisions about the best way to take an island held by an enemy. It was described as a task that imposed no structural limitations and permitted multiple solutions and multiple routes to those solutions. The concrete task was the Combat Information Center Task used by Altman and Haythorn (1967b), which required group members to plot inputs from a sonar scope (presumably) on a vertical plotting board. It was said to require single solutions and single routes to those solutions. In general, homogeneous groups performed slightly better than heterogeneous groups, although this was accounted for by the relatively better performance of the homogeneous System IV groups. The homogeneous System I groups performed more poorly than any other composition. The interpretation of these results is complicated by the fact that System IV individuals are more successful than System I individuals, and this effect is confounded with the group composition variable. This study was also complicated by the fact that dominance of group members was also varied in a complex manner, making it difficult to isolate conceptual system composition effects. However, the results generally supported Tuckman's hypothesis that groups in which abstract group members (System IV's) predominate outperform groups in which concrete group members (System I's) predominate, at least when the task is unstructured. No differences were observed on a concrete, structured task.

A more easily interpreted experiment was conducted by Stager (1967). As in Tuckman's study, the relative number of System I–System IV group members constituted the major composition variable. Four-person groups were composed to represent four levels of homogeneity-heterogeneity: 100 percent System IV members; 75 percent System IV and 25 percent System I members; 50 percent System IV and 50 percent System I members; and 25 percent System IV and 75 percent System I members. The groups were equated across composition conditions for intelligence and for dominance tendencies. The task used was the island problem (abstract task), which required that the group plan the capture of the island from the enemy. The group was instructed to act as an equal-status military field staff, and was required to make a series of decisions during seven half-hour periods. Observers coded the interaction of the group members and rated their performance. It was predicted that the amount of search for new information, the number of alternatives suggested, the use of conflict in synthesizing and evaluating alternatives, and role differentiation would increase with increasing percentage of group members of a high conceptual level. The results generally supported predictions, as shown in Figure 7-3. Complexity of communications and evaluations of alternatives increased with increased percentage of members of a high conceptual level, as expected. The generation of alternatives (suggestions) did not vary with group composition, but the ratio of suggestions to evaluations (S/E ratio) decreased with increasing high-conceptual membership. Role flexibility also increased with increased proportion of highs in the group.

The research data are consistent in showing that the heterogeneity of group composition is related to group function, although it is evident that much of this effect can be accounted for by the additivity of individual contributions to the group. That is, the group composition effects are produced by behavior attributable to the individual in any situation and do not depend upon the particular other persons with whom the individual is grouped. Presumably, a four-person group composed of three high-conceptual level persons and one intermediate would be as effective as one with three highs and one low, or even with two or more lows.

In summary, the limited evidence concerning trait homogeneity suggests that (1) groups composed of members heterogeneous with respect to abilities are more effective than those homogeneous in ability, (2) members of mixed-sex groups conform more than members of same-sex groups, and (3) heterogeneity of conceptual systems is not a determinant of group functioning, since such functioning is a result of the proportion of System IV individuals in the group. Studies utilizing profile homogeneity-heterogeneity measures are more promising.

PROFILE HOMOGENEITY

As noted earlier, group problem solving requires a variety of skills, abilities, and perspectives; hence, a group that is heterogeneous on a number of member characteristics is more likely to contain members having the needed attributes and is therefore more likely to be effective than a homogeneous

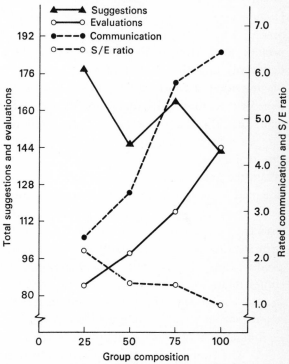

Figure 7-3 The Effect of an Increasing Percentage of Members of a High Conceptual Level in the Group on the Generation of Alternatives, Evaluation of Alternatives, Communication Complexity, and S/E Ratio. (Reprinted with permission from P. Stager. Conceptual level as a composition variable in small-group decision making. *Journal of Personality and Social Psychology,* 1967, **5,** 152–161.)

group. The profile approach to the study of homogeneity-heterogeneity considers several individual attributes rather than a single characteristic as in the trait approach; this enhances the probability that heterogeneous groups will perform more effectively than homogeneous groups. This effect has been demonstrated clearly by Hoffman (1959) and Hoffman and Maier (1961). In the first study, Hoffman composed groups upon the basis of personality profiles obtained by administering the Guilford-Zimmerman Temperament Survey (GZTS) (Guilford & Zimmerman, 1949). This survey measures ten personality traits that are relatively independent dimensions of the personality. Homogeneous groups were made up of individuals who had similar GZTS profiles and heterogeneous groups of individuals who had dissimilar GZTS profiles. Each group solved two problems: the mined road problem (already described) and the change of work problem (CWP). The CWP is a role-playing situation in which three workers report to a supervisor, who is the fourth man in the group. The supervisor requests, at the suggestion of a time-study man, that the three workers work at fixed positions instead of rotating as they have been doing in the past. The group must decide what to do about this request, since the workers would prefer to rotate to relieve monotony. When the group had finished the problem, they responded to a questionnaire designed to measure satisfaction with the solution reached by the group.

The heterogeneous groups performed better on both tasks. On the mined road problem, the heterogeneous groups earned a mean score of 63.1 compared with a mean score of 44.5 earned by the homogeneous groups. The solutions produced on the CWP were scored in terms of old solutions (the group continues rotation), new solutions (acceptance of the supervisor's suggestion), or inventive solutions (attempts to compromise between the old and the new). The heterogeneous groups produced more inventive solutions, although there was no difference between types of groups in satisfaction with the solution achieved.

The Hoffman and Maier (1961) study extended this approach to a variety of tasks in an attempt to determine whether heterogeneous groups would produce higher quality solutions on tasks involving conflicts in values and personal conflicts. The three problems that could be scored objectively were described on page 220. The results of this study were consistent with those reported by Hoffman. Heterogeneous groups produced a higher proportion of "good" solutions on most tasks and equally good solutions on others. The conclusion that high-quality solutions can be obtained more readily from heterogeneous than from homogeneous groups appears justified.

Two other studies may be considered to have adopted the profile approach in the sense that more than one personal attribute was considered in the determination of homogeneity-heterogeneity. Triandis, Hall, and Ewen (1965) conducted three experiments to investigate the relationship between group member heterogeneity and dyadic creativity. In the first experiment, subjects were given eighteen semantic differential scales concerning such issues as war, socialized medicine, and immortality. Dyads were then formed (on the basis of responses to these scales) that were high, medium, or low on cognitive similarity. The dyads were asked to consider social problems, such as how to reduce unemployment in the United States. Half of the dyads had had previous experience with such tasks and half had not. Group products were scored for originality, practicality, and quality. Heterogeneous dyads performed better when they had had experience, but were less effective when they were untrained. In the other two experiments, group composition was based upon attitudinal measures and measures of creativity. Dyads were formed that were (1) homogeneous on both attitudes and creative ability, (2) heterogeneous on both attitudes and creative ability, (3) homogeneous on attitudes but heterogeneous on ability, or (4) heterogeneous on attitudes but homogeneous on ability. The problems were similar to those used in Experiment I; dyads responded to such questions as "How can a person of average ability achieve fame, though he does not possess any particular talents?" Results showed that dyads that are heterogeneous in attitudes and homogeneous in abilities are more creative than other group compositions. The relatively complex manner in which the attitudes and creative abilities were measured and in which groups were formed makes these results difficult to interpret.

A study by Fiedler (1966) also may be considered a study of profile homogeneity, since he investigated groups differing in homogeneity of cultural background. Half of the groups were "homocultural" groups composed of either three French-speaking men or three Dutch-speaking men in the Belgian Navy. The other half were "heterocultural" groups composed of either a French-speaking leader and two Dutch-speaking followers or a Dutch-speaking leader and two French-speaking followers. Since the language difference correlated with wide cultural differences in the men's backgrounds, homogeneity-heterogeneity was actually based upon many personal attributes. Also, it should be evident that language heterogeneity would be expected to inhibit effective group performance, whereas heterogeneity of opinions and perspectives might be expected to enhance performance. This particular way of forming groups therefore produces two opposed forces relative to group effectiveness. This fact probably accounts for the "strikingly small" differences in performance by homogeneous and heterogeneous groups. However, Fiedler, Meuwese, and Oonk (1961) also failed to find a difference in the performance of Dutch groups differing in religious and subcultural homogeneity. It is possible that the characteristics studied by Fiedler and his associates were not relevant to the tasks the groups were assigned to complete.

In summary, groups that are heterogeneous in terms of personality profile usually perform more effectively than groups that are homogeneous in this respect. When the group members have a variety of opinions, abilities, skills, and perspectives, the probability is increased that the group as a whole will possess the characteristics necessary for efficient group performance. Obviously, there are some personal attributes on which group members should be similar for effective group functioning. For example, language homogeneity clearly facilitates group communication, which in turn facilitates group functioning. Heterogeneity on such characteristics can counteract the desirable effects of other types of member heterogeneity, a fact which reinforces our earlier assertion that the best approach to the study of homogeneity-heterogeneity of group membership involves both trait and profile analyses.

PLAUSIBLE HYPOTHESES ABOUT GROUP COMPOSITION

Our rather brief review of studies dealing with group composition effects makes it evident that the research in this area has only begun to reduce the number of plausible hypotheses concerning relations among group member characteristics and group processes. Nevertheless, several hypotheses have tentative support. Each of the following should be considered a plausible hypothesis, but further research is required before some of them can be regarded as *probably* valid.

Hypothesis 1   Individuals contribute differently to the group product, depending upon the particular other individuals in the group.
Although the evidence for Hypothesis 1 is limited largely to a single study (Rosenberg et al., 1955), the hypothesis gains strength from the fact that it is intuitively plausible. A given individual may be active and outspoken when in a group of friends or with submissive strangers, but be very inactive and uncommunicative when in a group of aggressive strangers. Such variations in behavior obviously mean differences in the amount of contribution to the group's products.

Hypothesis 2   Members of high-cohesive groups communicate with each other to a greater extent than members of low-cohesive groups.
Numerous studies have shown that the amount of interaction is greater in groups composed of members who are highly attracted to the group than

in groups composed of members who are less attracted to or are repelled by the group (Back, 1951; French, 1941; Lott & Lott, 1961). Persons who like each other talk with each other more than do individuals who dislike each other. This obvious fact has important implications for group behavior.

Hypothesis 3   *The pattern and content of interaction are more positively oriented in high-cohesive than in low-cohesive groups.*

When the group is highly cohesive, members tend to be friendly and co-operative and to engage in behaviors which facilitate group integration. Members of low-cohesive groups tend to function as individuals rather than as group members; their group-oriented behavior tends to be aggressive and uncooperative (Back, 1951; Shaw & Shaw, 1962).

Hypothesis 4   *High-cohesive groups exert greater influence over their members than do low-cohesive groups.*

One source of social power is interpersonal attraction; hence, it is reasonable to suppose that members of high-cohesive groups should have more power and therefore more influence over each other. This expectation is supported by studies showing that members of high-cohesive groups respond to attempted influence by other group members more than do members of low-cohesive groups (Berkowitz, 1954; Schachter et al., 1951), that members of high-cohesive dyads change their opinions in the direction of their partner's opinion more than members of low-cohesive dyads (Back, 1951), and that members of high-cohesive groups conform to majority judgments more than do members of low-cohesive groups (Bovard, 1951; Lott & Lott, 1961; Wyer, 1966).

Hypothesis 5   *High-cohesive groups are more effective than low-cohesive groups in achieving their respective goals.*

Evidence concerning the relationship between group cohesiveness and group effectiveness is not altogether consistent. Laboratory studies have shown only small increments in favor of the high-cohesive group (Schachter et al., 1951) or no difference in the productivity of high- and low-cohesive groups (Berkowitz, 1954). However, such failures to support Hypothesis 5 are probably due to the fact that groups do not always accept the goal specified by the experimenter. Results of field studies and field experiments generally support the hypothesis (Goodacre, 1951; Shaw & Shaw, 1962; Van Zelst, 1952a; Van Zelst, 1952b). The results of these studies suggest that the high-cohesive group is effective in achieving whatever goals its members establish, although these may not always be the ones of interest to the investigator.

Hypothesis 6   Members of high-cohesive groups are generally better satisfied than members of low-cohesive groups.

Results from both field studies (Gross, 1954; Marquis et al., 1951; Van Zelst, 1952b) and laboratory experiments (Exline, 1957) support the proposition that members of high-cohesive groups are better satisfied with the group and with its products than are members of low-cohesive groups. Members of high-cohesive groups are motivated to interact with others in the groups and to achieve group goals; this motivation leads to effective group functioning and to high member satisfaction.

Hypothesis 7   Compatible groups are more effective in achieving group goals than are incompatible groups.

Although there are some negative results, the bulk of the evidence suggests that groups that are compatible with respect to needs and personality characteristics are able to function more smoothly, devote less of their energy to group maintenance, and thus achieve their goals more effectively than groups whose members are incompatible with respect to needs and personality characteristics (Haythorn et al., 1956b; Sapolsky, 1960; Schutz, 1955; Schutz, 1958; M. E. Shaw, 1959b). However, much more theoretical work is required to determine which individual characteristics may be expected to be compatible and which incompatible; only then can empirical work establish valid hypotheses about specific aspects of group compatibility and group process.

Hypothesis 8   Members of compatible groups are better satisfied than members of incompatible groups.

The studies cited in connection with Hypothesis 7 also provide some support for Hypothesis 8. In addition, studies by Smelser (1961), Fry (1965), and A. R. Cohen (1956) indicate that members of incompatible groups experience anxiety and general dissatisfaction with the group. It seems inevitable that such factors will eventually interfere with effective group functioning.

Hypothesis 9   Other things being equal, groups composed of members having diverse abilities perform more effectively than groups composed of members having similar abilities.

This hypothesis has a firm theoretical foundation as well as adequate empirical support. Group performance usually calls for diverse skills and these are more likely to be found in groups whose members have diverse abilities than in groups whose members have similar abilities. Work by a number of researchers verifies this expectation (Goldman, 1965; Laughlin et al., 1969).

Hypothesis 10   Members conform more in mixed-sex groups than in same-sex groups.

The best evidence suggests that members of mixed-sex groups are more concerned about interpersonal relations and hence conform more than members of same-sex groups, who are more concerned with the task at hand. Despite some inconsistent results (Tuddenham et al., 1958), the empirical data generally support the above hypothesis (Reitan & Shaw, 1964).

Hypothesis 11   Groups whose members are heterogeneous with respect to personality profiles perform more effectively than groups whose members are homogeneous with respect to personality profiles.

Although the evidence supporting this hypothesis is relatively good (Hoffman, 1959; Hoffman & Maier, 1961), there is also some reason to believe that certain composition effects may be obscured by limiting attention to profiles. For example, Fiedler (1966) found little difference between the performance of homocultural and heterocultural groups, a finding which probably resulted from the combination of attributes which should be homogeneous (language) with those which should be heterogeneous (opinions, perspectives) for effective group functioning.

In brief summary: We have just begun the analysis of group composition effects. It is already clear that such effects are far more complex than they appeared to be initially. We may hazard a guess that interpersonal compatibility is the basic variable in group composition; the large task facing group dynamicists is the theoretical analysis of interpersonal relations so that the compatibility-incompatibility of individual characteristics can be identified.

SUGGESTED READINGS

ALTMAN, I., & HAYTHORN, W. W.   The effects of social isolation and group composition on performance. *Human Relations,* 1967, **20,** 313–340.

FRENCH, J. R. P., Jr.   The disruption and cohesion of groups. *Journal of Abnormal and Social Psychology*, 1941, **36**, 361–377.

FRY, C. L.   Personality and acquisition factors in the development of coordination strategy. *Journal of Personality and Social Psychology*, 1965, **2**, 403–407.

GOODACRE, D. M., III.   The use of a sociometric test as a predictor of combat unit effectiveness. *Sociometry*, 1951, **14**, 148–152.

HOFFMAN, L. R., & MAIER, N. R. F.   Quality and acceptance of problem solutions by members of homogeneous and heterogeneous groups. *Journal of Abnormal and Social Psychology*, 1961, **62**, 401–407.

LAUGHLIN, P. R., BRANCH, L. G., & JOHNSON, H. H.   Individual versus triadic performance on a unidimensional complementary task as a function of initial ability level. *Journal of Personality and Social Psychology*, 1969, **12**, 144–150.

LOTT, A. J., & LOTT, B. E.   Group cohesiveness, communication level, and conformity. *Journal of Abnormal and Social Psychology*, 1961, **62**, 408–412.

ROSENBERG, S., ERLICK, D. E., & BERKOWITZ, L.   Some effects of varying combinations of group members on group performance measures and leadership behaviors. *Journal of Abnormal and Social Psychology*, 1955, **51**, 195–203.

SCHUTZ, W. C.   What makes groups productive? *Human Relations*, 1955, **8**, 429–465.

TUCKMAN, B. W.   Group composition and group performance of structured and unstructured tasks. *Journal of Experimental Social Psychology*, 1967, **3**, 25–40.

VAN ZELST, R. H.   Sociometrically selected work teams increase production. *Personnel Psychology*, 1952, **5**, 175–186.

CHAPTER 8

THE SOCIAL ENVIRONMENT: GROUP STRUCTURE

Everyone has been impressed at one time or another by the very different behaviors enacted by an individual in different situations. The aggressive boss greets the demands of his wife with a meek "Yes, dear." The forthright, decisive senator becomes a confused incompetent in mixed-sex social groups. The person who confidently and accurately makes judgments alone often errs when faced with the unanimous wrong judgments of his fellow group members. It may be noted, upon closer examination, that these variations are associated with particular group memberships. A person's behavior is a function of his relationships to others in the group.

When several individuals come together for the first time and begin to interact, these consistent individual differences begin to appear. Some persons talk more than others; some exert more influence upon the group's decisions; some are generally more active than others; some appear to elicit greater respect from other group members; and so on. Differentiations occur among the members of the group such that inequalities exist among them along a variety of dimensions. These differentiations are the basis for the formation of group structure. As differentiations occur, relationships are established among the differentiated parts so that there exists a pattern of relationships in the group. This pattern of relationships among the differentiated parts of the group is often referred to as group structure (Cartwright & Zander, 1953). However, since the group may become differentiated along a variety of dimensions, this conception of group structure means that there is not a single group structure but rather many group structures—in fact, as many structures as there are dimensions along which the group may be differentiated (M. E. Shaw, 1961b). But in reality, the structure of a group is not merely a set of separate, albeit interrelated, patterns of relationships among diverse units; it is an integrated organizational pattern that reflects the totality of differentiated parts that inhere in each individual group member. An adequate conception of group structure must recognize this complexity.

THE NATURE OF GROUP STRUCTURE
Within any given group, the various differentiations result in parts of the group that reside in individual group members. That is, it is the group member who is differentiated from other group members with respect to the particular dimension under consideration. Hence, a given group member may simultaneously be the person who talks most, the person who is most active, the person who has least influence in the group, and so on. The total characterization of the differentiated parts associated with an individual group member may be referred to as the person's *position* in the group. Thus, each group member occupies a position in the group, and the pattern of relationships among the positions in the group constitutes a *group structure*.

Each position is evaluated by the members of the group, including the occupant, in terms of its prestige, importance, or value to the group. Although several positions may enjoy equal status, there almost always exist

status differences such that the group structure is hierarchical. The occupant
of each position is expected to carry out certain functions (enact certain
behaviors) during group interaction. The set of expected behaviors associated
with a position within the group constitutes the *social role* or, more briefly,
role of the occupant of that position. These aspects of group structure are
shown graphically in Figure 8-1. This diagram depicts the structure of a sales
department in a small business. The sales manager occupies the highest status
position; he exerts the greatest influence on the group, has the most power,
is the most respected group member, etc. He is expected to lead the group,
to set policy, to decide group goals, to serve as the final arbiter of disputes,
and to perform similar group functions. The deputy sales managers have
equal status but it is lower than that of the sales manager; they have some
power in the group, have an intermediate amount of influence on the group,
enjoy less respect than the sales manager, but more than others in the group,
etc. They are expected to advise the sales manager regarding policy matters,
to lead others in the group in the performance of their duties, and to perform similar functions for the group. The three salesmen are at the bottom
of the status hierarchy and are of equal status. They have little power, exert

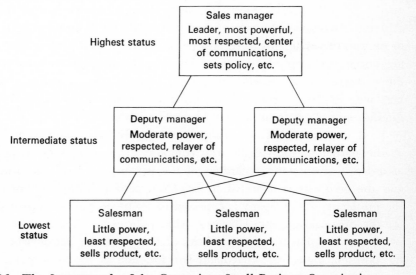

Figure 8-1 The Structure of a Sales Group in a Small Business Organization.

little influence on others in the group, and are generally less respected than the sales manager and his deputies. Their role requires that they carry out the instructions of the managers; that is, their primary function is to sell the product produced by the small business.

The example we have used represents a formal group structure. The positions, roles, and statuses are made explicit by the larger organization of which the group is a part. But the structure need not be explicit, and indeed is not in many informal groups. For example, the participants in a game of bridge may constitute an informal group in which each member has a definite position, and each position may be evaluated differently by the group members. There is a pattern of relationships among positions which constitutes the group structure, and the occupant of each position is expected to engage in certain kinds of behavior which constitute the role associated with that position. Each group member is more or less aware of this group structure and often can verbalize it quite clearly; yet there is no explicit statement concerning the organization of the group. Group structure may therefore be either formal or informal; it may be explicitly recognized and stated or merely implicit in the functioning of the group. In either case, the group structure exerts a pervasive influence upon the behavior of the members of that group.

In addition to the status accorded each position, the group establishes rules which specify acceptable behavior in the group. These "rules of conduct" are called *social norms* or, more simply, *norms*. Norms specify acceptable behavior in the group; they may apply to all members of the group or only to the occupants of certain positions in the group. Role specifications are norms that apply to positions, but not all norms are role specifications. Furthermore, there are wide variations in the degree to which group members may disobey norms without sanctions being administered. The many ramifications of group norms will be explored later.

The structure of the group, once established, is largely independent of the particular individuals who compose the group. A given position is accorded a given status regardless of the person who happens to occupy it, and the occupant is expected to carry out certain behaviors. For example, the president of a company is expected to set broad policy, to plan the goals for the organization, etc. However, what policies and goals are set may depend heavily upon the characteristics of the particular person who occupies the position. Thus, role enactment is a function of the structural aspects of the group (i.e., the expected behaviors associated with a position) *and* the personal characteristics of the occupant. Although the occupant of a position may alter the role associated with the position and the status ascribed to it, group structure tends to be stable over time even when group membership changes.

The stability of group structure has been demonstrated experimentally by Jacobs and Campbell (1961). After a cultural norm had been established with the help of confederates, confederates and old members were removed from the group one at a time as new members replaced them. The arbitrary norm persisted for four or five generations after the last confederate had been removed, after which it decayed. This study shows that at least one aspect of group structure does not depend upon the particular individuals who compose the group. It also suggests that purely arbitrary aspects of group structure, such as the norm in the Jacobs and Campbell experiment, probably will not be perpetuated indefinitely with changing group membership.

STATUS, POSITIONS, AND DIFFERENTIATED PARTS

The status assigned to a given position is a consequence of other characteristics which lead to the differentiation of that position from other positions in the group. The leadership position is ordinarily evaluated more highly than nonleadership positions; the position with the greatest amount of power is accorded higher status than less powerful positions; the position with the greatest communication potential is perceived as more important than other positions; and so on. Thus, the status attributed to a given position is a function of the differentiations that occur in the group and subsumes the various aspects of group structure that are commonly referred to as leadership structure, power structure, sociometric structure, communication structure, and the like. These different aspects· of group structure are intercorrelated such that the leader is usually the most powerful person in the group and has the greatest communication potential (that is, he is the center of the communication network), etc. However, these aspects are independent in the sense that they may be varied independently for experimental purposes, and a number of studies have examined the effects of "single structures." Some of these studies have already been discussed; others will be presented in later sections of this chapter.

It should now be evident that our analysis of group structure and the way we have used the terms *position, status, role,* and *group structure* are somewhat different from other analyses and usages. For example, status has been given a variety of conceptual meanings by group theorists, and it is often confused with position and/or with role. We have reserved a discussion of these differing viewpoints for a later part of this chapter.

ORIGINS OF GROUP STRUCTURE

The formation of group structure is one of the basic aspects of group development; hence, the emergence of positions, statuses, roles, and norms occurs during the process of group formation and development. It is not possible to consider the process of group formation without simultaneously considering the origins of group structure. In Chapter 4, we discussed some of the phases in group development as observed in problem-solving groups (Bales & Strodtbeck, 1951) and in sensitivity training groups (Bennis & Shepard, 1956). In both instances, groups were concerned with problems of relations within the group and the locus of control. We also noted instances of coalition formation and the ways subgroups are formed. In subsequent chapters, we observed the effects of the physical environment, the personal attributes of group members, and the composition of the group on such aspects of the group as the development of leadership, status, and power relations. Consequently, we have already said a great deal about the origins of group structure. Therefore, the present discussion will be restricted to a review of these earlier considerations and an attempt to show how they are interrelated.

According to Cartwright and Zander (1968), the factors that determine group structure can be classified into three major categories: (1) the requirements for efficient group performance; (2) the abilities and motivations of group members; and (3) the physical and social environments of the group. We have seen how each of these sets of variables influences various aspects of group structure, but we have also seen how one aspect of group structure may influence another aspect and thereby the nature of the structure as ·a whole. Thus, a fourth category must be considered: the "single structures" of the group.

REQUIREMENTS FOR EFFICIENT GROUP PERFORMANCE

Groups usually assemble for a purpose, be it to solve a problem of great magnitude or merely to engage in friendly social interaction. The kind of task that the group establishes or accepts as its goal becomes important to group members, who usually consider the best ways of organizing themselves to achieve the goal. This tendency was brought into sharp focus in a study of communication and leader choice in small groups (Shaw & Gilchrist, 1956). Groups of five subjects each were observed in an experiment requiring that group members select problems and solve them via written communication. Each group member was assigned a mailbox and the only way the group members could interact was by writing letters to each other. In eight of ten groups, one or more group members suggested early in the interaction period that the group needed to organize itself for efficient performance. In various ways, members suggested that the group needed a leader, a coordinator, etc., who would direct the activities of others. These suggestions were acted upon in every instance and the group organized itself in a way that group members believed would help them perform efficiently.

In Chapter 4, considerable evidence was cited to show that coalitions form in situations in which greater rewards can be achieved by subgroups than by individuals acting alone. Clearly, concern for outcomes influences the kinds of subgroupings that develop, although the overall efficiency of the group may sometimes be impaired.

CHARACTERISTICS OF GROUP MEMBERS

The kinds of differentiations that are likely to develop in neonate groups are clearly influenced by the attributes of individuals who compose them.

The individual who likes to dominate others will try to establish a centralized power structure with himself at the center; the person who enjoys social interaction will seek to establish an equalitarian structure that permits easy interpersonal exchange; the knowledgeable group member is likely to emerge as the task leader; and so on. In some individuals, a need for structure exists; the individual needs to structure relevant situations in meaningful and integrated ways (Cohen, Stotland, & Wolfe, 1955). When persons having such needs are in group situations, they attempt to structure the group to satisfy this need.

In Chapter 6, it was noted that characteristics of individual group members contribute to group structure in several important ways. Physical superiority, intelligence, and task-related skills were shown to be positively related to leadership emergence. Persons who are positively oriented toward others contribute to the development of group cohesiveness. The individual who is dependable contributes to goal achievement and is more likely to emerge as the leader. These member characteristics, and many other aspects of the group members which have not yet been carefully studied, contribute greatly to the development of group structure.

THE ENVIRONMENTS OF THE GROUP

That the environments of the group play a highly significant role in group process has been emphasized throughout this book. The physical surroundings provide the opportunity for other variables to influence group structure and also exert a direct effect upon the development of structure through the cultural connotations of spatial positions. For example, the well-known study of student housing (Festinger, Schachter, & Back, 1950) revealed clearly that the physical location of living quarters determined the sociometric structure of groups. In Chapter 5, we found that the status of group members was intimately related to their physical position in the group. Persons sitting at the head of the table, for instance, are typically accorded higher status than individuals who sit at the sides. Conversely, an individual who has high status in the group usually chooses to sit at the head of the table. Similarly, an individual who is arbitrarily assigned a central position in a communication network has a high probability of emerging as a leader. The pattern of communication also influences the sociometric structure of the group and the degree to which the occupant of any specific position in the communication network is perceived as having prestige in the group.

SINGLE STRUCTURES AS FACTORS IN THE ORIGINS OF GROUP STRUCTURE

Interaction among the various aspects of group structure also contributes to the development of structure. As noted earlier in this chapter, the group becomes differentiated along a variety of dimensions; hence one can view the group as having several structures—one for each dimension on which the group becomes differentiated. We have designated these structurings with respect to single dimensions as "single structures." Each single structure has an effect upon other such structures. A person who achieves a position of leadership in the group is usually accorded high status; the individual who is attractive to others in the group (a high sociometric status) is more likely to be given a high-status position and to become the leader; sociometric status is one source of power, as we shall see later; and so on. Each single structure is thus a factor in the development of other single structures and, ultimately, the structure of the group. In other words, differentiation along one dimension often is a determinant of differentiation along other group dimensions, each of which influences the total group structure.

In summary: Numerous factors influence the development of group structure; these range from the characteristics of the members who compose the group to the effects of one aspect of the structuring process on others. Although the general nature of these effects is known, few have been studied in careful detail. Perhaps more can be said about the effects of group structure upon group process.

STATUSES, ROLES, AND NORMS

Statuses, roles, and norms are significant concepts for the description and analysis of group structure, and they are interrelated in a variety of ways. Furthermore, these terms have been used with a variety of meanings and have been qualified by various prefixes which give them different connotations. In this section, we will explore the different meanings of status, role, and norm, and attempt to show some of their consequences for group behavior.

STATUS AND POSITION

Status and position are so closely interrelated that the two terms are often used interchangeably (Davis, 1940; Linton, 1936), but they are basically different aspects of group structure. A person's position in a group is the total characterization of the differentiated parts of the group associated with that person; it is his place in the social system. When one identifies a person's position in the group, one is at the same time identifying his relative standing with respect to such dimensions as power, leadership, and attractiveness. Status, on the other hand, refers to the evaluation of that position. It is the rank accorded the position by group members—the prestige of the position.

Some writers have made a distinction between *ascribed status* and *achieved status* (Davis, 1940; Linton, 1936). Ascribed status is attributed to the individual through no fault or merit of his own; it is based upon such arbitrary characteristics as sex, age, and kinship. The individual's personal qualities are the bases for attribution of ascribed status. For example, it is evident that a person who is "born to the color" has higher status than a person who has the misfortune to be born on "the wrong side of the tracks." A Rockefeller has more status than a Snuffy Smith. The person's own achievements or qualifications have little to do with this kind of status. On the other hand, achieved status is based upon individual achievement or failure. A person who is so unfortunate as to be born into an undistinguished family can achieve high status if he has the necessary abilities and motivations. Abraham Lincoln reportedly was born in a log cabin, yet he achieved high status in our society. When such a distinction is made, however, it is clear that status is being used in essentially the same way that we have used the term "position," although prestige rank is also implied. Hence, in the following discussions, the reader should remember that the term "position" refers to a person's place in the social structure and "status" refers to the group members' evaluation of that position.

STATUS EFFECTS

Since the status assigned to a position by group members is the resultant of many aspects of group structure, it is possible to study the effects of each aspect more or less independently of the others or to study the effects of status as such. In subsequent sections of this chapter we will discuss the effects of selected aspects of group structure, namely, power and leadership. Here we are interested in the effects of status differences in the group without regard to the source of these differences. That is, the data concerning these status effects have been derived from examination of various aspects of group structure; hence, any one measure of status differences usually samples only a portion of the total differences among group positions.

In earlier discussions we noted that status contributes to a number of group processes and member behaviors. The high-status person selects a culturally valued spatial position in the group; he conforms to group norms both more and less than the low-status group member, depending upon the situation; and he is likely to have greater influence upon the group's products than lower-status group members. For instance, several studies have shown that the high-status person tends to conform more than the low-status group member (Berg & Bass, 1961), and Homans (1950) suggested that a person must live up to all the norms of the group if he desires high status in the group. On the other hand, Harvey and Consalvi (1960) reported that under financial reward conditions the second-highest-status person in the group was found to conform more than either the highest- or the lowest-status person.

Similarly, Hollander (1958) noted that a group member may be permitted deviation from group norms to the extent that he has contributed to the group's goals in the past and has thus built up "idiosyncrasy credit." The conclusion to be drawn from these findings is that the high-status person, to a greater extent than the low-status person, is permitted to deviate from group norms in an attempt to aid in goal achievement, although he usually conforms more than low-status members.

Gergen and Taylor (1969) have identified another source of variation in conformity as a function of status: the degree to which the context emphasizes productivity or solidarity. When the situation stresses productivity, the high-status person is reluctant to conform to the expectations of low-status persons. According to Gergen and Taylor, this reluctance derives from the fact that success in achieving the goal depends upon the high-status person's freedom to marshal resources for goal attainment; however, conformity to the expectations of the low-status person may be seen as an erosion of the high-status person's standing in the group. Under conditions which emphasize solidarity, this effect does not occur, since conformity does not represent a threat to either goal achievement or status.

Status differences exert a powerful influence upon the pattern and content of communications in the group. In general, more communications are directed toward the high-status group member, and the content of such messages tends to be more positive than messages directed downward in the status hierarchy. Several laboratory and field studies have provided information concerning this effect. Thibaut (1950) varied status differences in groups composed of ten to twelve boys between the ages of ten and twelve. Some of the boys were assigned a menial task (so described by the experimenter to the boys) and the others an attractive task that was described in prestige terms. In some of the groups, it was indicated that perhaps statuses could be changed, whereas in others no such manipulation was introduced. With increasing status differences, the lows increased in total amount of communication addressed to the highs, but decreased in the proportion which was aggressively toned. In a study having a very similar design, Kelley (1951) observed a number of interesting effects of status upon communication: (1) Low-status group members communicated more task-irrelevant information than the high-status group members. (2) High-status persons appeared to be restrained from communicating criticisms of their own jobs to those of lower status; for example, their communications to low-status members contained relatively few expressions of negative attitudes or confusions about their own jobs. (3) Communication with high-status persons apparently served as a substitute for real upward locomotion for low-status persons who had little or no possibility of real upward locomotion.

The effect of status on message content was also demonstrated in a rather different experimental situation by Worchel (1957). Students were frustrated either by a high-status faculty member or by a low-status student, after which they were given an opportunity to communicate with the frustration agent. According to the frustration-aggression hypothesis, the target of the frustration should express aggression toward the frustration agent. Worchel found that the amount of verbal aggression directed toward the agent decreased with the increasing status of the agent.

The tendency for communications to be directed upward in the status hierarchy has been demonstrated in an ingenuous field experiment conducted by Back, Festinger, Hymovitch, Kelley, Schachter, and Thibaut (1950). Rumors were planted in an industrial organization containing five levels of status, and selected members of the organization cooperated in reporting from whom they first heard one of the rumors. Of seventeen communications, eleven were upward in the status hierarchy, four were at the same level, and two were downward. There also appeared to be restraining forces against the communication of rumors that were critical of high-status persons.

ROLE AND ROLE EFFECTS

Each position in the group structure has an associated role which consists of the behaviors expected of the occupant of that position. The principal of a school is expected to supervise the teachers of the school, to plan and organize the school's program, to assist teachers with tutorial and disciplinary problems, to deal with parent-teacher relations, and to engage in many other school-related activities. The school custodian, on the other hand, is expected to maintain the building and grounds, but has no responsibility for the school's educational program. The head of a city fire department is expected to carry out whatever behaviors will contribute to making the city safe from fires. These expected behaviors are generally agreed upon not only by the occupant of the position but also by other members of the group and often by members of other groups and of the larger society in which the group is embedded.

As in the case of status, the term "role" may be viewed in several ways. In addition to the definition that we are using, which might be designated the "expected role," some writers have identified a "perceived role" and an "enacted role." The perceived role is the set of behaviors that the occupant of the position believes he should enact. This may or may not correspond to the expected role, since the latter depends upon the perceptions of others. The enacted role is the set of behaviors an occupant actually carries out. Again, the perceived role may be different from the enacted role if the occupant fails to do some things that he believes he should do or if he does some things that he believes he should not do as the occupant of the position. To the extent that there are differences among these different aspects of role, the probability of conflict and group dysfunction is increased. In most instances, however, there is relatively good agreement between expected and perceived roles; when the enacted role departs too much from the expected role, the role will change or the occupant will be evicted. In the following discussions, we will use role in the sense of expected behaviors of a position occupant.

The effects of roles upon behavior and group process have not been studied extensively, perhaps because the definition of role specifies the kinds of behaviors that are expected. Furthermore, studies are difficult to interpret because the definition of role is confused with other aspects of the group structure. For example, Slater (1955) conducted a study of role differentiations in groups of high and low status-consensus. He studied twenty groups, varying in size from three to seven persons, as they discussed an administrative case for forty minutes. He found that three types of role structures emerged: (1) The rare case in which the leader performs all functions and essentially no differentiation occurs. This is found only in high-consensus groups. (2) Moderate specialization occurs in high-consensus groups when the specialists do not have the exceptional talent required to establish the first type of role structure. (3) Extreme specialization occurs when the individual performs a specialty because he *must* rather than because it is good for the group. This is a low-consensus phenomenon. As can be seen, this study dealt primarily with the development of role differentiations rather than with the effects of roles. However, it was observed that the extreme form of role differentiation disrupted the group, an effect which may be due to low status-consensus rather than to the form of role differentiation.

A study by Torrance (1954) gives some evidence of the consequences of role for influence on the group, although again there is confusion with other aspects of the group's structure. Torrance studied sixty-two permanent and thirty-two temporary air crews consisting of pilot, navigator, and gunner. The roles of these positions are clearly different: The pilot is supposed to fly the plane, the navigator to direct it to its destination, and the gunner to protect it. But there are also other differences: The pilot has the highest status (he is the commander of the ship and usually has the highest military rank), the navigator has the second highest status, and the gunner the lowest status. The Torrance study revealed that the amount of influence on the group's decisions was generally correlated with role, with the pilot having the greatest influence and the gunner least, an effect which was more pronounced in the permanent than in the temporary groups. As we have seen, however, this could be caused by status differences rather than role differences.

ROLE CONFLICT   A given individual occupies many different roles in many different groups. In most instances, the behaviors specified by the different roles are not incompatible (for example, the physician usually is not also an undertaker) so long as different roles are not made salient at the same time. The policeman may be expected to protect the property and lives of members of the community, but in the role of father he is expected to protect his family. Under normal circumstances, there is no role conflict since enactment of the policeman role is not required at the same time as enactment of the father role. Under unusual circumstances, however, the occupant of positions in different groups may be called upon to enact both roles simultaneously. When this happens, the individual will resolve the conflict in the direction of greatest group attraction; he will elect to enact the role required by the group which has the greatest importance for him. This form of resolution was revealed strongly in the disastrous Texas City fire (Killian, 1952). When oil refineries caught fire and endangered the entire city, policemen were faced with role requirements that were obviously conflicting: to enact the policeman role and help protect the community or to enact the father role and look to the needs of their families. In every case except one the conflict was resolved in favor of the father role; in the one exception it turned out that there was no conflict at all—the policeman knew that his family was safe in another town visiting friends. A similar conflict has been observed in a strike by telephone operators in a small town. As a member of the telephone union, the operator role required staying off the job for the duration of the strike, whereas the role associated with community membership required the operator to return to the job when failure to do so would be greatly detrimental to the community. In this instance, the direction of the resolution was not so consistent. Some of the operators remained away from the job throughout the strike despite sanctions by their community group; others returned to the job when the consequences for the community became serious.

NORMS AND BEHAVIOR

Norms are rules of conduct established by the members of the group to maintain behavioral consistency. If each member of the group decided for himself how he would behave on each interaction, no one would be able to predict the behavior of any other member, and chaos would reign. Norms provide a basis for predicting the behavior of others and thus enable the individual to anticipate the others' actions and to prepare an appropriate response. Such rules also serve as a guide for the group member's own behavior and thus reduce ambiguity, which many persons find intolerable.

Social norms represent standardized generalizations concerning expected behavior in matters that are of some importance to the group. Thus, they are special kinds of concepts and, like all concepts, refer to classes or groupings of items. That is, a norm usually does not identify a specific behavior, such as saying "Good morning" when one encounters an acquaintance; rather, the norm specifies that one should greet an acquaintance pleasantly with some acceptable form of address. Norms are distinguished from concepts in general by their evaluative nature; norms refer to what *should* be done. Norms thus represent value judgments with respect to modes of behavior in social situations.

Norms are social products which are formed during the course of social interaction. A standard may be imposed from without (for example, the school board may require that pupils dress in a certain way), but such imposed standards do not become norms unless they are accepted as right and proper by the pupils. This fact, of course, raises an important question that has not been answered satisfactorily: How many group members must accept a standard of conduct in order for it to become a norm? Everyone? A majority? It is clear that one cannot point to an arbitrary proportion of group members that must accept a rule before it becomes a norm, but it is also clear that a norm is rarely accepted by all members of the group. Most students of group dynamics regard a standard as a norm if more than half of the group members agree that it is a norm.

We can now identify some of the characteristics of norms that are important for understanding how norms develop and how they influence behavior in groups. First, a group does not establish norms about every conceivable situation; norms are formed only with respect to things that have some significance for the group. Second, norms may apply to every member of the group, or they may apply only to certain members. For example, all members of a bridge team are expected to follow suit whenever possible; however, only dummy is expected to display the faces of his cards. Those norms which apply to particular group members are usually norms which specify the role of the occupant of a position in the group structure. Third, norms vary in the degree to which they are accepted by the group; some norms are accepted by almost everyone (for instance, that an automobile driver should stop his vehicle for a red light) whereas others are accepted by some group members and not by others (for instance, that the driver of a slow-moving vehicle should drive in the outside lane). Fourth, norms vary in range of permissible deviation. When a person deviates from a norm, some form of sanction is usually directed toward him (Schachter, 1951). Sanctions vary from mild disapproval to the death penalty, depending upon the severity of the outcome of the deviation and the circumstances under which it occurs (see Shaw & Reitan, 1969). But norms differ with respect to the amount of deviation that is tolerable. Some norms require strict adherence to the rule (for example, thou shall not kill), whereas others permit a wide range of behavior that is regarded as acceptable (for example, gentlemen shall not be impolite to ladies).

CONFORMITY TO NORM REQUIREMENTS   Not only do norms vary in the degree to which conformity is required, but there are also variations in the degree of conformity to a particular norm under differing conditions. We have already noted many variables that influence degree of conformity, but we have not considered in detail the concept of "conformity" and the methods that have been used to study it in the laboratory. The everyday conception of conformity is that it consists of blind, unreasoning, slavish adherence to the patterns of behavior established by others or to the demands of authority. Even among social psychologists there is the pervasive conception of conformity as agreement with the majority only for the sake of agreement. Fortunately, some investigators (for example, Deutsch & Gerard, 1955) have begun to make a distinction between this kind of conformity (based upon normative social influence) and other kinds of conformity (for example, that based upon informational social influence). Whereas normative social influence results from a desire to conform to the expectations of the group, informational social influence is the result of the value that conformity may have for the individual. He uses the majority behavior as a source of information to help him make the best response that he can in the situation in which he finds himself. Although this conceptual distinction between types of conformity is logical and undoubtedly significant for the interpretation of conformity behavior, most investigators have not made the distinction. Nor have they adopted the everyday conception of conformity. In fact, they have simply ignored the individual's reasons for his behavior and have defined conformity as the agreement of the individual's response with that of the majority of the group.

The methods of study vary greatly in details, but most investigators adopt one or the other of two basic procedures. The first experimental paradigm is exemplified by the classical study of conformity conducted by Solomon Asch (1952). A naïve subject is exposed to obviously incorrect judgments of a unanimous majority in a face-to-face group. This is accomplished by means of confederates who have been instructed by the experimenter to make incorrect responses. In the Asch study, subjects were shown slides containing four lines, including a standard and three stimulus lines. The subject's task was to select the stimulus line which was the same length as the standard. Conformity is measured by the frequency with which the naïve subject's choice agrees with that of the unanimous majority. Since few errors in judgment occur when the subject faces the task alone, such agreement is presumed to be due to the influence of the majority.

The other method is a simulated group, of sorts, first suggested by Crutchfield (1955). Each group member is seated in an isolated cubicle from which he signals his judgments to the experimenter by throwing an electric switch. He has before him a response panel on which the choices of others in the group presumably are shown. Several persons may be present at any one session, but each person is designated as the last one to make his judgment; hence all other choices are "known" to him at the time he responds. Obviously, the "judgments" of the other group members are determined by the experimenter. Stimuli and method of estimating conformity are the same as in the Asch paradigm.

Although one may raise grave questions about this definition of conformity and these methods of studying the factors determining conformity, much has been learned by these procedures. Also, there is evidence that the results obtained agree very well with results obtained in natural settings, as we shall see later. We are now ready to consider the classes of variables that influence conformity behavior and to try to show how the forces toward uniformity combine to produce a given level of conformity behavior.

Four general classes of variables influence conformity to group norms: (1) personality characteristics of group members; (2) the kinds of stimuli evoking the response reflecting conformity; (3) situational factors; and (4) intragroup relationships (Reitan & Shaw, 1964). *Personality* factors refer to the characteristics of the individual group member that predispose him to conform to group norms. In Chapter 6 we noted that more intelligent persons are less likely to conform than less intelligent persons; women conform more than men; there is a curvilinear relationship between age and conformity; and authoritarians conform more than nonauthoritarians. It has also been shown that there is a general predisposition to acquiesce, which is positively related to conformity (Frye & Bass, 1963). In addition, Crutchfield (1955) reported negative correlations between conformity and measures of leadership ability $(r = -.30)$, tolerance $(r = -.30)$, social participation $(r = -.36)$, and responsibility $(r = -.41)$. All these correlations are relatively low, a result attributable in part to the unreliability of the personality measures, but due largely to the fact that personality factors are relatively less powerful in determining conformity behavior than other classes of variables listed above.

Stimulus factors include all those aspects of the problem faced by the individual; that is, the stimuli that are related to the norm to which the individual is presumably conforming. It will be recalled that, in the typical laboratory experiment on conformity behavior, the norm is established by exposing the subject to unanimously false (incorrect) responses to a stimulus by other group members (in fact or simulated). Conformity to this arbitrarily established "group norm" is measured by the extent of agreement of the subject's response to the stimulus with that reportedly made by other group members. Such stimuli include the autokinetic phenomenon (judgment of perceived movement of a stationary pinpoint of light in a dark room), counting a series of metronome clicks, estimating areas of geometric figures, judging the length of lines, and so on. In general, the more ambiguous the stimulus situation, the greater will be the conformity behavior. Consider the four stimuli mentioned above. The autokinetic situation requires the individual to judge the movement of a light that is really stationary, although it appears to move; hence, the individual is faced with a very ambiguous situation and he is very uncertain about the actual amount of perceived movement. Under these conditions, about eight of every ten subjects yield to unanimous group pressure (Sherif & Sherif, 1956). The ambiguity of metronome clicks can be varied greatly, but in the typical situation the stimulus is moderately ambiguous and the person is uncertain about the accuracy of his count. About six of every ten subjects conform to the perceived group norm with this kind of stimulus (Shaw, Rothschild, & Strickland, 1957). When geometric figures are used as stimuli, the task is to judge the relative areas of circles, squares, triangles, etc. In this instance, there is an objectively correct answer, but the subject would probably have to be a mathematical genius to compute the areas in the time allotted and under the conditions of stimulus presentation. Typically, about half of the subjects conform at least some of the time to unanimous group pressure (Nickols, 1964). The least ambiguous stimuli listed above are the lines originally used by Asch (1951) and later by many other investigators. The subject is asked to judge which of three vertical lines is the same length as a standard line which is presented at the same time. Typically, there is little doubt about the correct answer; when individuals respond in isolation, few errors of judgment are made. Nevertheless, about one-third of all subjects show some degree of conformity to unanimous group pressure in the form of a false norm. These four types of stimuli vary in degree of ambiguity roughly in the order presented here, and it is evident that the degree of conformity corresponds very closely to the degree of ambiguity. Clearly, then, the stimulus situation exerts a powerful influence upon conformity behavior; it appears to be the most powerful set of variables that has been identified.

Situational factors include all aspects of the group context except the stimulus situation; it refers to such variables as size of the group, unanimity of the majority, structure of the group, and so on. In his early studies, Asch (1951) found that conformity to unanimous false judgments increased with group size up to size four, and was essentially constant thereafter. Although this precise effect has been questioned (Gerard, Wilhelmy, & Conolley, 1968), it is evident that the size of the group is an important determinant of conformity. Conformity increases with size up to some maximum (size four or perhaps more), probably because the larger number of group members who give the same response simultaneously weakens the subject's confidence in his own judgment and strengthens his belief in the group norm. Asch also found that conformity was greater when the majority was unanimous than when one or more other group members (confederates) gave the correct response. For example, when one member was instructed to respond correctly to the lines stimulus, the percentage of conformity decreased from the usual 33 percent with a unanimous majority to 5.5 percent. Shaw et al. (1957) demonstrated that this effect was due to the lack of unanimity rather than to the support given by the instructed confederate. A group member who merely said that he was unable to make a judgment had similar effects on conformity behavior. These investigators also found greater conformity in a decentralized communication network than in a centralized one, a finding which has also been reported by Goldberg (1955). These several studies show clearly that the social context in which the group interaction occurs has a marked effect on conformity behavior of group members.

The term *intragroup relationships* refers to the relations among the members of the group. This category includes such variables as the kind of pressure exerted, the composition of the group, how successful the group has been in achieving past goals, the degree to which the person identifies with the group, and so on. All these variables have been shown to be related to conformity. Kelley (1952) suggested that the group serves both a normative function and a comparative function, a distinction which is similar to the Deutsch and Gerard (1955) distinction between normative and informational social influence. Normative social influence was defined as pressure to conform to the positive expectations of group members, whereas informational social influence was based upon the individual's use of others' responses as a source of information about the external world. Deutsch and Gerard were able to show that subjects respond differentially to these different kinds of pressure. We have already noted in Chapter 6 that conformity increases with identification with the group (cohesiveness) and that mixed-sex groups generally produce greater conformity than same-sex groups. Group composition effects were also revealed in a study by Costanzo, Reitan, and Shaw (1968), which found that conformity is influenced by both the perceived competence of the majority and the subject's perception of his own competence relative to the task. Figure 8-2 illustrates these effects. Perceived competence was manipulated by the experimenter reporting performance scores on nonpressure trials to the group members. When the subject (minority) has high confidence in his own competence, he conforms less than when he perceives his competence to be low, regardless of the competence of the group majority. However, he conforms more when the perceived competence of the majority is high than when it is low, regardless of the level of his own competence. This effect has also been demonstrated by several other investigators (Hollander, 1960). Kidd and Campbell (1955) have shown that the past success of the group also contributes to conformity behavior, and Schneider (1968) reported that both

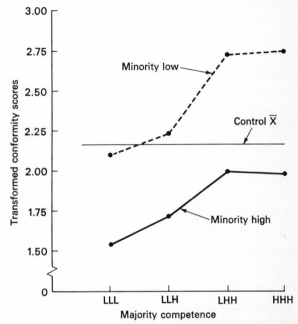

Figure 8-2 Conformity at Two Levels of Minority Competence as a Function of Majority Competence. (Reprinted with permission from P. R. Costanzo, H. T. Reitan, & M. E. Shaw. Conformity as a function of experimentally induced minority and majority competence. *Psychonomic Science,* 1968, **10**, 329–330.)

whites and blacks conformed more to a white majority than to a black majority.

In summary, it is clear that conformity to group norms is influenced by a variety of factors which can be classified into the four sets of variables outlined above. But an important question is raised by these findings: Are the effects of these variables independent and additive, or do they operate as alternative stimuli for conformity behavior? For example, if a given stimulus elicits 50 percent conformity behavior with a randomly selected population, can this degree of conformity be increased or decreased by varying the size of the group or by selecting more or less conformity-prone subjects? Or stated another way, if a given stimulus situation produces 50 percent conformity across a variety of group sizes and a unanimous majority of three produces 30 percent conformity (across a variety of stimulus situations), will the same stimulus plus a majority of three produce 80 percent conformity, or perhaps only 50 percent? This question was attacked experimentally by Nickols (1964). She systematically varied a personality variable (acquiescence), a stimulus variable (ambiguity), and a situational variable (size of the group). Acquiescence was varied by selecting subjects who scored either high or low on the Bass (1956) Social Acquiescence Scale; stimulus ambiguity was varied by using the Asch lines task (an unambiguous stimulus) and the autokinetic light (an ambiguous stimulus); and size of group was varied from two to four persons (a "majority" of one versus a majority of three). Since prior experimental evidence had indicated that stimulus factors have the greatest influence on conformity and personality factors the least effect, Nickols weighted the three variables in the following way: stimulus—3; group size—2; and personality of group member—1. She then arbitrarily assumed that the difference between the high and low level of each variable should be weighted by a factor of 2. Using these weights, she was able to compute a conformity index for purposes of predicting amount of conformity in each of the several experimental conditions. For example, if a given individual scored low on the acquiescence scale, was exposed to the unambiguous stimuli, and was a member of a two-person group, his conformity index would be $1 + 2 + 3 = 6$. If he happened to be at the other extreme (high on acquiescence, exposed to an ambiguous stimulus situation, and a member of a four-person group), each weight would be doubled and his conformity index would be 12. Figure 8-3 shows the relationship between this index and mean conformity under the various experimental conditions. It can be seen that the index predicted the amount of conformity extremely well, thus supporting the proposition that the effects of the variables influencing conformity behavior are additive. The curve shown in Figure 8-3 is slightly ogival. This probably reflects the fact that some minimal amount of pressure is required to elicit any conformity behavior, on the one hand, and the fact that when the forces are strong enough to elicit maximum conformity, additional force has no further effect, on the other hand.

The interested reader will probably ask at this point whether these laboratory findings have any relationship to behavior in natural situations. Fortunately, several field studies have shown that such behavior does indeed

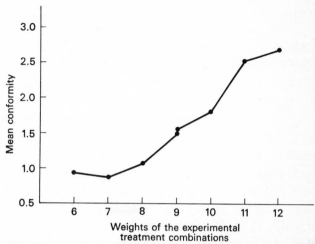

Figure 8-3 Mean Conformity Scores for the Experimental Treatment Combinations, Ordered in Terms of Weights Assigned to the Combinations of the Variables. (Reprinted with permission from S. A. Nickols. A study of the additivity of variables influencing conformity. Unpublished doctoral dissertation, University of Florida, Gainesville, 1964.)

occur in natural settings. Lefkowitz, Blake, and Mouton (1955) observed obedience and violations of traffic signals as a function of a model who either obeyed or violated the signal. Observations were made at three different street corners in Austin, Texas, on three afternoons during the hours of 12:00 to 1:00, 2:00 to 3:00, and 4:00 to 5:00. No policeman was on duty, although the study had the approval of the police department. The traffic lights at the experimental corners had a forty-second "wait" signal, followed by a fifteen-second "walk" signal. Observations were made during the "wait" period. The 2,103 pedestrians who happened by during the observation periods unknowingly served as subjects. Observations were made under five conditions: (1) a control (violations were merely recorded); (2) a high-status conformer (a well-dressed person approached the corner and waited for the walk signal); (3) a high-status violator (a well-dressed confederate violated the signal); (4) a low-status conformer (a poorly dressed confederate waited for the walk signal); and (5) a low-status violator (a poorly dressed confederate walked against the light). In the control condition subjects violated the signal only 8 times in 742 instances; in the conformer conditions subjects violated the signal only 4 times in 771 instances; but in the violator conditions the signal was violated 52 times in 526 instances. Clearly, the confederate who violated the traffic signal influenced others to do likewise. The bulk of the violations (40) occurred with the high-status violator. A conforming confederate had little effect, probably because there were few violators in the control condition.

A somewhat similar study was conducted by Barch, Trumbo, and Nangle (1957) in Greater Lansing, Michigan. They observed the signaling behavior of automobile drivers for a period of sixty-one hours over a four-week period. Pairs of cars were selected according to the following criteria: Both cars were turning, there was no car between them, and the second car was 100 feet or less behind the lead car. Altogether, 1,195 pairs were observed, of which 723 lead drivers signaled and 472 did not. Conformity was recorded if the follower either signaled when the lead car did or did not signal when the lead car did not. When the leader signaled, the follower signaled 432 times and failed to signal only 291 times; when the leader did not signal, the follower signaled only 226 times and failed to signal 246 times. Again, the effect of the behavior of others was demonstrated in a natural situation.

Similar effects have been observed by Freed, Chandler, Mouton, and Blake (1955) with respect to conformity to "do not enter" signs on doors, and by Rosenbaum and Blake (1955) with respect to volunteering behavior. There can be little doubt that conformity occurs not only in the laboratory but in "real-life" situations as well. In fact, the principles illustrated by these investigations have been put to practical, if somewhat questionable, use by organizations soliciting funds by mail. The target of the fund-raising scheme receives a request for money, along with a list of persons who reportedly have donated specified amounts of money to the cause. Presumably, this creates the perception of a social norm which influences the target person to also donate to the fund.

CONSEQUENCES OF CONFORMITY   Conformity is generally rewarded by the group; deviancy is punished, or at least not rewarded. Thus, it is not surprising that there is general conformity to group norms. To many observers, conformity is an undesirable outcome of group interaction. It is seen as leading to loss of individuality, restriction of creativity, and reduction of all group members to the level of mediocrity (cf. Asch, 1951; Milgram, 1964;

W. H. Whyte, 1957). These undesirable consequences undoubtedly would follow from a blind, unreasoning "follow the crowd" type of conformity. Fortunately, there is no evidence that behaving in accordance with group norms *necessarily*, or even usually, results from such Babbittry. In many, perhaps most, instances, there are good and sufficient reasons for conforming to group norms. Conformity introduces order into the group process and provides for the coordination of individual behaviors. If no one conformed, group members would not know what behavior to expect from others in the group and so would have no basis for determining appropriate courses of action for effective group functioning. Consider a society in which each automobile driver decided for himself which side of the road he would drive on at any given moment, or a bridge game in which each player decided for himself the meaning of any particular bid or the value of each contract. It is clear that effective group interaction would be impossible under such circumstances.

Although most studies have emphasized the negative consequences of conformity, some investigators have examined its positive effects. Berkowitz and Daniels (1963) have shown that conformity to a social norm can lead to desirable outcomes even when there are few or no social or material rewards to be gained by conforming to the norm. In their experiments each subject played the role of "worker," supposedly under the direct supervision of a peer (a stranger) who played the role of "supervisor." In one experimental condition, the subjects were told that the evaluation of the supervisor would depend upon the worker's productivity (high dependency), and in another condition that the evaluation would not be affected by his performance (low dependency). Berkowitz and Daniels postulated a social responsibility norm that should cause the worker to try to help the supervisor reach his goal even though there were no rewards for doing so. The results of this study supported the hypothesis: The workers produced significantly more in the high-dependency condition than in the low-dependency condition.

A somewhat different approach was used by Milgram to show that in some situations conformity frees the individual to behave in accordance with his own standards of conduct rather than in accordance with authoritative coercion. In one study (1963), he demonstrated that subjects in an experimental situation would administer exceedingly strong electric shock to another person when instructed to do so by the experimenter. In a later series of studies, Milgram (1965) observed similar effects, but the introduction of confederates who defied the experimenter's authority changed the subjects' behavior. In Experiment I, subjects were instructed to give increasingly strong shocks to a victim, despite the victim's protests and cries of anguish. Most of the subjects complied with the experimenter's commands, even though this behavior was incompatible with normal standards of conduct. In Experiment II, two confederates were instructed to defy the experimenter's authority when the shock to be administered reached the "very strong" level (about midway in the range, which went from "slight shock" to "danger: severe shock"). Under these conditions, only four of forty subjects continued to obey the experimenter. In a third experiment, the procedure was the same as in Experiment II except that the two confederates followed the experimenter's orders without question. The results were essentially the same as in Experiment I; the obedience of the confederates had little effect on the behavior of the naïve subjects. Thus, it can be seen that conformity to an experimentally established norm can sometimes free the individual from the pressures of authority and enable him to follow his own standards.

In conclusion, conformity to group norms can be either positive or negative. Some agreed-upon standards of conduct are essential for effective group action, and sometimes conformity can result in altruistic behavior or behavior that agrees with the individual's own moral or ethical standards. Conformity produces the undesirable negative effects so frequently attributed to it when the group member conforms only for the sake of conformity.

DEVIATION FROM NORM REQUIREMENTS   Obviously, not every group member conforms to the norms of the group, and deviancy usually brings some sanctions to the deviant. Many years ago, observers in industrial organizations noted that members of work groups typically established production standards (norms) which were adhered to by most group members (Homans, 1950; Roethlisberger & Dickson, 1939). When a worker deviated too much from the standard, he was subjected to ridicule and various other forms of sanction. If the worker produced too much, he was referred to as a "speed king" or "ratebuster"; if he produced too little, he was called a "chiseler." One especially interesting means of controlling the overproducer was referred to as "binging," a game in which one man hit another on the arm, whereupon the second man had the right to retaliate. The object was to see who could hit the harder, but obviously this could be used to interfere with productivity.

These kinds of sanctions have also been demonstrated in the laboratory. Schachter (1951) conducted a study designed to reveal some of the processes related to reactions to deviancy from an experimentally created group norm. Four types of clubs were established, each representing a different degree and combination of cohesiveness and relevance (importance of the discussion topic to the members of the club). Each club consisted of five to seven members, all of whom were male college students. Each member of the group read a case history of a juvenile delinquent and then indicated on a 7-point scale what he thought should be done with the delinquent. The opinion of each group member was then announced to the group, followed by the opinion of each of three paid participants. The paid participants (confederates) were assigned three different roles: (1) The *deviate* chose an extreme position and maintained it throughout the subsequent group discussion; (2) the *mode* chose the modal opinion of the group and maintained it throughout the discussion; and (3) the *slider* chose an extreme position but allowed himself to be influenced so that by the end of the discussion he was at the modal position. The case was then discussed for forty-five minutes, during which time an observer recorded selected aspects of the group interaction. Postexperimental questionnaires were also used to obtain measures of the group members' reactions to the confederates. The results indicated clearly that initially communications were directed primarily toward the deviates (the deviate and slider). Communications to the slider decreased as he approached the modal group opinion. Communications to the deviate increased up to a point and then decreased, but this effect was limited to group members who rejected the deviate. The magnitude of these effects varied with cohesiveness and relevance, but the general picture that emerged was one of increasing attempts to get the deviate to conform, followed by complete acceptance if he succumbed or rejection if he maintained his deviant position. The moral of this story seems to be that it is all right to be a deviate, so long as you are "flexible" enough to change your mind when the majority of the group points out the error of your ways!

In the preceding pages, we have seen how group structure is an inevitable consequence of group interaction, and we have noted the many ways in which group structure influences the behavior of group members. We are now ready to examine some specific aspects of group structure that play an especially important function in the determination of group process. In the next section we will consider the power associated with positions in the group structure (social power), and in the following section we will examine the leadership role in small groups.

SOCIAL POWER

There is usually some variation in the power associated with different positions in the group structure. Most group dynamicists would agree with this statement, but different persons would probably interpret its meaning differently. Everyone believes that there is something that can be called power, but there is little agreement about its characteristics. Social power is also sometimes confused with other aspects of group structure. For example, Emerson (1964) and Alkire, Collum, Kaswan, and Love (1968) appear to use "status" and "power" interchangeably; and in their analysis of authority relationships Adams and Romney (1959) use the term "authority" to mean the same thing that others label "power" (Bass, 1960; Mulder, 1959b). Despite these diverse uses of the term, it is possible to define power in a consistent manner and to study its consequences for group functioning.

THE NATURE OF SOCIAL POWER

The various conceptions of social power have in common the view that power involves at minimum the ability of one person to control or influence another person in some way. Lewin (1951) defined the power of person A over person B as the quotient of the maximum force which A can induce on B and the maximum resistance which B can mobilize against A. French (1956) modified this definition somewhat, although he also defined power in terms of force; the power of person A over person B was defined as the maximum force which A can induce on B *minus* the maximum force which B can mobilize to resist A. In both these definitions, power is a joint function of the forces controlled by A and B. The definitions were derived from field theory, but in many ways they are similar to definitions of power derived from reinforcement theory. For example, Bass (1960) defined power as control over others through the use of rewards and punishments, a definition which is not unlike that formulated by Thibaut and Kelley (1959) in their exchange theory. If one substitutes "power" for "authority," the Bass definition also agrees with that of Adams and Romney (1959).

In general, it appears appropriate to define power as the *control of reinforcers*. Thus, person A has power over person B to the extent that he controls reinforcers for B. In the industrial work group, the foreman has power over his men because he controls reinforcers for them, such as pay, work schedules, promotions, etc. The men also have some power over the foreman, since they control productivity, to some extent, and the foreman's reinforcements are closely related to the productivity of his work group. However, the foreman has greater power over his men than they have over him because he controls more reinforcers, and he controls them more directly.

This conception of social power permits a meaningful distinction among similar concepts, such as power, social influence, authority, and leadership. Thus, authority may be defined as legitimate power, or the control of reinforcers that is approved by members of the group. Social influence may be defined as the exercise of power or the use of reinforcers to control another person's behavior. Social influence is sometimes used to refer to a process, as in the definition given here, and sometimes to an outcome or end result of a social process. When social influence is used in the latter sense, we would define it as the consequence of the exercise of social power. Leadership is a special case of social influence; that is, leadership is the exercise of power in particular situations, as by the occupant of a particular position in the group structure.

The main problem with the conceptual scheme outlined above is the identification of reinforcers, since a reinforcer for one person is not necessarily a reinforcer for another. Nevertheless, it is generally the case that certain things, for example money, are reinforcing for most persons in a given group. Also, it is no more difficult to identify reinforcers than it is to identify the forces that one person can mobilize for or against another person, and it may be that "reinforcers" and "forces" are merely different labels for the same phenomenon. Certainly, the bases of social power specified by French and Raven (1959) apply equally well to power defined by the field theory orientation and by the reinforcement orientation. Five kinds of social power were identified: attraction power, reward power, coercive power, legitimate power, and expert power. Attraction power is based upon identification or a liking relationship: A person who is liked by another person has more power over the other person than one who is disliked. Reward power is based upon the ability to mediate rewards for the other person, and coercive power is based upon the ability to mediate punishments for the other person. Thus, reward power and coercive power, taken together, constitute our definition of power as control of reinforcers. Legitimate power is based upon the belief that one person has the right to prescribe the behavior of another person, and expert power is based upon the less powerful person's belief that the powerful person has greater resources with respect to a given area. It should be evident from an analysis of these bases of power that all represent some form of control over reinforcers. The attractive person can bestow favors that are reinforcing for the person who is attracted to him; the expert can reinforce the other person by providing resources that are unavailable to the other person; and legitimate power merely describes the group members' attitude toward the power held by the powerful group member. Thus, these three kinds of power reduce to reward power and coercive power, and we have already noted that these agree closely with the view of power as control of reinforcers. The distinction among types of power is nevertheless useful, since it is quite possible that the effects of power upon group process vary with the sources of power.

REACTIONS TO THE POWERFUL GROUP MEMBER

The reactions of group members to another member are determined in part by the power attributed to that person. Some reactions have been documented by carefully controlled studies, both in the laboratory and in natural settings. In general, the powerful group member is treated deferentially, he is the target of a disproportionate number of communications, and he is seen as more likable than the less powerful group member. All these effects may be seen in field studies conducted by Hurwitz, Zander, and Hymovitch (1953) and by Lippitt, Polansky, Redl, and Rosen (1952). Hurwitz et al. selected forty-two workers in the general area of mental hygiene on the basis of prestige rankings by two qualified persons. These rankings were assumed to reflect power differences among mental hygiene workers, and subsequent ratings of perceived power to influence others supported this assumption. The workers were subdivided into groups of six persons each, such that the groups varied in degree of power distribution. Each member subsequently rated the extent to which he liked each of the other group members, his perception of how well others liked him, and his perception of the amount of verbal participation of each group member. Observers kept a record of the pattern of participation. High-power members communicated more frequently and received more communications than low-power members. Powerful group members were also better liked than low-power members.

Similar effects were observed by Lippitt et al. in two studies of attributed power among members of fresh-air camps in Michigan and Wisconsin. The person with high attributed power was the target of more deferential, approval-seeking behavior than were the low-power members. Others also tended to accept influence attempts from high-power persons to a greater extent. These reactions suggest that powerful group members are seen as able to either help or hurt others with respect to their goals; such behaviors are thus designed to reduce the uneasiness aroused by this perception. This aspect is supported by a laboratory study by Butler and Miller (1965) which revealed that more rewards and fewer punishments were directed to subjects with higher power to reward others in the group.

The reactions of group members to a group leader as a function of his power have been investigated by Mulder, Van Dijk, Soutendijk, Stelwagen, and Verhagen (1964). Power was manipulated by varying the magnitude of rewards or fines that the leader could administer to group members. Three levels of power were created: (1) High power—the leader could administer rewards or punishments equal to 190 cents (where 250 cents was roughly equal to one American dollar); (2) medium power—the leader controlled rewards and punishments of 100 cents; and (3) low power—the leader controlled rewards and punishments equaling only 10 cents. After group interaction, members rated the leader on a number of attributes. The greater the leader's power the greater the self-confidence and satisfaction with self attributed to the leader. Two ratings, however, correlated negatively with leader power: ratings of the leader as "a nice fellow" and degree of preference as an associate in a social situation.

In summary: The studies of member reactions to a powerful group member show that he is seen as capable of helping or hindering others in the achievement of their goals; hence he is the target of communications and deferential behavior. The powerful person is better liked than the low-power group member, but he is not seen as an attractive person for social interaction—at least, not as attractive as less powerful group members.

REACTIONS OF THE POWERFUL GROUP MEMBER

The power possessed by a group member not only affects the reactions of others in the group to him, but also the powerful person's own behavior. Compared with other group members, the more powerful member is more highly attracted to the group, he perceives that he has greater influence upon it, he is better satisfied with his position, etc. Some of these reactions of the powerful member can be demonstrated quite easily in a laboratory or classroom setting. In Zander and Cohen's experimental demonstration (1955), groups of seven persons each were formed in a classroom. The groups were told to assume that their "committee" had been appointed by the vice president of the university to advise him on the use of a large sum of money that had been donated anonymously. Then two of the members were asked to leave the room for a time so that they could experience the feelings of a new member in a previously organized group. While they were out of the room, the remaining five members were told that one of the new members was to play the role of dean and the other the role of freshman; however, the members were to make no mention of the positions held by the new members. The assumption was that the dean would have greater power in an academic community, although it is evident that other differences might also exist. After the new members rejoined the group, the problem was discussed for a short time, and then members filled out questionnaires about their reactions to the group. The results showed that, relative to the freshman, the dean (1) was more attracted to the group (means = 6.2 versus 4.1), (2) believed that he had made a better first impression on the group (means = 5.0 versus 3.9), (3) believed that the group gave greater "social validity" to his opinions (means = 5.4 versus 3.9), and (4) believed that he had more influence on the group (means = 6.8 versus 4.4).

These findings are consistent with those reported by Lippitt et al. (1952) in the study cited earlier. Similar results were also reported by Watson and Bromberg (1965). Power was manipulated in laboratory groups by appointing one member "coordinator" and giving him the power to issue commands which the other group members were required to obey. Each group solved a series of problems in which interaction was limited to written communications. Under these conditions, the high-power member indicated that he had greater opportunity to influence the group and to be helpful in the attainment of group goals than did low-power members. He also expressed greater enjoyment of his position than did low-power members.

An interesting study by W. P. Smith (1967) demonstrated that the powerful group member is more likely to use his power than are less powerful persons. Each of seventy-two subjects was told that he must work through an intermediary in order to affect his rewards from another person. Each was told that he had either high or low power over the intermediary and that the intermediary had either high or low power over the source of rewards. The subjects used their power more when they thought that they had high power and also when they thought the intermediary had high power. The empirical evidence thus reveals that the more powerful group member not only enjoys his position more and perceives that he has greater influence on the group, but he also tends to use his power in direct proportion to the amount of power that he believes he possesses.

EFFECTS OF POWER DIFFERENCES ON THE GROUP'S PRODUCTS

The behaviors of the powerful group member and the reactions of others to him inevitably influence the functioning of the group. It is curious that few studies have been directed toward an analysis of this effect. Most investigators have been interested in the effects of other variables upon the consequences of power differences among group members. For example, it seems obvious that greater conformity should be observed in a group characterized by a power hierarchy than in an equal-power structure, at least on the part of low-power group members. Studies in this area have been largely limited to comparisons of reward and coercive power, with special reference to other variables. Kipnis (1958) exposed grammar school children to propaganda regarding comic books, administered by an adult who could either reward or punish the children for conformity. In some cases the propaganda was presented in a group discussion and in others via lecture. Initial compliance was equal for all conditions, but a check one week later revealed that in the group discussion reward power was more effective in maintaining conformity than coercive power, whereas in the lecture sections the opposite was true. Kipnis suggested that group discussion made the coercive forces more salient and thus reduced their long-range effects on conformity.

Empirical investigations concerning group productivity are also limited in number and tend to be concerned with the effects of other variables relative to power. For instance, G. B. Cohen (1968a) examined the effects of power as a function of communication network and "weight" of the group member in the determination of group output. In each three-person group, member A was given the greatest amount of power in that his decisions limited the alternatives available to member B, whose decisions in turn limited the alternatives of member C. The power structure was therefore always hierarchical, with member A having the greatest restriction power and member C the least. In the first experiment, two communication networks were imposed: B-A-C and A-B-C. Thus the two networks were chains, with member A in the central position in one and member B in the central position in the other. In the second experiment, a third chain was introduced (A-C-B), with member C in the central position. The "weight" of each member was determined by formulas which gave the greatest weight either to A's yield or to C's yield in determining the value of the final group product. In a sense, then, two aspects of power were varied: restriction power and influence power. A prediction that the communication network with member A in the central position would be more effective was not supported. However, the results of both experiments supported the prediction that group productivity would be higher when member A, who had the most restriction power, also had the greatest weight relative to the group's output. The finding that giving the greatest weight to the inputs of the member having the most influence over the group's alternatives produces higher productivity scores is probably not too surprising, but it does show that power differences are determinants of group productivity.

The emphasis upon other variables relative to the effects of power differences is also noticeable in studies of bargaining behavior. Komorita, Sheposh, and Braver (1968) investigated the effects of different perceptions of the more powerful member of a dyad on the level of cooperation of the less powerful member. Subjects were asked to play the prisoner's dilemma game in which the best outcomes for both members can be obtained only through cooperation in response choices. The low-power member was led to believe that the high-power member intended to use his power either benevolently, malevolently, or passively (nonuse of power). The benevolent condition elicited the greatest amount of cooperation (and hence the greatest rewards for both members), and the malevolent condition the least amount of cooperation. The consequences of power differences in this situation are thus seen to be a function of the group member's perceptions of the powerful member's intentions. In a somewhat similar situation, Thibaut and Gruder (1969) noted that groups with an attractive alternative to interdependent negotiation formed agreements regulating their bargaining behavior; however, groups with an unattractive alternative formed such agreements only if the low-power member could in some way compensate the high-power member for his loss of power.

In brief summary, the power differences among group members influence the reactions of other group members to the powerful member, the powerful member's reactions to the group, and the group's products. The particular effects of power differences upon the group's products are determined by a number of other variables, such as the weight given to the outputs of group members, the perceptions of the intentions of the powerful group member, and the kinds of alternatives that are available to the group.

LEADERSHIP

The leadership role is one of the most important roles associated with positions in the group structure. It has been studied more extensively than any other role and with the greatest variety of research techniques. It is probably also true that "leader" and "leadership" have been defined in more different ways than almost any other concept associated with group structure. For these reasons, it is important to consider some definitional problems in the studies of leadership before we examine the outcomes of such studies.

THE DEFINITION OF LEADERSHIP

The problem of defining leadership was attacked by Carter (1953), who identified five distinctly different views of leadership that have appeared in the literature. First, a leader may be defined as a person who is the focus of group behaviors. This definition emphasizes the polarization of group members around the leader. As we have already noted, the leader is likely to receive more communications than others, have more influence upon the group's decisions, etc. Hence, the leader usually is the center of attention in the group. As Carter noted, however, there are many situations in which an individual who is the focus of attention is not the person most researchers would identify as the leader. He cited the example of an obnoxious drunk at a social gathering. The behavior of all members of the group might be centered around the drunk, but few would be willing to call him the leader. In the studies of deviancy cited earlier in this chapter, the deviant was initially the center of group interaction, but again, few would call him the leader.

A second approach defines leadership in terms of group goals. Thus, the leader is the person who is able to lead the group toward its goals. Most people would probably agree with this definition, although Carter found it unsatisfactory because of the difficulty of identifying group goals. This is indeed a problem, as we shall see in the next chapter; however, it is probably not an impossible task. Carter also noted that such a definition would exclude persons who lead the group away from its goals, as in the case of leaders like Hitler.

A third approach defines the leader as the person so named by the members of the group. This definition of leadership is thus based upon sociometric choice. Carter objected that this definition only points to a person who occupies the leadership role, but says nothing about the characteristics of leadership. This is obviously true, but the views of group members may nevertheless be useful in identifying the group leader.

A fourth approach was proposed by Cattell (1951b) in connection with his theory of group syntality (see Chapter 2). Accordingly, a leader is defined as a person who has demonstrable influence upon group syntality, that is, a person who causes syntality change. It will be recalled that syntality was said to be for the group what personality is for the individual, and also that it could be thought of as the measured performance of the group. In terms of the latter interpretation of syntality, the definition of leader as one who produces syntality change would mean that the leader is one who changes the level of group performance. Unfortunately, Cattell did not provide precise methods for determining when a given person has produced such a change, and Carter rejected this definition as impractical. However, there is another assumption implicit in Cattell's definition that is worthy of note, namely, that any group member is a leader to the extent that he influences group syntality. Thus, there is not a single group leader; instead, each member is a leader to some degree, depending upon the amount of influence he has upon syntality change. This is undoubtedly true; when we speak of *the leader* we mean the group member who has exerted the *greatest* influence upon the group's performance.

The fifth definition of leadership cited by Carter is the one that he preferred: leadership defined in terms of leadership behaviors. Thus, the leader is a person who engages in leadership behaviors. This is an operational definition that is pragmatic with respect to research. That is, the researcher can identify the specific kinds of behaviors that he calls leadership behaviors; others can accept or reject them as evidences of leadership, but at least it is clear what is being discussed. Nevertheless, this approach leads to a heterogeneous mass of specific acts that supposedly identify leadership in the group. What constitutes leadership depends upon the view of the person who is listing leadership behaviors.

There are other definitions that Carter did not mention. For example, many investigators have defined the leader as the person who occupies a position of leadership in a group. The president of a company, the foreman of a work group, the platoon sergeant in military organizations, etc., are therefore leaders by virtue of the positions they hold. This definition really refers to headship rather than leadership. That is, this kind of role occupant is supported by forces outside the group and may or may not be able to function as a leader of the group. Psychologically, a leader is a person who has the support of the members of his group and is able to influence their behavior without invoking external authority. Therefore, we prefer to define the *leader* as that group member who exerts positive influence over other group members, or as that member who exerts more positive influence over others than they exert over him. The term "positive" indicates that the direction of the influence is that desired by the leader. This definition permits the inclusion of leaders who lead the group away from the group goal, so long as that is the direction the leader intends to go—whether or not he believes the outcome will be goal achievement. It excludes the person who exerts negative influence on the group, that is, the group member who always manages to get the group to do just the opposite of what he desires them to do.

THE TRAIT APPROACH TO THE STUDY OF LEADERSHIP

The study of leadership has been influenced greatly by the dominant philosophical orientations of the Western world. In the latter part of the nineteenth century and the first part of the twentieth, the Western world was dominated by an individualistic position which held that a man could become whatever he wished to become, so long as he worked hard and persevered. Thus, the leader became a leader because of his own personal efforts and attributes. Perhaps it is not surprising that students of leadership looked first to individual characteristics as the major determinants of leadership. Thus, in the early part of this century, hundreds of empirical studies attempted to identify the personal attributes or traits of leaders. In Chapter 6 we cited the results of many of these studies, and we will not repeat them here. A brief summary of the conclusions that may be drawn from the trait approach will suffice.

Although the correlations between individual traits and leadership measures are not large, there is nevertheless enough consistency to permit some generalizations. The leader of the group, to a greater extent than other group members, exemplifies traits related to ability, sociability, and motivation. Thus, Stogdill (1948) observed that the average group leader exceeds the average group member in such *abilities* as intelligence, scholarship, knowing how to get things done, insight into situations, verbal facility, and adaptability. The leader exceeds the group member in regard to such *sociability* factors as dependability in exercising responsibilities, activity and social participation, cooperativeness, and popularity. *Motivational* characteristics are indicated by the findings that leaders exceed other group members with respect to initiative and persistence. When the great variety of groups, leader definitions, and research techniques are considered, it is remarkable that the results of the trait approach yielded enough consistency to permit these generalizations. Confidence in these results is enhanced if we consider factor analytic studies which revealed three factors that are essentially the same as the three kinds of traits listed above.

LEADERSHIP STYLES*

Since characteristics of individuals presumably reflect behavioral tendencies, it has seemed to many students of leadership that investigations should deal with behavior directly. Even casual observation of leaders at work reveals tremendous differences in leadership style. Some leaders give orders, demand obedience, make all decisions without regard to the opinions of others, etc., whereas other leaders are considerate, request the cooperation of others, ask their opinions before making decisions, etc. Such differences in leadership style obviously should affect group process, and a number of studies have been conducted to determine the exact nature of the effects.

The pioneering study of leadership styles was conducted by Lewin and his associates (Lewin, Lippitt, & White, 1939; Lippitt & White, 1943). Four comparable groups of ten-year-old boys were observed as they successively experienced autocratic, democratic, and "laissez faire" adult leadership. The group task was to engage in hobby activities, such as making paper masks. Each group met after school for 3 six-week periods, with a different adult leader and a different leadership style for each period. Four adult leaders were trained to play each of the three leadership roles. The autocratic leader determined all policy for the group, dictated techniques and actions— one at a time to ensure that future actions would always be uncertain, usually dictated the particular work task and work companions, and was subjective in praise and criticism of the work of group members. His attitude was impersonal and aloof, but not openly hostile. The democratic leader allowed the group to determine matters of policy, the general steps to the goal were sketched and alternative procedures suggested when appropriate, the mem-

---

* Leadership style is used here to refer to a set of behaviors that characterize the leader's activities during the time of investigation. This set of behaviors may or may not reflect a personality attribute of the leader (cf. Fiedler, 1967).

bers were free to work with whomever they chose, and the leader was objective in his praise and criticism of group members. The laissez faire leader was essentially a nonparticipant in group activities. The group was given complete freedom to make its own decisions, materials and information were supplied when asked for, and comments on members' activities were very infrequent.

Relatively complete records were kept of group behavior, and included observations, structure analysis, interpretation of significant member actions, stenographic records of all conversation, interpretation of member relationships, movies of several parts of group interaction, and comments by the leader and by visitors. The results showed markedly different patterns of interaction as a function of leadership style. Hostility was thirty times as great in the autocratic as in the democratic groups, and aggression was eight times as great in the autocratic as in the democratic. There was more scapegoating in the autocratic groups than in either of the other two; one group member was frequently made the target of hostility and aggression until he left the group, and then another boy would be chosen for this honor. Nineteen of twenty boys liked the democratic leader better than the autocrat, and seven of ten liked the laissez faire leader better than the autocrat. There was no reliable difference in the number of products produced, but the products of the democratic groups were judged to be qualitatively superior to those of other groups.

There were some very interesting sequential effects associated with the change in leadership style, although, unfortunately, the design did not permit their precise interpretation. The most interesting effects occurred when the group experienced the autocratic leader first in the sequence, followed by the laissez faire leader in the second period. The rise in aggression under laissez faire leadership can be seen in Figure 8-4. This was attributed to repressed aggression during the autocratic period. Under the freer group atmosphere, the boys expressed the pent-up aggressive tendencies that they had not been able to express under the autocratic leader. Sequential effects of this kind are probably very important for interaction in natural groups, and merit further study. For instance, consider the reaction of a worker who has been a member of a work group led by an autocratic foreman, who now finds himself in a group with a democratic leader. Perhaps he will be ineffective in such a group because his aggressive responses now dominate his behavior.

Many of the findings reported by Lewin et al. have been replicated in

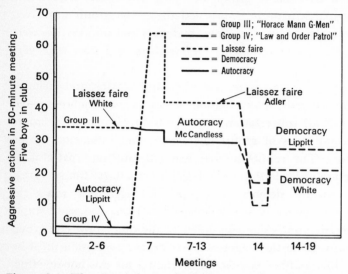

Figure 8-4 The Same Group in Different Atmospheres. Group IV Shows Changes to the Levels Typical for Each Atmosphere. It Shows also the "Release of Tension" on the First Day of Freedom (7) after Apathetic Autocracy. Group III Seemed Resistant to Change; It Was Relatively Aggressive Even in Democracy. (Reprinted with permission from K. Lewin, R. Lippitt, & R. K. White. Patterns of aggressive behavior in experimentally created "social climates." *Journal of Social Psychology*, 1939, **10**, 271–299.)

widely divergent settings. Preston and Heintz (1949) asked members of several laboratory classes to rank twelve potential presidential candidates in order of individual preference. Class members were then divided into groups of four or five members each, and asked to rank the candidates, working as a group. Assigned leaders were instructed to play either a participatory or a supervisory role. The participatory leader was told to be sure that each name was considered, to encourage all members to take part in the discussions, to discourage chance methods of deciding doubtful cases, and to complete the work in half an hour. The supervisory leaders were instructed not to participate in the discussion and to limit their responsibility to seeing that the work was done in the allotted time. The results showed that participatory leadership was more effective in changing attitudes than was supervisory leadership. Participatory group members also were better satisfied with the group's ranking, found the task more interesting and meaningful, and rated their group discussions as more friendly and enjoyable than did members of supervisory groups.

The effects of authoritarian and nonauthoritarian leadership were also examined in a laboratory setting by M. E. Shaw (1955). Groups of four college males were assembled and assigned instructed leaders who played either an authoritarian or a nonauthoritarian leadership role. The authoritarian leader was asked to issue orders, to accept no suggestion uncritically, and to make it clear that he was boss of the group. The nonauthoritarian leader was instructed to solicit suggestions, make requests instead of issuing orders, and make it clear that he wanted the group to function democratically. Each group solved three arithmetic problems via written communication. The authoritarian groups made fewer errors, required fewer messages for problem solution, and required less time than did the nonauthoritarian groups; however, the ratings of satisfaction with the group were higher in nonauthoritarian groups.

Similar effects have been reported from studies conducted in natural settings. Morse and Reimer (1956) selected four work groups from a nonunionized industrial organization. The four groups were matched as closely as possible with respect to satisfaction and productivity measures taken before the study began. Two of the four groups were assigned to an autonomy condition in which they were given greater control over all aspects of the work situation except their salary. The others were assigned to a hierarchically controlled situation in which greater control was given to the supervisor. The task was clerical work which required that the groups process whatever material came to them. Hence, productivity was measured by the number of workers required to handle a given number of units. After the groups had spent one year under the experimental conditions, measures of satisfaction and productivity were again obtained. As in laboratory experiments, satisfaction increased in the autonomy groups but decreased in the hierarchically controlled groups. Productivity increased in both groups, but the increase was greater in the hierarchically controlled groups (+14.1) than in the autonomy groups (+10). In interpreting this difference in productivity, we must remember that one restriction was that no worker could be fired because he was not needed. However, a worker who resigned did not have to be replaced and a worker could be transferred to another department in the company. It is possible that members of the autonomy work group were more reluctant to transfer a worker who was no longer needed than the supervisor in the hierarchically controlled groups was.

It is evident that, although different terms are used, these several researchers are dealing with similar leadership variables. In each instance, a directive leader is compared with a nondirective one. The results concerning the group members' reactions to the group are entirely consistent across a wide range of situations and groups: Members of groups with nondirective leaders react more positively to the group than do members of groups led by directive leaders. The evidence concerning productivity is inconsistent; however, it appears that either the directive-led groups are usually more productive than the nondirective-led groups or there is no difference in productivity.

Laboratory studies have indicated one other interesting aspect of autocratic versus democratic leadership: It is apparently much easier to be a good autocratic leader than a good democratic leader. For example, in the study by M. E. Shaw (1955) both the most and least effective groups had democratic leaders; there was relatively little variance among autocratic groups. It is easy to issue orders, but difficult to utilize effectively the abilities of group members. If a leader doubts his ability to be an effective democratic leader, then he probably is well advised to play the autocratic role.

SITUATIONS AND LEADERSHIP

We have noted that relationships between specific traits and leadership tend to be consistent, but moderately weak. That is, a person who possesses a particular personality trait is more likely to become a leader than a person who lacks that trait, but there are many instances in which he is not the leader. Murphy (1941) argued that leadership traits are fluid in that individual characteristics may change with the situation. For example, a person who is usually dominant may become shy if placed in an unfamiliar situation. This is obviously true, but possession of a given characteristic does not imply that the individual will behave as expected in every conceivable situation. Nevertheless, it is a mistake to think of the relationship between a trait and leadership as universal. A trait that is positively related to leadership in one situation may be unrelated or even negatively related in another. This fact led many researchers to conclude that leadership traits, and indeed leadership behaviors, are relative to the situation.

This conclusion is justified if it is stated with qualification. It will be recalled that the traits associated with leadership were rather general: Abilities, for instance, includes not only general ability (intelligence) but many specific abilities. The leader must have the abilities that are relevant to the situation in which he finds himself. A person who has great ability with respect to building bridges would have a better chance of becoming an effective leader of a bridge-building crew than one without such skills, but his chances of becoming the leader of a chemical research team might be very low indeed. Hence, we would qualify an earlier statement to read, "Abilities relevant to the group's task are positively correlated with effective leadership."

Similar criticism may be directed toward the conclusions drawn from the investigations of leadership styles. The kind of leadership behavior that is most effective depends upon the situation in which the leader finds himself. Data from Fiedler's (1964) studies of the relationship between LPC scores and effective leadership lead to a similar conclusion. According to his contingency model, which is outlined in the following section, directive leadership is more effective when the task situation is either very favorable or very unfavorable to the leader, whereas nondirective leadership is more effective when the situation is moderately favorable (see Figure 8-5, page 279). This may be one of the reasons for the lack of consistency among findings relative to differences in the productivity of groups under autocratic and democratic leadership. Although the identification of the favorability dimension is a step in the right direction, considerably more information is needed concerning the specific characteristics and behaviors of leaders required for group efficiency in different kinds of situations.

THE CONTINGENCY MODEL OF LEADERSHIP EFFECTIVENESS

One of the most promising analyses of leadership was proposed by Fiedler (1964, 1967), who attempted to integrate the effects of leadership styles and situational variables. In this model of leadership effectiveness, leadership styles are identified by the ASo/LPC scores of the leaders, as described in Chapter 6. It will be recalled that ASo and LPC scores are obtained from responses to a questionnaire which requires that the respondent rate his most preferred and least preferred coworkers on a number of characteristics. The ASo (assumed similarity of opposites) score is derived from a comparison of most and least preferred coworker ratings: the greater the difference between the two sets of ratings the higher the ASo score. The LPC score is based on the ratings of least preferred coworker, and correlates highly with the ASo score. Hence, the two scores are used interchangeably. The high ASo/LPC person perceives his least preferred coworker in a relatively favorable manner. Fiedler (1967) describes him as a person who derives his major satisfaction from successful interpersonal relationships. The low ASo/LPC person perceives his least preferred coworker in very unfavorable terms, and is described as a person who derives his major satisfaction from task performance.

> Thus, high-LPC leaders are concerned with having good interpersonal relations and with gaining prominence and self-esteem through these interpersonal relations. Low-LPC leaders are concerned with achieving success on assigned tasks, even at the risk of having poor interpersonal relations with fellow workers. The behaviors of high- and low-LPC leaders will thus be quite different if the situation is such that the satisfaction of their respective needs is threatened. Under these conditions the high-LPC leader will increase his interpersonal interaction in order to cement his relations with other group members while the low-LPC leader will interact in order to complete the task successfully. The high-LPC person is concerned with gaining self-esteem through recognition by others, the low-LPC person is concerned with gaining self-esteem through the successful performance of the task. Both types of leaders may thus be concerned with the task and both will use interpersonal relationships, although the high-LPC leader will concern himself with the task in order to have successful interpersonal relationships, while the low-LPC leader will concern himself with interpersonal relations in order to achieve task success (Fiedler, 1967, pp. 45–46).

The relationship between ASo/LPC score and effectiveness as a group leader was examined in numerous investigations, with varying results. Correlations between leader ASo/LPC scores and measures of group effectiveness ranged from −.67 to .69. Since these correlations were obtained from a variety of groups operating in widely different settings, the interpretation of ASo/LPC scores described above suggests that the effects of leadership styles on group effectiveness can only be understood by considering situational variables. In other words, some system of classifying group situations is required. Fiedler's proposed classification system was based on the belief that the leader's style of interacting with his followers is affected by the degree to which the leader can wield power and influence over them. His proposed system postulated three major factors: (1) the leader's position power, (2) the structure of the task, and (3) the personal relationships between leader and members.

Position power was defined as the degree to which the position itself enables the leader to get his followers to comply with his wishes and to accept his leadership. This conception of position power is closely related to French and Raven's (1959) concepts of legitimate power, reward power, and coercive power, which were discussed earlier (see page 261). It is also related to Adams and Romney's (1959) conception of authority as control of reinforcers. In general, the situation is more favorable for the leader when he occupies a strong power position. Fiedler assessed position power by means of an eighteen-item checklist which contains various indices of position power.

The structure of the task refers to the degree to which the task requirements are clearly specified, that is, the degree to which the task is capable of being programmed. Fiedler defined task structure operationally in terms of four task dimensions: decision verifiability, goal clarity, goal-path multiplicity, and solution specificity. Briefly, decision verifiability is the degree to which the correctness of a decision can be verified by appeal to authority, by logical procedures, or by feedback; goal clarity is the degree to which the requirements of the task are known to group members; goal-path multiplicity refers to the degree to which the task can be completed by a variety of procedures; and solution specificity (or more appropriately, solution multiplicity) is the degree to which there is more than one correct solution or decision. (Task dimensions are discussed in greater detail in Chapter 9.) The task is structured to the extent that the goal is clear, there is a single path to the goal, there is only one correct solution or decision, and the decision is easily verified. In general, the more structured the task, the more favorable the situation is for the leader.

The personal relationship between the leader and his followers depends upon his affective relations with group members, the acceptance he is able to obtain, and the loyalty he is able to elicit. When the leader has good personal relations with his fellow group members the situation is more favorable for him than when relations are poor. Leader-member relations are assessed by sociometric ratings and/or ratings of group atmosphere.

Leader-member relations presumably exert the strongest effect on the favorability dimension, followed by task structure, and finally position power of the leader. By taking into account these differences, one can order group situations according to degree of favorability to the leader. For example, the most favorable situation for the leader is one in which leader-member relations are good, the task is highly structured, and the leader's position power is strong; the most unfavorable situation is one in which leader-member relations are poor, the task is unstructured, and the leader's position power is weak. According to Fiedler's theory, the low ASo/LPC leader is more effective when the situation is either highly favorable or unfavorable to the leader, whereas the high ASo/LPC leader is more effective when the situation is moderately favorable. That is, when the situation is very favorable, the leader can be managing and controlling without arousing negative responses by group members; because things are going well, there is no reason to reject the directive behaviors of the leader. On the other hand, when the situation is highly unfavorable, things are going badly, and the group is in danger of falling apart, then directive leadership is required and again the low ASo/LPC leader is more effective. But if the situation is only moderately favorable, the group expects to be treated with consideration, and the permissive, high ASo/LPC leader is more effective. The data presented by Fiedler and reproduced in Figure 8-5 reveal that these expectations are supported by empirical findings. Although the data presented in Figure 8-5 are post hoc, later investigations support the analysis (Fiedler, 1967).

It is now evident that the behavior of the leader depends not only upon his personality attributes but also upon the characteristics of the situation. In moderately favorable group situations, the relationship-oriented (high ASo/LPC) leader has his needs gratified by good interpersonal relations and the favorable power position he occupies; therefore, he devotes more of his energy to the task. In the same situation, the task-oriented (low ASo/LPC) leader becomes more concerned with building good interpersonal relationships. In general, high ASo/LPC persons behave in a relationship-relevant manner in situations that are unfavorable for them, and low ASo/LPC leaders act in a task-relevant manner in situations that are unfavorable to them. These patterns of behavior determine the relative effectiveness of leaders in various situations. The task-oriented leader tends to be more effective when the situation is either highly favorable or highly unfavorable for the leader, whereas the relationship-oriented leader tends to be more effective in situations that are only moderately favorable or moderately unfavorable.

Although there are still some problems and unanswered questions, the contingency model is a promising start toward the integration of leadership styles and situational factors as determinants of group effectiveness. The model is important in that it not only asserts that the kind of leadership behavior that is most effective depends upon the situation, but it also attempts to specify what behaviors are likely to be most effective in which situations.

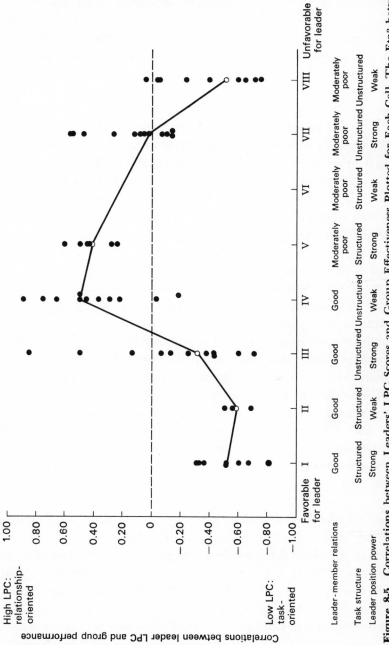

Figure 8-5 Correlations between Leaders' LPC Scores and Group Effectiveness Plotted for Each Cell. The Eta^2 between the Correlations LPC/ASo and Performance and Favorableness is .586, $r^2 = .007$. (Reprinted with permission from F. E. Fiedler. *A theory of leadership effectiveness*. New York: McGraw-Hill, 1967.)

PLAUSIBLE HYPOTHESES ABOUT GROUP STRUCTURE

The discussions of group structure have considered many aspects of this feature of groups. They have shown that there has been no concerted attack on the variables determining the development of group structure or its effects on group behavior. The many individual bits of research nevertheless suggest a number of plausible hypotheses that merit further consideration.

Hypothesis 1   The perception that organization facilitates goal achievement is a determinant of group structure.

Many group members believe that some form of organization is necessary if the group is to attain its goals. A study by Shaw and Gilchrist (1956) revealed that one or more members of problem-solving groups suggested some form of organization in eight of ten groups studied. This belief in the efficacy of structure with respect to goal achievement leads group members to establish structural relations among parts of the group.

Hypothesis 2   The formation of group structure is facilitated to the extent that group members have a need for structure.

This hypothesis concerns a different determinant of group structure from that referred to in Hypothesis 1. The need of group members for structure is a general need rather than a belief concerning the efficacy of structure for goal attainment. Cohen, Stotland, and Wolfe (1955) have demonstrated that certain individuals need to structure relevant situations in meaningful and integrated ways. To the extent that the group is relevant, such persons also experience a need to structure the group. Hence, the more group members who have such a need and the greater the strengths of their needs for structure, the greater will be the tendency for them to structure the group. The observations of Bennis and Shepard (1956) are also in accord with this hypothesis.

Hypothesis 3   The kind of structure that the group develops is influenced by the physical environment of the group.

The effects of the physical environment are pervasive, and relate to so many specific aspects of group structure that it is difficult to formulate a general hypothesis concerning them. Festinger et al. (1950) noted the effects of physical arrangements of housing units upon friendship formations (an aspect of structure), and in Chapter 5 we noted many instances of the culturally mediated influences of spatial arrangements on group differentiation. The close relationship between spatial position and perceived status of the group member is an outstanding example of this effect (Lott & Sommer, 1967; Sommer, 1969).

Hypothesis 4   *A high-status group member may deviate from group norms without being sanctioned if his deviancy contributes to goal attainment.*

The high-status person generally conforms to the norms of the group more than most other group members; however, if he has contributed to goal attainment in the past, he may build up idiosyncrasy credit (Hollander, 1958) which permits greater deviancy under certain circumstances. Studies by Gergen and Taylor (1969) suggest that this effect is especially strong when the group is concerned primarily with productivity.

Hypothesis 5   *Communications tend to be directed upward in the status hierarchy.*

Numerous studies have shown that more communications tend to be directed toward the high-status than toward the low-status person (Kelley, 1951; Thibaut, 1950). Such upward communication has been interpreted as a substitute for real upward locomotion. It may also reflect an attempt to attain vicarious rewards through interaction with high-status persons.

Hypothesis 6   *Communications directed upward in the status hierarchy have more positive content than communications directed downward.*

This effect is reflected in the communications of both high- and low-status group members. In the studies by Thibaut and by Kelley cited above, it was observed that communications directed to high-status persons contained fewer aggressive comments and more task-irrelevant information than did communications directed to peers; on the other hand, high-status persons refrained from communicating negative attitudes or confusion concerning their own jobs. Worchel (1957) also noted that the amount of verbal aggression directed toward a high-status person following frustration was less than that directed toward a low-status person under similar circumstances. The low-status person is probably restrained from aggressive communication by fear of punishment, whereas the high-status person may fear a loss of status if he expresses any concern about his own effectiveness.

Hypothesis 7   *Role conflicts will ordinarily be resolved in favor of the group that is most important to the role occupant.*

In addition to the validity indicated by the logic of common sense, the studies of disasters reported by Killian (1952) clearly support this hypothesis. Faced with role requirements from two different roles that cannot be met simultaneously, the group member responds to the requirements of the role associated with the group that he is most attracted to.

Hypothesis 8   *There is a general, but weak, predisposition toward conformity to group norms.*

There is good evidence that there are individual differences in susceptibility to social influence. Although there are many factors related to these differences (such as intelligence and social responsibility), Frye and Bass (1963) have shown that there is a general tendency to agree with diverse propositions, and that this general tendency toward acquiescence is correlated with conformity behavior. This tendency appears to be real, but its effect is relatively weak.

Hypothesis 9   *The more ambiguous the stimulus situation, the greater the probability that a group member will conform to the perceived norms of the group.*

Numerous studies have demonstrated that ambiguous stimuli, such as judging movement of the autokinetic light (Sherif & Sherif, 1956), produce greater conformity than unambiguous stimuli, such as judging the length of lines (Asch, 1951). When the individual has little objective evidence about reality, he must rely upon others to validate his opinions. On the other hand, if the objective evidence is clear, he does not need to rely upon normative standards. This is probably the most powerful set of variables with respect to conformity behavior.

Hypothesis 10   *Conformity increases with increasing size of the majority up to some maximum size and remains constant thereafter.*

For many years, the conclusion drawn by Asch (1951) that a majority of three produces maximum conformity was accepted as valid. Recently, that conclusion has been called into question by studies showing increases in conformity with majorities larger than three (Gerard, Wilhelmy, & Conolley, 1968). Nevertheless, it is evident that there is a limit to the amount of conformity that can be elicited by increasing majority size.

Hypothesis 11   *A group member is more likely to conform to group judgment when other members are in unanimous agreement than
when they are not.*

Asch (1951) demonstrated conclusively that introducing a confederate who
agreed with the naïve group member reduced conformity dramatically and
that the inclusion of two or more uninstructed group members resulted in a
significant decrease in conformity. His results could have been due to the fact
that the subject had support or to the mere fact that the majority was not
unanimous. Shaw, Rothschild, and Strickland (1957) found that even a subject who declined to make a judgment led to reduced conformity by the
naïve group member. Hence, it appears that the critical variable is the
unanimity or nonunanimity of the opinions of other group members.

Hypothesis 12   *Greater conformity occurs in groups with decentralized communication networks than in groups with centralized communication networks.*

In a decentralized network all group members can exert direct pressure on
each other member in the group, whereas in a centralized network pressure
can be exerted by some members on some others only through intermediaries.
Direct contact should be more influential than contact via another person.
At least four separate studies have demonstrated this effect. Goldberg (1955)
found greater group influence on the group member's estimation of the
number of dots on a card in a decentralized than in a centralized network.
Shaw et al. (1957) conducted three experiments using human relations discussion tasks and counting metronome clicks, again finding greater conformity
in the decentralized network.

Hypothesis 13   *Conformity varies positively with the perceived competence
of the majority relative to the individual's perception of his
own competence.*

The effects on conformity of the competence of the group member relative
to that of others in the group is shown most clearly in Figure 8-2. It can be
seen that conformity is influenced by both the perceived competence of the
majority and the individual's perception of his own competence. When the
member believes that he is more competent than others in the group, he is
less inclined to conform to their standards. This effect is probably the result
of a number of intervening variables: (1) The competent person feels more
confident of his own judgments; (2) the member of a group composed of a

majority of relatively incompetent members will not be as attractive to a person as a group composed of relatively competent others; (3) the judgments of a competent majority are seen as more valid representations of reality than the judgments of a less competent majority; etc.

Hypothesis 14   *The effects of personality, situational, and stimulus variables are additive within the normal ranges of conformity behavior.*

The general import of this hypothesis is that the effects of several variables summate in the production of conformity behavior up to some maximum level. For example, if the personality factor "acquiescence" elicits 10 percent conformity, an ambiguous stimulus 40 percent conformity, and a given majority size 20 percent conformity, the three variables operating together should elicit approximately 70 percent conformity. The additivity of conformity variables is illustrated in Figure 8-3.

Hypothesis 15   *Conformity introduces order into the group process and provides for the coordination of individual behavior.*

There are only observational data available to support this hypothesis, but the data are so logically imperative that the validity of Hypothesis 15 can scarcely be doubted.

Hypothesis 16   *Under certain circumstances, conformity frees the individual from the coercive influence of authority.*

It is an unfortunate fact of social life that the individual is sometimes the victim of coercive forces which elicit behaviors that are not in accord with the individual's own standards of conduct. Milgram (1963) demonstrated the extreme consequences of such forces and later demonstrated that conformity can operate to liberate the individual so that he can resist authority (Milgram, 1965). The desirable consequences of conformity under some conditions have also been revealed by the Berkowitz and Daniels (1963) experiment which showed that conformity to a norm of social responsibility often leads to helping a dependent other.

Hypothesis 17   *Deviation from group norms usually elicits sanctioning behavior by other group members. Continued or habitual deviation may lead to rejection by other group members.*

Many observations of work groups reveal that such groups typically establish norms concerning a proper day's output (e.g., Homans, 1950; Roethlisberger & Dickson, 1939) and that deviation from these norms elicits various forms of sanction. Laboratory studies indicate a similar effect. Schachter (1951) found that deviation from normative group opinion initially elicited many communications directed toward the deviate. If the deviate continued to maintain a divergent opinion, communications decreased, and the deviate was apparently rejected as an acceptable group member.

Hypothesis 18 High-power group members are usually better liked than low-power group members.
Field studies with young people (boys and girls in fresh-air camps) and with older people (mental hygiene workers) indicate that group members express greater liking for high-power than for low-power group members (Hurwitz et al., 1953; Lippitt et al., 1952). The high-power person is seen as the source of rewards and punishments; a liked other is perceived as more likely to reward and less likely to punish than a disliked other.

Hypothesis 19 The high-power group member is the target of more deferential, approval-seeking behavior than low-power group members.
The basis for the effects referred to in Hypothesis 19 is probably the same as for the effects specified by Hypothesis 18: The high-power person is potentially threatening because he is capable of hurting the weaker group member. Deferential, approval-seeking behavior reduces the uneasiness aroused by this potential threat (Lippitt et al., 1952). This interpretation is also supported by the findings of Butler and Miller (1965) that more rewards and fewer punishments are directed toward the high-power group member than toward low-power group members.

Hypothesis 20 The high-power person has greater influence upon the group than low-power group members.
This very reasonable hypothesis is also supported by studies reported by Lippitt et al. (1952) and Hurwitz et al. (1953). The person who controls more reinforcements obviously should be able to influence others more than the one who controls fewer reinforcements.

Hypothesis 21 The high-power group member is more highly attracted to the group than are low-power group members.

A group member who is highly accepted by the group, who is the target of deferential treatment from others, who has great influence upon the group process, etc., undoubtedly finds the group more attractive than a member who is not treated so favorably. That the above hypothesis is a valid one is supported by the results of several empirical investigations. For instance, Zander and Cohen (1955) demonstrated this phenomenon clearly in their classroom exercise: The person whom the group identified as a dean was much more highly attracted to the group than a member identified as a freshman, although neither knew that these role identifications had been made. Results reported by Lippitt et al. (1952) and by Watson and Bromberg (1965) are also consistent with Hypothesis 21.

Hypothesis 22   The more power a group member has, the greater the probability that he will use it.

This interesting hypothesis does not have a great deal of supporting empirical evidence, but the one study reporting the effect is reasonably convincing (W. P. Smith, 1967). The phenomenon merits further empirical analysis.

Hypothesis 23   Effective leaders are characterized by task-related abilities, sociability, and motivation to be a leader.

To be effective, the leader of a group must have knowledge and skills related to the group's task so that he may guide group members toward their goal. He must also have interpersonal skills (sociability) in order to deal effectively with the inevitable friction and conflict between group members. But possession of these necessary abilities and skills will not guarantee that the individual will become an effective leader. In addition, he must *want* to be a leader or at least want the group to achieve its goals badly enough to be willing to serve as a leader in order to achieve those goals. Evidence from a variety of studies provides support for this conclusion (Stogdill, 1948).

Hypothesis 24   A task-oriented leader is more effective when the group-task situation is either very favorable or very unfavorable for the leader, whereas a relationship-oriented leader is more effective when the group-task situation is only moderately favorable or unfavorable for the leader.

Fiedler (1964, 1967) has provided a substantial amount of empirical evidence to support this hypothesis, which is central to his contingency model of leadership effectiveness. Additional evidence has been obtained in a laboratory study using procedures that differ greatly from those used by Fiedler and his associates (Shaw & Blum, 1966). Although the definition of favorability may require some further consideration, the hypothesis is well supported by present knowledge.

SUGGESTED READINGS

ADAMS, J. S., & ROMNEY, A. K.   A functional analysis of authority. *Psychological Review,* 1959, **66**, 234–251.

CRUTCHFIELD, R. S.   Conformity and character. *American Psychologist,* 1955, **10**, 191–198.

GERARD, H. B., WILHELMY, R. A., & CONOLLEY, E. S.   Conformity and group size. *Journal of Personality and Social Psychology,* 1968, **8**, 79–82.

HARVEY, O. J., & CONSALVI, C.   Status and conformity to pressures in informal groups. *Journal of Abnormal and Social Psychology,* 1960, **60**, 182–187.

HOLLANDER, E. P.   Conformity, status, and idiosyncrasy credit. *Psychological Review,* 1958, **65**, 117–127.

JACOBS, R. C., & CAMPBELL, D. T.   The perpetuation of an arbitrary tradition through several generations of a laboratory microculture. *Journal of Abnormal and Social Psychology,* 1961, **62**, 649–658.

LEFKOWITZ, M., BLAKE, R. R., & MOUTON, J. S.   Status factors in pedestrian violation of traffic signals. *Journal of Abnormal and Social Psychology,* 1955, **51**, 704–706.

LEWIN, K., LIPPITT, R., & WHITE, R. K.   Patterns of aggressive behavior in experimentally created "social climates." *Journal of Social Psychology,* 1939, **10**, 271–299.

MILGRAM, S.   Liberating effects of group pressure. *Journal of Personality and Social Psychology,* 1965, **1**, 127–134.

MORSE, N. C., & REIMER, E.   The experimental change of a major organizational variable. *Journal of Abnormal and Social Psychology,* 1956, **52**, 120–129.

MULDER, M., VAN DIJK, R., SOUTENDIJK, S., STELWAGEN, T., & VERHAGEN, J.   Non-instrumental liking tendencies toward powerful group members. *Acta Psychologica,* 1964, **22**, 367–386.

TORRANCE, E. P.   Some consequences of power differences on decision making in permanent and temporary three-man groups. *Research Studies, Washington State College,* 1954, **22**, 130–140.

CHAPTER 9

THE TASK ENVIRONMENT

A group forms and continues its existence for some purpose; when this purpose no longer exists, the group disintegrates unless a new purpose can be established. There may, of course, be more than one group purpose. The purpose is usually labeled "group goal," but sometimes it is referred to as "group task." Actually, group goal and group task are not coextensive, although they are interrelated and may in some instances be identical. That is, the task faced by the group may constitute its goal, and when that task is completed, the group will have no further basis for existence. An example of this is a committee appointed for the purpose of making recommendations concerning the disposition of money available for student support. The task of the group is to prepare a statement of recommendations, and completion of such a statement is its goal. But in many instances, the task may be only to achieve a subgoal that must be attained in order to reach the ultimate goals of the group. For instance, a group may have as its goal the improvement of the educational system in a particular community. In attempting to realize this goal, the group may have to complete a number of tasks, such as raising money for library books, recruiting highly qualified teachers, etc. Whether the task faced by the group at any particular moment is direct achievement of its ultimate goal, as in the example of the committee making recommendations, or whether it is merely to achieve a subgoal, as in the example of the educational improvement group, the characteristics of the task may be expected to exert a strong influence upon group process.

Throughout this book we have discussed the effects of variables upon group productivity and task solution, and we have noted how the particular effects of variables frequently depend upon the task of the group. It may seem odd that we have waited until this point to consider task environment. Although it would have been helpful to consider task characteristics before taking up other aspects of the group such as member characteristics, group composition, and group structure, it would have been exceedingly difficult to analyze the task environment without the background information provided in earlier portions of this book. And the *task* of analyzing the task environment will not be easy even at this stage. We must begin by asking what is meant by the term "group goal" so that we may relate it properly to the task environment. Next, we must inquire whether and to what extent group members establish goals for the group and whether they react to group goals as they do to individual goals. Finally, we will need to consider the analysis of group tasks and review the relationships of task characteristics to group functioning. Only then will we begin to understand the complexity of the task environment and its consequences for group process.

THE NATURE OF GROUP GOALS

Everyone seems to agree that groups have goals, and almost all writers and researchers appear to assume that everyone knows what is meant by the term "group goal." In any event, group goal usually is not defined beyond the identification of a particular goal for a particular group. For example, a researcher may state that the goal of the group was to solve an assigned problem in the shortest possible time, when, in fact, although he instructed the group to adopt such a goal, he has no reliable evidence that the group members indeed established problem solution as their goal. Thus, both the definition of group goal and the identification of the goal for a particular group are based upon unverified assumptions by the investigator. However, there is one noteworthy exception; Cartwright and Zander (1953, 1960, 1968) have made heroic attempts to deal with this knotty problem. The difficulties involved in formulating an acceptable definition of group goal are reflected in the changing views of these writers. In the first edition of their book, an entire section was devoted to "Group Goals and Group Locomotion," and four conceptions of group goals were presented. When the book was revised in 1960, the section heading was changed to "Individual Motives and Group Goals"; and the four conceptions, although still presented, were embedded in a general discussion of motivational influences. By the third edition (1968), the section on goals had been eliminated altogether, and the discussion of group goals appeared in a section dealing with motivational processes in groups. Since Cartwright and Zander's analysis represents the most extensive attempt to deal with the problem of group goals, it will be helpful to consider their conceptions.

Cartwright and Zander (1953) began their analysis by assuming that the formal properties of group goals do not differ in essentials from the properties of individual goals. Thus, the activities of group members with respect to group goals are similar to the activities of individuals with respect to individual goals. (We will see later that this assumption has a firm empirical basis.) Hence, they regarded the major problem as how to link individual goals with group goals. Their four conceptions represent different attempts to solve this problem.

The first conception proposes that a group goal is merely the composite of similar individual goals. Cartwright and Zander found this definition most unsatisfactory. They cited the example of two young men who want to marry the same girl. Although the individual goals of the men are indeed similar, few would agree that they have established a group goal. Even the qualification that the individual goals must be shared was rejected in view of the above example. On closer examination, however, it becomes clear that the two young men have very different end results in mind; young man A desires a goal of "A married to young lady C," whereas young man B desires a goal of "B married to C." Although the two goals are similar in that C is involved in both, they are really quite dissimilar. However, there are other problems associated with this conception of group goal. First, how are the individual goals to be "composited." Are they additive? Or should more weight be given to some individual goals than to others? Second, how is similarity to be determined, and just how similar must the individual goals be before they constitute a group goal. Third, Cartwright and Zander noted that sometimes a group goal exists even when the goals of individual group members are not at all similar. They cited the example of three boys who joined forces to build a lemonade stand, although A's goal was to make enough money to buy a baseball glove, B's goal was to use carpenter tools that he had received for his birthday, and C's goal was merely to join in the others' activities. Again, the objection disappears if one considers the entire situation. It is evident that a distinction must be made between immediate and long-range goals. A shared immediate goal of each of the three boys can be identified: the construction of a lemonade stand. True, this is merely a means to an end which is different for each of the three boys, and as such might be considered a subgoal. For A, the desired end constitutes a long-range goal, whereas for B and C, the desired ends are also immediate goals since they can be achieved simultaneously with the achievement of the goal "completed lemonade stand." Whether or not a group goal can appear to exist when individual goals are different thus depends upon whether immediate or long-range goals are considered.

The second conception of goal discussed by Cartwright and Zander holds that the group goal consists of individual goals for the group. This approach begins with a phenomenological point of view, and asks how the group members see the situation. Accordingly, this definition provides an operational procedure for identifying group goals: Ask the group members to specify the group goal; the degree of consensus reflects the degree to which the group has a unitary goal. It also meets Cartwright and Zander's criterion of linking individual and group goals. On the other hand, they objected that it is limited to consciously reportable goals and does not reveal hidden agenda. Also, it does not tell how the individual goals are to be combined.

The third conception views the group goal as depending upon a particular interrelation among motivational systems of group members. This formulation is not at all clear, either conceptually or operationally. Presumably, when the relations between two or more persons are such that the actions of any one satisfy the needs or reduce the need tensions of others, a group goal exists. The major problems with this conception are: (1) There is no easy way to determine when such a relationship exists; the group members must engage in goal-directed activities before the goal can be identified with confidence. (2) It does not identify what the group goal is, but merely asserts the existence of some goal.

The fourth and final conception identifies the group goal as an inducing agent. This view takes into account the fact that the group goal can influence group members to engage in goal-directed activities. Group members are expected to work toward the achievement of the group goal. Although it is true that the group goal can induce motivational forces upon group members, this cannot be seriously considered a *definition* of group goal.

The reader will undoubtedly find himself experiencing a strong feeling of dissatisfaction with these attempts to define group goals. Apparently Cartwright and Zander were also less than happy with their analysis; in their third edition (1968) they defined group goal simply as a preferred location of the group in its environment. That is, a group occupies some location in its environment which can be changed by certain activities of group members. When the group engages in such activities, it is assumed that another location is preferred by all or some of the group members. The location of the group when these activities terminate is regarded as the preferred one and therefore the group's goal. This formulation is conceptually clear, but it merely asserts that whatever end state is achieved through the actions of group members constitutes the group's goal. It, therefore, provides no basis for identifying group goals prior to goal attainment. Furthermore, it makes no distinction between achievement of the end state *attained* by group action and the end state *desired* by group members. It is conceivable that a group could engage in activities designed to reach location A but which actually led to location B, at which time the activities ceased because locomotion to A appeared impossible.

Group goals probably are best regarded as some composite of individual goals, despite the difficulties associated with such a conception. It is obvious that whatever goals can be attributed to the group must reside in the members of the group. It also seems clear that groups whose members all agree upon a single goal to the exclusion of all other goals, both individual and group, are extremely rare. In the typical group, there exists at least one goal which is acceptable to a majority of the group and which can properly be identified as the group goal. Group members who accept this goal are motivated to enact activities that are expected to aid in the achievement of this goal, and they are pleased (experience tension reduction?) when there is movement toward the goal or when the goal is achieved. Even those members who are not enthusiastic about this goal may nevertheless work toward it for a variety of individual goals or subgoals. Thus, a group goal is an end state desired by a majority of the group members. It can be identified by observing the activities of group members or, usually, by asking the members of the group to specify it.

In defining group goal in this way, one should take care to avoid the assumption that the group must have only one goal. A group may indeed have a single goal, but it is also common for a group to have several goals. A city planning committee may at one and the same time have the goals of paving city streets, obtaining federal funds for a control tower for the municipal airport, and building city parks. All these goals might be subsumed under the more general goal of city improvement. This consideration again raises the question concerning immediate and long-range goals. The achievement of city improvement constitutes a long-range goal, whereas paving city streets is a more immediate goal. In attempting to understand the behavior of group members, one must remember that it is the immediate goal that is of greatest significance. The activities of the group members are directly related to immediate goals, but are only indirectly related to long-range goals. As indicated earlier, the immediate goal or subgoal is often identical with the task of the group.

Finally, it is important to recognize that individual goals that are not a part of the group goal do not cease to influence an individual's behavior just because he becomes a member of a group and accepts the goal or goals of that group. The group member may be trying to achieve only individual goals, only group goals, or both individual and group goals when he engages in a particular set of activities. Usually, he is attempting to achieve both simultaneously. The relative strengths of individual and group goals, and the degree to which both can be achieved by the same activities, determine how effective the group will be in achieving its goal.

DO INDIVIDUALS SET GOALS FOR THE GROUP?

It is now time to return to the assumption that is implicit in our earlier discussions of the task environment, namely, that individuals establish goals for the group and respond to those goals in essentially the same way that they respond to individual goals. If this is a valid assumption, then it should be possible to demonstrate that group members do set goals for the group which have predictable consequences for behavior in the group. An early study by Shelley (1954) approached this problem by means of the level of aspiration paradigm. The level of aspiration is defined as the level of difficulty of that task which the individual sets as his goal for the next action. In the typical experiment, the individual attempts a particular task and achieves some level of success or failure; that is, he earns a particular score. He is then asked to state the score he expects (predicts, believes, etc.) that he will achieve on the next trial. This statement of the expected score on the next attempt is his level of aspiration. Although the level of aspiration is influenced by many factors, such as intelligence, knowledge of others' performance, etc., empirical findings generally show that the level of aspiration is raised following success and lowered following failure, where success is defined as a performance equaling or exceeding the previous level of aspiration and failure as a performance that is lower than the previous level or aspiration (Lewin, Dembo, Festinger, & Sears, 1944). In an experiment conducted for another purpose, Shelley (1954) elicited levels of aspiration for the group from members of four-person groups that had experienced varying degrees of success and failure. Success was manipulated through a trained assistant who served as a fifth group member. During the solution of five problems, the assistant guided certain groups to success and the experimenter assured failure for others by presenting them with unsolvable tasks. Some of the groups were led to succeed on the first four problems (success group); some were made to fail on the first four problems (failure group); some succeeded on the first problem, failed on the second, succeeded on the third, and failed on the fourth (SFSF groups); and some failed on the first, succeeded on the second, failed on the third, and succeeded on the fourth (FSFS groups). After the third problem and again after the fourth, each group member was asked to rate how well he thought the group would do on the next problem, using an 11-point rating scale. The ratings were used as a measure of level of aspiration for the group. The mean levels of aspiration for the fourth problem were 7.1 for the success groups, 2.3 for the failure groups, 6.0 for the SFSF groups, and 4.5 for the FSFS groups. The pattern thus corresponded closely to the degree of success and failure experienced by the groups on the problems previously attempted. The mean levels of aspiration for problem 5 were 7.2, 1.9, 4.9, and 5.6, respectively. Again, the pattern corresponded to degree of success and failure; the level of aspiration increased for those groups experiencing success on problem 4 and decreased for those experiencing failure on problem 4. Members of Shelley's experimental groups thus established goals for their group and responded to success or failure of the group in much the same way that individuals respond to individual success or failure.

Zander and his associates (Zander, 1968; Zander & Medow, 1963; Zander & Newcomb, 1967) also adopted the level of aspiration procedure for the study of group goal setting. However, these investigators' approach was somewhat different from Shelley's procedure. Instead of asking each group member to set a level of aspiration for the group, Zander et al. required that group members agree upon a joint level of aspiration, which they called the group's level of aspiration. Zander and Medow (1963) used a group ball-propelling task which requires all group members to stand in single file, to grasp a long pole, and to swing it collectively so that the end of the pole strikes a wooden ball and drives it down a channel. Numbers are painted on the side of the channel; the group's score is the number nearest the ball when it stops. Each group is given five shots per trial and may earn a maximum of 50 on each trial. When groups performed this task, the group level of aspiration was raised following a success and lowered following a failure. Thus group members set goals for the group very much as they do individual goals, whether asked to do so as individuals or as a group.

Zander and Medow also noted that the group level of aspiration was more often raised following success than it was lowered following failure, an asymmetry that has also been observed in some studies of individual levels of aspiration (Lewin et al., 1944). This finding was interpreted as reflecting both the perceived probability of succeeding and the attractiveness of doing so. It was assumed that when an individual must decide whether to engage in a solitary activity, he does so on the basis of the satisfaction that he may obtain from engaging in it. In a similar fashion, when the group member chooses a level of aspiration for his group, he does so on the basis of expected satisfaction, which in turn derives from both the satisfaction that it is possible to attain and the probability that this possible satisfaction actually will be attained by the group's action relative to that task. It is interesting to note that the stronger tendency to raise the group level of aspiration following success than to lower it following failure has also been observed in natural situations. Zander and Newcomb (1967) studied changes in the official goals of United Fund campaigns in 149 cities over a four-year period. A successful campaign was almost always followed by the setting of a higher goal the next year, whereas a failing campaign was rarely followed by a lowered goal the next year.

The studies of levels of aspiration in groups reveal that individuals establish goals for the group and respond to goal achievement in essentially the same way that they respond to personal goal achievement. Group goals serve as an inducing agent in that they motivate group members to work toward their attainment. Thus, it appears that many of the motivational concepts that apply to individuals working toward their own goals also apply to individuals working toward group goals. A further test of this expectation was reported by Horwitz (1954). He began with the assumption that no individual group member can achieve the group goal acting alone, although each group member may contribute in some degree to the movement of the group toward its goal. A group goal is like an individual goal in that it terminates a sequence of group activities. Since individual goals usually presuppose the existence of an internal system of tension, such as a need, then it follows that the existence of a group goal should also be based upon tension systems. Following Lewin (1951), Horwitz adopted the "interrupted task" experimental paradigm to test his hypothesis that tension systems can be aroused for goals which the individual holds for the group. Lewin and his associates have shown that when an individual works on a series of tasks, some of which are completed and some of which are interrupted, the individual tends to recall more of the incompleted tasks than the completed ones. This greater recall of the interrupted tasks is interpreted as reflecting unreduced tension associated with the goal of task completion.

Horwitz recruited eighteen five-person groups from sororities at the University of Michigan. Each group was exposed to several experiences designed to arouse a feeling of group solidarity among its members. First, the groups were told that they were engaged in a contest in which each team represented its sorority and that each group would be judged by the quality of its cooperative performance on jigsaw puzzles. Next, group members were involved in a group discussion designed to increase their awareness as group members. Finally, they were given a questionnaire entitled "Test on Group Loyalty" which included items dealing with team spirit, willingness to go along with the group, etc. Following these procedures, each group worked on seventeen jigsaw puzzles. A 14- by 14-inch cardboard poster was exposed to the group. The group's task was to direct the experimenter in filling in the parts of the figure one piece at a time. Each group member was seated in a separate booth so that she could see the poster and the experimenter, but could not see the other group members. Each person had four differently shaped cardboard pieces, each corresponding to a section of the figure. On each trial, each group member indicated which piece the experimenter should fill in by holding up the corresponding piece. According to the rules, if a specified number of group members—and no more—held up a given piece, then the experimenter placed the piece in the figure. This procedure permitted those who did not hold up the piece to take credit for successful task completion, since their *not* holding up the piece resulted in the correct number. The actual determination of whether the correct number of subjects had held up a piece was, of course, made by the experimenter. At the midpoint of each task, the experimenter explained that he had the basic score, and asked if the group wanted to stop or to complete the puzzle. Group members voted by holding up the right hand for completion and the left hand for stopping. The experimenter then announced the majority vote; if the vote was "yes," work was continued, if "no," the puzzle was set aside and work was started on the next one. The first two puzzles were practice. On the last fifteen trials, the announced majority vote was "no" on five and "yes" on ten puzzles. Group members were allowed to continue five of the "yes" puzzles to completion, whereas the other five "yes" puzzles were interrupted by the experimenter midway in the work on the third piece, with the explanation that they would return to it later. Thus, there were three experimental conditions: a "no" vote followed by work stoppage (N); a "yes" vote followed by task completion (Y-C); and a "yes" vote followed by task interruption (Y-I).

According to Horwitz's analysis, the psychological situation for the "yes" conditions is very different from that of the "no" condition. These differences are shown graphically in Figure 9-1. The group goal was characterized as earning as many points as possible, which is represented in Figure 9-1a as a region toward which the group is locomoting. If the group votes "yes," this region has a positive valence; that is, the group is motivated to move toward that region, thus reducing tension. If the group votes "no," then the region representing task completion has a negative valence, as shown in Figure 9-1b, and the goal is to avoid completion; that is, tension will be increased if the group locomotes toward task completion. These considerations suggest that task completion should lead to tension reduction in the Y-C condition, whereas tension reduction should occur in the N condition when the task is not completed. Tension reduction should not occur in the Y-I condition, since the group did not achieve its goal. Therefore, Horwitz predicted that the Y-I condition should result in the greatest recall of interrupted tasks, with the N and Y-C conditions equal in this respect. The results

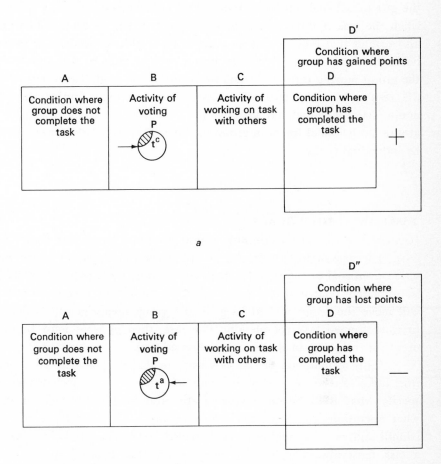

Figure 9-1 The Psychological Situation for Group Members Who Vote "Yes" (*a*) and for Group Members Who Vote "No" (*b*). (Reprinted with permission from M. Horwitz. The recall of interrupted group tasks: An experimental study of individual motivation in relation to group goals. *Human Relations*, 1954, **7**, 3–38.)

verified this prediction: The Y-I condition resulted in 55.9 percent recall of interrupted tasks as compared with 44.4 percent and 46.0 percent in the Y-C and N conditions, respectively.

This investigation has been outlined in detail because it represents a particular orientation to group goal and reveals so clearly some of the consequences of group goals for the individual group member. The results show that tension systems can be aroused for goals which the individual holds for the group and that tension is reduced by task completion but is not reduced when the task is interrupted—at least not to the same extent. The findings also suggest that tension may be aroused for avoidances which the individual holds for the group and that the tension will be reduced if the possibility of the group moving into the avoidance region is removed. Taken together with the results from the level of aspiration studies, these findings leave little doubt that individuals do establish goals for the group and that such goals arouse motivational forces in group members that are similar to those aroused by individual goals.

TASKS AND GROUP GOALS

It is unlikely that group members would attempt a group task if they had no goal. The reason for attempting a task is task completion, which may be either a subgoal or the ultimate goal. In any case, the task faced by the group is intimately related to the group goal; to the extent that task completion will move the group toward its goal, the group members will be motivated to work toward task completion. The *task*, then, is what must be done in order for the group to achieve its goal or subgoal.

This formulation of task is similar to that proposed by Hackman: "It (the task) consists of a stimulus complex and a set of instructions which specify what is to be done vis-à-vis the stimuli. The instructions indicate what operations are to be performed by the subject(s) with respect to the stimuli and/or what goal is to be achieved" (Hackman, 1969, p. 113). Thus, a task must always include identifiable stimulus material and instructions about what to do about this material. According to Hackman, instructions to think would not be a task, whereas instructions to think about a specific picture and relate its meaning would be.

In the following pages, we will be concerned primarily with the analysis of group tasks and the consequences of task environment for group process. However, the reader should keep one thing firmly in mind: The fact that group members work at a task implies that some goal is held for the group. The ultimate goal of each group member might be no more than a desire to escape from an unpleasant experimental situation; but for the group collectively, there must be at least a subgoal which can be attained through task completion.

THE PROBLEM OF TASK ANALYSIS

For many years, most group dynamicists commented upon the importance of the task for group functioning, but continued to use a wide variety of unanalyzed tasks in their empirical investigations. The result was an almost complete lack of systematization of task-related information about group behavior. This made it very difficult to establish general principles that could be applied to specific task situations. In recent years, however, a number of theorists and researchers have attempted to introduce some order into the task environment. Although the attempts have taken many forms, they can be represented by three general approaches: (1) the development of a standard group task; (2) the classification of tasks into specific categories (a typology of tasks); and (3) the dimensional analysis of group tasks.

STANDARD GROUP TASKS

A standard group task is a task with known characteristics that is adaptable to the study of a variety of problems relative to small group behavior. That is, the inputs can be described, the operations required of group members for successful task completion can be specified, and the outputs (group products or performance measures) can be observed and quantified. For the standard task to be generally useful, it should be possible to study different kinds of questions about group behavior by suitably modifying elements of the task. For example, a standard task might be equally useful for the study of leadership, of social facilitation, or of conformity behavior.

The design of a standard group task usually arises from a consideration of the great difficulty of comparing experimental results derived from heterogeneous group tasks. The need for some systematic assessment becomes obvious, and the adoption of a standard task is a relatively easy way of making a minimal response to this need. The term "minimal" is used deliberately, since the problems created by the use of a standard task are almost as great as those resulting from task heterogeneity. Nevertheless, standard tasks are useful for certain purposes and should not be dismissed summarily.

Several standard tasks have been proposed and used in research with some success. For example, McCurdy and Lambert (1952) designed an apparatus which they said could appropriately be called a group maze. The device could be adapted for use with a single person or with groups of varying size. The model described was designed for three-person groups. It consists of six 2-position rotary switches mounted on separate panels that can be attached to the edge of a work table for convenient operation by group members. These switches are connected to six matching switches on a control panel. When the member's switches are set in the same way as the corresponding switch on the control panel, a signal lamp on the table lights up, as well as a signal light on the control panel. The member's switches are connected via the control panel to a kymograph which records each person's response on each trial. The experimenter controls the setting of the switches on the control panel, and thus can set up tasks varying in degree of difficulty. This task has clearly defined inputs, the operations required for task completion are easily understood, and the group's performance can be recorded and quantified. It is also adaptable to different problems; McCurdy and Lambert used it to compare individual and group performance and to study the effects of autocratic leadership on group performance. A similar task was used by M. E. Shaw (1958a) in a study of cooperation and competition.

Another switch-setting task was designed by Lanzetta and Roby (1957) and used with some success in studying various aspects of group performance. This task also can be adapted for use with groups of varying size, but was described for the three-person group. It consisted of three major components: displays, controls, and communication system. The displays were six AC voltmeters, modified to simulate aircraft instrument dials. Dial readings were programmed from a central control, each having three positions. The controls were six 2-position switches labeled to represent aircraft controls. An operating card near each control gave the correct settings for different dial readings, each correct setting being determined by the readings of two dials. Each group member occupied a separate booth which contained two displays, two controls, and a communication box. All communication was by interphone, which was attached to an operations recorder that provided a record of all communication. Switch settings were recorded on an Esterline-Angus operations recorder. The immediate task of the group was to adjust and readjust switch settings in response to changing dial readings. Since each booth contained only part or none of the information needed to adjust the controls, group interaction was required. This is obviously adaptable to a variety of problems, and has the added advantage of permitting wide variations in difficulty and distribution of task load among group members.

A rather different kind of standard task was described by Zajonc (1965b), although it also was mechanical. In describing this task, Zajonc provided the most detailed statement of the requirements of a standard group task that is available. It will be instructive to review his analysis at this point. Zajonc asserted that group performance depends directly on the performance of individual group members and the pattern of task assignments. His analysis, therefore, attempted to identify requirements relevant to these two classes of variables. These requirements may be paraphrased as follows:

1 A standard group task should involve individual behavior that has already been studied extensively on an individual basis so that its antecedents are reasonably well known.

2 The task should involve individual responses that are known or easily acquired by members of any population.

3 It should allow precise and independent measurement of both individual capability and group performance, using the same units of measurement.

4 The task should permit the experimenter to evaluate individual contributions independently of the measurement of group performance, again using the same units.

5 The task should allow manipulation of group member interdependence without altering the basic characteristics of the task or the responses required by it.

6 A standard group task should permit manipulation of task difficulty, task complexity, and knowledge of results (performances) without altering the character of the task or the required responses.

7 The task should involve units of measurement that are commensurate with units of individual measurement. (This is essentially the same as requirement 3.)

8 It should allow many varieties of division of labor.

In addition to these requirements, Zajonc suggested other desirable characteristics of a standard group task, including economy of data collection, stability of observations, adaptability with respect to a large variety of problems, the possibility of repeated measurements of the same behavior from the same individual, and portability.

With these requirements in mind, Zajonc proposed a Group Reaction Time Apparatus which he believed met most or all of his specifications. It consists of seven individual panels, one for each group member, and a control panel for the experimenter. This permits study of groups ranging up to seven persons, but the apparatus can be expanded to fit groups of any size. Each subject panel is placed in a separate cubicle or on a table with partitions between group members. Each panel has two reaction keys and eight stimulus displays. One of the stimulus displays is the subject's own and another is the group display. The remaining displays provide feedback about the behavior of other group members. Each stimulus display has two stimulus lights and a red failure light. Each reaction key can be coordinated with either of the two stimulus lights, so that the pattern of required responses can be varied at will. The stimulus lights are turned on by the experimenter. The task of the group members is to turn off, as quickly as possible, any stimulus light that appears on their panel. Reaction time is measured by a clock attached to each reaction key. The difficulty of the task, feedback about own and others' achievement, etc., can be manipulated, and both individual and group responses can be studied using the same task.

The task proposed by Zajonc has many advantages and has been used successfully to study various aspects of group and individual behavior. Nevertheless, like the other standard tasks reviewed here, this is a mechanical task requiring mechanical responses by group members. It seems highly doubtful that complex group behavior can be investigated with such a task, nor is it probable that the findings of research using such a task can be generalized to tasks such as group discussion, intellectual analyses, or clerical operations.

TASK TYPOLOGIES

A task typology consists of a set of categories or classifications into which group tasks can be sorted, more or less exclusively. In the simplest typology, tasks may be classified into two mutually exclusive categories, such as simple and complex (M. E. Shaw, 1964) or conjunctive and disjunctive (Thibaut & Kelley, 1959). The same set of tasks, of course, may be classified according to several different sets of categories. Essentially the same kind of classification is represented by the six types identified by Carter, Haythorn, and Howell (1950): clerical, discussion, intellectual construction, mechanical assembly, motor coordination, and reasoning. This grouping of tasks is based upon obvious differences in tasks, such as the instructions given the subjects and the kinds of operations they are expected to perform. Such "qualitative" differences are important, and this kind of typology is useful for many purposes.

A much more complex typology involving two-category classifications on three dimensions was proposed by Thibaut and Kelley. These authors defined task as "a problem, assignment, or stimulus complex to which the individual or group responds by performing various overt or covert operations which lead to various outcomes" (Thibaut & Kelley, 1959, p. 150). Tasks fitting this definition were held to vary with respect to state, requirements, and correspondence. The *state* of the task refers to the fact that the stimuli and situations presented to an individual confronting the task vary from time to time. A variation may occur because of external forces or because of the person's own actions, but in either case, states are different only if the variation makes a difference to the person. That is, different states yield different outcomes for one or more behaviors that the person might enact. The state of any given task may be either *steady* or *variable*. "Steady state" means only that the task has one state and no more, whereas "variable state" means that the task has multiple states. For example, a task in which the teacher can present only one arithmetic problem would be a steady state task, but if she could present either of two problems of different types, it would be a variable state task.

Task *requirements* may be either *conjunctive* or *disjunctive*. A conjunctive task requires that more than one group member make responses before the task can be completed, whereas a disjunctive task allows the task to be completed if any group member makes the required response. For example, human relations problems that require consensus involve conjunctive task requirements; all group members must make some response before consensus can be achieved. On the other hand, tasks such as jigsaw puzzles are disjunctive in that the task can be completed if any group member places the pieces in the proper place. Thibaut and Kelley noted that conjunctiveness or disjunctiveness is usually determined by the structure of the task, although it may depend upon a group member's relation to his comembers. That is, if the relationship is such that person A gains as much satisfaction from task completion by his coworker B as he does from task completion by his own efforts, then the task requirements are conjunctive even though the structure of the task implies disjunctivity. This member-relation analysis appears to confuse task structure and interpersonal relations, thus making it extremely difficult to determine whether the requirements of a given task are conjunctive or disjunctive.

Tasks may also vary with respect to *correspondence* or *noncorrespondence* of outcomes. The outcomes available to person A may correspond to those available to person B or not. That is, if the task permits both A and B to achieve good outcomes simultaneously, the task is characterized by correspondence of outcomes; if they cannot, it is characterized by noncorrespondence. This particular classification is most relevant when the investigator adopts Thibaut and Kelley's theory of interaction outcomes (see Chapter 2).

A given group task can be classified according to any one or all of the three dimensions. For example, a task may be classified as steady state, conjunctive, and correspondent, indicating that it has only one state, requires responses by all group members, and is characterized by correspondence of outcomes. This kind of typology is certainly superior to global classifications based on qualitative aspects of the task, and it begins to introduce some order into the task environment of groups. The value of the analysis would be enhanced, however, if tasks were scaled along these three dimensions rather than treated in an all-or-none fashion.

Another typology, suggested by G. B. Cohen (1968b), is similar to that of Thibaut and Kelley in that it is based upon operational requirements of the task; however, it differs in that Cohen divided tasks into three mutually exclusive classes. According to his analysis, group tasks require three basically different kinds of operations: (1) intake of information; (2) transformation of information; and (3) execution. Although all or most tasks require all three kinds of operations, the emphasis is usually upon one of the three. Tasks that emphasize the intake of information are called *sensor-type tasks*. Tasks that require the generation of a great many different ideas, recall of information, verbal associations, etc., are sensor-type tasks because the main emphasis is on information intake. It is regarded as irrelevant whether the information comes from memory or from perception of the environment or whether the data consist of isolated facts or more complex patterns of cognitions.

Tasks that place the main emphasis upon the transformation of information are called *control-type tasks*. These tasks may permit several choices initially, but once the first decision has been made, choices at later points in task completion are limited. This means that the group must consider the consequences of each decision for later events and must, therefore, evaluate relatively long cognitive chains. The major difficulty in such tasks is the monitoring of unfinished cognitive sequences, although, of course, information must be received before control-type activities can begin. Examples of this kind of task are the construction of a crossword puzzle, solution of complicated mathematical problems, and the like.

Finally, some tasks emphasize execution of operations according to rules or instructions. These are called *effector-type tasks.* Again, these tasks require both information collection and control-type activities, but the major requirement is one of execution. A task requiring the construction of a simple object from Tinkertoy pieces is an example of an effector-type task.

The Cohen typology is also useful for certain purposes. For instance, the classification of tasks used in the individual versus group performance studies (see Chapter 3) enabled Cohen to interpret the findings more systematically. He found that individuals usually performed better than groups on control-type tasks, whereas groups usually performed better than individuals on sensor-type tasks.* However, like other typologies, Cohen's typology is a rather gross form of analysis that does not reflect the multiplex character of group tasks.

The Cohen classification is similar to one adopted by Hackman and Jones (1965). Their typology included production tasks, discussion tasks, and problem-solving tasks. *Production* tasks require group members to elicit images and to synthesize them into an integrated unit. *Discussion* tasks require the members to resolve some issue and to summarize their consensus. *Problem-solving* tasks require group members to generate and evaluate procedural implementation.

A much more complex typology was proposed by Roby and Lanzetta (1958). In fact, they developed a rational framework for task description which may be called a typology only because tasks are described in categories or classes. According to their analysis, task performance involves a chain of events which include task input and output variables and group input and output variables. *Task input variables* (T_i) are those events which occur in the environment of the group. This set of events includes such things as variations in input displays and stress-inducing stimuli. *Group input activities* (G_i) consist of a correlative set of events that occurs within the group; it

---

* Note that Cohen used "man-minutes" as the measure of quality of performance. Other measures yield different conclusions, as will be recalled from Chapter 3.

includes such things as observational responses of group members and communication processes. *Group output activities* (G_o) are events resulting from group input activities. Examples cited included decisions to make certain motor responses as well as the motor responses themselves. *Task output variables* (T_o) are events which occur in the group surroundings following the group performance.

Roby and Lanzetta further proposed three properties for the description of these four classes of events: descriptive aspects, distribution of component events, and functional behavior of the events. *Descriptive aspects* concern the qualitative nature of events as well as quantitative properties, such as numerousness. *Distribution* of component events refers to the distribution of events in physical space *or* to their distribution in relation to other events. The *functional behavior* of events deals with the recurrence of events over time or as a result of preceding events. Thus, it is theoretically possible to describe any group task by describing the four classes of events in terms of the three properties.

To illustrate this form of description, Roby and Lanzetta selected the common symbol task used by Leavitt (1951) in his study of communication networks. It will be recalled from Chapter 5 that this task consists of five cards containing such symbols as stars and triangles. These cards are distributed among the members of a five-person group. One, and only one, symbol appears on each and every card; the group's goal is to identify this commonly held symbol, communicating only via written messages. Their description of this task is given in Table 9-1. It can be seen that this analysis yields a relatively complete description of the task, but it does not provide a ready basis for comparing the task with some other task described in the same way. Nevertheless, such a description highlights task characteristics and reveals at least some of the "critical demands" of the task. Such a description also enables the researcher to note the similarities and differences of group tasks. Furthermore, the Roby-Lanzetta descriptive analysis could be converted into a form of dimensional analysis if the properties of the event classes were subjected to scale analysis.

DIMENSIONAL ANALYSIS OF GROUP TASKS

Dimensional analysis of group tasks represents an attempt to specify differences among tasks along a variety of relatively independent dimensions. It differs from the typology approach primarily in degree of differentiation. For

TABLE 9-1 Description of the Common-symbol Task

	Descriptive properties	Spatial distribution	Functional behavior
T_i	Easily distinguished symbols on cards	Uniformly distributed except for missing symbols	Independent of output present throughout task performance
G_i	Determine missing symbol and transmit to other station(s)	Uniform except that central persons may relay from distant persons	Reporting ad lib. or by request
G_o	Report on common symbol to other group member or experimenter	Essentially uniform	Dependent on G_i through network channels. No fixed phasing.
T_o	Experimenter corroboration of answer	Uniform	Occurs at termination of performance

SOURCE: Reprinted with permission from T. B. Roby and J. T. Lanzetta, Considerations in the analysis of group tasks. *Psychological Bulletin*, 1958, **55**, 88–101.

example, it would not be inaccurate to treat the Thibaut and Kelley analysis as a form of dimensional analysis, since tasks were differentiated on three different dimensions. On the other hand, the Cohen typology cannot properly be regarded as representing dimensional analysis because no dimensions are involved, unless "task emphasis" is viewed as a dimension.

A form of dimensional analysis was described by the author several years ago (M. E. Shaw, 1963). The proposed method is an adaptation of the Thurstone and Chave (1929) method for the construction of attitude scales. First, ten potential task dimensions were identified by a review of the literature on small group research and discussions with prominent investigators in the field of group dynamics. Next, a sample of 104 group tasks was assembled and each task described as clearly as possible. Third, forty-nine judges familiar with the field of psychology were asked to sort the tasks along the ten potential task dimensions, using eight categories or "piles." Each dimension was described as clearly as possible to each judge in order to reduce interjudge variability in the interpretation of dimension labels. Fourth, scale values were computed for each task on each dimension as the median of the distribution of judgments (categories) by the forty-nine judges, and interjudge consistency was estimated by the interquartile range. Fifth, intercorrelations among the a priori task dimensions were computed and a factor analysis was carried out. The results of this analysis are given in Table 9-2. The correlations among dimensions that are heavily loaded on the

TABLE 9-2   Intercorrelations among A Priori Task Dimensions (104 tasks, 10 dimensions)

	1	2	3	4	5	6	7	8	9	10
1. Difficulty			I							
2. Goal clarity	−.54									
3. Operation requirements	.65	−.68								
4. Decision verifiability	.02	.29	−.52			II				
5. Goal-path multiplicity	.05	−.31	.59	−.89						
6. Intrinsic interest	.05	−.28	.58	−.70	.67					
7. Solution multiplicity	−.15	−.20	.38	−.90	.91	.59				
8. Cooperation requirements	.05	−.28	.32	−.14	.18	.26	.10		III	
9. Intellectual-manipulative requirements	.13	.16	.04	−.22	.20	.05	.07	−.40		
10. Population familiarity	−.12	.08	.25	−.47	.44	.42	.33	.04	.46	IV

NOTE: Correlations among dimensions heavily loaded on a common factor are enclosed in boxes. The common factor is indicated by a roman numeral.

same factor are enclosed in boxes. A second factor analysis using only the most reliable data yielded similar results.

On the basis of these data, plus certain theoretical considerations, six of the ten a priori task dimensions were retained as representing relatively independent dimensions. These dimensions may be described briefly as follows:

Difficulty (Factor I) may be defined as the amount of effort required to complete the task. (This was the original definition of difficulty given judges.) Difficulty is influenced by (or perhaps determined by) the number of operations, skills, and knowledges required for successful task completion. Goal clarity is negatively loaded on Factor I and hence may be regarded as one aspect of lack of difficulty or the ease with which a task may be completed. Tasks may vary on the difficulty dimension from easy (requiring few operations, skills, and knowledges, and/or having a clear goal) to difficult (requiring many operations, skills, and knowledges and/or having an unclear goal).

Solution multiplicity (Factor II) may be defined as the degree to which there is more than one correct solution to the task. It is a complex dimension involving the number of acceptable solutions, the number of alternatives for task completion, and the degree to which acceptable solutions can be verified, i.e., can be demonstrated to be correct. Solution multiplicity was chosen as the label for this dimension not only because the a priori dimension bearing that label had the heaviest factor loading, but also because the number of acceptable solutions appeared to be the most basic aspect of this dimension. Goal-path multiplicity (number of alternatives for task completion) and decision verifiability (degree to which acceptable solutions can be demonstrated to be correct) are probably the consequences of solution multiplicity. A task that has numerous acceptable solutions will almost necessarily have several alternatives for arriving at those solutions, and it is improbable that any one solution can be demonstrated to be correct. Thus, a task that has a high scale value on solution multiplicity is one that has many possible acceptable solutions, many alternatives for attaining those solutions, and no solution that can be easily verified, whereas a task that has a low scale value on this dimension will have a single acceptable solution that can be easily demonstrated to be correct and a single path to this goal.

Intrinsic interest is defined as the degree to which the task in and of itself is interesting, motivating, or attractive to the group members. Although moderately loaded on Factor II, intrinsic interest is not regarded as a necessary aspect of solution multiplicity. This conclusion was based upon two considerations. First, the second factor analysis, using only the most reliable data from the task-sorting procedure, revealed intrinsic interest to be at least partially independent. Second, it is possible that the correlation between intrinsic interest and solution multiplicity might have been due to the particular judges used in the collection of data. Graduate students undoubtedly find the complex problems more interesting, and they may have judged the tasks on the basis of their own feelings.

Cooperation requirements (Factor III) may be defined as the degree to which integrated action of group members is required to complete the task. Tasks at the upper end of this dimensional continuum require that group members coordinate their actions so that each member is performing the appropriate function at the right time relative to the actions of other members, whereas a task at the other end of the continuum could be completed by each group member working independently and at his own speed. This dimension is thus quite similar to Thibaut and Kelley's conjunctive-

disjunctive category. However, while a task with high cooperative requirements is clearly conjunctive, so is one with moderately low cooperation requirements. Only tasks with very low scale values on cooperation requirements could be classified as disjunctive.

Intellectual-manipulative requirements is defined as the ratio of mental
requirements to motor requirements of the group task. It is regarded as a
separate dimension even though it did not emerge as an independent factor.
This decision was based largely upon the low correlations between this
dimension and other a priori dimensions, but consideration was also given
to the fact that no good theoretical basis could be found for combining it
with any other dimension. Tasks at the upper extreme of this dimension require only mental activities (reasoning, thinking, etc.) for task completion,
whereas those at the low end of the continuum require only motor activities
for successful completion. Of course, most group tasks require a combination
of both kinds of activities, but there are wide variations in the relative
amounts of each activity required.

Population familiarity may be defined as the degree to which the task
is encountered by members of the larger society. It correlated moderately
with intellectual-manipulative requirements in the second factor analysis,
but this could be due to an artifact in the judging procedure. That is,
graduate students in psychology are more familiar with intellectual than with
manipulative tasks.

The validity of the scale values derived from the scaling method was
initially tested for the difficulty dimension, since its effects upon certain
aspects of group performance are most predictable. For instance, groups
should require more time to solve difficult tasks than to solve easy ones.
Measures of time to solve were obtained on four tasks and correlated with
scale values for difficulty, yielding a correlation coefficient of .80. Difficulty
scale values were also obtained for six tasks used in a study reported by
Lawson (1961) and correlated with time scores reported by Lawson. A correlation coefficient of .79 was obtained. These correlations are moderately
high and provide some evidence for the validity of the scaling procedure.

The usefulness of the dimensional analysis approach has already been
illustrated in our discussion of the contingency model of leadership effectiveness (Fiedler, 1964; see Chapter 8). Fiedler theorized that the effectiveness of
a particular leadership style depends upon the favorability of the situation
for the leader, which in turn depends upon affective leader-group relations,
task structure, and position power. Task structure was operationally defined

by four of the a priori task dimensions used in the above analysis: decision verifiability, goal clarity, goal-path multiplicity, and solution multiplicity. (According to our analysis, these are reducible to solution multiplicity, with perhaps some variation in difficulty.) Tasks used in Fiedler's research and theory were scaled according to the procedure outlined above, and scale values combined with measures of affective leader-group relations and position power to define the favorability continuum. It will be remembered that this analysis enabled Fiedler to make a more reasonable interpretation of his findings than had been possible before. Thus, scale analysis of group tasks proved to be helpful in at least one problem area. Other evidences of its usefulness will be cited in the next section, as well as evidences of the values of other approaches to task analysis.

TASK CHARACTERISTICS AND GROUP PROCESS

Standard tasks have been used in research with some success, as indicated earlier. However, when standard tasks have been used, other task parameters have been varied also. For instance, Zajonc and Taylor (1963) used the Group Reaction Time Apparatus to investigate the effects of task difficulty; in a similar way, Lanzetta and Roby (1956, 1957) used their dial-setting task to study the consequences of task demands. Therefore, we will discuss research using standard tasks in connection with the appropriate typology or dimensional analysis approach. By far, the greatest number of investigations of the effects of task characteristics have involved some form of task typology.

TYPE OF TASK AND GROUP PROCESS

We have already discussed rather extensively the differences resulting from task simplicity-complexity (see Chapter 5). The reader will recall that one major consequence of this gross difference in type of task is in relation to the group's communication network: Centralized networks are more effective when the task is simple, whereas decentralized communication networks are more effective when the task is complex. Conformity behavior was also seen to vary directly with task difficulty, and type of task was assumed to be responsible for a variety of other differences in group process. Concern for the effects of type of task has been secondary in most studies, but several researchers have been primarily interested in such effects. The bulk of their work, unfortunately, deals with only two aspects of the task. The first of these is the classification of tasks according to their global characteristics, including such categories as reasoning tasks, mechanical assembly tasks, etc. These categories might be called *general types* of tasks. The other kind of classification is with respect to *task difficulty;* tasks are typed as either difficult or easy, or sometimes into sets of high, moderate, or low levels of difficulty.

GENERAL TYPES AND GROUP PROCESS   One of the earliest studies of general types of tasks and group behavior was conducted by Carter, Haythorn, and Howell (1950). They were interested in the degree to which different kinds of tasks call for different leadership abilities. The six kinds of tasks mentioned earlier were used: reasoning, intellectual construction, clerical, discussion, motor cooperation, and mechanical assembly tasks. The reasoning task was a true-false form of syllogistic reasoning task which required group members to determine the correct conclusion from four "given statements." The intellectual construction task required that group members plot a field, such as a basketball court, on the floor, using strings and cellophane tape. They were given some dimensions, but had to determine others from those given. The clerical tasks required that group members sort a large number of cards according to several dimensions. This task demanded considerable coordination of efforts. Discussion tasks required that group members discuss an issue to consensus and write a statement of their conclusions. The motor coordination task was the ball and spiral task that we have encountered in other research. The mechanical assembly tasks required construction of simple objects, such as goal posts, using precut lumber. Leadership ratings of group members were obtained by five different methods: the leaderless group discussion technique, nominations, ratings by faculty members, ratings by friends, and assessment of leadership in other activities. Correlations of leadership ratings across tasks indicated a certain degree of generality of leadership ability, but they also revealed wide variations from task to task. A factor analysis suggested that there were two different kinds of tasks requiring different kinds of leadership abilities: intellectual tasks and manipulative tasks. This dichotomy is very similar to the intellectual-manipulative requirements dimension derived from the scale analysis of group tasks.

Hackman (1968) investigated differences in group behavior as a function of type of task, using production, discussion, and problem-solving tasks. The study involved 108 three-person groups and 108 different tasks, 12 for each combination of the three types of tasks with three levels of difficulty.

Groups produced written products in response to questionnaires, which were then analyzed according to six general dimensions: action orientation, length, originality, optimism, quality of presentation, and issue involvement. In addition, group products were evaluated on two "task-dependent dimensions": adequacy and creativity. Type of task was shown to be systematically related to all these dimensions except adequacy. "In general, problem-solving tasks were characterized by high action orientation, production tasks by high originality, and discussion tasks by high issue involvement" (Hackman, 1968, p. 169). A study by Morris (1965) used the same three types of tasks and found that leaders were more active on problem-solving tasks than on production tasks or on discussion tasks. In general, discussion tasks and problem-solving tasks produced similar effects upon group process and contrasted with production tasks. However, production tasks seemed to lead to an emphasis by the group on getting the job done, whereas discussion tasks produced more process-oriented activity, such as clarifying, explaining, and defending. Problem-solving tasks combined both output-oriented activity and process-oriented activities. Morris concluded that about 60 percent of a group's or a leader's behavior is highly sensitive to type of task.

These several studies make it abundantly clear that the general type of task faced by the group will have important consequences for group interaction. It has been shown that the type of task, grossly determined, influences the kinds of leadership abilities that are required for successful task completion, the amount of leader activity, and the particular kinds of interactions that occur during the process of task completion.

TASK DIFFICULTY AND GROUP FUNCTIONING   Many of the studies of task difficulty merely demonstrate that the more difficult the task, the more time the group requires for solution and the greater the probability that the group product will be inferior. These findings are certainly not astounding, although they may be significant for methodological purposes. That is, it may be necessary to demonstrate that tasks do indeed differ in difficulty, or that a particular method of measuring task difficulty is valid, before one can investigate other effects of task difficulty. An interesting variation in the study of the effects of task difficulty on group performance was reported by Zajonc and Taylor (1963). Using the Group Reaction Time Apparatus, they varied difficulty either by varying the time permitted for reaction before failure or by varying the number of group members required to make the response before failure time elapsed. The probability of success under each level of difficulty was computed, and performance was evaluated relative to the probability of success. The results showed that both individual and group reaction times decreased with increasing difficulty for both manipulations of task difficulty. Thus, task difficulty does not inevitably impair group performance; the relationship between difficulty and performance depends upon the nature of the task and the performance measure. In the Zajonc and Taylor study, the effects were probably mediated by motivation; that is, increasing difficulty may increase the motivation of group members, thus increasing speed of reaction.

However, task difficulty affects other aspects of group process as well as group performance. Bass, Pryer, Gaier, and Flint (1958) studied 51 five-person groups as they solved easy and difficult tasks. The task required that group members rank-order lists of words in terms of familiarity. Easy tasks were lists of familiar words and difficult tasks were lists of less familiar words. They found that less leadership was attempted by group members when the task was easy than when it was difficult.

Task difficulty in relation to self-esteem of group members and conformity behavior was investigated by Gergen and Bauer (1967). They speculated that the relationship between self-esteem and conformity should vary with the difficulty of the task, since the relevance of self-confidence to conformity should become greater with increasing task difficulty. The conformity behavior of persons having low, medium, or high self-esteem was measured, using tasks that were low, medium, or high with respect to difficulty. The task involved comparisons of pairs of paintings on criteria of varying clarity, e.g., amount of color when one painting clearly had more color than the other (low difficulty), degree of creativeness (moderate difficulty), and degree of aesthetic goodness (high difficulty). The results are depicted in Figure 9-2. It can be seen that conformity was curvilinearly related to self-esteem when task difficulty was either low or medium, whereas it was essentially unrelated to self-esteem when task difficulty was high. When the task becomes very difficult, one might suppose that self-esteem would not be threatened by failure in any case; hence degree of conformity would not be influenced by the person's general attitude toward himself.

The various studies by Lanzetta and Roby (1956, 1957) on task demands are closely related to the studies of task difficulty. When the information-processing demands upon the group are increased, it is plausible to suspect that the difficulty of the task also increases. In approaching the question of how task demands influence group process, Lanzetta and Roby used the

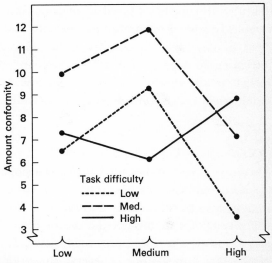

Figure 9-2   Conformity as a Function of Self-esteem Level and Task Difficulty. (Reprinted with permission from K. J. Gergen & R. A. Bauer. Interactive effects of self-esteem and task difficulty on social conformity. *Journal of Personality and Social Psychology*, 1967, **6,** 16–22.)

standard dial-setting task described earlier, although the manipulations of task demands were based upon their descriptive analysis outlined on pages 307–309. Thus, their approach to task characteristics involves all three of the general approaches to task analysis discussed earlier. In the first study (Lanzetta & Roby, 1956), task demands were varied in three ways. First, the location of controls relative to instruments was varied so that two different amounts of information transmission were required. Second, the rate of change of instrument readings was varied, and third, the predictability and sequence of instrument changes were varied. Two 3-person groups performed under each combination of "work group structures" created by the task variations. Performance was measured by the number of times each control was incorrectly set. Errors increased linearly with amount of information transmission required, increasing rate of change of instrument readings, and decreasing predictability of changes of instrument readings. The second study (Lanzetta & Roby, 1957) verified these findings and also demonstrated that the proportion of time spent in communication varied with input load.

Studies of task difficulty reveal the expected effects upon time to complete the task, number of errors, and similar performance measures. Task difficulty also increases speed of reaction and attempted leadership, and it is complexly related to conformity behavior and self-esteem. Although measurement of task difficulty was far from precise, these findings are sufficiently intriguing to suggest that other aspects of group process are undoubtedly related to the difficulty of the group task and that studies of these effects should yield rich rewards in the understanding of group behavior.

DIMENSIONS OF TASKS AND GROUP PROCESS

There are fewer studies involving dimensional analysis than involving types of tasks, but some of the results suggest that the more detailed form of analysis may be much more fruitful. First, let us present data relative to task difficulty obtained through the use of dimensional analysis so that findings may be related to those presented above. In Hackman's study (1968) cited earlier, difficulty was one of several dimensions evaluated by the scaling technique and related to dimensions of group products. Task difficulty was found to be related to action orientation, originality, optimism, quality of presentation, issue involvement, and adequacy. Products from more difficult tasks were generally more original and issue-involved, whereas products from easier tasks met specific task requirements more adequately and the quality of presentation was higher. The relationships between difficulty and action orientation and between difficulty and optimism depended upon the general type of the task. For example, products from medium-difficulty production tasks showed more action orientation than did other difficulty levels of that type of task, whereas difficulty level and action orientation were essentially unrelated for problem-solving and discussion tasks. On the other hand, difficulty level of production tasks had little effect on optimism, whereas medium-difficulty discussion tasks produced relatively low optimism. On problem-solving tasks, difficulty level was positively correlated with the degree of optimism reflected in group products. These data demonstrate clearly that task characteristics are important determinants of the group's products, and identify some of their effects on product dimensions.

Difficulty was also manipulated through task selection based upon scale analysis in a study of group awareness of member satisfaction and group performance (Shaw & Blum, 1965). This study used three tasks varying in level of difficulty (scale values were 2.5, 4.2, and 6.1) but approximately equal on other task dimensions (i.e., cooperation requirements, solution multiplicity, population familiarity, intrinsic interest, and intellectual-manipulative requirements). Five-person groups completed each of the three tasks, under three feedback conditions. In one condition, group members indicated their satisfaction with the group by identifiable signals (overt feedback); in a second condition, they indicated satisfaction by signals that could not be identified as coming from any particular group member (covert feedback); and in the third condition, no feedback was permitted. The results showed the expected differences in time to solve, with the easy tasks requiring less time than the difficult tasks (means = 7.7, 18.4, and 29.2 minutes). Much more interesting is the fact that the effects of satisfaction feedback varied with the difficulty of the task. It can be seen in Table 9-3 that group performance was higher under feedback conditions than under no-feedback conditions for all tasks, but the effect was most pronounced for the most difficult task. These findings were interpreted in terms of "pluralistic ignorance." When the task is being solved, one group member may be dissatisfied with the proposed solution but believe that he is the only dissatisfied member—so he remains silent. Or more than one member may react this way. A solution or decision may be accepted that most members find unsatisfactory. This result is most likely to occur with difficult tasks where the correct solution or procedure is not so readily discovered by the group. When a member can signal his feelings about proposed solutions without disrupting group interaction, he presumably feels freer to do so, and this information leads the group to reconsider faulty decisions, thus resulting in better group performance.

At least two other studies have investigated the effects of task characteristics employing the dimensional analysis approach. In one study (Shaw

TABLE 9-3 Mean Performance Scores for Task and Satisfaction Feedback Conditions

Condition	Easy	Medium	Difficult
No feedback	.66	3.02	.89
Overt feedback	.83	3.65	1.11
Covert feedback	.88	3.39	2.44

NOTE: Scores are not comparable across tasks.

SOURCE: Reprinted with permission from M. E. Shaw and J. M. Blum, Group performance as a function of task difficulty and the group's awareness of member satisfaction. *Journal of Applied Psychology*, 1965, **49**, 151–154.

& Blum, 1966) five-person groups attempted three tasks varying on the dimension of solution multiplicity, working under either directive or nondirective leadership. Task A required group members to list the five most important traits needed for success in our culture; hence, solution multiplicity was high (scale value = 7.4). Task B was intermediate with respect to solution multiplicity (scale value = 4.1); it required subjects to decide which of five alternatives was best for a young politician burdened with an alcoholic wife. Task C was similar to the parlor game "twenty questions" and was very low on solution multiplicity (scale value = .9). The three tasks were approximately equal on other task dimensions. Findings were in general agreement with Fiedler's theory: Directive leadership was more effective on the low solution multiplicity task, whereas nondirective leadership was more effective on the other two (see Table 9-4).

The second study dealt with the cooperation requirements of the task (Shaw & Briscoe, 1966). Two tasks varying in degree of cooperation requirements (scale values = 2.04 and 6.25) were attempted by three-, four-, and five-person groups. It was predicted that the larger groups would be relatively less effective in dealing with the task having high cooperation requirements, because the difficulty of coordinating activities increases with size of group. The hypothesis was not supported by the data. However, the high-cooperation-requirements task required more time than did the low-cooperation-requirements task (means = 1.5 versus .3). Since the difficulty of the two tasks was approximately equal, these differences must be attributed to the fact that the tasks differed in the amount of intermember coordination required for successful completion.

TABLE 9-4 Mean Time Scores (Minutes) for Leadership and Task Conditions

Leadership style	Task		
	A	B	C
Directive	23.42	13.36	24.67
Nondirective	16.76	5.29	34.73

SOURCE: Reprinted with permission from M. E. Shaw and J. M. Blum, Effects of leadership style upon group performance as a function of task structure. *Journal of Personality and Social Psychology*, 1966, **3**, 238–242. Slightly adapted.

Before leaving the discussion of the effects of task characteristics, we shall note two further studies. Although the authors did not use dimensional analysis, they did attempt to evaluate one of the a priori dimensions used in the original dimensional analysis of tasks (M. E. Shaw, 1963) and, in fact, provided the stimulus for this dimension being included in that analysis. A. R. Cohen (1959) examined the effects of goal-path clarity upon certain individual behaviors. He studied telephone operators who were being evaluated by a supervisor. From the standpoint of the telephone operators, the goal was clear: to get a good rating from the supervisor. The way to achieve this desirable outcome, i.e., the path to the goal, was not always clear. For some of the operators, the supervisor gave a single clue that presumably would help them get a good rating; for others, various inconsistent clues were given throughout the test session. Thus, the path to the goal was considerably less clear under the second set of conditions than under the first. Under the low goal-path clarity conditions, operators were less motivated, less secure, evaluated themselves lower, and worked less efficiently than operators in the higher condition.

In a related study, Raven and Rietsema (1957) conducted a laboratory study in which they manipulated clarity of the group goal. Through tape recordings, some group members were given a clear picture of the goal, whereas others received only vague and ambiguous information about it. Members of high-clarity groups were more attracted to the task, showed less nontask-directed tension, were more involved with the group, and conformed more to group expectations than low-clarity group members.

It will be remembered that goal clarity was revealed to be an aspect of difficulty in the dimensional study cited earlier. Furthermore, it is questionable whether goal clarity and goal-path clarity represent two aspects of the task situation or only one. Therefore, it is probable that the findings of A. R. Cohen and Raven and Rietsema can be validly interpreted as further evidence concerning the effects of task difficulty on group process.

In brief summary, the empirical investigations of the effects of task characteristics upon group process are unsystematic, loosely controlled, and restricted to relatively few task dimensions and group situations. The identification and measurement of task dimensions have been haphazard, for the most part, and only recently has there been some promise of advances in research sophistication. Nevertheless, the evidence amassed thus far provides strong support for those who expect significant benefits to derive from detailed analysis of task characteristics and group process.

HETEROGENEITY-HOMOGENEITY OF GROUP GOALS

To this point, we have tacitly assumed that the group goal is known to group members and that all accept it and work toward its attainment. Although this situation undoubtedly does occur, group members commonly differ, to some extent, in their perceptions of the group goal and, especially, in the degree to which they are committed to achieving it. In some instances, group members hold different goals for the group, or they hold different individual goals that can only be achieved through group action. These differing individual orientations have powerful effects upon the behaviors of group members and upon the products of the group.

Perhaps the most extensive studies of heterogeneity of group goals are those dealing with "cooperation and competition." It requires only a brief consideration of the definitions of cooperation and competition to observe that in a cooperative situation group goals are homogeneous (i.e., members hold the same goal for the group), and in a competitive situation group goals are heterogeneous (i.e., group members hold differing goals for the group). This conclusion is illustrated by the definitions offered by M. Deutsch (1949a). A competitive social situation was defined as one in which the goal regions of each group member are such that if the goal region is entered by any individual group member, other group members will, to some degree, be unable to reach their respective goal regions. A cooperative social situation was defined as one in which the goal regions of individual group members are such that if a goal region is entered by any given individual, all other group members are facilitated in reaching their respective regions. In other words, in a competitive situation, goal achievement by one group member to some extent hinders the goal achievement of other members, whereas in a cooperative situation, goal achievement by one member facilitates goal achievement by all others. A competitive situation clearly cannot exist if group goals are homogeneous; it is theoretically possible for a cooperative situation to exist without homogeneous group goals, but this situation is relatively rare.

M. Deutsch (1949b) also conducted an extensive empirical study of cooperation and competition. The subjects were drawn from an introductory course in psychology at the Massachusetts Institute of Technology. There were ten 5-person groups, five groups working in a cooperative situation and five in a competitive situation. Each group met once a week for five weeks, to work on puzzles and human relations problems. Competitive groups were told that individual contributions to the puzzle solutions would be ranked from 1 to 5, with 5 being assigned to the person who contributed the most. The individual who received the highest average was excused from one term paper and given an automatic H (the highest grade awarded at MIT). The five cooperative groups were told that they would be ranked and that all members of the group with the highest rank would be excused from a term paper and given an automatic H. Similar instructions were given with respect to the human relations problems, except that the ranks were to be used in determining the final grade in the course. Observers recorded selected portions of the group interaction and rated certain aspects of the group process at the conclusion of each task. Group members completed questionnaires designed to provide data on a wide range of group perceptions and products.

Deutsch divided his hypotheses into "basic hypotheses" and "specific hypotheses about group functioning." Experimental evidence supported the following basic hypotheses, grossly paraphrased:

1. Members of cooperative groups perceive the group situation to be cooperative, and members of competitive groups perceive the group situation to be competitive; that is, the perceptions of group members are veridical.

2. There will be more substitutable actions in the cooperative than in the competitive situation; that is, an action of one member in the cooperative situation relieves another member from performing the same action to a greater extent than in the competitive situation.

3. A larger percentage of actions of others will be positively cathected (acquire positive valence) in the cooperative than in the competitive situation.

4. There will be greater positive inducibility in the cooperative than in the competitive situation. (Positive inducibility referred to the production of additional own forces and the channeling of existing own forces in a new direction.)

5. Members of cooperative groups will exhibit greater helpfulness than will members of competitive groups.

The effects of cooperation and competition upon group functioning were quite considerable. In summary, the cooperative situation showed more of the following characteristics than did the competitive situation:

(i) coordination of efforts; (ii) diversity in amount of contributions per member; (iii) subdivision of activity; (iv) achievement pressure; (v) production of signs in the puzzle problem; (vi) attentiveness to fellow members; (vii) mutual comprehension of communication; (viii) common appraisals of communication; (ix) orientation and orderliness; (x) productivity per unit time; (xi) quality of product and discussions; (xii) friendliness during discussions; (xiii) favorable evaluation of the group and its products; (xiv) group functions; (xv) perception of favorable effects upon fellow members; and (xvi) incorporation of the attitude of the generalized other" (M. Deutsch, 1949a, p. 230).

On the other hand, the competitive situation showed more production of signs (i.e., the utterance of good ideas) in the human relations problems and more individual functions. In short, the cooperative groups engaged in more specialized activities, were more productive, and had higher morale than the competitive groups.

Several other studies of the relative effectiveness of cooperation and competition yielded findings that are in general agreement with those reported by Deutsch. For instance, the author (M. E. Shaw, 1958a) attempted to separate the effects of task requirements and motivational requirements in cooperative and competitive situations. Members of dyads were led to believe they were cooperating, competing, or working individually, whereas their performance score actually depended upon their own efforts. In one task situation, two hand cranks controlled a pointer which was to be kept in alignment with a moving target. Performance was measured by time on target during fifteen-second test periods. The results are shown graphically in Figure 9-3. Clearly, the cooperative situation resulted in the most proficient tracking behavior, whereas the competitive situation was least effective. Contrary to Deutsch's findings, satisfaction was rated higher in the competitive than in the cooperative situation. These results were replicated using a task requiring less eye-hand coordination and greater mental activity. In a very different situation, Willis and Joseph (1959) observed that cooperative instructions to dyads playing nonzero sum games resulted in more agreements (and greater mutual rewards) than did competitive instructions.

Cooperation has also been observed to be more effective than competition in natural situations. Blau (1954) compared two groups of interviewers in a public employment agency whose task was to place as many job applicants as possible, as quickly as possible. In one group, a cooperative atmosphere existed such that each member helped others to place an applicant that he had interviewed. In the other, a competitive atmosphere emerged such that each member attempted to place as many applicants as he could

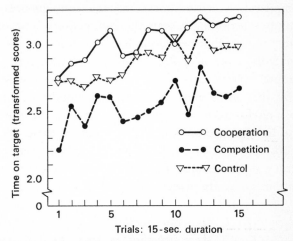

Figure 9-3 Mean Time on Target as a Function of Practice in the Three Motivational Conditions. (Reprinted with permission from M. E. Shaw. Some motivational factors in cooperation and competition. *Journal of Personality*, 1958, **26,** 155–169.)

on an individual basis. Job openings were hoarded rather than distributed among the group in accordance with approved practices. The result was reduced productivity by the competitive group. According to Blau, anxiety over productivity led to behaviors which interfered with group effectiveness.

These empirical studies make it abundantly clear that homogeneity of group goals facilitates group functioning, whereas heterogeneity of group goals interferes with group functioning. This effect is produced by the specialization of task behaviors and helpful actions of group members in the cooperative situation. Members of groups with homogeneous group goals are usually happier than members of groups with heterogeneous goals. Homogeneity of goals generally has positive effects upon group functioning, both in the laboratory and in natural situations.

PLAUSIBLE HYPOTHESES ABOUT THE TASK ENVIRONMENT

In the preceding pages we have reviewed the various conceptions of group task in relation to group goals and have tried to show that individuals establish group goals which function in much the same way as individual goals. Empirical evidence concerning the consequences of task environment for group functioning reveals the rudimentary state of research on group tasks. Only the smallest beginning has been made on the enormous problem of task analysis—a problem which must be solved before a detailed analysis of small group behavior can become a reality. Nevertheless, it is important to recognize that some general conclusions can be drawn about the effects of the task environment and that these general conclusions are at least plausible in the light of present knowledge. Some of these hypotheses are intuitively obvious but have limited empirical support; some are less obvious but have strong support from empirical investigations; and most have significant implications for group process.

Hypothesis 1   Individuals establish goals for their groups which influence their behavior in ways similar to the influence of personal goals.

The evidence for this hypothesis is reasonably extensive and is quite consistent. The work of Shelley (1954) on the establishment of individual levels of aspiration for the group and that of Zander and his associates (Zander, 1968; Zander & Medow, 1963; Zander & Newcomb, 1967) on the setting of group levels of aspiration demonstrate conclusively that group members set goals for the group and that these goals exert a measurable influence upon behavior in the group.

Hypothesis 2   Tension systems can be aroused for goals which the individual holds for the group.

Hypothesis 3   Tension systems can be aroused for avoidances which the individual holds for the group.

These two interrelated hypotheses are derived from the work by Horwitz (1954) on incompleted group tasks. His work revealed that once a group goal is established, group members experience task-related tension which is reduced by task completion. Group members recalled more incompleted tasks than completed ones in situations where the majority of group members had voted to complete the task, but they recalled no more incompleted tasks than completed ones in situations where the majority of group members had voted to discontinue working toward completion. Whether group members hold goals for task completion or goals for task incompletion, tension systems are aroused which influence the members' reactions to movement relative to the group goal.

Hypothesis 4   *The kinds of leadership abilities that are required for effective group action vary with type of task.*

Although Hypothesis 4 appears obvious in light of present knowledge, this was not always so. Early studies of leadership traits implicitly assumed that the kind of task faced by the group was irrelevant, and the failure of these studies to predict leadership effectiveness accurately can be attributed in large measure to this neglect of the task environment. Studies by Carter et al. (1950) provided strong empirical support for this hypothesis.

Hypothesis 5   *The characteristics of group products are a function of the kind of task faced by the group.*

The phrase "kind of task" in Hypothesis 5 refers to the global classification of tasks into such categories as discussion tasks, problem-solving tasks, and production tasks. Hypothesis 5 is based primarily upon a single study (Hackman, 1968), which found that the products of groups working on discussion tasks are characterized by high issue involvement, those of groups working on problem-solving tasks are characterized by high action orientation, and those of groups working on production tasks by high originality. The results of the study by Morris (1965) are consistent with Hackman's result, although the two investigators did not use the same dimensions in their analyses of group products.

Hypothesis 6   *The activity of group leaders varies with the kind of task faced by the group.*

This hypothesis also has minimal empirical support. Morris (1965) found that leaders were more active on problem-solving tasks than on production tasks or on discussion tasks. More data are required to determine whether this represents a realistic response of the leader to the requirements of the task or whether such a response is maladaptive with respect to at least some aspects of the task environment.

Hypothesis 7   *The quality of group performance, as measured by time and errors, decreases with increasing task difficulty.*

This hypothesis is supported not only by logical considerations but also by a large amount of empirical evidence. Various studies of task difficulty measured by scale analysis provided uniform data supporting this proposition (e.g., M. E. Shaw, 1963; Shaw & Blum, 1965). Studies of the effects of task demands upon group performance also are in agreement with Hypothesis 7 (Lanzetta & Roby, 1956, 1957). However, all these studies used tasks requiring some degree of problem solving; there is some doubt regarding the validity of this hypothesis when the task requires only a motor response.

Hypothesis 8   Reaction time decreases with increased task difficulty.
Zajonc and Taylor (1963) found that increasing the difficulty of a task requiring rapid reaction time led to increased group effectiveness. This contrasts sharply with the findings cited above when the task requires problem-solving activities. Probably Hypothesis 7 should be qualified to apply only to problem-solving tasks, and Hypothesis 8 to apply only to motor-reaction tasks.

Hypothesis 9   Group members attempt leadership more frequently when the task is difficult than when it is easy.
Again, the evidence is limited to a single investigation (Bass et al., 1958), although the hypothesis appears eminently reasonable. The question of the adaptiveness of the response, however, has not been answered; hence, the meaning of this relationship for group functioning is unclear.

Hypothesis 10   When task difficulty is low or moderate, conformity is curvilinearly related to the self-esteem of the group member.
When the task is not too difficult, failure may be attributed to personal deficiencies and, hence, is ego-threatening to some individuals. A person who has low self-esteem is not concerned about his performance because he expects to fail regardless of the difficulty of the task, whereas a person with high self-esteem does not anticipate failure. Hence neither of these group members conforms excessively to the standards of the majority. Group members of intermediate self-esteem experience some doubt about their effectiveness and feel threatened by failure; hence, they tend to conform to group norms more closely than either low or high self-esteem members. When the task is difficult, failure may be attributed to the task rather than to the person and so is not ego-threatening to anyone. The group member need not conform regardless of his self-esteem. Gergen and Bauer (1967) demonstrated these effects quite clearly, although the interpretation given above is somewhat different from their proposals.

*Hypothesis 11   The quality of group performance decreases with increasing
            task demands.*

This is another fairly obvious hypothesis which nevertheless has important
consequences for group behavior. When the demands of the task are increased, group members must distribute their activities more broadly and
thus cannot give the same amount of attention to each aspect of the task as
they can when demands are fewer. The work of Lanzetta and Roby (1956,
1957) illustrates these effects.

*Hypothesis 12   The characteristics of group products vary with the difficulty
            of the group task.*

In the study of group products as a function of type of task and task characteristics, Hackman (1968) also examined the effects of task difficulty as
measured by the scale analysis procedure. He found that products from more
difficult tasks were generally more original and issue-involved, whereas products from easier tasks met specific task requirements more adequately. Quality
of presentation was also higher for easy tasks than for difficult ones.

*Hypothesis 13   On difficult tasks, group performance is facilitated to the ex-
            tent that group members can freely communicate their feel-
            ings of satisfaction or dissatisfaction with the group's progress
            toward goal achievement.*

A group member often disagrees with a proposed decision or action of the
group, but believes incorrectly that he is the only group member who is dissatisfied. He is, therefore, reluctant to express his views lest he become a
disruptive force or be viewed as a nonconformist. When he is encouraged to
express his disagreement (Maier, 1950) or when he can do so without disrupting the group (Shaw & Blum, 1965), the group's performance is superior.
Effective group functioning can be facilitated by providing an opportunity
for group members to express their feelings and opinions in an uninhibited
manner. This opportunity can be provided either through a leader who encourages the expression of minority opinion or by some device which permits an indication of satisfaction or dissatisfaction without focusing attention
on the group member.

*Hypothesis 14   The style of leadership that is most effective varies with task
            solution multiplicity.*

Hypothesis 14 may be taken as a more specific instance of the functional relationship stated in Hypothesis 24 in Chapter 8, which asserted that a directive leader is more effective when the group-task situation is either very favorable or very unfavorable for the leader, whereas a nondirective leader is more effective when the situation is moderately favorable. Given that leader-member affective relations are at least moderately good and that the power position of the leader is at least moderately strong, then a task with low solution multiplicity should constitute a favorable group-task situation for the leader, and directive leadership should be more effective. On the other hand, a task high on solution multiplicity should create a group-task situation of intermediate favorability, and nondirective leadership should be more effective. These effects were demonstrated clearly in the study reported by Shaw and Blum (1966). Thus one must conclude that the kind of behavior that a leader should enact for efficient group performance depends in part upon the degree to which the group task has one or many acceptable outcomes; or, conversely, the kind of leader selected for a group should be determined in part by the solution-multiplicity characteristics of the task.

Hypothesis 15   The quality of group performance, as measured by time and errors, is negatively correlated with the cooperation requirements of the group task.

The evidence for this hypothesis is limited to a single study (Shaw & Briscoe, 1966) but is strongly supportive. A task having high cooperation requirements required approximately four times as long as a similar task having lower cooperation requirements. Groups made approximately five times as many errors on the high than on the low cooperation requirements task. Increasing the requirements for cooperation among group members also increases coordination problems and, hence, reduces the quality of group performance.

Hypothesis 16   Goal clarity and goal-path clarity are positively related to motivational characteristics of group members.

Hypothesis 17   Goal clarity and goal-path clarity are positively correlated with the efficiency of group members.

These two related hypotheses are based upon findings from a field study (A. R. Cohen, 1959) and from a laboratory study (Raven & Rietsema, 1957). The field study showed that telephone operators were more highly motivated, felt more secure, and worked more efficiently when the path to the goal was relatively clear than when it was ambiguous. The laboratory study generally agreed with those findings and also reported similar effects with respect to goal clarity. Although it seems obvious that group members are more highly motivated and perform more efficiently when they know what is expected of them, it is important to remember this obvious fact when attempting to understand group processes.

*Hypothesis 18   Homogeneous group goals facilitate effective group function-
ing, whereas heterogeneous group goals hinder effective
group functioning.*

Numerous studies of cooperation and competition have shown that groups perform more efficiently when the situation is cooperative than when it is competitive (Blau, 1954; M. Deutsch, 1949b; M. E. Shaw, 1958a). Since cooperation is defined as a situation in which the goals of the group are homogeneous, and competition as a situation in which the goals are heterogeneous, these studies support Hypothesis 18. This effect is produced largely through the specialization of individual contributions and through helpful actions of each member vis-à-vis other members in the cooperative situation. Motivational factors also play a role; the competitive situation may arouse greater motivation than the cooperative situation, but this increased motivation does not always improve group performance (M. E. Shaw, 1958a). Planners for group action are well advised to provide homogeneous group goals if efficient group performance is the desired outcome of group process.

In brief summary, a multitude of factors related to task environment influence group interaction, group effectiveness, and group products. Empirical data relative to these factors and their effects are sparse indeed, and much remains to be done before one can confidently predict the consequences of task environment for many aspects of group behavior. Even at this early stage, however, it is clear that the characteristics of a task cannot be ignored in the analysis of group process.

SUGGESTED READINGS

CARTWRIGHT, D., & ZANDER, A. (Eds.)   *Group dynamics: Research and theory.* Evanston, Ill.: Row, Peterson, 1953. Pp. 305–318.

DEUTSCH, M.   An experimental study of the effects of co-operation and competition upon group process. *Human Relations,* 1949, **2,** 199–232.

HACKMAN, J. R.   Effects of task characteristics on group products. *Journal of Experimental Social Psychology,* 1968, **4,** 162–187.

HORWITZ, M.   The recall of interrupted group tasks: An experimental study of individual motivation in relation to group goals. *Human Relations,* 1954, **7**, 3–38.

LAWSON, E. D.   Reinforced and non-reinforced four-man communication nets. *Psychological Reports,* 1964, **14**, 287–296.

ROBY, T. B., & LANZETTA, J. T.   Considerations in the analysis of group tasks. *Psychological Bulletin,* 1958, **55**, 88–101.

SHELLEY, H. P.   Level of aspiration phenomena in small groups. *Journal of Social Psychology,* 1954, **40**, 149–164.

ZAJONC, R. B.   The requirements and design of a standard group task. *Journal of Experimental Social Psychology,* 1965, **1**, 71–88.

ZANDER, A., & MEDOW, H.   Individual and group levels of aspiration. *Human Relations,* 1963, **16**, 89–105.

PART IV

EPILOGUE

CHAPTER 10

ISSUES, APPLICATIONS, AND PROSPECTS

The great complexity of group process is surely evident from our explorations of the relationships among the various environments of the group. We have attempted to identify the convoluted relationships among the many variables influencing group behavior. We have seen that the characteristics of individuals influence group performance both directly and indirectly via group structure and that the physical environment may influence group formation and structure as well as behavior. But have we learned anything more than this? Our various explorations led to the formulation of 105 plausible hypotheses, but in far too many instances it was necessary to "hedge" concerning the validity of hypotheses beyond the specific situation in which data were collected. The student may justly ask about the significance of the "scientific" study of group dynamics. The two questions most frequently asked deal with (1) the validity of hypotheses established in the laboratory for natural situations, and (2) the practical value of the findings of studies of group process. We will try to deal with each of these questions, first, by showing that investigations conducted in the laboratory and in the field yield comparable results, and second, by showing how research findings can contribute to practical problems. A final section deals with past mistakes and suggestions for the future.

LABORATORY AND NATURAL SITUATIONS

Questions concerning the relevance of laboratory findings for natural situations revolve about two major issues:

1   Does the psychology of the college sophomore correspond to the psychology of human beings in general? This puts it strongly, but fairly represents the position taken by many critics. Somehow, it is assumed that the college student—and the college sophomore in particular—cannot be taken as representative of the human race. It is believed that his behavior is governed by a set of psychological laws that do not apply to others and particularly to those others who are engaged in "real" activities in "real life." It is true that the college student differs in certain significant ways from the general population. On the average, he is more intelligent, better educated, and younger than the general population of adults. These differences may, indeed, result in behavioral differences of significance for group behavior. Whether these differences exist, and to what extent they invalidate conclusions drawn from the study of groups of college students, can be determined empirically. An armchair answer is no more likely to be correct here than armchair answers to other questions about psychological events.

2   Do the results obtained from "artificial" groups functioning in a laboratory have any relevance for natural groups functioning "out there" in the "real world"? The argument of critics is that laboratory groups cannot hope to re-create the richness of groups in natural situations; and, hence, a principle that operates in such ad hoc groups cannot be expected to operate in ongoing groups exposed to the complex pattern of variables that exists in the larger society. Furthermore, it is asserted that members of such groups are probably not motivated, that the whole situation is regarded as a game, that

the typical "subject" is motivated to please the experimenter, or, conversely, to deliberately foul up the experiment, and so on. It is certainly true that laboratory groups differ in many ways from natural groups, although it is not at all certain that the differences are those pointed to by the critics. For example, an individual need only observe the involvement of a member of a laboratory group in the task assigned the group to become convinced that the question of motivation is not a legitimate one. On the other hand, natural groups are clearly exposed to many more variables than laboratory groups. Indeed, Festinger (1953b) noted many years ago that the great advantage of studying laboratory groups is that the number of variables influencing group behavior at any one time can be reduced to manageable proportions. Only by controlling some variables while allowing others to operate can we identify the effects of such variables. But once again, we are dealing with empirical questions that cannot be resolved by polemics. The basic question is: Do laboratory studies and field studies yield similar results?

In practice, the two questions raised above resolve to a single issue. The great bulk of laboratory investigations involve college students as group members, whereas the majority of field studies involve noncollege personnel. We shall try to show that investigations of similar problems lead to similar conclusions, whether the subjects be college students or members of the larger population and whether the groups are ad hoc laboratory groups or natural groups functioning in the "real world." Comparison of laboratory and field studies dealing with several aspects of group behavior will illustrate this point.

ALONE VERSUS TOGETHER

The comparability of results from laboratory and field studies was demonstrated as early as 1897 in the studies of Triplett dealing with behavior of the individual acting alone and in the presence of others. The initial studies were based upon data taken from official records of bicycle races and compared unpaced, paced, and competitive situations. In the unpaced situation, the bicycle rider was alone on the track as he attempted to beat an established time; in the paced, the rider attempted to beat an established time, but with another cycle setting the pace; and in the competitive situation, several riders competed, as in an ordinary race. Triplett found that the competitive situation produced the fastest time and the unpaced the slowest time. He then conducted a laboratory study in which forty children, working alone or in pairs, operated a gadget constructed of fishing reels. As in the initial study, the together situation produced the faster performance rates. These studies differed not only in setting (laboratory versus field) but also in kind of task and subject population. Nevertheless, the results agreed perfectly.

BRAINSTORMING

Osborn (1957) reported that group participation results in more new and radical ideas than individual work when special procedures are followed. These procedures, called "brainstorming," consist of a set of rules about acceptable group participation. The basic rules are that any idea should be mentioned and that no idea should be evaluated until all ideas have been expressed. Evidence supporting the proposition concerning the effects of brainstorming was cited from research conducted in an industrial organization, with employees of the company serving as group members as a part of their regular work activities. At least two laboratory studies were conducted to test Osborn's conclusions. Meadow, Parnes, and Reese (1959) conducted a study with college students who worked alone under either brainstorming or nonbrainstorming instructions. Brainstorming instructions produced almost twice as many "good solutions" to the unusual uses task as the nonbrainstorming instructions. The other study (Cohen, Whitmyre, & Funk, 1960) compared pairs of individuals working together with nominal pairs (i.e., the pooled results of two individuals working alone.) All subjects followed brainstorming instructions. Again the results were in accord with Osborn's findings. Taken together, these studies make it clear that the effects of following brainstorming instructions are similar, whether in natural situations or in the laboratory. There is some question, however, about the effects of group participation per se.

These conclusions are bolstered by studies by Taylor, Berry, and Block (1958) and by Dunnette, Campbell, and Jaastad (1963). Taylor et al. compared real and nominal laboratory groups working under brainstorming instructions and found that nominal groups produced almost twice as many ideas as real groups. Dunnette et al. conducted a similar study in a mining company and found essentially the same results. These two studies, of course, say nothing about the effectiveness of brainstorming instructions, but do cast doubt on the value of group participation. The main point here, however, is that the same conclusions may be drawn from a laboratory study using college students and from a study conducted in an industrial organization using research scientists and administrative personnel as subjects.

INTERPERSONAL ATTRACTION

Studies of interpersonal attraction provide evidence of the comparability of laboratory and natural group studies with respect to at least two variables: similarity and physical attractiveness. A long-range study of the acquaintance process (Newcomb, 1961) revealed that perceived similarity of attitudes was an important determinant of attraction. Students were invited to live in a house rent-free in exchange for serving as research subjects. The students were initially unacquainted; hence, it was possible to study the variables related to friendship formation. Newcomb concluded that ". . . as individuals acquired more information about each others' attitudes, their high attraction preferences tended to change in favor of individuals with whom they were more closely in agreement" (Newcomb, 1961, p. 254). Certainly these students were members of "real groups" living in the "real world." The same conclusions may be drawn from the many studies reported by Byrne and his associates, using strictly laboratory groups. The basic procedure required subjects to respond to attitude scales, after which fake conditions were established which led them to believe that their attitudes agreed with those of another to varying degrees. Subsequent measures of attraction correlated highly with degree of perceived similarity of attitudes (see, for example, Byrne, 1961; Byrne & Nelson, 1964; Byrne & Nelson, 1965b; Byrne & Rhamey, 1965). Attitude similarity has thus been demonstrated to be an important determinant of attraction, both in the laboratory and in natural situations.

Physical attractiveness of the other person has also been shown to be a determinant of interpersonal attraction. Walster, Aronson, Abrahams, and Rottman (1966) conducted a field study utilizing a procedure they called a "computer dance." Ostensibly, males and females were paired by a computer for a dance, after which the investigators obtained measures of the degree to which a subject was attracted to his partner. The results showed that how much the subject liked his partner, how much he wanted to see her again, and how often he actually asked her out again were a function of his date's physical attractiveness. A laboratory study by Schlosser (1969) revealed the same results. A confederate was made up to be either attractive or unattractive and paired with a naïve subject to work on a laboratory task. The physically attractive confederate was rated more highly than the less attractive version, even when she behaved in a manner that interfered with task completion.

The empirical evidence thus yields consistent results with respect to both attitude similarity and physical attractiveness as determinants of interpersonal attraction, whether the studies are conducted in natural situations or in the laboratory.

CONFORMITY BEHAVIOR

The numerous studies conducted in the laboratory demonstrating that individual group members tend to conform to a perceived group standard scarcely need mentioning (see, for example, Asch, 1951; Berg & Bass, 1961). Conformity also has been demonstrated in many field studies. For example, Freed, Chandler, Mouton, and Blake (1955) observed considerable conformity behavior among automobile drivers: Signaling before making a turn depended to a marked extent upon the behavior of the driver in the car immediately ahead of the driver being observed. The reader may have viewed the behavior of elevator occupants on "Candid Camera." Confederates of the program director deliberately turned to face in a particular direction after entering the elevator; other passengers obediently turned to face in the same direction. This show may have been "rigged," but the behavior of the elevator passengers corresponded closely to behavior demonstrated in the laboratory and in other field situations. The study by Rosenbaum and Blake (1955) concerning volunteer behavior also demonstrated conformity in a nonlaboratory situation. An investigator entered the reading room of a college library, approached a confederate already seated there, and invited him to participate in an experiment. The confederate either agreed or refused. Others seated at the table were approached with the same request. Considerably more naïve students volunteered following the confederate's agreement than following his refusal.

Much more interesting, however, is the fact that amount of conformity has been shown to vary with the status of the other person, both in the laboratory and in natural settings. Mausner (1953) tested subjects alone or with a partner who was introduced as either a fellow student or an "art authority." The task was the Meier Art Judgment Test. The partner, who was a confederate of the experimenter, made choices that were incorrect according to the scoring key for the art test. Significantly greater conformity to the partner's erroneous choices occurred when the partner was introduced as an art authority than when he was introduced as a fellow student. The study by Lefkowitz et al. (1955) dealing with pedestrian violation of traffic signals also demonstrated greater conformity to a high-status person. A confederate dressed either as a high-status or as a low-status person violated a "don't walk" signal. Other persons waiting to cross the street violated the signal considerably more frequently when the confederate-violator was dressed as a high-status person than when he was dressed as a low-status person.

In summary, there is strong evidence that the effects of others on an individual's behavior are essentially the same in both laboratory and natural situations.

LEADERSHIP STYLES

The correspondence between laboratory and field data is shown most clearly in the many studies of the effects of leadership style upon group behavior. The initial study by Lewin, Lippitt, and White (1939) might be considered a field study, since it was conducted in a laboratory school. It was experimental, however, in that the behavior of the leaders was systematically varied. It will be recalled that the morale of the autocratic groups was considerably lower than that of the democratic groups; there was more scapegoating, more aggression and hostility, and less liking for the autocratic leader. The productivity of the autocratic groups was slightly higher than that of the democratic groups, although the difference was not statistically reliable. Similar results have been obtained in a number of studies employing ad hoc laboratory groups. For instance, Preston and Heintz (1949) compared participatory and supervisory leadership in groups composed of four or five students. The assigned task was to rank potential presidential candidates in order of merit. The results showed that participatory leadership resulted in higher group morale (satisfaction) than did supervisory leadership. Supervisory leadership revealed less influence on the final product than participatory leadership, but the meaning of this result with respect to productivity is difficult to interpret. M. E. Shaw (1955) conducted a laboratory study of four-person ad hoc groups solving problems under either autocratic or democratic leadership. The instructions to the leaders attempted to stimulate behaviors similar to those displayed by the autocratic and democratic leaders in the Lewin et al. study. The subjects were college students who worked in the groups for approximately fifty minutes. Thus, the experimental situation differed considerably from that of the Lewin et al. study; it differed, in fact, in just about all respects except that the leaders behaved either autocratically or democratically. And yet the results of the two studies were in close agreement. Morale was considerably higher in the democratic than in the autocratic groups, whereas the quality of group performance was higher in the autocratic groups. The autocratic groups required less time and made fewer errors than the democratic groups.

Although the correspondence between the Lewin et al. study and the Shaw study suggests that similar conclusions may be drawn from both laboratory and natural group data, there is one other study that reveals this fact even more clearly. Morse and Reimer (1956) conducted a study in an industrial organization in which changes were made that corresponded to a change in the direction of either greater autocratic behavior on the part of the leader or greater democratic behavior. Four groups were selected by pretest to be as nearly alike as possible. In two of the groups, a change was introduced which led to greater "hierarchical control"; that is, the change led to greater control by upper management of decisions affecting group members. In the other two groups, members were given greater autonomy with respect to matters affecting their work. After six months of training to create the experimental conditions, the groups functioned for one year under the autonomy or hierarchically controlled conditions. Then morale and productivity were measured a second time. Differences between initial and final measures were taken as evidence of the effects of the experimentally introduced changes. Several measures of satisfaction were obtained, with the general finding that satisfaction increased under the autonomy conditions and decreased under the hierarchically controlled conditions. For example, one question asked for a global estimate of how well the worker liked working for the company. Ratings increased in the autonomy condition (+.17) and decreased in the hierarchical condition (−.27), a highly reliable difference. Other indices of job satisfaction and satisfaction with supervision revealed a similar pattern. The measure of productivity was indirect, since group members were required to process whatever materials were assigned to them. Thus, productivity was measured in terms of the cost of doing a given volume of work. The results showed an increase in productivity in both situations, but the increase was greater in the hierarchically controlled groups. The results of this long-range field study are, therefore, in close agreement with findings of studies conducted in other settings.

It is very interesting that investigations conducted under such diverse conditions should yield essentially the same results. It may be noted that (1) the subjects differed in age, experience, and familiarity with the group, (2) the leaders were either highly trained or untrained with respect to their role, and were either peers of groups members or of higher status, (3) the groups were either traditioned or ad hoc, (4) the settings were either field or laboratory, and (5) the tasks differed widely from study to study. Despite these many differences, the conclusions that may be drawn are basically identical. Regardless of the circumstances, autocratic leadership leads to reduced group morale or satisfaction, whereas democratic leadership leads to improved morale; the productivity of autocratic groups is either superior to that of democratic groups or equivalent.

THE SETTING OF GROUP GOALS

The study by Shelley (1954) revealed that members of laboratory groups set levels of aspiration (goals) for their groups and react to achievement or non-achievement of the goals in much the same way that individuals react relative to personal goals. That is, levels of aspiration are raised after success and lowered after failure, whether these are personal or group levels of aspiration. Zander (1968) and Zander and Medow (1963) reported similar results when group members were asked to arrive at group consensus concerning a level of aspiration for the group. The one difference was that groups lowered the level of aspiration for the group less after failure than they raised it after success. These studies were conducted in the laboratory with ad hoc groups composed of college students. Essentially the same effects were observed by Zander and Newcomb (1967) in their study of fund-raising campaigns. Over a period of several years, it was found that United Fund groups in charge of fund-raising activities almost always raised their goal after a successful campaign, but were much less likely to lower it after a failing campaign.

In the preceding discussions, we have shown that the findings of laboratory studies using ad hoc groups suggest conclusions about many aspects of group behavior that are the same as the conclusions suggested by the findings of field studies using natural groups. These investigations included the following areas: (1) behaviors in alone situations compared with behaviors in the presence of others; (2) the effects of brainstorming; (3) variables influencing interpersonal attraction; (4) conformity behavior; (5) the effects of leadership styles; and (6) the setting of group goals. These are diverse forms of behavior, indeed, and the demonstration that principles identified in the laboratory also operate in natural settings reduces the force of critics who argue that the results of studies of artificial groups in an artificial atmosphere have no relevance to natural groups in natural social situations. We have shown that in many instances the same functional relationships apply to both situations.

However, let the reader beware. We do *not* wish to maintain that there are no differences between laboratory and natural groups or situations, nor do we intend to imply that the findings of laboratory investigations can be generalized automatically to the field situation. On the contrary, principles established in the laboratory must be tested in the field before we can know whether or not they can be generalized to natural groups. By the same token, principles derived from observations of groups functioning in natural settings, with the lack of control of variables inherent in such situations, cannot be accepted as valid until they are tested under controlled conditions. The important point is that many of the findings from controlled studies of ad hoc groups also apply to natural groups, but the only way this can be known is through similar studies in *both* settings. It cannot be asserted a priorily either that the results of laboratory studies are irrelevant to "real life" or that they can be generalized directly to natural situations.

CAN EFFECTIVE GROUPS BE "CONSTRUCTED"?

If findings from the study of small groups are valid, it is reasonable to suppose that they should have some practical value. One might justifiably ask, Can the results from such research be used to form groups that will be efficient in achieving group purposes? We believe that an affirmative answer can be given to this question, however tentative the suggestions may be. In the following pages an example is offered of the kinds of recommendations that a student of group dynamics might make if he were asked for advice concerning the construction of a group for the effective performance of a particular task.

In responding to this self-imposed challenge, we must begin at the end; that is, we must begin by asking: What task or tasks must be completed by the group in order for it to achieve its goal or goals? In Chapter 9, data were cited which made it painfully evident that the kind of task faced by the group is an important determinant of group effectiveness or, at least, that the kind of task determines the characteristics of the group that is more likely to be effective in completing that task. We will, therefore, try to show how the empirical data cited in earlier chapters may be used to construct effective groups for the completion of a task that is highly structured in that the goal is clear, the steps required for task completion are readily identifiable, and there is only one acceptable outcome.

We should constantly keep in mind that these recommendations represent the best guess that can be made, given the present state of knowledge of group process. Certainly, no one should assume that these are final answers to the complex problem of building effective groups.

AN EFFECTIVE GROUP FOR A STRUCTURED TASK

Let us assume that the task of the group is to solve a mathematical problem such as the "appliance-manufacturing" task cited by M. E. Shaw (1963). This task requires the group to reach a decision concerning which of four types of appliances a manufacturing company should produce for a given production year. The one selected should be that appliance which will yield the greatest total net profit for that year. Information relative to the number of appliances of each type that can be produced per day and the amount of profit per unit is distributed among the group members. There is only one acceptable solution (i.e., only one solution can be demonstrated to be correct), and the operations required to achieve this solution are known to most adults. The characteristics of this task, as measured by scale analysis (M. E. Shaw, 1963), are shown in Table 10-1. It can be seen that the task is moderately familiar to the population, moderately difficult, and moderately interesting. It is high on cooperation requirements and on intellectual-manipulative requirements, but it is very low on solution multiplicity. It, therefore, meets our description of a structured task.

TABLE 10-1 Characteristics of the Appliance-manufacturing Task

Dimension	Scale value
Cooperation requirements	6.32
Difficulty	4.25
Intellectual-manipulative requirements	6.21
Intrinsic interest	3.35
Population familiarity	4.94
Solution multiplicity	0.56·

It is also necessary to specify the size of the group as a prerequisite for the determination of other group characteristics. It is probable that a single individual working alone, given all the necessary information, could solve the appliance-manufacturing task more efficiently than any group. However, we are interested in group behavior, and the task is a prototype of many tasks faced by groups in which the needed information is not available to any single individual, hence the specification that the necessary information be distributed among the group members. With these conditions in mind, we must consider the size of group that is most likely to perform effectively. In fact, evidence regarding size of group and effectiveness in problem solving is inconsistent. For instance, Taylor and Faust (1952) found four-man groups more effective than two-man groups in solving a task similar to the "twenty questions" game, a moderately structured task. Ziller (1957b) reported a positive relationship between group size (two to six Air Force officers) and the quality of group decisions about the importance of military facts, but he found a curvilinear relationship between group size and accuracy of judgment of number of dots on a card. The first of these tasks is moderately unstructured, whereas the latter is moderately structured. On the negative side, Lorge and Solomon (1959, 1960) found no evidence of a relationship between group size and effectiveness in solving a structured problem.

It appears that the choice of size of group must be made either arbitrarily or on the basis of other factors. One other factor that should be considered is the satisfaction of group members. Evidence related to this factor is not extensive. but there is some indication that members of larger groups are less satisfied than members of smaller groups (Hare, 1952; Slater, 1958). In one study, group members suggested that five members are optimum for discussing human relations problems (Slater, 1958). On the basis of these findings, and because the scale values cited in Table 10-1 were determined for a five-person group, the following analysis will assume that the group under consideration is a five-man group.

The task environment faced by the group is now reasonably well defined, and the next factor to be considered is optimal group composition. This must be considered from the standpoint of both the personal environment and the structural environment. It is probably easier to begin with the selection of a population of potentially acceptable group members, based upon their personal characteristics. Reference to Chapter 6 provides considerable evidence concerning the desirable characteristics of group members. First, potential group members should be adults rather than children: Adults are more sensitive to the behavior of others and are less likely to conform to inappropriate group norms. Second, to simplify matters all the members should be of the same sex; all-male groups will be chosen, somewhat arbitrarily, although men do appear to have slightly higher mathematical skills than women. There is also good evidence that women generally conform more than men, and some evidence that same-sex groups are more task-oriented than mixed-sex (although this latter is really a structural variable). Group members should also be physically superior, in good health, etc., and they should have at least average intellectual ability. (With more difficult tasks, the intellectual ability of group members becomes more critical.)

In addition, there are many personality characteristics that must be considered in selecting potential group members. With respect to *interpersonal orientation*, potential group members should be high on approach tendencies (such as cyclothymia and adventurous cyclothymia) and low on avoidance tendencies (such as paranoid schizothymia), in order to maximize social interaction, cohesiveness, and morale. They also should be low on authoritarianism in order to reduce excessive conformity behavior (see Table 6-1). Potential group members should be high on *social sensitivity* (such as empathy, social activeness, sociability, etc.), in order to enhance friendliness, leadership attempts and success, and group effectiveness (see Table 6-2). In general, group members should be high on *ascendant* tendencies (see Table 6-3), since such persons tend to participate in group activities, emerge as leaders, promote group cohesiveness, and influence group decisions. On the other hand, they sometimes are dissatisfied with less than the leadership role and may conform to group norms more than is desirable. On balance, however, characteristics such as ascendance, assertiveness, dominance, and individual prominence contribute to group effectiveness. Table 6-4 suggests that potential group members should be dependable, a reasonably obvious desirable personal characteristic. *Dependability* is reflected by such personality traits as integrity, responsibility, self-reliance, and will control. Desirable group members should be emotionally stable (see Table 6-5), since *emotional stability* is generally positively correlated with such desirable group processes as cohesiveness, morale, leadership behavior, and group effectiveness. This means that potential group members should score high on measures of adjustment, emotional control, and emotional stability, and should score low on measures of anxiety, defensiveness, neuroticism, paranoid tendencies, and the like.

In summary, the population of potentially acceptable group members should be composed of adult males in good physical condition and of at least average intellectual ability. They should be approach-oriented, socially sensitive, ascendant, dependable, and emotionally stable.

Given a population of potential group members with these characteristics, our next task is to select members for the effective group in such a way that group members can work together effectively. In Chapter 7, it was shown conclusively that the particular assembly of individuals is an important determinant of group effectiveness, and evidence was amassed concerning the particular aspects of assembly that are related to effective group functioning. In the first place, group members should be selected to ensure group cohesiveness. Members who are attracted to the group are more highly motivated to work toward group goals, are better satisfied, and exert greater influence upon one another than members who are not attracted to the group. Cohesive groups also achieve their goals more effectively than noncohesive groups. It seems obvious that members of cohesive groups should be more compatible than members of noncohesive groups, but it is also important that group members be compatible with respect to interpersonal needs (Schutz, 1955, 1958). For example, if one group member needs to be emotionally close to others and another member needs to be distant, they will be incompatible with respect to such needs, and this incompatibility will tend to reduce group effectiveness. Therefore, group members should be selected to be compatible with respect to their interpersonal needs. (Some measure, such as FIRO-B, could be used in making this selection.) Finally, group members should be chosen to be heterogeneous with respect to personality profiles (Hoffman, 1959; Hoffman & Maier, 1961) and abilities (Goldman, 1965; Laughlin et al., 1969). Other things equal, groups composed of persons having diverse personality characteristics and diverse abilities perform more effectively than homogeneous groups.

In summary, group members should be selected to compose a group that is cohesive, compatible with respect to interpersonal needs, and heterogeneous with respect to abilities and personality attributes.

The composition of the group represents only one aspect of the social environment. The other aspect of the social environment, the group's structure, is equally important, although it is in some ways more difficult to control than group composition. To the extent that it is possible to control the structure of the group, empirical evidence suggests that a leader should be arranged for, preferably by member choice, who has task-related skills, who is high on sociability, and who is motivated to be a leader. If his position power can be made strong, then he should behave in a directive manner toward other group members (Fiedler, 1964). Social status of group members should be equal, except for the status differences created by the leadership-followership roles. The decision structure [defined as who takes decision for whom (Mulder, 1960)] should be centralized, with the leader in the central position. Since so much of the structure of the group develops during group interaction, it is probably unrealistic to believe that it can be "constructed" beyond the gross variations outlined here.

Finally, we return to the physical environment. With respect to the kind of task and group that we have established, the physical environment can be very simple indeed: a circular or oval work table, with no marked status differences implied by the seating arrangements, and a decentralized communication network. The table and seating arrangements may be inferred from Sommer's work (1969), whereas the communication network may be selected on the basis of the several studies of communication patterns reviewed by M. E. Shaw (1964). Both undifferentiated seating arrangements and decentralized communication networks facilitate group performance on the kind of task we have been considering.

We have now described the various characteristics or environments of an effective group faced with a structured task. The major aspects of these environments are outlined in Table 10-2. Although these exercises demonstrate that something can be said about the "design" of an effective group, the tentative nature of these recommendations should be evident. It should also be clear that the effort required to compose such a group may be greater than the benefits derived from the increased group effectiveness. On the other hand, we have used a very simple task as a prototype of the kinds of tasks that natural groups may be called upon to complete, with the clear recognition that the tasks of natural groups may be considerably more complex than the one we have used. Under such conditions, the complicated operations required to construct an effective group may well be worth the effort.

In summary, the effectiveness of a group probably can be improved greatly if attention is given to the various factors that have been shown to be related to group effectiveness. Selection of group members in such a way that their abilities, opinions, and personality attributes promote efficient group functioning obviously improves performance, but it is also clear that the particular combination of individuals must be taken into account, as well as other structural features of the group. Even the physical setting or spatial arrangement of the group may markedly influence its efficiency. Finally, it is

TABLE 10-2 The Environments of an Effective Group Assigned a Structured Task

The task environment*	The personal environment	The social environment		The physical environment
		Composition	Structure	
Cooperation requirements: high	Five persons	Cohesive	Leader: strong, having task and social skills, motivated to be a leader	Work area: undifferentiated
Difficulty: moderate	Adults	Compatible with respect to interpersonal needs	Followers: of equal status	Communication network: decentralized
Intellectual-manipulative requirements: high	Physically sound	Heterogenous with respect to abilities and personality	Decision structure: centralized	
Intrinsic interest: moderate	Intelligence: at least average			
Population familiarity: moderately high	Approach oriented			
Solution multiplicity: very low	Socially sensitive			
	Ascendant			
	Dependable			
	Emotionally stable			

* The task environment is "given"; i.e., when the task to be completed has the characteristics listed in this column, the characteristics listed in the other columns represent the "best guess" about the other environments of an effective group.

evident that the group's task often determines the relative influence of other characteristics of the group upon group process. And this fact suggests another practical consideration. In many instances, it is not feasible or it is impractical to manipulate all the variables influencing group effectiveness; hence, it is necessary to be selective with respect to the variables that are manipulated. Since the relative importance of the determinants of group functioning varies with the kind of task, those variables which exert the greatest effect upon the performance of the particular task can be selected for consideration. For instance, group-member compatibility may be more important for a task requiring much cooperation among members, whereas leadership structure may be more important for an unstructured task, such as a discussion task. In short, the data from research on group dynamics provide a minimal basis for the formation of effective groups, but many other factors that are essentially unrelated to group effectiveness often need to be considered in practical situations.

EFFECTIVE PARTICIPATION IN GROUPS

The preceding discussions have assumed that the major interest lies in the construction or formation of effective working groups. But there is another practical consideration that is at least equally important, namely, effective participation in group activities as a group member. Evidence concerning the many variables which determine group process provides many guidelines for the individual who wishes to become a more effective group member. It is not our purpose to engage in an extended discussion of the application of the principles of group dynamics to effective participation in groups; instead, we will consider a limited number of practical implications to suggest how knowledge about group processes can be used to improve one's effectiveness as a group member. Let us examine some data concerning each of the several environments of the group.

THE PHYSICAL ENVIRONMENT AND EFFECTIVE PARTICIPATION

To be an effective group member, one must recognize that each individual has a personal space into which others may not intrude and which varies with the relationship between that individual and other persons. To the extent that a group member is sensitive to the personal space of other group members, and respects it, his chances of being effective in the group are increased. Intrusion into the personal space of another will arouse negative reactions that interfere with effective interaction. In a similar way, group members establish territorial rights that must be respected by the individual who wishes to be accepted and admired by other persons in the group. Recognition and respect of territorial rights of others will increase the group member's chances of being an effective group member.

Spatial arrangements must also be considered by the aspiring effective group member. Spatial positions are associated with status in the group, and the group member must behave accordingly. For example, suppose that a member of low status sits at the head of the table, a high-status seating position. Other group members will regard him as unduly arrogant or impolite or perhaps a bit stupid. On the other hand, suppose he is high status, say the leader of the group, but sits at the side of the table. Others will probably regard him as trying to show that he does not take his position too seriously. Especially in neonate groups, behavior that is inconsistent with norms relative to spatial position may produce undesirable consequences for effective group participation.

Conversely, suppose that the group is so new that structural differentiations have not occurred. The group member may enhance his opportunities for a position of leadership or high status in the group simply by choosing a favorable spatial position. Insofar as there is no basis for judging the selection of a particular position as inappropriate, the position that a person occupies at the initial meeting of a group probably determines to some extent the social position (role, status) he will have in the established group.

THE PERSONAL ENVIRONMENT AND EFFECTIVE PARTICIPATION

It is difficult for an individual to change his personality when he becomes a member of a particular group, but it is not too difficult to become aware of the characteristics of other group members and to adjust one's own behavior accordingly. For example, a group member may discover that others in the group lack certain abilities required for task completion. He might fail to act on this information for fear of appearing aggressive or supercilious; such a response would reduce his effectiveness as a group member. On the other hand, he could offer his suggestions in a way that would aid the group in achieving its objectives, and hence increase his own effectiveness as a member of the group. In a similar way, a group member might adjust his behavior to other attributes of his fellow group members. For instance, it is known that women are less assertive and less competitive in groups than are men. When the group is composed of women, therefore, the individual group member might become more effective by behaving in a less self-assertive, ascendant fashion than might be necessary in all-male groups. Also, a recognition that assertiveness and competitiveness are characteristic of men should serve as an aid in determining the appropriate responses to such behavior by other group members.

When a group member is also the leader of the group, it is important for him to evaluate the favorability of the group-task situation. When the group-task situation is either very favorable or very unfavorable, he will probably be a more effective leader if he adopts a directive leadership style. On the other hand, when the group-task situation is only moderately favorable or unfavorable for the leader, he is more likely to be effective if he adopts a nondirective leadership style. The group leader often errs in this respect, especially when the group-task situation becomes highly unfavorable. Empirical evidence suggests that he should become more directive, whereas all too often he becomes less directive in his interactions with other members of the group.

The socially sensitive group member is more effective than the less sensitive member. It is at least theoretically possible for an individual to deliberately attend to the moods, feelings, and emotions of others, and therefore become more sensitive to them. When this is done, the probability is increased that the group member will behave in ways that enhance his acceptance in the group and also the effectiveness of the group.

Finally, it is evident that a member who behaves either in an unconventional manner or in an unusually conforming manner is likely to interfere with effective group action. Hence, the effective group member will be alert to the problems of conformity-nonconformity: He will conform when it appears that conformity is desirable for effective group performance, but he will also recognize the occasions on which nonconformity is the better course.

GROUP COMPOSITION AND EFFECTIVE PARTICIPATION

As in the case of the personal environment, group composition depends upon the characteristics of group members or, more specifically, upon the relationships among the characteristics of group members. Since it is difficult to change one's characteristics, improvement in effectiveness of group membership can be achieved primarily through a modification of behavior, which usually requires that the person behave in uncharacteristic ways. For example, suppose that a person finds himself a member of a noncohesive group. His "natural" reaction probably would involve behaviors that reveal his disenchantment with the group. However, if he is seriously interested in becoming more effective in the group and in making the group more effective, he can modify his behaviors so as to communicate a more favorable orientation toward the group or at least to conceal his lack of enthusiasm for it.

In a similar way, a group member may increase his effectiveness in incompatible groups by attending to the interpersonal needs of other group members. If another group member expresses a need for affection, one might satisfy this need by showing him affection even though such behavior is contrary to one's own desires or typical ways of reacting to others. Or if others in the group indicate a need for dominance, one might become more submissive in the interests of effective group action.

Heterogeneity of abilities and opinions probably cannot be increased at will, but it is possible for the group member to encourage the use of available abilities and the expression of diverse opinions. This is especially important when the group member is in a position of leadership. The degree to which he encourages the expression of minority opinion is an important determinant of group effectiveness. The follower may also improve his effectiveness as a group member by encouraging others to contribute to the group process.

GROUP STRUCTURE AND EFFECTIVE PARTICIPATION

Behaviors that contribute to effective group membership are obviously related to group structure. The position an individual occupies in a group specifies the behaviors expected of him and the reactions of others to his actions. This expectation is stated explicitly in the case of social roles; the role is the set of behaviors expected of an individual who occupies a particular position in the group. To be an effective group member, therefore, one must be fully aware of the role specifications associated with one's position in the group. In general, the more nearly the occupant's behavior coincides with role requirements, the more effective he is likely to be as a member of his group.

But there are also some implicit expectations associated with the individual's position that may be equally important for effective group participation. For example, the high-status group member is usually accorded greater latitude with respect to degree of conformity to group norms. Hence, a high-status group member may be more effective under certain circumstances by *not* conforming to group norms, whereas a low-status group member may be less effective if he deviates. This means that the group member who aspires to be effective in the group must consider his status and what this means with respect to deviation from group norms. Either conformity or nonconformity may be indicated, depending upon the person's status in the group.

The pattern of communication in the group is also related to status structure. Communications tend to be directed upward in the status hierarchy, and the communications directed upward have more positive content than those directed downward. These facts mean (1) that the individual who is in a low-status position must recognize that his source of information is relatively limited, and (2) that the high-status person must be aware of the potentially distorted nature of the information he receives. The low-status person can enhance his effectiveness in the group by making a special effort to learn about those things that are of importance to the group and to his own effectiveness as a group member. The high-status person, on the other hand, must be alert to the possibility that things are not as rosy as implied by the communications directed toward his position in the status hierarchy. To be most effective as a group member, he must make a special effort to determine the validity of the information he receives.

Since conformity is sometimes desirable and sometimes undesirable with regard to group effectiveness, it is important for the group member not only to ascertain when conformity is indicated and when it is counterindicated, but also for him to recognize the factors which determine conformity behavior. For instance, when he is faced with an ambiguous stimulus situation and there is unanimous agreement among other group members, he may improve his effectiveness in the group by considering the consequences of conformity and nonconformity. If nonconformity is judged to be the better course, then he will improve his effectiveness by resisting pressures toward uniformity.

Finally, if the group member has power in the group, it is important to remember that others may be responding in ways designed to maximize their own reinforcements, rather than in ways designed to ensure the achievement of group goals. When another group member enacts deferential, approval-seeking behavior, this may be entirely unrelated to the effectiveness of the powerful group member. To be effective, the powerful group member must use his power to enhance group effectiveness, and this usually means arranging the situation in such a way that individual group member reinforcement and goal achievement are congruent.

THE TASK ENVIRONMENT AND EFFECTIVE PARTICIPATION

It is obvious that the effective group member must be responsive to the demands of the task faced by the group. Effective behaviors with respect to one task may be completely ineffective with a task having different characteristics. It is important, therefore, for the group member to become thoroughly familiar with the particularities of the group task and to adjust his behaviors to its demands.

It is also important for the group member to recognize that other members set goals for the group which arouse tension systems that influence behavior in much the same way as tensions associated with personal goals. The behaviors of others may become more understandable, and hence less irritating, when it is evident that these behaviors are related to goals held for the group. The effective group member will behave in ways designed to reduce these tensions through goal achievement.

Most significant, perhaps, is the fact that goals held for the group may be heterogeneous; not every group member perceives the goal of the group in the same way. When this is the case, the group is likely to be ineffective in achieving its goals. A group member may improve his effectiveness by working toward goal clarification and unification. If he is successful in identifying differences among group members with respect to the goals they have established for the group, many of the difficulties associated with heterogeneity of goals may be solved. And if he is successful in bringing about goal unification so that all group members are working toward the same goal, he will have increased not only his own effectiveness as a group member, but the effectiveness of the group as well.

PAST MISTAKES AND RECOMMENDATIONS FOR THE FUTURE

The history of science is to a large extent the history of the mistakes of man, and the history of group dynamics is no exception to this general rule. It is inevitable that the researcher who seeks to push back the frontiers of knowledge will make many false starts, that he will do some things he should not do (because they fail to accomplish his purpose) and leave undone some things that should be accomplished. To some extent, these statements are cliches—mere assertions of the obvious. But it is important to keep them in mind, lest we become unduly critical of those who have preceded us. The discussion that follows is not intended as an indictment of group dynamics and/or those who have attempted to solve the riddles of small group behavior; instead, it is *intended* as an unbiased analysis of the field as it has developed over the past several years.

From this point in time, it seems evident that students of small group behavior have allowed themselves to be overly influenced by certain viewpoints and orientations and that they have failed to deal with certain significant issues. The field of group dynamics has been characterized by (1) an overemphasis on laboratory research and a corresponding lack of emphasis on research in natural settings, (2) an overemphasis on ad hoc groups, with a corresponding lack of concern for traditioned groups, (3) a tendency toward the elegant treatment of trivial problems, (4) an overdependence on arbitrary statistical standards, (5) a lack of application of research findings to current social problems, (6) a restriction of research to intragroup processes, and (7) a failure to develop integrative theories. These aspects of group dynamics are not independent, of course, and several of them probably reflect a single orientation. For example, the first four are probably consequences of the emphasis upon the rigorous control of variables that has characterized general psychology throughout the twentieth century. Therefore, the major shortcomings of group dynamics may be subsumed under four major headings: preference for rigor, restriction of the scope of research, lack of a theory, and failure to apply research findings.

PREFERENCE FOR RIGOR

Several years ago, Seeman and Marks (1962) wrote an amusing article about a white rat that wanted to be a psychologist. This white rat, after much "soul-searching" activity, chose as his dissertation topic a comparison of the rigor with which a problem could be attacked and the interest value of the problem. After constructing reliable measures of rigor (RIGS) and interest (INTS), he was able to demonstrate a strong inverse relationship between

RIGS and INTS: the greater the rigor that could be applied to the problem, the lower its interest value. This little story illustrates a not-so-amusing aspect of research in group dynamics. There has been an overconcern for rigorous research methods, and this has often led to concern for trivial, uninteresting problems.

The preference for rigor over problem significance is reflected in a variety of ways in research. In the first place, it has led to an overemphasis on laboratory studies. In general, laboratory studies can be conducted with a great deal more rigor than field studies. Variables can be controlled, manipulated, etc., to a much greater extent in the laboratory than in natural settings. It is not surprising, then, that those who place greater emphasis upon rigor than upon problem significance should also emphasize laboratory research. The problem is not that there has been too much laboratory research, but rather that there has been too little research in the field. As noted in Chapter 2, both laboratory and field studies are needed to completely understand small group phenomena. Field studies help in the identification of significant problems; laboratory studies permit a more precise determination of functional relationships; and finally, field studies are again necessary to determine whether laboratory-established principles can be generalized to natural situations. There is a need for constant interchange between the laboratory and the field; group dynamicists have tended to neglect the field.

The overemphasis upon laboratory research probably accounts for another mistake, namely, the tendency to study ad hoc groups of short duration and to avoid studies of extant groups over long periods. There are two undesirable consequences of this limited approach. First, newly formed groups do not have a set of traditions, nor do they have expectations about future interactions. In some instances, these factors may not be important; that is, the same principles may operate in both ad hoc and traditioned groups. On the other hand, these variables may be extremely important in some cases, and this can be determined only by studying both kinds of groups. Second, the study of fifty-minute groups does not permit the observation of long-term changes. Although it is possible to conduct longitudinal studies in the laboratory, this is difficult to do and it is rare for a laboratory study to span even a week.

Finally, the emphasis upon rigor has led to an almost servile dependence upon arbitrary statistical standards; $p < .05$ has become a cruel master. Consider for a moment the meaning of statistical probabilities. When a difference between two experimental treatments is found to be significant at the 5 percent level of confidence (p = .05), this means that the chances that the observed difference is due to uncontrolled factors are only 5 in 100. Since .05 is an arbitrary standard that, by convention, allows the rejection of the null hypothesis (the hypothesis that there is no difference between the treatments except that caused by uncontrolled variables), it is then inferred that the observed difference was due to the experimental treatments. But if the probability value is greater than .05, convention holds that the difference is not significant; hence the null hypothesis is accepted. But suppose the significance level is p = .10. This means that the chances are only 10 in 100 that the observed difference was due to chance factors, or conversely, that the chances are 90 in 100 that the observed difference was *not* due to chance factors. When the null hypothesis is accepted, the researcher is putting his faith in the lower probability. In effect, he is betting on an event that has only 10 chances in 100 of occurring in preference to one that has 90 chances in 100. The argument here is not that the researcher should accept probabilities higher than .05 for establishing truth, but rather that he should *not* accept even much higher probabilities for this purpose. In far too many instances, the group dynamicist has interpreted a failure to establish a relationship as a demonstration that the relationship does not exist. Everyone who has had an elementary course in statistics knows that this conclusion is not valid, but it appears to be one of the undesirable consequences of the demand for rigorous experimental procedures.

RESTRICTION OF THE SCOPE OF RESEARCH

The complete analysis of group behavior must include not only the investigation of intragroup processes, but also the behavior of groups vis-à-vis other groups. Research on group dynamics, however, has been limited almost entirely to the study of intragroup effects. If we are to make a contribution to the solution of the vexing problems of society, attention must be given to intergroup processes. Failure to do so means that group dynamics can say little about such significant issues as international relations, industrial negotiations, peace talks, political machinations, interracial conferences, and the like. Studies of interpersonal bargaining (e.g., Deutsch & Krauss, 1962; McGrath & Julian, 1963), international relations (e.g., Guetzkow et al., 1963), and coalition formation (see Chapter 4) represent the kind of research that needs to be done. Unfortunately, such investigations are indeed rare.

LACK OF A THEORY

In the first few chapters of this book, it was argued that research data are unlikely to be very useful if they are not organized in a theoretically meaningful way. Theory is a convenient way of organizing experiences so that a large amount of empirical data can be treated with relatively few propositions. Theoretical organization of data also allows us to discover implications and relationships that are not evident from isolated bits of information. Thus, any discipline must provide for the integration of its data by the development of adequate theoretical formulations. Group dynamics has largely failed in this respect. As noted in Chapter 2, a few attempts have been made, with varying degrees of success. But for the most part, these theories are capable of encompassing only limited amounts of the information gleaned from small group research. One can appeal to the complexity of the phenomena as a reason for the failure of group dynamicists to devise an adequate theory, but the fact remains that no existing theory can adequately organize the empirical data of group dynamics. Such a theory is sorely needed.

FAILURE TO APPLY RESEARCH FINDINGS

Historically, the scientist has maintained a position of aloofness with regard to the use of his research findings. The "pure" scientist has not been concerned with the application of his findings to events outside the laboratory. If he discovered a lifesaving drug, it was not his responsibility to see that it was used by physicians, or if he discovered a device that could destroy the world, it was no concern of his if some maniac used it. Application simply has not been viewed as a proper function for the scientist. This view is being seriously questioned today. No longer can the researcher remain in his ivory tower and ignore the consequences of his work. With an ever-increasing demand for "relevance," those who support research expect the scientist to aid in relating his work to the problems of society. And this demand is being made especially of the social scientist, including the group dynamicist.

Students of group behavior have not been noted for their overwhelming response to the needs of society. With the exception of a concern for sensitivity training, which has been spearheaded by clinically oriented group theorists, little attention has been given to the possible application of research findings to small groups in everyday life. In the first part of this chapter, an attempt was made to show some of the possible applications of research-established principles. This attempt was tentative, a first step taken with a great deal of trepidation. But one must begin somewhere, and only by implementing such tentative proposals in natural situations can we hope to discover whether applications can be effective.

WHAT NOW?

Suggestions for future activities in group dynamics are embedded in the preceding discussions. First, there is a need to place greater emphasis upon the significance of the research problem than has been done in the past. This is not to say that there should be a decreased concern for rigorous research procedures. On the contrary, the most rigorous research methods available must be adopted. But significant problems must not be avoided simply because elegant research techniques are not available to study them, nor are sophisticated research methods sufficient justification for investigating meaningless problems. Significant problems must be attacked even if this means using less than perfect research procedures. This "mandate" probably means that there must be an increase in experimentation in natural settings, an increase in the study of traditioned groups, an increase in longitudinal studies, and a greater concern for the logic of statistical analysis.

Second, the future researcher should be willing to expand his outlook with respect to both appropriate areas of research and possible application of his findings to the problems of society. In particular, there is a need to enlarge the scope of research to include many aspects of intergroup relations that have been all but neglected in the past.

Finally, there must be a greater concern for theory. Theory and research are equal partners in the advancement of knowledge. One without the other can only be a sterile exercise of the intellect. In far too many instances the two endeavors have traveled different roads, with few interconnecting pathways. Let the researcher give heed to theory and the theorist take account of research data. By this cooperative endeavor, perhaps an adequate theoretical integration of empirical data can be accomplished.

CONCLUDING STATEMENT

The field of group dynamics is still in its infancy, but even so, a tremendous amount of information has been amassed through empirical investigations. Much of this information is unreliable and lacking in validation; theoretical integration is practically nonexistent. Nevertheless, a beginning has been made and available data reveal the great complexity of small group behavior. The interrelations among the many parts of the group and the variables that influence group process almost defy comprehension. But hope springs eternal; we are beginning to gain some understanding of this multiplex phenomenon.

In the preceding pages, we have examined the many environments in which the group functions and have shown some of the effects of these environments upon the group process. These environments are sometimes unique in that the group is at one and the same time exposed to the environment and is a part of the environment. That is, parts of the group form the environment to which the remainder of the group is exposed and to which it responds. It might be more precise to say that the group is often intertwined with an environment, rather than embedded in it. For example, the personality of a given group member forms a part of the environment to which the rest of the group is exposed. The unraveling of the consequences of this kind of environment is difficult indeed. Despite these complexities, data obtained from empirical studies permit the formulation of relatively precise plausible hypotheses. These hypotheses have been shown to be useful not only for the understanding of group process, but also for practical purposes. Given the data at hand, an effective group can be described; the formation of effective groups then becomes limited by lack of control over variables rather than by lack of knowledge about the characteristics of an effective group. The knowledge that is available concerning group behavior is also useful for the person who wishes to improve his effectiveness as a group member. By being aware of the internal functioning of small groups, the individual can adjust his own behavior to improve the effectiveness of his group.

Group dynamicists have thus made progress in the analysis of group interaction and group functioning. But much remains to be done before the group process can be completely understood. The greatest need today is an adequate theory for the organization of data, so that the implications of the data at hand can be spelled out more definitively and deficiencies revealed more clearly. When this is done, we may learn much more about small group behavior.

SUGGESTED READINGS

COHEN, D. J., WHITMYRE, J. W., & FUNK, W. H. Effect of group cohesiveness and training upon group thinking. *Journal of Applied Psychology*, 1960, **44**, 319–322.

MEADOW, A., PARNES, S. J., & REESE, H. Influence of brainstorming instructions and problem sequence on a creative problem solving test. *Journal of Applied Psychology*, 1959, **43**, 413–416.

NEWCOMB, T. M. *The acquaintance process.* New York: Holt, 1961.

TRIPLETT, N. The dynamogenic factors in pacemaking and competition. *American Journal of Psychology*, 1897, **9**, 507–533.

ZANDER, A., & NEWCOMB, T., Jr. Group levels of aspiration in United Fund campaigns. *Journal of Personality and Social Psychology*, 1967, **6**, 157–162.

REFERENCES

ABELSON, R. P. Simulation of social behavior. In G. Lindzey & E. Aronson (Eds.), *The handbook of social psychology*. (2d ed.) Reading, Mass.: Addison-Wesley, 1968. Pp. 274–356.

ADAMS, J. S., & ROMNEY, A. K. A functional analysis of authority. *Psychological Review*, 1959, **66**, 234–251.

ADORNO, T. W., FRENKEL-BRUNSWIK, E., LEVINSON, D. J., & SANFORD, R. N. *The authoritarian personality*. New York: Harper, 1950.

ALKIRE, A. A., COLLUM, M. E., KASWAN, J., & LOVE, L. R. Information exchange and accuracy of verbal communication under social power conditions. *Journal of Personality and Social Psychology*, 1968, **9**, 301–308.

ALLPORT, F. H. The influence of the group upon association and thought. *Journal of Experimental Psychology*, 1920, **3**, 159–182.

ALLPORT, F. H. *Social psychology*. Boston: Houghton Mifflin, 1924.

ALLPORT, G. W., & ALLPORT, F. H. *The A-S reaction study: A scale for measuring ascendance-submission in personality*. Boston: Houghton Mifflin, 1928.

ALTMAN, I., & HAYTHORN, W. W. The ecology of isolated groups. *Behavioral Science*, 1967a, **12**, 169–182.

ALTMAN, I., & HAYTHORN, W. W. The effects of social isolation and group composition on performance. *Human Relations*, 1967b, **20**, 313–340.

ANDERSON, H. H. Domination and social integration in the behavior of kindergarten children and teachers. *Genetic Psychology Monographs*, 1939, **21**, 287–385.

ARGYLE, M., & DEAN, J. Eye contact, distance, and affiliation. *Sociometry*, 1965, **28**, 289–304.

ASCH, S. E. Effects of group pressure upon the modification and distortion of judgments. In H. Guetzkow (Ed.), *Groups, leadership and men*. Pittsburgh: Carnegie Press, 1951. Pp. 177–190.

ASCH, S. E. *Social psychology*. Englewood Cliffs, N.J.: Prentice-Hall, 1952.

BACK, K. W. Influence through social communication. *Journal of Abnormal and Social Psychology*, 1951, **46**, 9–23.

BACK, K. W., FESTINGER, L., HYMOVITCH, B., KELLEY, H. H., SCHACHTER, S., & THIBAUT, J. W. The methodology of studying rumor transmission. *Human Relations*, 1950 **3**, 307–312.

BALES, R. F. *Interaction process analysis: A method for the study of small groups*. Cambridge, Mass.: Addison-Wesley, 1950.

BALES, R. F. Factor analysis of the domain of values in the value profile test. Mimeographed report, Laboratory of Social Relations, Harvard University, 1956.

BALES, R. F., & STRODTBECK, F. L.   Phases in group problem solving. *Journal of Abnormal and Social Psychology*, 1951, 46, 485–495.

BARCH, A. M., TRUMBO, D., & NANGLE, J.   Social setting and conformity to a legal requirement. *Journal of Abnormal and Social Psychology*, 1957, 55, 396–398.

BARNLUND, D. C.   A comparative study of individual, majority, and group judgment. *Journal of Abnormal and Social Psychology*, 1959, 58, 55–60.

BARTON, W. A., Jr.   The effect of group activity and individual effort in developing ability to solve problems in first-year algebra. *Journal of Education Administration and Supervision*, 1926, 12, 512–518.

BASS, B. M.   An analysis of the leaderless group discussion. *Journal of Applied Psychology*, 1949, 33, 527–533.

BASS, B. M.   Development and evaluation of a social acquiescence scale. *Journal of Abnormal and Social Psychology*, 1956, 53, 296–299.

BASS, B. M.   *Leadership, psychology, and organizational behavior*. New York: Harper & Row, 1960.

BASS, B. M., & KLUBECK, S.   Effects of seating arrangement on leaderless group discussions. *Journal of Abnormal and Social Psychology*, 1952, 47, 724–727.

BASS, B. M., McGEHEE, C. R., HAWKINS, W. C., YOUNG, P. C., & GEBEL, A. S.   Personality variables related to leaderless group discussion. *Journal of Abnormal and Social Psychology*, 1953, 48, 120–128.

BASS, B. M., PRYER, M. W., GAIER, E. L., & FLINT, A. W.   Interacting effects of control, motivation, group practice and problem difficulty on attempted leadership. *Journal of Abnormal and Social Psychology*, 1958, 56, 352–358.

BASS, B. M., & WURSTER, C. R.   Effects of company rank on LGD performance of oil refinery supervisors. *Journal of Applied Psychology*, 1953a, 37, 100–104.

BASS, B. M., & WURSTER, C. R.   Effects of the nature of the problem on LGD performance. *Journal of Applied Psychology*, 1953b, 37, 96–99.

BASS, B. M., WURSTER, C. R., DOLL, P. A., & CLAIR, D. J.   Situational and personality factors in leadership among sorority women. *Psychological Monographs*, 1953, 67, No. 16 (Whole No. 366).

BAVELAS, A.   A mathematical model for group structures. *Applied Anthropology*, 1948, 7, 16–30.

BAVELAS, A.   Communication patterns in task-oriented groups. *Journal of the Acoustical Society of America*, 1950, 22, 725–730.

BEATY, W. E., & SHAW, M. E.   Some effects of social interaction on probability learning. *Journal of Psychology*, 1965, 59, 299–306.

BEAVER, A. P.   The initiation of social contacts by pre-school children. *Child Development Monographs*, 1932, No. 7.

BECKWITH, J., IVERSON, M. A., & RENDER, M. E. Test anxiety, task relevance of group experience, and change in level of aspiration. *Journal of Personality and Social Psychology*, 1965, 1, 579–588.

BEGUM, B. O., & LEHR, D. J. Effects of authoritarianism on vigilance performance. *Journal of Applied Psychology*, 1963, 47, 75–77.

BELL, G. B., & HALL, H. E., Jr. The relationship between leadership and empathy. *Journal of Abnormal and Social Psychology*, 1954, 49, 156–157.

BELOFF, H. Two forms of social conformity: Acquiescence and conventionality. *Journal of Abnormal and Social Psychology*, 1958, 56, 99–104.

BEM, D. J., WALLACH, M. A., & KOGAN, N. Group decision making under risk of aversive consequences. *Journal of Personality and Social Psychology*, 1965, 1, 453–460.

BENNIS, W. G., & SHEPARD, H. A. A theory of group development. *Human Relations*, 1956, 9, 415–437.

BERENDA, R. W. *The influence of the group on the judgments of children.* New York: King's Crown, 1950.

BERG, I. A., & BASS, B. M. (Eds.) *Conformity and deviation.* New York: Harper, 1961.

BERGER, E. The relation between expressed acceptance of self and expressed acceptance of others. *Journal of Abnormal and Social Psychology*, 1952, 47, 778–782.

BERKOWITZ, L. Group standards, cohesiveness, and productivity. *Human Relations*, 1954, 7, 509–519.

BERKOWITZ, L., & DANIELS, L. R. Responsibility and dependency. *Journal of Abnormal and Social Psychology*, 1963, 66, 429–436.

BERNHARDT, K. S., MILLICHAMP, D. A., CHARLES, M. W., & McFARLAND, M. P. An analysis of the social contacts of pre-school children with the aid of motion pictures. *University of Toronto Studies of Child Development*, 1937, No. 10.

BIXENSTINE, V. E., & DOUGLAS, J. Effects of psychopathology on group consensus and cooperative choice in a six-person game. *Journal of Personality and Social Psychology*, 1967, 5, 32–37.

BIXENSTINE, V. E., POTASH, H. M., & WILSON, K. V. Effects of level of cooperative choice by the other player on choices in a prisoner's dilemma game. Part I. *Journal of Abnormal and Social Psychology*, 1963, 66, 308–313.

BLAU, P. M. Co-operation and competition in a bureaucracy. *American Journal of Sociology*, 1954, 59, 530–535.

BLAU, P. M.   Social integration, social rank, and the process of interaction. *Human Relations,* 1959–1960, **18**, 152–157.

BOND, J. R., & VINACKE, W. E.   Coalitions in mixed-sex triads. *Sociometry,* 1961, **24**, 61–75.

BONNER, H. *Group dynamics: Principles and applications.* New York: Ronald, 1959.

BORG, W. R.   Prediction of small group role behavior from personality variables. *Journal of Abnormal and Social Psychology,* 1960, **60**, 112–116.

BORGATTA, E. F.   Sidesteps toward a nonspecial theory. *Psychological Review,* 1954, **61**, 343–352.

BORGATTA, M. L.   Power structure and coalitions in three person groups. *Journal of Social Psychology,* 1961, **55**, 287–300.

BORKO, H. (Ed.) *Computer applications in the behavioral sciences.* Englewood Cliffs, N.J.: Prentice-Hall, 1962.

BOUCHARD, T. J., Jr.   Personality, problem-solving procedure, and performance in small groups. *Journal of Applied Psychology,* 1969, **53**, 1–29.

BOVARD, E. W.   Group structure and perception. *Journal of Abnormal and Social Psychology,* 1951, **46**, 398–405.

BOVARD, E. W.   Conformity to social norms and attraction to the group. *Science,* 1953, **118**, 598–599.

BOVARD, E. W.   Interaction and attraction to the group. *Human Relations,* 1956, **9**, 481–489.

BOWEN, A. J., Jr.   Coalition patterns in three-person family and non-family groups. Unpublished doctoral dissertation, University of Florida, Gainesville, 1966.

BROWN, R. *Social psychology.* New York: Fress Press, 1965.

BURGESS, E. W., & COTTRELL, L. S. *Predicting success or failure in marriage.* Englewood Cliffs, N.J.: Prentice-Hall, 1939.

BURTON, A.   The influence of social factors upon the persistence of satiation in school children. *Child Development,* 1941, **12**, 121–129.

BURTT, H. E.   Sex differences in the effect of discussion. *Journal of Experimental Psychology,* 1920, **3**, 390–395.

BUTLER, D. C., & MILLER, N.   Power to reward and punish in social interaction. *Journal of Experimental Social Psychology,* 1965, **1**, 311–322.

BYRNE, D.   Interpersonal attraction and attitude similarity. *Journal of Abnormal and Social Psychology,* 1961, **62**, 713–715.

BYRNE, D., & BUEHLER, J. A.   A note on the influence of propinquity upon acquaintanceships. *Journal of Abnormal and Social Psychology,* 1955, **51**, 147–148.

BYRNE, D., CLORE, J. L., Jr. & WORCHEL, P.   Effect of economic similarity-dissimilarity on interpersonal attraction. *Journal of Personality and Social Psychology*, 1966, **4**, 220–224.

BYRNE, D., & GRIFFITT, W. A developmental investigation of the law of attraction. *Journal of Personality and Social Psychology*, 1966, **4**, 699–702.

BYRNE, D., GRIFFITT, W., & STEFANIAK, D. Attraction and similarity of personality characteristics. *Journal of Personality and Social Psychology*, 1967, **5**, 82–90.

BYRNE, D., LONDON, O., & GRIFFITT, W. The effect of topic importance and attitude similarity-dissimilarity on attraction in an intrastranger design. *Psychonomic Science*, 1968, **11**, 303–304.

BYRNE, D., & NELSON, D. Attraction as a function of attitude similarity-dissimilarity: The effect of topic importance. *Psychonomic Science*, 1964, **1**, 93–94.

BYRNE, D., & NELSON, D. Attraction as a linear function of proportion of positive reinforcements. *Journal of Personality and Social Psychology*, 1965a, **1**, 659–663.

BYRNE, D., & NELSON, D. The effect of topic importance and attitude similarity-dissimilarity on attraction in a multi-stranger design. *Psychonomic Science*, 1965b, **3**, 449–450.

BYRNE, D., NELSON, D., & REEVES, K. Effects of consensual validation and invalidation on attraction as a function of verifiability. *Journal of Experimental Social Psychology*, 1966, **2**, 98–107.

BYRNE, D., & RHAMEY, R. Magnitude of positive and negative reinforcements as a determinant of attraction. *Journal of Personality and Social Psychology*, 1965, **2**, 884–889.

CAMPBELL, D. T. Common fate, similarity, and other indices of the status of aggregates of persons as social entities. *Behavioral Science*, 1958, **3**, 14–25.

CAMPBELL, D. T., KRUSKAL, W. H., & WALLACE, W. P. Seating aggregation as an index of attitude. *Sociometry*, 1966, **29**, 1–15.

CAMPBELL, D. T., & STANLEY, J. C. Experimental and quasi-experimental designs for research on teaching. In N. L. Gage (Ed.), *Handbook on research on teaching*. Chicago: Rand McNally, 1963. Pp. 171–246.

CAPLOW, T. Further development of a theory of coalitions in the triad. *American Journal of Sociology*, 1959, **64**, 488–493.

CARTER, L. F. On defining leadership. In M. Sherif & M. O. Wilson (Eds.), *Group relations at the crossroads*. New York: Harper & Row, 1953, Pp. 262–265.

CARTER, L. F., HAYTHORN, W. W., & HOWELL, M. A. A further investigation of the criteria of leadership. *Journal of Abnormal and Social Psychology*, 1950, **45**, 350–358.

CARTWRIGHT, D., & ZANDER, A. (Eds.) *Group dynamics: Research and theory.* Evanston, Ill.: Row, Peterson, 1953.

CARTWRIGHT, D., & ZANDER, A. (Eds.) *Group dynamics: Research and theory.* (2d ed.) Evanston, Ill.: Row, Peterson, 1960.

CARTWRIGHT, D., & ZANDER, A. (Eds.) *Group dynamics: Research and theory.* (3d ed.) New York: Harper & Row, 1968.

CATTELL, R. B. Concepts and methods in the measurement of group syntality. *Psychological Review,* 1948, **55,** 48–63.

CATTELL, R. B. Determining syntality dimension as a basis for morale and leadership measurement. In H. Guetzkow (Ed.), *Groups, leadership and men.* Pittsburgh: Carnegie Press, 1951a. Pp. 16–27.

CATTELL, R. B. New concepts for measuring leadership, in terms of group syntality. *Human Relations,* 1951b, **4,** 161–184.

CATTELL, R. B., SAUNDERS, D. R., & STICE, G. F. The dimensions of syntality in small groups. *Human Relations,* 1953, **6,** 331–356.

CATTELL, R. B., & STICE, G. F. The dimensions of groups and their relations to the behavior of members. Champaign, Ill.: Institute for Personality and Ability Testing, 1960.

CATTELL, R. B., & WISPE, L. G. The dimensions of syntality in small groups. *Journal of Social Psychology,* 1948, **28,** 57–78.

CERVIN, V. Individual behavior in social situations: Its relation to anxiety, neuroticism, and group solidarity. *Journal of Experimental Psychology,* 1956, **51,** 161–168.

CHANEY, M. V., & VINACKE, W. E. Achievement and nuturance in triads varying in power distribution. *Journal of Abnormal and Social Psychology,* 1960, **60,** 175–181.

CHERTKOFF, J. M. The effects of probability of future success on coalition formation. *Journal of Experimental Social Psychology,* 1966, **2,** 265–277.

COCH, L., & FRENCH, J. R. P., JR. Overcoming resistance to change. *Human Relations,* 1948, **1,** 512–532.

COE, R. M. Conflict, interference and aggression: Computer simulation of a social process. *Behavioral Science,* 1964, **9,** 186–197.

COHEN, A. M. Changing small group communication networks. *Journal of Communication,* 1961, **11,** 116–124 and 128.

COHEN, A. M. Changing small-group communication networks. *Administrative Science Quarterly,* 1962, **6,** 443–462.

COHEN, A. R. Experimental effects of ego-defense preference on interpersonal relations. *Journal of Abnormal and Social Psychology,* 1956, **52,** 19–27.

COHEN, A. R. Situational structure, self-esteem, and threat-oriented reactions to power. In D. Cartwright (Eds.), *Studies in social power.* Ann Arbor, Mich.: Institute for Social Research, 1959.

COHEN, A. R., STOTLAND, E., & WOLFE, D. M. An experimental investigation of need for cognition. *Journal of Abnormal and Social Psychology,* 1955, **51,** 291–294.

COHEN, D. J., WHITMYRE, J. W., & FUNK, W. H. Effect of group cohesiveness and training upon group thinking. *Journal of Applied Psychology,* 1960, **44,** 319–322.

COHEN, G. B. Communication network and distribution of "weight" of group members as determinants of group effectiveness. *Journal of Experimental Social Psychology,* 1968a, **4,** 302–314.

COHEN, G. B. *The task-tuned organization of groups.* Amsterdam: Swets en Zeitlinger, 1968b.

COLLINS, E. B., & GUETZKOW, H. *A social psychology of group processes for decision-making.* New York: Wiley, 1964.

COOK, S. W., HAVEL, J., & CHRIST, J. R. The effects of an orientation program for foreign students. Mimeographed report, Research Center for Human Relations, New York University, 1957. (Cited in Selltiz, Jahoda, Deutsch, & Cook, 1961).

COSTANZO, P. R., REITAN, H. T., & SHAW, M. E. Conformity as a function of experimentally induced minority and majority competence. *Psychonomic Science,* 1968, **10,** 329–330.

COSTANZO, P. R., & SHAW, M. E. Conformity as a function of age level. *Child Development,* 1966, **37,** 967–975.

CRONBACH, L. J., & GLESER, G. C. Assessing similarity between profiles. *Psychological Bulletin,* 1953, **50,** 456–473.

CRUTCHFIELD, R. S. Conformity and character. *American Psychologist,* 1955, **10,** 191–198.

DASHIELL, J. F. An experimental analysis of some group effects. *Journal of Abnormal and Social Psychology,* 1930, **25,** 190–199.

DAVIS, J. H., & RESTLE, F. The analysis of problems and prediction of group problem solving. *Journal of Abnormal and Social Psychology,* 1963, **66,** 103–116.

DAVIS, K. The child and the social structure. *Journal of Educational Sociology,* 1940, **14,** 217–229.

DEUTSCH, K. W. *Political community at the international level.* Garden City, N.Y.: Doubleday, 1954.

DEUTSCH, M. An experimental study of the effects of co-operation and competition upon group process. *Human Relations,* 1949a, **2**, 199–232.

DEUTSCH, M. A theory of co-operation and competition. *Human Relations,* 1949b, **2**, 129–152.

DEUTSCH, M., & COLLINS, M. E. *Interracial housing: A psychological evaluation of a social experiment.* Minneapolis: University of Minnesota Press, 1951.

DEUTSCH, M., & GERARD, H. B. A study of normative and informational social influences upon individual judgment. *Journal of Abnormal and Social Psychology,* 1955, **51**, 629–636.

DEUTSCH, M., & KRAUSS, R. Studies of interpersonal bargaining. *Conflict Resolution,* 1962, **1**, 52–76.

DOWNING, J. Cohesiveness, perception, and values. *Human Relations,* 1958, **11**, 157–166.

DUNNETTE, M. D., CAMPBELL, J., & JAASTAD, K. The effect of group participation on brainstorming effectiveness for two industrial samples. *Journal of Applied Psychology,* 1963, **47**, 30–37.

DURKHEIM, E. Représentations individuelles et représentations collectives. *Revue de Métaphysique,* 1898, **6**, 274–302. (Translated by D. F. Pocock, *Sociology and philosophy.* New York: Free Press, 1953).

DYMOND, R. S., HUGHES, A. S., & RAABE, V. L. Measurable changes in empathy with age. *Journal of Consulting Psychology,* 1952, **16**, 202–206.

EMERSON, R. M. Power-dependence relations: Two experiments. *Sociometry,* 1964, **27**, 282–298.

EXLINE, R. V. Group climate as a factor in the relevance and accuracy of social perception. *Journal of Abnormal and Social Psychology,* 1957, **55**, 382–388.

EXLINE, R. V. Explorations in the process of person perception: Visual interaction in relation to competition, sex, and need for affiliation. *Journal of Personality,* 1963, **31**, 1–20.

EXLINE, R. V., GRAY, D., & SCHUETTE, D. Visual behavior in a dyad as affected by interview content and sex of respondent. *Journal of Personality and Social Psychology,* 1965, **1**, 201–209.

FARNSWORTH, P. R. Concerning so-called group effects. *Journal of Genetic Psychology,* 1928, **35**, 587–594.

FESTINGER, L. A theory of social comparison processes. *Human Relations,* 1954, **7**, 117–140.

FESTINGER, L. Group attraction and membership. In D. Cartwright and A. Zander (Eds.), *Group dynamics: Research and theory.* Evanston, Ill.: Row, Peterson, 1953a. Pp. 92–101.

FESTINGER, L.   Informal social communication. *Psychological Review,* 1950, **57,** 271–282.

FESTINGER, L.   Laboratory experiments. In L. Festinger & D. Katz (Eds.), *Research methods in the behavioral sciences.* New York: Dryden Press, Inc., 1953b. Pp. 136–172.

FESTINGER, L., GERARD, H., HYMOVITCH, B., KELLEY, H. H., & RAVEN, B. The influence process in the presence of extreme deviates. *Human Relations,* 1952, **5,** 327–346.

FESTINGER, L., SCHACHTER, S., & BACK, K. W.   *Social pressure in informal groups.* New York: Harper, 1950.

FIEDLER, F. E.   A method of objective quantification of certain counter-transference attitudes. *Journal of Clinical Psychology,* 1951, **7,** 101–107.

FIEDLER, F. E.   Assumed similarity measures as predictors of team effectiveness. *Journal of Abnormal and Social Psychology,* 1954, **49,** 381–388.

FIEDLER, F. E.   A contingency model of leadership effectiveness. In L. Berkowitz (Ed.), *Advances in experimental social psychology.* Vol. 1. New York: Academic, 1964. Pp. 149–190.

FIEDLER, F. E.   The effect of leadership and cultural heterogeneity on group performance: A test of the contingency model. *Journal of Experimental Social Psychology,* 1966, **2,** 237–264.

FIEDLER, F. E.   *A theory of leadership effectiveness.* New York: McGraw-Hill, 1967.

FIEDLER, F. E., HUTCHINS, E. B., & DODGE, J. S.   Quasi-therapeutic relations in small college and military groups. *Psychological Monographs,* 1959, **73,** No. 473.

FIEDLER, F. E., MEUWESE, W. A. T., & OONK, S.   Performance of laboratory tasks requiring group creativity. *Acta Psychologica,* 1961, **18,** 100–119.

FIEDLER, F. E., WARRINGTON, W. G., & BLAISDELL, F. J.   Unconscious attitudes as correlates of sociometric choice in a social group. *Journal of Abnormal and Social Psychology,* 1952, **47,** 790–796.

FREED, A. M., CHANDLER, P. J., MOUTON, J. S., & BLAKE, R. R.   Stimulus background factors in sign violation. *Journal of Personality,* 1955, **23,** 499.

FREEMAN, E. *Social psychology.* New York: Holt, 1936.

FRENCH, J. R. P., JR.   The disruption and cohesion of groups. *Journal of Abnormal and Social Psychology,* 1941, **36,** 361–377.

FRENCH, J. R. P., JR.   A formal theory of social power. *Psychological Review,* 1956, **63,** 181–194.

FRENCH, J. R. P., JR., & RAVEN, B.   The bases of social power. In D. Cartwright

(Ed.), *Studies in social power*. Ann Arbor, Mich.: Institute for Social Research, 1959. Pp. 150–167.

FRY, C. L.   Personality and acquisition factors in the development of coordination strategy. *Journal of Personality and Social Psychology*, 1965, **2**, 403–407.

FRYE, R. L., & BASS, B. M.   Behavior in a group related to tested social acquiescence. *Journal of Social Psychology*, 1963, **61**, 263–266.

GAMSON, W. A.   An experimental test of a theory of coalition formation. *American Sociological Review*, 1961a, **26**, 565–573.

GAMSON, W. A.   A theory of coalition formation. *American Sociological Review*, 1961b, **26**, 373–382.

GAMSON, W. A.   Experimental studies of coalition formation. In L. Berkowitz (Ed.), *Advances in experimental social psychology*. Vol. 1. New York: Academic, 1964. Pp. 82–110.

GARDNER, R. A.   Probability-learning with two and three choices. *American Journal of Psychology*, 1957, **70**, 174–185.

GARDNER, R. A.   Multiple-choice decision-behavior. *American Journal of Psychology*, 1958, **71**, 710–717.

GARNER, W. R., HAKE, H. W., & ERIKSEN, C. W.   Operationism and the concept of perception. *Psychological Review*, 1956, **63**, 149–159.

GERARD, H. B., WILHELMY, R. A., & CONOLLEY, E. S.   Conformity and group size. *Journal of Personality and Social Psychology*, 1968, **8**, 79–82.

GERGEN, K. J., & BAUER, R. A.   Interactive effects of self-esteem and task difficulty on social conformity. *Journal of Personality and Social Psychology*, 1967, **6**, 16–22.

GERGEN, K. J., & TAYLOR, M. G.   Social expectancy and self-presentation in a status hierarchy. *Journal of Experimental Social Psychology*, 1969, **5**, 79–92.

GEWIRTZ, J. L., & BAER, D. M.   Deprivation and satiation of social reinforcers as drive conditions. *Journal of Abnormal and Social Psychology*, 1958a, **57**, 165–172.

GEWIRTZ, J. L., & BAER, D. M.   The effect of brief social deprivation on behaviors for a social reinforcer. *Journal of Abnormal and Social Psychology*, 1958b, **56**, 49–56.

GILCHRIST, J. C.   The formation of social groups under conditions of success and failure. *Journal of Abnormal and Social Psychology*, 1952, **47**, 174–187.

GILCHRIST, J. C., SHAW, M. E., & WALKER, L. C.   Some effects of unequal distribution of information in a wheel group structure. *Journal of Abnormal and Social Psychology*, 1954, **49**, 554–556.

GOLDBERG, S. C.   Influence and leadership as a function of group structure. *Journal of Abnormal and Social Psychology*, 1955, **51**, 119–122.

GOLDMAN, M. A comparison of individual and group performance for varying combinations of initial ability. *Journal of Personality and Social Psychology,* 1965, 1, 210–216.

GOODACRE, D. M., III. The use of a sociometric test as a predictor of combat unit effectiveness. *Sociometry,* 1951, 14, 148–152.

GOODNOW, J. J. Determinants of choice-distribution in two-choice situations. *American Journal of Psychology,* 1955, 68, 106–116.

GORDON, K. A study of aesthetic judgments. *Journal of Experimental Psychology,* 1923, 6, 36–43.

GORDON, K. Group judgments in the field of lifted weights. *Journal of Experimental Psychology,* 1924, 7, 389–400.

GREEN, E. H. Friendships and quarrels among pre-school children. *Child Development,* 1933a, 4, 237–252.

GREEN, E. H. Group play and quarreling among pre-school children. *Child Development,* 1933b, 4, 302–307.

GREER, F. L. Small group effectiveness. Institute Report No. 6, Contract Nonr-1229(00), Institute for Research in Human Relations, Philadelphia, 1955.

GRIFFITT, W. Interpersonal attraction as a function of self concept and personality similarity-dissimilarity. *Journal of Personality and Social Psychology,* 1966, 4, 581–584.

GROSS, E. Primary functions of the small group. *American Journal of Sociology,* 1954, 60, 24–30.

GROSS, E. Symbiosis and consensus as integrative factors in small groups. *American Sociological Review,* 1956, 21, 174–179.

GUETZKOW, H., ALGER, C. F., BRODY, R. A., NOEL, R. C., & SNYDER, R. C. *Simulation in international relations.* Englewood Cliffs, N.J.: Prentice-Hall, 1963.

GUETZKOW, H., & DILL, W. R. Factors in the organizational development of task-oriented groups. *Sociometry,* 1957, 20, 175–204.

GUETZKOW, H., & SIMON, H. A. The impact of certain communication nets upon organization and performance in task-oriented groups. *Management Science,* 1955, 1, 233–250.

GUILFORD, J. P., & ZIMMERMAN, W. S. *The Guilford-Zimmerman Temperament Survey.* Beverly Hills: Sheridan Supply, 1949.

GULLAHORN, J. T., & GULLAHORN, J. E. A computer model of elementary social behavior. *Behavioral Science,* 1963, 8, 354–362.

GULLAHORN, J. T., & GULLAHORN, J. E. Computer simulation of human interaction in small groups. *American Federation of Information Societies Conference Proceedings,* 1964, 25, 103–113.

GUNDLACH, R. H. Effects of on-the-job experiences with Negroes upon racial attitudes of white workers in union shops. *Psychological Reports,* 1956, **2**, 67–77.

GURNEE, H. A comparison of collective and individual judgments of facts. *Journal of Experimental Psychology,* 1937, **21**, 106–112.

GURNEE, H. The effect of collective learning upon the individual participants. *Journal of Abnormal and Social Psychology,* 1939, **34**, 529–532.

HACKMAN, J. R. Effects of task characteristics on group products. *Journal of Experimental Social Psychology,* 1968, **4**, 162–187.

HACKMAN, J. R. Toward understanding the role of tasks in behavioral research. *Acta Psychologica,* 1969, **39**, 97–128.

HACKMAN, J. R., & JONES, L. E. Development of a set of dimensions for analyzing verbal group products. Technical Report No. 23, ONR Contract NR 177–472, Nonr-1834(36), University of Illinois, 1965.

HARDING, J., & HOGREFE, R. Attitudes of white department store employees toward Negro coworkers. *Journal of Social Issues,* 1952, **8**, 18–28.

HARE, A. P. Interaction and consensus in different sized groups. *American Sociological Review,* 1952, **17**, 261–267.

HARE, A. P., & BALES, R. F. Seating position and small group interaction. *Sociometry,* 1963, **26**, 480–486.

HARVEY, O. J., & CONSALVI, C. Status and conformity to pressures in informal groups. *Journal of Abnormal and Social Psychology,* 1960, **60**, 182–187.

HARVEY, O. J., HUNT, D. E., & SCHRODER, H. M. *Conceptual systems and personality organization.* New York: Wiley, 1961.

HAYTHORN, W. The influence of individual members on the characteristics of small groups. *Journal of Abnormal and Social Psychology,* 1953, **48**, 276–284.

HAYTHORN, W. W. The composition of groups: A review of the literature. *Acta Psychologica,* 1968, **28**, 97–128.

HAYTHORN, W. W., COUCH, A., HAEFNER, D., LANGHAM, P., & CARTER, L. F. The behavior of authoritarian and equalitarian personalities in groups. *Human Relations,* 1956a, **9**, 57–74.

HAYTHORN, W. W., COUCH, A., HAEFNER, D., LANGHAM, P., & CARTER, L. F. The effects of varying combinations of authoritarian and equalitarian leaders and followers. *Journal of Abnormal and Social Psychology,* 1956b, **53**, 210–219.

HEARN, G. Leadership and the spatial factor in small groups. *Journal of Abnormal and Social Psychology,* 1957, **54**, 269–272.

HEIDER, F. *The psychology of interpersonal relations.* New York: Wiley, 1958.

HELSON, H. Adaptation-level as a basis for a quantitative theory of frames of reference. *Psychological Review*, 1948, **55**, 297–313.

HEMPHILL, J. K., & SECHREST, L. A comparison of three criteria of air crew effectiveness in combat over Korea. *American Psychologist*, 1952, **7**, 391.

HIROTA, K. Group problem solving and communication. *Japanese Journal of Psychology*, 1953, **24**, 176–177.

HOFFMAN, L. R. Homogeneity of member personality and its effect on group problem-solving. *Journal of Abnormal and Social Psychology*, 1959, **58**, 27–32.

HOFFMAN, L. R., & MAIER, N. R. F. Quality and acceptance of problem solutions by members of homogeneous and heterogeneous groups. *Journal of Abnormal and Social Psychology*, 1961, **62**, 401–407.

HOLLANDER, E. P. Authoritarianism and leadership choice in a military setting. *Journal of Abnormal and Social Psychology*, 1954, **49**, 365–376.

HOLLANDER, E. P. Conformity, status, and idiosyncrasy credit. *Psychological Review*, 1958, **65**, 117–127.

HOLLANDER, E. P. Competence and conformity in the acceptance of influence. *Journal of Abnormal and Social Psychology*, 1960, **61**, 365–369.

HOMANS, G. C. *The human group.* New York: Harcourt, Brace & World, 1950.

HOROWITZ, M. J., DUFF, D. F., & STRATTON, L. O. Body buffer zone. *Archives of General Psychiatry*, 1964, **11**, 651–656.

HORWITZ, M. The recall of interrupted group tasks: An experimental study of individual motivation in relation to group goals. *Human Relations*, 1954, **7**, 3–38.

HOWELLS, L. T., & BECKER, S. W. Seating arrangement and leadership emergence. *Journal of Abnormal and Social Psychology*, 1962, **64**, 148–150.

HOYT, G. C., & STONER, J. A. F. Leadership and group decisions involving risk. *Journal of Experimental Social Psychology*, 1968, **4**, 275–284.

HURWITZ, J. I., ZANDER, A. F., & HYMOVITCH, B. Some effects of power on the relations among group members. In D. Cartwright & A. Zander (Eds.), *Group dynamics: Research and theory.* Evanston, Ill.: Row, Peterson, 1953. Pp. 483–492.

HUSBAND, R. W. Cooperative versus solitary problem solution. *Journal of Social Psychology*, 1940, **11**, 405–409.

ISCOE, I., WILLIAMS, M., & HARVEY, J. Modification of children's judgments by a simulated group technique: A normative developmental study. *Child Development*, 1963, **34**, 963–978.

IZARD, C. E. Personality similarity and friendship. *Journal of Abnormal and Social Psychology*, 1960a, **61**, 47–51.

IZARD, C. E. Personality similarity, positive affect, and interpersonal attraction. *Journal of Abnormal and Social Psychology*, 1960b, **61**, 484–485.

JACOBS, R. C., & CAMPBELL, D. T.   The perpetuation of an arbitrary tradition through several generations of a laboratory microculture. *Journal of Abnormal and Social Psychology*, 1961, **62**, 649–658.

JAHODA, M.   Race relations and mental health. In UNESCO, *Race and science.* New York: Columbia, 1961.

JAMES, J.   A preliminary study of the size determinant in small group interaction. *American Sociological Review*, 1951, **16**, 474–477.

JELLISON, J. M., & ZEISSET, P. J.   Attraction as a function of the commonality and desirability of a trait shared with another. *Journal of Personality and Social Psychology*, 1969, **11**, 115–120.

JENNESS, A.   The role of discussion in changing opinion regarding a matter of fact. *Journal of Abnormal and Social Psychology*, 1932, **27**, 279–296.

JOHNSON, R. H., Jr., & HUNT, J. J.   *Rx for team teaching.* Minneapolis: Burgess, 1968.

JUSTICE, M. T.   Field dependency, intimacy of topic and interaction distance. Unpublished doctoral dissertation, University of Florida, Gainesville, 1969.

KATZ, D.   *Animals and men.* London: Longmans, 1937.

KELLEY, H. H.   Communication in experimentally created hierarchies. *Human Relations*, 1951, **4**, 39–56.

KELLEY, H. H.   Two functions of reference groups. In G. E. Swanson, T. M. Newcomb, & E. L. Hartley (Eds.), *Readings in social psychology.* (2d ed.) New York: Holt, 1952. Pp. 410–414.

KELLEY, H. H., & ARROWOOD, A. J.   Coalitions in the triad: Critique and experiment. *Sociometry*, 1960, **23**, 231–244.

KELLEY, H. H., & THIBAUT, J. W.   Group problem solving. In G. Lindzey & E. Aronson (Eds.), *The handbook of social psychology.* (2d ed.) Vol. 4. Reading, Mass.: Addison-Wesley, 1969. Pp. 1–101.

KELLY, E. L.   Consistency of adult personality. *American Psychologist*, 1955, **10**, 659–681.

KIDD, J. S., & CAMPBELL, D. T.   Conformity to groups as a function of group success. *Journal of Abnormal and Social Psychology*, 1955, **51**, 390–393.

KILLIAN, L. M.   The significance of multiple-group membership in disaster. *American Journal of Sociology*, 1952, **57**, 309–314.

KIPNIS, D.   The effects of leadership style and leadership power upon the inducement of an attitude change. *Journal of Abnormal and Social Psychology*, 1958, **57**, 173–180.

KLECK, R.   Physical stigma and task-oriented interaction. *Human Relations*, 1969, **22**, 51–60.

KLEINER, R. J.   The effect of threat reduction upon interpersonal attractiveness. *Journal of Personality*, 1960, **28**, 145–155.

KNIGHT, H. C.   A comparison of the reliability of group and individual judgments. Unpublished master's thesis, Columbia University, 1921. (Cited in Lorge et al., 1958).

KOGAN, N., & WALLACH, M. A.   Group risk taking as a function of members' anxiety and defensiveness. *Journal of Personality*, 1967a, **35**, 50–63.

KOGAN, N., & WALLACH, M. A.   Risky-shift phenomenon in small decision-making groups: A test of the information-exchange hypothesis. *Journal of Experimental Social Psychology*, 1967b, **3**, 75–84.

KOMORITA, S. S., SHEPOSH, J. P., & BRAVER, S. L.   Power, the use of power, and cooperative choice in a two-person game. *Journal of Personality and Social Psychology*, 1968, **8**, 134–142.

LANA, R. E.   *Assumptions of social psychology.* New York: Appleton-Century-Crofts, 1969.

LANZETTA, J. T., & ROBY, T. B.   Effects of work-group structure and certain task variables on group performance. *Journal of Abnormal and Social Psychology*, 1956, **53**, 307–314.

LANZETTA, J. T., & ROBY, T. B.   Group learning and communication as a function of task and structure "demands." *Journal of Abnormal and Social Psychology*, 1957, **55**, 121–131.

LATANE, B., ECKMAN, J., & JOY, V.   Shared stress and interpersonal attraction. *Journal of Experimental Social Psychology*, 1966, **1**, 80–94.

LAUGHLIN, P. R., BRANCH, L. G., & JOHNSON, H. H.   Individual versus triadic performance on a unidimensional complementary task as a function of initial ability level. *Journal of Personality and Social Psychology*, 1969, **12**, 144–150.

LAWSON, E. D.   Change in communication nets and performance. Paper read at Eastern Psychological Association Convention, 1961.

LAWSON, E. D.   Reinforced and non-reinforced four-man communication nets. *Psychological Reports*, 1964a, **14**, 287–296.

LAWSON, E. D.   Reinforcement in group problem-solving with arithmetic problems. *Psychological Reports*, 1964b, **14**, 703–710.

LAWSON, E. D.   Change in communication nets, performance, and morale. *Human Relations*, 1965, **18**, 139–147.

LEAVITT, H. J.   Some effects of certain communication patterns on group performance. *Journal of Abnormal and Social Psychology*, 1951, **46**, 38–50.

LEFKOWITZ, M., BLAKE, R. R., & MOUTON, J. S.   Status factors in pedestrian violation of traffic signals. *Journal of Abnormal and Social Psychology*, 1955, **51**, 704–706.

LEUBA, C. J. An experimental study of rivalry in young children. *Journal of Comparative Psychology*, 1933, **16**, 367–378.

LEVENTHAL, G. S., ALLEN, J., & KEMELGOR, B. Reducing inequity by reallocating rewards. *Psychonomic Science*, 1969, **14**, 295–296.

LEVENTHAL, G. S., & BERGMAN, J. T. Self-depriving behavior as a response to unprofitable inequity. *Journal of Experimental Social Psychology*, 1969, **5**, 153–171.

LEVINGER, G., & SCHNEIDER, D. J. Test of the "risk is a value" hypothesis. *Journal of Personality and Social Psychology*, 1969, **11**, 165–169.

LEWIN, K. Forces behind food habits and methods of change. *Bulletin of the National Research Council*, 1943, **108**, 35–65.

LEWIN, K. *Field theory in social science.* New York: Harper, 1951.

LEWIN, K. Studies in group decision. In D. Cartwright & A. Zander (Eds.), *Group dynamics: Research and theory.* Evanston, Ill.: Row, Peterson, 1953. Pp. 285–301.

LEWIN, K., DEMBO, T., FESTINGER, L., & SEARS, P. S. Level of aspiration. In J. McV. Hunt (Ed.), *Personality and the behavior disorders.* New York: Ronald, 1944. Pp. 333–378.

LEWIN, K., LIPPITT, R., & WHITE, R. K. Patterns of aggressive behavior in experimentally created "social climates." *Journal of Social Psychology*, 1939, **10**, 271–299.

LINTON, R. *The study of man.* New York: Appleton-Century-Crofts, 1936.

LIPMAN, A. Building design and social interaction. *The Architects Journal*, 1968, **147**, 23–30.

LIPPITT, R., POLANSKY, N., REDL, F., & ROSEN, S. The dynamics of power. *Human Relations*, 1952, **5**, 37–64.

LIPPITT, R., & WHITE, R. K. The "social climate" of children's groups. In R. G. Barker, J. Kounin, & H. Wright (Eds.), *Child behavior and development.* New York: McGraw-Hill, 1943. Pp. 485–508.

LITTLE, K. B. Personal space. *Journal of Experimental Social Psychology*, 1965, **1**, 237–247.

LOEHLIN, J. C. A computer program that simulates personality. In S. S. Tomkins & S. Messick (Eds.), *Computer simulation of personality.* New York: Wiley, 1963. Pp. 189–211.

LOEHLIN, J. C. "Interpersonal" experiments with a computer model of personality. *Journal of Personality and Social Psychology*, 1965, **2**, 580–584.

LORGE, I., AIKMAN, L., MOSS, G., SPIEGEL, J., & TUCKMAN, J. Solutions by teams and by individuals to a field problem at different levels of reality. *Journal of Educational Psychology,* 1955, **46**, 17–24.

LORGE, I., FOX, D., DAVITZ, J., & BRENNER, M.   A survey of studies contrasting the quality of group performance and individual performance, 1920–1957. *Psychological Bulletin,* 1958, **55**, 337–372.

LORGE, I., & SOLOMON, H.   Individual performance and group performance in problem solving related to group size and previous exposure to the problem. *Journal of Psychology,* 1959, **48**, 107–114.

LORGE, I., & SOLOMON, H.   Group and individual performance in problem solving related to previous exposure to the problem, level of aspiration, and group size. *Behavioral Science,* 1960, **5**, 28–39.

LOTT, A. J., & LOTT, B. E.   Group cohesiveness, communication level, and conformity. *Journal of Abnormal and Social Psychology,* 1961, **62**, 408–412.

LOTT, D. F., & SOMMER, R.   Seating arrangements and status. *Journal of Personality and Social Psychology,* 1967, **7**, 90–95.

LUCHINS, A. S., & LUCHINS, E. H.   On conformity with true and false communications. *Journal of Social Psychology,* 1955, **42**, 283–304.

LYMAN, S. M., & SCOTT, M. B.   Territoriality: A neglected sociological dimension. *Social Forces,* 1967, **15**, 236–249.

McBRIDE, G., KING, M. G., & JAMES, J. W.   Social proximity effects on GSR in adult humans. *Journal of Psychology,* 1965, **61**, 153–157.

McCLELLAND, D. C., ATKINSON, J. W., CLARK, R. A., & LOWELL, E. L.   *The achievement motive.* New York: Appleton-Century-Crofts, 1953.

McCURDY, H. G., & LAMBERT, W. E.   The efficiency of small human groups in the solution of problems requiring genuine co-operation. *Journal of Personality,* 1952, **20**, 478–494.

McDAVID, J. W.   Personality and situational determinants of conformity. *Journal of Abnormal and Social Psychology,* 1959, **58**, 241–246.

McDAVID, J. W., & HARARI, H.   *Social psychology: Individuals, groups, societies.* New York: Harper & Row, 1968.

McDAVID, J. W., & SISTRUNK, F.   Personality correlates of two kinds of conforming behavior. *Journal of Personality,* 1964, **32**, 420–435.

McGRATH, J. E., & ALTMAN, I.   *Small group research.* New York: Holt, 1966.

McGRATH, J. E., & JULIAN, J. W.   Interaction process and task outcome in experimentally-created negotiation groups. *Journal of Psychological Studies,* 1963, **14**, 117–138.

MACK, R. W.   Ecological patterns in an industrial shop. *Social Forces,* 1954, **32**, 351–356.

McWHINNEY, W. H. Simulating the communication network experiments. *Behavioral Science*, 1964, **9**, 80–84.

MACY, J., Jr., CHRISTIE, L. S., & LUCE, R. D. Coding noise in a task-oriented group. *Journal of Abnormal and Social Psychology*, 1953, **48**, 401–409.

MAIER, N. R. F. The quality of group decisions as influenced by the discussion leader. *Human Relations*, 1950, **3**, 155–174.

MAIER, N. R. F. An experimental test of the effect of training on discussion leadership. *Human Relations*, 1953, **6**, 161–173.

MAISSONNEUVE, J., PALMADE, G., & FOURMENT, C. Selective choices and propinquity. *Sociometry*, 1952, **15**, 135–140.

MANDLER, G., & SARASON, S. B. A study of anxiety and learning. *Journal of Abnormal and Social Psychology*, 1952, **47**, 166–173.

MANN, R. D. A review of the relationships between personality and performance in small groups. *Psychological Bulletin*, 1959, **56**, 241–270.

MARINE, G. I've got nothing against the colored, understand. *Ramparts*, 1966, **5**, 13–18.

MARPLE, C. H. The comparative susceptibility of three age levels to the suggestion of group versus expert opinion. *Journal of Social Psychology*, 1933, **10**, 3–40.

MARQUART, D. I. Group problem solving. *Journal of Social Psychology*, 1955, **41**, 103–113.

MARQUIS, D. G. Individual responsibility and group decision involving risk. *Industrial Management Review*, 1962, **3**, 8–23.

MARQUIS, D. G., GUETZKOW, H., & HEYNS, R. W. A social psychological study of the decision-making conference. In H. Guetzkow (Ed.), *Groups, leadership and men*. Pittsburgh: Carnegie Press, 1951. Pp. 55–67.

MARSTON, W. M. Studies in testimony. *Journal of Criminal Law and Criminology*, 1924, **15**, 5–31.

MAUSNER, B. Studies in social interaction: III. Effect of variation in one partner's prestige on the interaction of observer pairs. *Journal of Applied Psychology*, 1953, **37**, 391–393.

MEAD, M. *Male and female: A study of the sexes in a changing world*. New York: Morrow, 1949.

MEADOW, A., PARNES, S. J., & REESE, H. Influence of brainstorming instructions and problem sequence on a creative problem solving test. *Journal of Applied Psychology*, 1959, **43**, 413–416.

MEDOW, H., & ZANDER, A. Aspirations for the group chosen by central and peripheral members. *Journal of Personality and Social Psychology*, 1965, **1**, 224–228.

MEUNIER, C., & RULE, B. G. Anxiety, confidence, and conformity. *Journal of Personality*, 1967, **35**, 498–504.

MEYER, H. H. Factors related to success in the human relations aspect of work-group leadership. *Psychological Monographs*, 1951, **65**, No. 3 (Whole No. 320).

MILGRAM, S. Behavioral study of obedience. *Journal of Abnormal and Social Psychology*, 1963, **67**, 371–378.

MILGRAM, S. Group pressure and action against a person. *Journal of Abnormal and Social Psychology*, 1964, **69**, 137–143.

MILGRAM, S. Liberating effects of group pressure. *Journal of Personality and Social Psychology*, 1965, **1**, 127–134.

MILL, C. R. Personality patterns of sociometrically selected and sociometrically rejected male college students. *Sociometry*, 1953, **16**, 151–167.

MILLS, T. M. Power relations in three-person groups. *American Sociological Review*, 1953, **18**, 351–357.

MILLS, T. M. *The sociology of small groups*. Englewood Cliffs, N.J.: Prentice-Hall, 1967.

MOORE, O. K., & ANDERSON, S. B. Search behavior in individual and group problem solving. *American Sociological Review*, 1954, **19**, 702–714.

MOOS, R. H., & SPEISMAN, J. C. Group compatibility and productivity. *Journal of Abnormal and Social Psychology*, 1962, **65**, 190–196.

MORAN, G. Dyadic attraction and orientational consensus. *Journal of Personality and Social Psychology*, 1966, **4**, 94–99.

MORRIS, C. G., II. Effects of task characteristics on group process. Technical Report No. 2. AFOSR Contract AF 49(638)-1291, University of Illinois, 1965.

MORSE, N. C., & REIMER, E. The experimental change of a major organizational variable. *Journal of Abnormal and Social Psychology*, 1956, **52**, 120–129.

MULDER, M. Group-structure and group-performance. *Acta Psychologica*, 1959a, **16**, 356–402.

MULDER, M. Power and satisfaction in task-oriented groups. *Acta Psychologica*, 1959b, **16**, 178–225.

MULDER, M. Communication structure, decision structure and group performance. *Sociometry*, 1960, **23**, 1–14.

MULDER, M., VAN DIJK, R., SOUTENDIJK, S., STELWAGEN, T., & VERHAGEN, J. Non-instrumental liking tendencies toward powerful group members. *Acta Psychologica*, 1964, **22**, 367–386.

MURPHY, A. J. A study of the leadership process. *American Sociological Review*, 1941, **6**, 674–687.

MYERS, R. K.   Some effects of seating arrangements in counseling. Unpublished doctoral dissertation, University of Florida, Gainesville, 1969.

NADLER, E. B.   Yielding, authoritarianism, and authoritarian ideology regarding groups. *Journal of Abnormal and Social Psychology*, 1959, **58**, 408–410.

NAKAMURA, C. Y.   Conformity and problem solving. *Journal of Abnormal and Social Psychology*, 1958, **56**, 315–320.

NEWCOMB, T. M.   The prediction of interpersonal attraction. *American Psychologist*, 1956, **11**, 575–586.

NEWCOMB, T. M.   *The acquaintance process.* New York: Holt, 1961.

NICKOLS, S. A.   A study of the additivity of variables influencing conformity. Unpublished doctoral dissertation, University of Florida, Gainesville, 1964.

NOVAK, D. W., & LERNER, M. J.   Rejection as a consequence of perceived similarity. *Journal of Personality and Social Psychology*, 1968, **9**, 147–152.

ORT, R. S.   A study of role-conflicts as related to happiness in marriage. *Journal of Abnormal and Social Psychology*, 1950, **45**, 691–699.

OSBORN, A. F.   *Applied imagination.* New York: Scribner, 1957.

PALMER, G. J., JR.   Task ability and effective leadership. Technical Report No. 4, Contract Nonr 1575(05), Louisiana State University, 1962a.

PALMER, G. J., JR.   Task ability and successful and effective leadership. Technical Report No. 6, Contract Nonr 1575(05), Louisiana State University, 1962b.

PALMORE, E. B.   The introduction of Negroes into white departments. *Human Organization*, 1955, **14**, 27–28.

PARTEN, M. B.   Social participation among preschool children. *Journal of Abnormal and Social Psychology*, 1932, **27**, 243–269.

PATEL, A. A., & GORDON, J. E.   Some personal and situational determinants of yielding to influence. *Journal of Abnormal and Social Psychology*, 1960, **61**, 411–418.

PEPITONE, A., & KLEINER, R. J.   The effects of threat and frustration on group cohesiveness. *Journal of Abnormal and Social Psychology*, 1957, **54**, 192–199.

PERLMUTTER, H. V., & DE MONTMOLLIN, G.   Group learning of nonsense syllables. *Journal of Abnormal and Social Psychology*, 1952, **47**, 762–769.

PESSIN, J., & HUSBAND, R. W.   Effects of social stimulation on human maze learning. *Journal of Abnormal and Social Psychology*, 1933, **28**, 148–154.

PETERS, H. N., & MURPHREE, O. D.   A cooperative multiple-choice apparatus. *Science*, 1954, **119**, 189–191.

PIAGET, J.   *The moral judgment of the child.* New York: Basic Books, 1954.

POLANSKY, N., LIPPITT, R., & REDL, F.   An investigation of behavioral contagion in groups. *Human Relations*, 1950, **3**, 319–348.

PRESTON, M. Note on the reliability and validity of group judgment. *Journal of Experimental Psychology*, 1938, 22, 462–471.

PRESTON, M. G., & HEINTZ, R. K. Effects of participatory vs. supervisory leadership on group judgment. *Journal of Abnormal and Social Psychology*, 1949, 44, 345–355.

PRUITT, D. G., & TEGER, A. I. The risky shift in group betting. *Journal of Experimental Social Psychology*, 1969, 5, 115–126.

RADKE, M., & KLISURICH, D. Experiments in changing food habits. *Journal of the American Dietetics Association*, 1947, 23, 403–409.

RAINIO, K. A study of sociometric group structure: An application of a stochastic theory of social interaction. In J. Berger, M. Zelditch, Jr., & B. Anderson (Eds.), *Sociological theories in progress*. Vol. 1. Boston: Houghton Mifflin, 1966. Pp. 102–123.

RAVEN, B. H., & RIETSEMA, J. The effects of varied clarity of group goal and group path upon the individual and his relation to the group. *Human Relations*, 1957, 10, 29–44.

REITAN, H. T., & SHAW, M. E. Group membership, sex-composition of the group, and conformity behavior. *Journal of Social Psychology*, 1964, 64, 45–51.

RICE, S. A. *Quantitative methods in politics*. New York: Knopf, 1928.

RIM, Y. Social attitudes and risk-taking. *Human Relations*, 1964, 17, 259–265.

ROBY, T. B. The influence of subgroup relationships on the performance of group and subgroup tasks. *American Psychologist*, 1952, 7, 313–314.

ROBY, T. B. Computer simulation models for organization theory. In E. V. Vroom (Ed.), *Methods of organizational research*. Pittsburgh: Pittsburgh Press, 1967. Pp. 171–211.

ROBY, T. B. *Small group performance*. Chicago: Rand McNally, 1968.

ROBY, T. B., & LANZETTA, J. T. Considerations in the analysis of group tasks. *Psychological Bulletin*, 1958, 55, 88–101.

ROETHLISBERGER, F. J., & DICKSON, W. J. *Management and the worker*. Cambridge, Mass.: Harvard, 1939.

ROSE, A. *Union solidarity*. Minneapolis: University of Minnesota Press, 1952.

ROSENBAUM, M. E., & BLAKE, R. R. Volunteering as a function of field structure. *Journal of Abnormal and Social Psychology*, 1955, 50, 193–196.

ROSENBERG, S., ERLICK, D. E., & BERKOWITZ, L. Some effects of varying combinations of group members on group performance measures and leadership behaviors. *Journal of Abnormal and Social Psychology*, 1955, 51, 195–203.

ROSENFELD, H. M. Effect of an approval-seeking induction on interpersonal proximity. *Psychological Reports*, 1965, 17, 120–122.

ROSS, I., & ZANDER, A.   Need satisfaction and employee turnover. *Personnel Psychology,* 1957, **10**, 327–338.

RUSSO, N. F.   Connotations of seating arrangements. *Cornell Journal of Social Relations,* 1967, **2**, 37–44.

RYAN, E. D., & LAKIE, W. L.   Competitive and noncompetitive performance in relation to achievement motive and manifest anxiety. *Journal of Personality and Social Psychology,* 1965, **1**, 342–345.

RYCHLAK, J. F.   The similarity, compatibility, or incompatibility of needs in interpersonal selection. *Journal of Personality and Social Psychology,* 1965, **2**, 334–340.

SAMPLE, J. A., & WILSON, T. R.   Leader behavior, group productivity, and rating of least preferred co-worker. *Journal of Personality and Social Psychology,* 1965, **1**, 266–270.

SAPOLSKY, A.   Effect of interpersonal relationships upon verbal conditioning. *Journal of Abnormal and Social Psychology,* 1960, **60**, 241–246.

SCHACHTER, S.   Deviation, rejection, and communication. *Journal of Abnormal and Social Psychology,* 1951, **46**, 190–207.

SCHACHTER, S.   *The psychology of affiliation.* Stanford, Calif.: Stanford University Press, 1959.

SCHACHTER, S., ELLERTSON, N., McBRIDE, D., & GREGORY, D.   An experimental study of cohesiveness and productivity. *Human Relations,* 1951, **4**, 229–238.

SCHEIN, E. H.   The development of organization in small problem-solving groups. Final Report, Sloan Project No. 134, Massachusetts Institute of Technology, 1958.

SCHELLING, T. C.   The strategy of conflict: Prospectus for a reorientation of game theory. *Journal of Conflict Resolution,* 1958, **2**, 203–264.

SCHLOSSER, M.   Liking as a function of physical attractiveness and task performance. Unpublished master's thesis, University of Florida, Gainesville, 1969.

SCHNEIDER, F. W.   Differences between Negro and white school children in conforming behavior. Unpublished doctoral dissertation, University of Florida, Gainesville, 1968.

SCHUTZ, W. C.   What makes groups productive? *Human Relations,* 1955, **8**, 429–465.

SCHUTZ, W. C.   *FIRO: A three-dimensional theory of interpersonal behavior.* New York: Rinehart, 1958.

SCHUTZ, W. C.   On group composition. *Journal of Abnormal and Social Psychology,* 1961, **62**, 275–281.

SCHUTZ, W. C.   *JOY: Expanding human awareness.* New York: Grove Press, 1967.

SEASHORE, S. E. *Group cohesiveness in the industrial work group.* Ann Arbor: University of Michigan Press, 1954.

SEEMAN, W., & MARKS, P. A. The behavior of the psychologist at a choice point. *American Scientist,* 1962, **50**, 538–547.

SELLTIZ, C., JAHODA, M., DEUTSCH, M., & COOK, S. W. *Research methods in social relations.* (rev. ed.) New York: Holt, 1961.

SHAW, MARJORIE E. A comparison of individuals and small groups in the rational solution of complex problems. *American Journal of Psychology,* 1932, **44**, 491–504.

SHAW, M. E. Some effects of problem complexity upon problem solution efficiency in different communication nets. *Journal of Experimental Psychology,* 1954a, **48**, 211–217.

SHAW, M. E. Some effects of unequal distribution of information upon group performance in various communication nets. *Journal of Abnormal and Social Psychology,* 1954b, **49**, 547–553.

SHAW, M. E. A comparison of two types of leadership in various communication nets. *Journal of Abnormal and Social Psychology,* 1955, **50**, 127–134.

SHAW, M. E. Some effects of irrelevant information upon problem-solving by small groups. *Journal of Social Psychology,* 1958a, **47**, 33–37.

SHAW, M. E. Some motivational factors in cooperation and competition. *Journal of Personality,* 1958b, **26**, 155–169.

SHAW, M. E. Acceptance of authority, group structure, and the effectiveness of small groups. *Journal of Personality,* 1959a, **27**, 196–210.

SHAW, M. E. Some effects of individually prominent behavior upon group effectiveness and member satisfaction. *Journal of Abnormal and Social Psychology,* 1959b, **59**, 382–386.

SHAW, M. E. A note concerning homogeneity of membership and group problem solving. *Journal of Abnormal and Social Psychology,* 1960, **60**, 448–450.

SHAW, M. E. Group dynamics. *Annual Review of Psychology,* 1961a, **12**, 129–156.

SHAW, M. E. Some factors influencing the use of information in groups. *Psychological Reports,* 1961b, **8**, 187–198.

SHAW, M. E. Implicit conversion of fate control in dyadic interaction. *Psychological Reports,* 1962, **10**, 758.

SHAW, M. E. Scaling group tasks: A method for dimensional analysis. Technical Report No. 1, ONR Contract NR 170–266, Nonr-580(11), University of Florida, 1963.

SHAW, M. E. Communication networks. In L. Berkowitz (Ed.), *Advances in experimental social psychology.* Vol. 1. New York: Academic, 1964. Pp. 111–147.

SHAW, M. E.   Social psychology and group processes. In J. B. Sidowski (Ed.), *Experimental methods and instrumentation in psychology.* New York: McGraw-Hill, 1966. Pp. 607–643.

SHAW, M. E., & BLUM, J. M.   Group performance as a function of task difficulty and the group's awareness of member satisfaction. *Journal of Applied Psychology,* 1965, **49**, 151–154.

SHAW, M. E., & BLUM, J. M.   Effects of leadership styles upon group performance as a function of task structure. *Journal of Personality and Social Psychology,* 1966, **3**, 238–242.

SHAW, M. E., & BRISCOE, M. E.   Group size and effectiveness in solving tasks varying in degree of cooperation requirements. Technical Report No. 6, ONR Contract NR 170-266, Nonr-580(11), University of Florida, 1966.

SHAW, M. E., & COSTANZO, P. R.   *Theories of social psychology.* New York: McGraw-Hill, 1970.

SHAW, M. E., & GILCHRIST, J. C.   Repetitive task failure and sociometric choice. *Journal of Abnormal and Social Psychology,* 1955, **50**, 29–32.

SHAW, M. E., & GILCHRIST, J. C.   Intra-group communication and leader choice. *Journal of Social Psychology,* 1956, **43**, 133–138.

SHAW, M. E., & NICKOLS, S. A.   Group effectiveness as a function of group member compatibility and cooperation requirements of the task. Technical Report No. 4, ONR Contract NR 170-266, Nonr-580(11), University of Florida, 1964.

SHAW, M. E., & PENROD, W. T., JR.   Does more information available to a group always improve group performance? *Sociometry,* 1962a, **25**, 377–390.

SHAW, M. E., & PENROD, W. T., Jr.   Validity of information, attempted influence, and quality of group decisions. *Psychological Reports,* 1962b, **10**, 19–23.

SHAW, M. E., & REITAN, H. T.   Attribution of responsibility as a basis for sanctioning behaviour. *British Journal of Social and Clinical Psychology,* 1969, **8**, 217–226.

SHAW, M. E., & ROTHSCHILD, G. H.   Some effects of prolonged experience in communication nets. *Journal of Applied Psychology,* 1956, **40**, 281–286.

SHAW, M. E., ROTHSCHILD, G. H., & STRICKLAND, J. F.   Decision processes in communication nets. *Journal of Abnormal and Social Psychology,* 1957, **54**, 323–330.

SHAW, M. E., & SHAW, L. M.   Some effects of sociometric grouping upon learning in a second grade classroom. *Journal of Social Psychology,* 1962, **57**, 453–458.

SHELLEY, H. P.   Level of aspiration phenomena in small groups. *Journal of Social Psychology,* 1954, **40**, 149–164.

SHERIF, M.   Experimental study of intergroup relations. In J. H. Rohrer & M.

Sherif (Eds.), *Social psychology at the crossroads.* New York: Harper & Row, 1951. Pp. 388–426.

SHERIF, M., HARVEY, O. J., WHITE, B. J., HOOD, W. R., & SHERIF, C. W. *Intergroup conflict and cooperation: The Robbers Cave experiment.* Norman:. Institute of Group Relations, University of Oklahoma, 1961.

SHERIF, M., & HOVLAND, C. I. *Social judgment.* New Haven, Conn.: Yale, 1961.

SHERIF, M., & SHERIF, C. W. *Groups in harmony and tension.* New York: Harper & Row, 1953.

SHERIF, M., & SHERIF, C. W. *An outline of social psychology.* (rev. ed.) New York: Harper & Row, 1956.

SHERIF, M., WHITE, B. J., & HARVEY, O. J. Status in experimentally produced groups. *American Journal of Sociology,* 1955, **60**, 370–379.

SHEVITZ, R. N. *Leadership acts: IV. An investigation of the relation between exclusive possession of information and attempts to lead.* Columbus: Ohio State University Research Foundation, 1955.

SINGER, J. E., & SHOCKLEY, V. L. Ability and affiliation. *Journal of Personality and Social Psychology,* 1965, **1**, 95–100.

SLATER, P. E. Role differentiation in small groups. *American Sociological Review,* 1955, **20**, 300–310.

SLATER, P. E. Contrasting correlates of group size. *Sociometry,* 1958, **21**, 129–139.

SMELSER, W. T. Dominance as a factor in achievement and perception in cooperative problem solving interactions. *Journal of Abnormal and Social Psychology,* 1961, **62**, 535–542.

SMITH, C. R., WILLIAMS, L., & WILLIS, R. H. Race, sex, and belief as determinants of friendship acceptance. *Journal of Personality and Social Psychology,* 1967, **5**, 127–137.

SMITH, M. Social situation, social behavior, social group. *Psychological Review,* 1945, **52**, 224–229.

SMITH, W. P. Power structure and authoritarianism in the use of power in the triad. *Journal of Personality,* 1967, **35**, 64–90.

SOMMER, R. Studies in personal space. *Sociometry,* 1959, **22**, 247–260.

SOMMER, R. *Personal space: The behavioral basis of design.* Englewood Cliffs, N.J.: Prentice-Hall, 1969.

SOUTH, E. B. Some psychological aspects of committee work. *Journal of Applied Psychology,* 1927, **11**, 348–368.

SPENCE, R. B. Lecture and class discussion in teaching educational psychology. *Journal of Educational Psychology,* 1928, **19**, 454–462.

SPENCER, H. *Principles of sociology.* New York: Appleton, 1876.

SPEROFF, B., & KERR, W.   Steel mill "hot strip" accidents and interpersonal desirability values. *Journal of Clinical Psychology*, 1952, **8**, 89–91.

STAGER, P.   Conceptual level as a composition variable in small-group decision making. *Journal of Personality and Social Psychology*, 1967, **5**, 152–161.

STEINZOR, B.   The spatial factor in face-to-face discussion groups. *Journal of Abnormal and Social Psychology*, 1950, **45**, 552–555.

STEVENSON, H. W., & CRUSE, D. B.   The effectiveness of social reinforcement with normal and feebleminded children. *Journal of Personality*, 1961, **29**, 124–135.

STEVENSON, H. W., & ODOM, R. D.   The effectiveness of social reinforcement following two conditions of social deprivation. *Journal of Abnormal and Social Psychology*, 1962, **65**, 429–431.

STEWART, F. A.   A study of influence in Southtown: II. *Sociometry*, 1947, **10**, 273–286.

STOGDILL, R. M.   Personal factors associated with leadership: A survey of the literature. *Journal of Psychology*, 1948, **25**, 35–71.

STOGDILL, R. M.   *Individual behavior and group achievement*. New York: Oxford, 1959.

STONER, J. A. F.   A comparison of individual and group decisions involving risk. Unpublished master's thesis, Massachusetts Institute of Technology, 1961. (Cited in Wallach, Kogan, & Bem, 1962.)

STONER, J. A. F.   Risky and cautious shifts in group decisions: The influence of widely held values. *Journal of Experimental Social Psychology*, 1968, **4**, 442–459.

STOTLAND, E., & COTTRELL, N. B.   Similarity of performance as influenced by interaction, self-esteem, and birth order. *Journal of Abnormal and Social Psychology*, 1962, **64**, 183–191.

STOTLAND, E., COTTRELL, N. B., & LAING, G.   Group interaction and perceived similarity of members. *Journal of Abnormal and Social Psychology*, 1960, **61**, 335–340.

STOUFFER, S. A., SUCHMAN, E. A., DeVINNEY, L. C., STAR, S. A., & WILLIAMS, R. M., Jr.   *The American soldier: Adjustment during army life*. Vol. 1. Princeton, N.J.: Princeton, 1949.

STRODTBECK, F. L., & HOOK, L. H.   The social dimensions of a twelve man jury table. *Sociometry*, 1961, **24**, 397–415.

STROOP, J. R.   Is the judgment of the group better than that of the average member of the group? *Journal of Experimental Psychology*, 1932, **15**, 550–562.

STRUPP, H. H., & HAUSMAN, H. J.   Some correlates of group productivity. *American Psychologist*, 1953, **8**, 443–444.

TAYLOR, D. W., BERRY, P. C., & BLOCK, C. H.   Does group participation when using brainstorming facilitate or inhibit creative thinking? *Administrative Science Quarterly,* 1958, **3,** 23–47.

TAYLOR, D. W., & FAUST, W. L. Twenty questions: Efficiency of problem solving as a function of the size of the group. *Journal of Experimental Psychology,* 1952, **44,** 360–363.

TAYLOR, J. A. A personality scale of manifest anxiety. *Journal of Abnormal and Social Psychology,* 1953, **48,** 285–290.

TEGER, A. I., & PRUITT, D. G. Components of group risk taking. *Journal of Experimental Social Psychology,* 1967, **3,** 189–205.

TERMAN, L. M. *Manual for Concept Mastery Test.* New York: Psychological Corporation, 1956.

TERMAN, L. M., & MILES, C. C. *Sex and personality: Studies in masculinity and femininity.* New York: McGraw-Hill, 1936.

THIBAUT, J. W. An experimental study of the cohesiveness of underprivileged groups. *Human Relations,* 1950, **3,** 251–278.

THIBAUT, J. W., & GRUDER, C. L. Formation of contractual agreements between parties of unequal power. *Journal of Personality and Social Psychology,* 1969, **11,** 59–65.

THIBAUT, J. W., & KELLEY, H. H. *The social psychology of groups.* New York: Wiley, 1959.

THIBAUT, J. W., & STRICKLAND, L. Psychological set and social conformity. *Journal of Personality,* 1956, **25,** 115–129.

THIE, T. W. The efficiency of the group method. *English Journal,* 1925, **14,** 134–137.

THOMAS, E. J., & FINK, C. F. Effects of group size. *Psychological Bulletin,* 1963, **60,** 371–384.

THORNDIKE, R. L. On what type of task will a group do well? *Journal of Abnormal and Social Psychology,* 1938, **33,** 408–412.

THURSTONE, L. L., & CHAVE, E. J. *The measurement of attitudes.* Chicago: University of Chicago Press, 1929.

TORRANCE, E. P. Some consequences of power differences on decision making in permanent and temporary three-man groups. *Research Studies, Washington State College,* 1954, **22,** 130–140.

TRAVIS, L. E. The effect of a small audience upon eye-hand coordination. *Journal of Abnormal and Social Psychology,* 1925, **20,** 142–146.

TRAVIS, L. E. The influence of the group upon the stutterer's speed in free association. *Journal of Abnormal and Social Psychology,* 1928, **23,** 45–51.

TRESSELT, M. E.   The influence of amount of practice upon the formation of a scale of judgment. *Journal of Experimental Psychology,* 1947, **37,** 251–260.

TRIANDIS, H. C., HALL, E. R., & EWEN, R. B.   Member heterogeneity and dyadic creativity. *Human Relations,* 1965, **18,** 33–55.

TRIPLETT, N.   The dynamogenic factors in pacemaking and competition. *American Journal of Psychology,* 1897, **9,** 507–533.

TROTTER, W.   *Instincts of the herd in peace and war.* (rev. ed.) London: Allen, 1920.

TUCKER, J., & LORGE, I.   Individual ability as a determinant of group superiority. *Human Relations,* 1962, **15,** 45–51.

TUCKMAN, B. W.   Group composition and group performance of structured and unstructured tasks. *Journal of Experimental Social Psychology,* 1967, **3,** 25–40.

TUDDENHAM, R. D.   The influence of a distorted norm upon individual judgment. *Journal of Psychology,* 1958, **46,** 227–241.

TUDDENHAM, R. D., MacBRIDE, P., & ZAHN, V.   The influence of the sex composition of the group upon yielding to a distorted norm. *Journal of Psychology,* 1958, **46,** 243–251.

TURNER, R. H., & KILLIAN, L. M.   (Eds.) *Collective behavior.* Englewood Cliffs, N.J.: Prentice-Hall, 1957.

UESUGI, T. T., & VINACKE, W. E.   Strategy in a feminine game. *Sociometry,* 1963, **26,** 75–88.

VAN ZELST, R. H.   Sociometrically selected work teams increase production. *Personnel Psychology,* 1952a, **5,** 175–186.

VAN ZELST, R. H.   Validation of a sociometric regrouping procedure. *Journal of Abnormal and Social Psychology,* 1952b, **47,** 299–301.

VINACKE, W. E.   Sex roles in a three-person game. *Sociometry,* 1959, **22,** 343–360.

VINACKE, W. E., & ARKOFF, A.   Experimental study of coalitions in the triad. *American Sociological Review,* 1957, **22,** 406–415.

WALLACH, M. A., & KOGAN, N.   The roles of information, discussion, and consensus in group risk taking. *Journal of Experimental Social Psychology,* 1965, **1,** 1–19.

WALLACH, M. A., KOGAN, N., & BEM, D. J.   Group influence on individual risk taking. *Journal of Abnormal and Social Psychology,* 1962, **65,** 75–86.

WALLACH, M. A., KOGAN, N., & BEM, D. J.   Diffusion of responsibility and level of risk taking in groups. *Journal of Abnormal and Social Psychology,* 1964, **68,** 263–274.

WALLACH, M. A., KOGAN, N., & BURT, R. B.   Can group members recognize the effects of group discussion upon risk taking? *Journal of Experimental Social Psychology,* 1965, **1,** 379–395.

WALLACH, M. A., & WING, C. W., JR.   Is risk a value? *Journal of Personality and Social Psychology*, 1968, **9**, 101–106.

WALSTER, E., ARONSON, V., ABRAHAMS, D., & ROTTMAN, L.   Importance of physical attractiveness in dating behavior. *Journal of Personality and Social Psychology*, 1966, **4**, 508–516.

WALTERS, R. H., & KARAL, P.   Social deprivation and verbal behavior. *Journal of Personality*, 1960, **28**, 89–107.

WALTERS, R. H., & RAY, E.   Anxiety, social isolation, and reinforcer effectiveness. *Journal of Personality*, 1960, **28**, 358–367.

WARRINER, C. H.   Groups are real: A reaffirmation. *American Sociological Review*, 1956, **21**, 549–554.

WATSON, D., & BROMBERG, B.   Power, communication, and position satisfaction in task-oriented groups. *Journal of Personality and Social Psychology*, 1965, **2**, 859–864.

WATSON, G. B.   Do groups think more effectively than individuals? *Journal of Abnormal and Social Psychology*, 1928, **23**, 328–336.

WESTON, S. B., & ENGLISH, H. B.   The influence of the group on psychological test scores. *American Journal of Psychology*, 1926, **37**, 600–601.

WHYTE, W. F.   *Street corner society*. Chicago: University of Chicago Press, 1943.

WHYTE, W. F.   The social structure of the restaurant. *American Journal of Sociology*, 1949, **54**, 302–308.

WHYTE, W. H., Jr.   *The organization man*. Garden City, N.Y.: Doubleday, 1957.

WILLERMAN, B., & SWANSON, L.   Group prestige in voluntary organizations. *Human Relations*, 1953, **6**, 57–77.

WILLIS, F. N., JR.   Initial speaking distance as a function of the speaker's relationship. *Psychonomic Science*, 1966, **5**, 221–222.

WILLIS, R. H.   Coalitions in the tetrad. *Sociometry*, 1962, **25**, 358–376.

WILLIS, R. H., & JOSEPH, M. L.   Bargaining behavior. I. "Prominence" as a predictor of the outcome of games of agreement. *Conflict Resolution*, 1959, **3**, 102–113.

WINCH, R. F.   The theory of complementary needs in mate selection: A test of one kind of complementariness. *American Sociological Review*, 1955, **20**, 52–56.

WORCHEL, P.   Cartharsis and the relief of hostility. *Journal of Abnormal and Social Psychology*, 1957, **55**, 238–243.

WYER, R. S., JR.   Effects of incentive to perform well, group attraction, and group acceptance on conformity in a judgmental task. *Journal of Personality and Social Psychology*, 1966, **4**, 21–26.

WYER, R. S., JR.   Behavioral correlates of academic achievement: Conformity under achievement- and affiliation-incentive conditions. *Journal of Personality and Social Psychology,* 1967, **6,** 255–263.

YUKER, H. E.   Group atmosphere and memory. *Journal of Abnormal and Social Psychology,* 1955, **51,** 17–23.

ZAJONC, R. B.   The requirements and design of a standard group task. *Journal of Experimental Social Psychology,* 1965a, **1,** 71–88.

ZAJONC, R. B.   Social facilitation. *Science,* 1965b, **149,** 269–274.

ZAJONC, R. B., & SALES, S. M.   Social facilitation of dominant and subordinate responses. *Journal of Experimental Social Psychology,* 1966, **2,** 160–168.

ZAJONC, R. B., & TAYLOR, J. J.   The effects of two methods of varying group task difficulty on individual and group performance. *Human Relations,* 1963, **16,** 359–368.

ZANDER, A.   Group aspirations. In D. Cartwright & A. Zander (Eds.), *Group dynamics: Research and theory.* (3d ed.) New York: Harper & Row, 1968. Pp. 418–429.

ZANDER, A., & COHEN, A. R.   Attributed social power and group acceptance: A classroom experimental demonstration. *Journal of Abnormal and Social Psychology,* 1955, **51,** 490–492.

ZANDER, A., & HAVELIN, A.   Social comparison and interpersonal attraction. *Human Relations,* 1960, **13,** 21–32.

ZANDER, A., & MEDOW, H.   Individual and group levels of aspiration. *Human Relations,* 1963, **16,** 89–105.

ZANDER, A., & NEWCOMB, T., JR.   Group levels of aspiration in United Fund campaigns. *Journal of Personality and Social Psychology,* 1967, **6,** 157–162.

ZANDER, A., & WULFF, D.   Members' test anxiety and competence: Determinants of a group's aspirations. *Journal of Personality,* 1966, **34,** 55–70.

ZELENY, L. D.   Characteristics of group leaders. *Sociology and Social Research,* 1939, **24,** 140–149.

ZELENY, L. D.   Experimental appraisal of a group learning plan. *Journal of Educational Research,* 1940, **34,** 37–42.

ZILLER, R. C.   Four techniques of group decision making under uncertainty. *Journal of Applied Psychology,* 1957a, **41,** 384–388.

ZILLER, R. C.   Group size: A determinant of the quality and stability of group decisions. *Sociometry,* 1957b, **20,** 165–173.

ZILLER, R. C., & BEHRINGER, R.   Assimilation of the knowledgeable newcomer under conditions of group success and failure. *Journal of Abnormal and Social Psychology,* 1960, **60,** 288–291.

GLOSSARY

ACHIEVED STATUS. Status attributed to an individual on the basis of his own performance.

AFFECTION NEED. A need for close personal and emotional relations with others.

ANXIETY. A general worry or concern about some uncertain or future event. The event may be definite or diffuse in form, and it may be realistic or unrealistic.

ASCRIBED STATUS. Status attributed to an individual on the basis of arbitrary characteristics, such as age, sex, and kinship.

ASSEMBLY EFFECT. Variations in group behavior that are a consequence of the particular combinations of persons in the group, excluding the effects of specific characteristics of group members.

ASSUMED SIMILARITY OF OPPOSITES (ASo). The degree to which an individual sees his most preferred and least preferred coworkers as being alike.

BEHAVIOR REPERTOIRE. All the possible behavior sequences that a person might enact during interaction with another person, including all possible combinations of possible behavior sequences.

BEHAVIOR SEQUENCE. A number of specific motor and verbal acts that are sequentially organized and directed toward some immediate goal.

BRAINSTORMING. A technique for the production of new ideas in which all ideas are expressed without regard to quality, evaluations of ideas are withheld until the end of the production period, and the elaboration of one person's ideas by others is encouraged.

COALITION. The joint use of resources by a subgroup to determine the outcome of a group decision.

COMMUNICATION NETWORK. The arrangement (or pattern) of communication channels among the members of a group.

COMPARISON LEVEL (CL). The standard against which an individual evaluates the attractiveness of an interpersonal relationship.

COMPARISON LEVEL FOR ALTERNATIVES (CL_{alt}). The standard that an individual uses to decide whether to remain in or to leave an interpersonal relationship.

COMPUTER SIMULATION STUDY. A research technique in which the variables are programmed and behavior is "enacted" by the computer rather than by groups of real persons.

CONCEPTUAL SYSTEM. The individual's characteristic ways of conceptualizing and organizing his world.

CONFORMITY. The degree to which an individual's behavior corresponds to the norms of his group.

CONTROL NEED. A need to dominate others and to have power and authority over them.

DECISION STRUCTURE. Defined by Mulder as "who takes decisions for whom" in the group; the pattern of decision making in the group.

DESCRIPTIVE-EXPLORATORY STUDY. A research technique for describing small groups, often for the purpose of identifying relationships among variables.

DIMENSIONAL ANALYSIS. A form of analysis designed to identify dimensions of group tasks and to assign tasks to appropriate positions with respect to those dimensions.

EFFECTIVE SYNERGY. The amount of energy available to the group after it has satisfied its maintenance requirements; total synergy minus maintenance synergy.

ENTITATIVITY. The degree of having real existence; the degree of being an entity.

EXCHANGE THEORY. A theory which attempts to explain interpersonal behavior in terms of the exchange of rewards and costs.

FAVORABILITY CONTINUUM. The range of group situations with respect to leader advantages.

FIELD EXPERIMENT. A study conducted in a natural setting in which the investigator deliberately produces variations in the natural situation in order to examine their effects upon group behavior.

FIRO. A theory of interpersonal behavior based upon three interpersonal needs: inclusion, control, and affection needs.

GOAL CLARITY. The degree to which the requirements of the task are clearly stated or known to the group members.

GOAL-PATH MULTIPLICITY. The degree to which the task can be completed by a number of alternative procedures.

GROUP. Two or more persons who are interacting with one another in such a manner that each person influences and is influenced by each other person.

GROUP COHESIVENESS. The resultant of all those forces acting upon group members to remain in or to leave the group.

GROUP COMPATIBILITY. The extent to which the needs and behaviors of group members are mutually satisfying.

GROUP COMPOSITION. The relationships among the characteristics of individuals who compose the group.

GROUP GOAL. An end state desired by a majority of the members of a group. The group may have a single goal or multiple goals.

GROUP STRUCTURE. The pattern of relationships among the differentiated parts of the group. The group may be differentiated along a variety of dimensions; hence, the group structure consists of a set of separate, highly interrelated relationships among diverse units of the group.

GROUP SYNTALITY. The personality of the group; any effect that the group has as a totality.

GROUP TASK. That which must be done in order for the group to achieve its goal or subgoal. It consists of a stimulus complex and a set of "instructions" concerning what is to be done with respect to the stimuli.

INCLUSION NEED. The need for togetherness; the need to associate with others, to be a member of a group.

INDEPENDENCE. The degree of freedom with which an individual may function as a member of a group.

INFORMATIONAL SOCIAL INFLUENCE. Influence exerted upon a group member which is based upon the value that conformity may have for the individual. The majority opinion serves as a source of information.

INTERACTION. An interpersonal exchange in which each person emits behavior in the presence of the other, with at least the possibility that the behaviors of each person affect the other person.

INTERCHANGE COMPATIBILITY. Compatibility based upon the mutual expression of inclusion, control, or affection needs. Interchange compatibility exists when two persons are similar with respect to the amount of exchange desired.

INTERPERSONAL ORIENTATION. The particular way or ways that an individual views or reacts to other persons.

INTERPERSONAL RELATIONSHIP. A relationship between two or more persons developed through interaction on a number of specific occasions.

LEADER. The group member who exerts more positive influence on others in the group than they exert on him.

LEADERSHIP. A process in which one group member exerts positive influence over other group members.

LEADERSHIP STYLE. The pattern of behaviors adopted by the leader of a group; the leader's orientation toward the group.

LEVEL OF ASPIRATION. The level of difficulty of that task chosen as the goal for the next action.

MAINTENANCE SYNERGY. That portion of the total energy available to the group that must be devoted to the establishment of cohesion and harmony in the group.

NATURAL EXPERIMENT. An investigation that capitalizes upon naturally occurring changes in variables in order to examine their effects upon group process.

NORMATIVE SOCIAL INFLUENCE. The influence of the group upon a group member which is based upon his desire to conform to the normative expectations of other group members.

ORIGINATOR COMPATIBILITY. Compatibilty based upon the originator-receiver dimension of interaction. Two persons are compatible to the degree that the expression of inclusion, control, or affection needs corresponds to that which the other person wishes to receive in each of the three need areas.

PERSONAL ENVIRONMENT. That aspect of the group's environment which is created by the personal characteristics of each group member, without regard to the characteristics of others in the group.

PERSONAL SPACE. That space surrounding each individual into which others may not enter.

PHYSICAL ENVIRONMENT. That aspect of the group's environment which is created by the physical objects, and the relations among them, that are of importance to the group's members.

POSITION. The person's standing in the group; the total characterization of the differentiated parts of the group that are associated with a given member of the group.

PROFILE HOMOGENEITY. The degree to which the members of a group are similar on a variety of individual characteristics, considered collectively; the similarity of the personality profiles of group members.

RECIPROCAL COMPATIBILITY. The degree to which two persons satisfy each other's behavior preferences.

RESPONSE COMPATIBILITY. The extent to which the behaviors of two or more persons are mutually agreeable, i.e., can coexist without conflict.

RISKY SHIFT. The tendency for decisions made in groups to be less conservative than the decision of the average group member.

ROLE CONFLICT. Conflict that results when the expectations associated with two or more positions in different groups that an individual occupies are incompatible, or when the various expectations associated with a single position that a person occupies are incompatible.

SATURATION. The degree to which a communication network is overloaded by the total requirements imposed upon the group by such aspects of group process as communication demands, organizational decisions, and data manipulations.

SOCIAL ENVIRONMENT. That aspect of the group's environment which is created by the pattern of relationships among the personal characteristics of group members.

SOCIAL FACILITATION. The effect that the mere presence of others has upon the behavior of individuals. At one time, this effect was believed to be facilitative, but it is now known that the presence of others may either facilitate or impede individual performance, depending upon other factors.

SOCIAL NORMS. Rules of conduct; standards which specify appropriate behavior in the group.

SOCIAL POWER. The control of reinforcers for other members of one's group. Person A has power over person B to the extent that he controls reinforcers for B.

SOCIAL ROLE. The behaviors expected of the occupant of a given position in a group by other group members.

SOCIAL SENSITIVITY. The ability to perceive and respond to the needs, emotions, and preferences of others.

SOLUTION MULTIPLICITY. The degree to which there is more than one "correct" solution to a problem or task.

STANDARD GROUP TASK. A task with known characteristics that is adaptable to a variety of problem situations relative to small group behavior.

STATUS. The evaluation of a position in a group; the prestige of a position in a group.

SYNERGY. The vectorial resultant of the attitudes of members toward the group; the total amount of energy that is available to the group.

TASK ENVIRONMENT. That aspect of the group's environment which is created by the goal(s) and/or task(s) of the group; the goal-task characteristics influencing the group's behavior.

TENSION SYSTEM. A psychological state produced by opposing forces in the life space; for example, an internal state created by the establishment of a personal or group goal.

TERRITORIALITY. The assumption of a proprietary orientation toward a geographical area by a person or by a group, either legitimately (as by purchase) or illegitimately (as by "squatting").

THEORY. A set of interrelated hypotheses or propositions concerning a phenomenon or set of phenomena.

TRAIT HOMOGENEITY. The degree to which the members of a group are similar with respect to a single individual characteristic.

VALID COMMUNICATION. A stage in group development in which each group member is able to freely express his true feelings about himself and about others in the group, and can accept other group members as individuals who have the right to express their feelings, their beliefs, and their values.

NAME INDEX

SUBJECT INDEX